Self-Compassion

for
dummies®
A Wiley Brand

Self-Compassion

by Steven Hickman, PsyD

A Wiley Brand

Self-Compassion For Dummies®

Published by: **John Wiley & Sons, Inc.**, 111 River Street, Hoboken, NJ 07030-5774, www.wiley.com

Copyright © 2021 by John Wiley & Sons, Inc., Hoboken, New Jersey

Published simultaneously in Canada

For general information on our other products and services, please contact our Customer Care Department within the U.S. at 877-762-2974, outside the U.S. at 317-572-3993, or fax 317-572-4002. For technical support, please visit https://hub.wiley.com/community/support/dummies.

Wiley publishes in a variety of print and electronic formats and by print-on-demand. Some material included with standard print versions of this book may not be included in e-books or in print-on-demand. If this book refers to media such as a CD or DVD that is not included in the version you purchased, you may download this material at http://booksupport.wiley.com. For more information about Wiley products, visit www.wiley.com.

Library of Congress Control Number: 2021938953

ISBN 978-1-119-79668-8 (pbk); ISBN 978-1-119-79669-5 (ebk); ISBN 978-1-119-79670-1 (ebk)

Manufactured in the United States of America

SKY10027803_062521

Contents at a Glance

Table of Contents

Introduction

I t's simple really. You just want to be happy and free from unnecessary struggle and suffering. Am I right? I can make that statement so boldly because this is actually true of every human being who has ever lived and ever will live. The issue, though, is that perhaps you are struggling more than you would like. Something doesn't feel right about how you feel, and in particular something doesn't feel right about how you treat yourself much of the time. Perhaps you have a constant virtual companion that provides negative commentary on your every move, often referred to as an inner critic. Or maybe you find yourself feeling isolated and alone or lost in rumination and worry. If any of this sounds familiar, and you've thought that perhaps more self-compassion might help, your instincts are right on target.

When your dear friends have a hard time, struggle, fail, or fall short, you know just how to be there for them, support them, and encourage them. But somehow, when you face the same kinds of challenges in *your* life, the narrative is different. You beat yourself up, you demand perfection, or you simply surrender, feeling defeated, isolated, and overwhelmed.

But at the same time, there is a part of you watching this all unfold and whispering in your ear that there has to be a better way. That part of you that simply wants to be happy is the part of you that saw self-compassion as a way out of this painful cycle, and it was that part of you that picked up this book. Bravo! You've made perhaps the most important step you can take toward building a kinder and more productive relationship with yourself.

Self-compassion has been scientifically demonstrated to promote resilience, improve mood, promote nourishing relationships, and motivate people to make positive changes in their life. Most importantly, greater self-compassion promotes joy and satisfaction, and who doesn't want more joy and satisfaction in their life!

About This Book

I have taken to telling colleagues that I have written the most ironic title in the *For Dummies* series. Think about it, *Self-Compassion For Dummies* seems like the ultimate oxymoron (like "jumbo shrimp" or "deafening silence"), and really the worst way to start an adventure in treating yourself with kindness and respect.

After all, calling yourself a *dummy* seems a lot like yelling at your kid to make them quiet down.

But taken another way, being willing to purchase a book called *Self-Compassion For Dummies* means that you are humble and receptive to change, which is actually exactly where you need to be to get the most out of this book.

This book will help you explore the possibility of cultivating a kinder and more supportive relationship with yourself and then guide you through a whole series of exercises, meditations, and reflections designed to help you cultivate greater self-compassion over time. The road ahead will not necessarily be easy, but the potential rewards are significant. Each chapter tackles a different aspect of life and gives you concrete and specific tools and tips for helping self-compassion truly make a difference in your life.

Don't feel confined to progressing through the book chapter by chapter systematically if that isn't your style, but do know that to some degree, each chapter builds a bit on the ones preceding it. And since I have established that you are a humble person by nature, be willing to notice when you feel stuck and simply go back and reread or repractice something that didn't land quite right. You can even go back to previous chapters and reexperience them with fresh eyes from time to time.

Also, feel free to skip sidebars that pop up throughout the book. If the subject doesn't resonate, maybe it doesn't apply to you right now. You won't miss anything crucial if you skip them. Follow your heart and see where it leads. Your practice of self-compassion hopefully won't end with this book, but instead will have only just begun . . .

Foolish Assumptions

In writing this book, I made a few assumptions about who you are and why you are here:

>> You have an intuition or an idea that self-compassion may be good for you, but you aren't quite sure where to start or if you're up to the challenge.

>> You are willing to be humble and receptive and maintain an open mind about this sort of thing, and "give it a go" as they say in England.

>> You have a sense that you are kinder to other people than you are to yourself, especially when encountering adversity, failure, and pain.

>> You are cautiously curious about meditation and self-compassion practice, but you have a few lingering reservations about this whole endeavor.

There is nothing tricky or technical about treating yourself with compassion, but it does require a willingness to approach it warmheartedly and with curiosity. All I ask for is your open heart and mind and some patience — not only with me, but more importantly, with yourself.

Icons Used in This Book

In writing this book, I have provided you with little "flags" or pointers to draw your attention to particular kinds of information that may be noteworthy for different reasons. Here's a key to what those icons mean:

TIP

From years of teaching people mindfulness, meditation, and self-compassion, I have identified certain helpful hints or ways of getting unstuck when you find yourself struggling. Think of these icons as pointing to words for the wise.

REMEMBER

Sometimes things bear repeating so that they stay with you when you really need them. These are those kinds of important points that can never be repeated enough.

TECHNICAL
STUFF

This icon denotes information that you may find interesting, but it isn't critical to your practice of self-compassion. Feel free to skip over it if you like.

PLAY

You'll see this icon next to exercises that have downloadable online audio.

Beyond the Book

In addition to the material in the print or e-book you're reading right now, this product comes with a number of companion downloadable audio recordings of key meditations, reflections, and exercises that you will encounter in the book. You are invited to make full use of them along the way or after you've finished reading the book.

To access or download the audio tracks, go to dummies.com/go/selfcompassionfd.

It's wise to bookmark the link so you can easily access the recordings when you need them. Most often, the practice of self-compassion happens in "real time," meaning in moments of difficulty, challenge, or even overwhelm. Thus, having the practices at your fingertips is very handy because life doesn't wait to serve up its challenges until you are sitting safely at home in front of your computer with your bunny slippers on.

This book also comes with an online Cheat Sheet with additional tips. To access this info, go to `http://www.dummies.com` and type "Self-Compassion For Dummies Cheat Sheet" in the Search box.

Where to Go from Here

The fundamental practice of self-compassion is to ask yourself, "What do I need?" and then to act on that question. Let that be the guiding principle for how you approach this whole book. Look over the table of contents and ask yourself, "What do I need just now?" I only ask you to be patient with yourself and this process, to not be overly ambitious or to try too hard to "get it right." Often those who need self-compassion the most are also incredibly ambitious and perfectionistic, so if you recognize this tendency in you, maybe "Whoa, big fella! Hold on there a minute," may be in order.

Whatever you feel you need in this practice of self-compassion, I urge you to consider at least taking some time with Part 2, Chapter 3 before you venture too far into the practice. This chapter sets the stage for the challenges as well as the opportunities of self-compassion practice, and it provides some useful tips for how to get the most out of your journey while also taking good care of yourself on the way.

If you are someone who likes to focus and go deep with a new skill or ability, you have my enthusiastic permission to spend a fair amount of time on Part 2 to build up your resources of self-compassion and help to make them a part of your way of being. Returning again and again to some of these core practices and concepts is a great way to be reminded that, while it isn't always easy, the practice of self-compassion can be quite simple. Think of Part 2 as the fundamentals of self-compassion and the later chapters as more advanced topics or applications of the core elements.

All in all, I invite you to browse, meander, and dip in and out of this book like a delicious buffet of goodness, which it is. Above all, be kind and patient with yourself, and be brave as well. If you have the intrepid spirit of an adventurer, set forth boldly and explore! If you are of a milder, more hesitant nature, come on in and dip your toe in the water. Everyone is welcome, and everyone belongs.

Finally, I would love to hear from you and about your experience in this book. Check out my website at `www.drstevenhickman.com` or email me at `steve@centerformsc.org`.

1

Getting Started with Self-Compassion

Discover how to begin to ask yourself the fundamental question of self-compassion: What do I need?

Find out what science tells us about self-compassion.

Explore how self-compassion may not be what you think and may actually be the opposite of what you think!

Develop some basic skills to create the best "inner space" and equip you to get the most from self-compassion practice.

Chapter **1**

Exploring Self-Compassion

Welcome to the next step on a journey to greater self-compassion in your life. Take a moment to appreciate the road you have traveled thus far and how you came to be holding this book. It is probably safe to say that, if you are reading these words, you do not consider yourself skilled at being kind to yourself or treating yourself compassionately when you have a hard time. After all, *those* people don't buy books like this. Maybe you're "self-compassion-curious," and you are here because you have become increasingly aware that being hard on yourself, perfectionistic, and prone to bouts of shame and maybe even self-loathing is not serving you. In fact, this way of being with yourself has caused you a great deal of emotional pain and impacted your ability to do what you want to do in life and to have the things you most desire, like joy, happiness, and satisfaction. Maybe you've observed a repeating pattern of destructive relationships, unfulfilling jobs, or unhealthy habits that you engage in to mute the pain you feel.

It may be pain or struggle or stress that brought you through the door, so to speak, but before you move on, consider looking just a little bit below the surface of those painful challenges. Specifically, the reason you took action and are seeking to find out about self-compassion is actually *not* because of the discomfort or pain that you feel. Instead, it is another part of you, that deeply understands that you deserve better, that motivated and moved you. At your very core is a deep desire to be happy and free from suffering. It is this quiet but persistent voice and inclination of the heart that moves you to seek out something better for yourself.

The practice of self-compassion is really about accessing that small voice and giving it space to grow and expand. Becoming more self-compassionate is like pulling weeds around a tender seedling full of potential and beauty and bounty so that it can reach its full potential. In this metaphor, you are both the seedling and the gardener, so with a fair amount of patience, persistence, and kind intention toward yourself, you can tend this garden and harvest the fruits of your labor. You actually have everything you need inside of you to do this kindhearted, important work, and my intention is to support you in accessing those inner resources (that you may doubt that you possess) and discover how to embrace them to fulfill your potential as a living, loving human being no less deserving of your own love and affection than any other person on the planet.

Befriending Yourself: A Splendid New Relationship

If you're like most people, you are a really good friend. When your pals have a hard time, when they miss out on a promotion or go through a divorce, you know how to respond in just the right way. You can comfort and soothe if needed, you may inspire self-confidence or cheer them on at other times, and you're generally their "rock" when times are tough. It's what you do. You're a mensch as they say in Yiddish, a good person, a stand-up guy. Not always, not perfectly, but you do your best, and friends appreciate your kind intention.

But maybe something different happens when the one who struggles is *you*. Take a moment to pause and consider this brief, guided reflection drawn from the Mindful Self-Compassion program:

1. **Pause for a moment to allow your mind to settle and to become aware of your body as it sits just where it is.**

    Create a brief pause between reading and reflecting.

2. **Call to mind a situation when a close friend was having a hard time.**

    Perhaps they failed a test in school, or they interviewed for a desirable job and they didn't get it, or they accidentally said something that made someone angry at them.

3. **See if you can recall how you responded to your friend in this situation.**

   Maybe recall how you found out about the situation and what you did upon hearing of it. What were the kinds of things you said to your friend? See if you can remember the tone of voice you used or your body posture at the time.

4. **Now take a moment to consider another scenario. Think of a time when *you* faced a misfortune.**

   Maybe you made a proposal at work that was rejected by management, or you said something that upset a romantic partner and they ended the relationship.

5. **Call to mind what went on inside your mind and heart at the time.**

   Again, how did you react? See if you can recall the words you used with yourself in the aftermath of the event. And even if you can't recall the exact words, you may recall the tone of your inner voice. You may even recall how your body felt to hear this or what emotions came up.

6. **Compare these two situations. Is there a difference in how you respond to a friend versus how you respond to yourself under similar circumstances?**

If what you discovered in the previous reflection was that you are harder on yourself than you are on your friends when things go wrong, you are in very good company. Researchers have found that the vast majority (78 percent) of the general population (at least in the United States) shares your bias toward cutting more slack to your friends. Sixteen percent report that they are more balanced in their treatment of themselves and others. And finally, 6 percent say that they are more compassionate to themselves than others (those folks are unlikely to buy this book!).

But the point of this reflection is not to highlight yet another way that you are not perfect or to imply that there is something wrong with you for being so hard on yourself. Instead, you can actually take heart! Consider the fact that you already know how to cultivate compassion and kindness, because you admitted you can do it for your dear friends.

TIP

All you have to do is orchestrate a U-turn on that compassion for others and, bingo, you've befriended yourself and you are on the road to more self-compassion. Simple. But of course, not so easy. Whenever you may struggle to offer yourself compassion in a difficult moment, consider starting by asking yourself, "How would I treat a good friend if they were going through what I'm going through? What would I say? What tone of voice would I use? What might I do to let them know that I'm here for them?" Asking yourself this question can "jump-start" your practice when your self-compassion "battery" has run down.

Understanding Self-Compassion

It's important to begin by being completely clear on what, exactly, self-compassion *is*, so that you can then proceed to cultivate it in your life. By necessity, this discussion must begin with Dr. Kristin Neff, an author and social psychologist who is the world's leading researcher and authority on self-compassion. Kristin's work, in collaboration with clinical psychologist Dr. Chris Germer, who is a pioneer in exploring the integration of psychology and contemplative practice, has resulted in the empirically supported Mindful Self-Compassion (MSC) program (described later in this chapter). But beyond the development of MSC, Neff and Germer (through their writing, speaking, and research) have raised the profile of self-compassion in the popular consciousness and contributed to a new appreciation in clinical and contemplative circles for the role of self-compassion in resilience, well-being, and the relief of human suffering. (*Note:* Much of what I know about this topic, and write about in this book, is a direct result of studying the work of Chris and Kristin, and working closely with them as friends and colleagues, and as a teacher and teacher trainer of MSC.)

Kristin Neff's research on the topic of self-compassion arose out of her own experience of discovering just how hard she was on herself as a graduate student. She thought it might be possible to cultivate a more harmonious relationship with herself through cultivating self-compassion. This direct personal experience led her to want to study the concept and understand it in a way that had not yet been researched. In turn, this led to a remarkable body of research that is cited widely around the globe, pointing to the benefits of self-compassion. Kristin developed the empirically supported Self-Compassion Scale (I present a version of it in Chapter 2), which enabled her and her colleagues to more directly study self-compassion and begin to understand how it is related to various other things like mood, well-being, motivation, behavior change, and so on.

TIP

If you're particularly interested in the research aspect of this topic, see Kristin's website (self-compassion.org) for a huge bibliography of published research studies on self-compassion.

Compassion at the core

REMEMBER

First and foremost, it's important to be completely clear that compassion is the foundation for everything that you discover and practice in this book. Whether you direct that compassion at others or yourself, the definition of compassion remains the same. A number of different authorities, from the Merriam-Webster Dictionary to the Dalai Lama, essentially define compassion in similar terms: the awareness of distress and the desire to alleviate that distress. (Some use the term "suffering" instead of "distress," but again, it's easiest to think of these as equivalent: distress, suffering, stress, pain.)

This two-part definition (awareness of distress and the desire to alleviate it) helps to also clarify the difference between empathy and compassion, which is another question that people often have. In simple terms, empathy is the first part of the definition of compassion, without the second part. Empathy is the human capacity to relate to and sense another person's pain. Period. I often say that "empathy is a one-way street" in this regard, and it lacks the action component of compassion. One can have empathy for another person's struggle without having compassion.

Most people tend to think of compassion as it relates to compassion for other people, which is probably why self-compassion gets lost in the shuffle and so many of us are in need of a "booster" when it comes to directing this warmth toward ourselves! Self-compassion is simply the capacity to include ourselves within the circle of our compassion, a kind of "compassionate U-turn." This may sound simple on the one hand, but if you've tried, you know that it can be challenging. To appreciate the elements involved in self-compassion, it may help to start with unpacking the experience of compassion for others. By doing so, you begin to see the connection between this and self-compassion.

Take a moment to imagine a scenario where you are walking down the street and encounter a homeless woman sitting on the curb, rumpled, dirty, holding a paper cup for donations, and clearly suffering. As you consider this situation, what do you think would have to be present in you for compassion for this woman to arise? I often present this exercise when I speak about self-compassion, and invariably, the responses that I get are very similar, group after group. One can easily group the responses into three general areas that, remarkably enough, align with what Kristin Neff's research has uncovered regarding self-compassion:

>> **"You have to even notice that the person is there."** This is a way of saying that one has to first be mindful to actually notice that there is a person in front of you who is suffering. Without awareness, there is no possibility of compassion, and this awareness is referred to as mindfulness. The simple capacity to notice what is present in the moment, without judgment, is not so easy sometimes, but each of us possesses the ability.

>> **"I realize that there but for the grace of God go I."** The recognition that this person is a fellow human being, who just like me, wants to be happy and free from suffering, is a powerful acknowledgement of what Kristin Neff calls common humanity. This ability to remember that all of us are human, all of us are imperfect, and that we need each other to survive is often forgotten when you are feeling isolated and different from others. But when you connect with it, it provides a solid support.

>> **"I feel the desire to do something to help them out."** Simply being aware, or even noticing the common humanity, does not automatically mean that compassion has arisen, unless it includes that action component of wanting to relieve the suffering or the difficulty. You can't always actively change the circumstances, but even in this scenario, noting the desire to relieve her suffering or offering the simple gift of eye contact or a smile may be an act of kindness that is possible in the moment.

Mindfulness, common humanity, and kindness. These are the three components of self-compassion that have emerged from Kristin Neff's research, and they point the way forward for developing self-compassion if they are directed inwardly in the same way that most of us easily direct them outwardly. One way to capture this self-compassionate stance is by boiling it down to what my dear colleague Michelle Becker coined as a "loving, connected presence."

REMEMBER

When you can be a loving (self-kindness), connected (common humanity) presence (mindfulness) for yourself, you are practicing self-compassion. Much, much easier said than done, but a nice way to keep a simple vision of your intention going forward.

Mindfulness

Chapter 4 explores the topic of mindfulness in greater depth, but for now it's helpful to get a basic grasp of how mindfulness plays a role in self-compassion and to contrast it with other ways of being that are less helpful or counterproductive to becoming more self-compassionate. With each of the three components — mindfulness, common humanity, and self-compassion — you may find it helpful to think of it as falling in the center of a continuum. In the case of mindfulness, it is the middle point between over-identification and being completely avoidant and checking out.

For example, consider the situation where your partner is facing a difficult medical procedure and you are concerned, worried, or afraid about the outcome of the procedure. From the standpoint of awareness, you would be most supported by finding a space between the two possible extremes:

>> Constantly ruminating over potential outcomes and becoming paralyzed with anxiety constitutes over-identification

>> Being totally checked out and in denial that something significant is happening to your beloved partner

Instead, you would want to stay connected, in tune with your reasonable fears but not overwhelmed by them, so that you can be present and supportive of your partner in the process. This attentional middle ground is mindfulness.

Common humanity

I cover the important role of common humanity in more detail in Chapter 5, but getting a general sense of it here can help ground you in the foundation of self-compassion. Returning to the metaphor of balance when looking at common humanity, you can probably relate to all points on that continuum. The extremes look like this:

>> On one end of the scale is a deep and painful sense of isolation, loneliness, and feeling different from others, especially when you fail or fall short. When something goes wrong, you are convinced it is because *you* are somehow wrong or flawed or uniquely imperfect.

>> On the other end of the spectrum are those times when you become so swallowed up in another's troubles that you lose yourself in the process and become overwhelmed.

Calmly in the middle between these two extremes is a balanced sense of connection and commonality with your fellow human beings, a deep awareness that at times we all suffer, fall short, and fail. When you are resting in a sense of common humanity after having flubbed an important job interview, you recognize that your imperfections are not actually *yours* in the sense that all humans (and the other candidates for the job) are imperfect. Rather than feeling uniquely flawed and fatally doomed to a life of mediocrity and solitude, you see this as one episode in a larger life. You can learn from your errors and perhaps seek the comfort of friends and colleagues who can relate with having had unfortunate experiences in key important situations. This is the healing power of common humanity.

Self-kindness

Our innate inclination toward kindness and happiness is further explored in Chapter 6, and as the third component of self-compassion, it is the warm ribbon that ties all three together into a package of goodwill in the face of difficulty. As nice as you may feel when you can muster up some kindness for yourself in challenging times, it may feel incredibly elusive at other times. Opposite ends of the self-compassion spectrum look like this:

>> Many people are more acutely aware of self-criticism, self-deprecation, and self-recrimination. You may be someone who lives with the voice of a harsh

and judgmental inner critic: a constant badgering, undermining, and demeaning voice that pokes you unmercifully and may have been with you for as long as you can remember (more on working with the inner critic in Chapter 9).

>> The other end of the spectrum is slightly more seductive and seems quite nice at first glance, but self-indulgence, just doing what feels good in the moment regardless of whether it is exactly what you need or even in your best interests, is another extreme that does not support self-compassion.

Self-kindness is that middle space that you might think of as the good parenting that you may or may not have had growing up. As an adult, you understand how to keep the big picture in mind when your son stays out past curfew because he was with friends having fun and lost track of the time. You know that berating him for being irresponsible and lazy is not a helpful way to react (however afraid you were that something had happened to him when he wasn't home at the appointed time). On the other hand, simply shrugging it off and saying, "That's ok, I'm just glad you're fine" may not be appropriate either if you want him to develop responsibility and maturity. The reasonable, compassionate response is somewhere in between, where you make clear your expectations and how he violated them, provide appropriate consequences, and emphasize your love and respect for him. This is the balanced essence of kindness that is not indulgent but not overly critical either.

Looking at the Yin and Yang of Self-Compassion

Self-compassion suffers from what people in the public relations business call "an image problem." Think about what comes to mind when you first see the phrase "self-compassion," or what a stranger might think when they see the title of this book. I would be willing to bet that something comforting or soothing or cuddly springs to mind. Maybe the term conjures up the image of a rustic hot tub on a chilly autumn evening or a warm cup of cocoa by the fire in the ski lodge. You might think of this practice as soothing, comforting, and nurturing — something to do when you hit a bumpy stretch that helps you settle down and meet yourself with patience and kindness, the way you would counsel a good friend to handle such a situation. And you would not be wrong about that. But there is a whole other side of the practice that balances out this softer side of self-compassion and is equally important.

You may have tendency to see self-compassion as nurturing and soothing because our mental model of what compassion looks like usually comes from the example of how a mother may nurture or comfort her child when the child is upset or suffering. As a result, you are likely to link compassion more broadly to a more traditional feminine gender role, and therein lies the flaw in our appreciation of what compassion really includes.

My goal here is to help illuminate your understanding of self-compassion so that you can appreciate its full expression, which will likely dispel some myths or misunderstandings you may have about the practice and allow you to open up to it more easily.

Compassion can best be thought of as a complete whole that has a complementary side to this soft side as well. The other side of compassion (including self-compassion) is more stereotypically masculine and linked to action-oriented gender roles.

Consider the job of a brave Coast Guardsmen (the official title for a uniformed member of the U.S. Coast Guard, irrespective of gender). These individuals risk their lives, dangling out of helicopters to pluck hapless boaters from the icy waves and pulling shivering fishermen from the hulls of capsized boats. It's hard to imagine a more compassionate act than putting aside one's own safety for the good of another. There's nothing warm and fuzzy about that!

Or, in another scenario, imagine facing someone making an unwanted and uninvited romantic advance, and needing to firmly say "no!" to protect yourself. This is also an act of self-compassion that is more about strength and speaking your truth than soothing or comforting yourself.

Taken together, we can appreciate that self-compassion has both tender (stereotypically feminine) and fierce (stereotypically masculine) sides. They complement each other in a beautiful dance between "being with" ourselves in a compassionate way and "acting in the world" to get things done. In Chinese philosophy this combination is represented by yin and yang, and indicates that all seemingly opposite attributes, like masculine-feminine, light-dark, and active-passive, are complementary and interdependent. This idea is represented by the familiar symbol shown in Figure 1-1.

FIGURE 1-1:
The yin-yang
symbol.

The *yin* side is most associated with the tender aspect of comforting, soothing, and validating ourselves in times of great difficulty. On the flip side, the *yang* aspect of self-compassion is linked to fiercely protecting ourselves, providing for our needs, and motivating ourselves to take action. All of these are self-compassion, and all are ultimately in our own best interests, but in quite different and complementary forms.

REMEMBER

It is notable that each side of the symbol contains a dot of the other side within it, showing that neither side loses touch with the other. For example, imagine finding out that you failed an important test because your professor accidentally told you to read the wrong chapter in the textbook. You are fuming over the unfairness of it and considering writing a nasty email to the professor that vents a semester's worth of frustration in a couple of paragraphs. You pause for a moment and simply acknowledge the situation by saying to yourself, "This is really unfair, and it hurts to feel this anger right now." In this moment you are both validating your anger in a yin way by naming it and acknowledging that it is hard, but it also requires a "dot" of yang strength and resolve to be willing to turn toward your anger first, when you really want to discharge it with a nasty email that will certainly make things worse.

Taken together, the yin and the yang energy of self-compassion support us in making wiser, more effective choices that are ultimately in our best interests.

"Yin-sights"

Make no mistake, the fact that you are considering becoming more self-compassionate is a big deal, and it won't always be easy. It will be especially hard because you have a lifetime's experience of probably being less compassionate with yourself than you could have been, or even downright mean to yourself at times. If you've experienced a breakup initiated by the other person, maybe you ruminate for hours, days, or even weeks over what you must have done wrong or how you could have been so terrible. Do you hear the voice of an inner critic berating you for not being *enough* . . . tolerant enough, loving enough, fun enough? For any one of a million reasons and a multitude of life experiences, you may have developed a tendency to be less than yin with yourself when you encounter failure, frustration, disappointment, or imperfection in yourself. It happens. Could you possibly even pause and forgive yourself just now, simply because that has been your experience in the past?

At first, when you make a commitment to be as kind to yourself as you are with your dear friends when they face the same hardships, it may feel weird, unfamiliar. It may feel like you just slipped your left foot into your right shoe. But see if you can be patient with yourself and the discomfort and continue to offer the natural kindness that you show your friends. Let it envelop you and warm your heart. Stay curious and see what may arise if, this time, you let yourself receive a little bit of your own kindness. Again, patience is the key.

Perhaps your go-to response when you face difficulties is to beat yourself up for falling short, harangue yourself for being imperfect, or take action that you may later regret. See if you can, for just this moment, let those harsh voices be there, but in the background, and make a little space for another voice that may be very quiet or timid just now. For *just this one moment* try simply soothing yourself for having a hard time, for no other reason than you are having it.

TIP

The next time you are aware that you're feeling uncomfortable or upset in some way, try the simple experiment of simply placing a hand on your body someplace that is soothing or supportive and notice how that feels. Nothing else. Notice if you have any thoughts and see if you can see them just scroll across your awareness like those stock tickers on Wall Street. Don't give them any importance by trying to argue with them or answer them. Just focus on what it feels like to comfort and soothe yourself in a moment of difficulty. It's perfectly natural to do this. Give yourself full permission to feel your own compassion, in the form of warm, supportive touch, for as long as you like. What are you aware of when you do this? What is the "yin-sight" that you discover by accessing, even for a moment, the warm, feminine, nurturing side of self-compassion?

WHAT FIERCE AND TENDER SOUND LIKE IN YOUR HEAD

It's all well and good to talk about yin and yang compassion in the abstract, but if you're like me, you're a practical person and you want to know how it actually plays out in real life. You can't always stop and affectionately place your hands on your heart in a moment of suffering (imagine doing that while making a presentation to the board of directors or with your fellow firefighters on the way to a fire). And other times you need to give yourself a kick in the pants, but despite the fact that that term is a cliché, I haven't yet figured out how to physically pull it off.

So sometimes the best way to recognize the quality of your attention is to take note of what you say to yourself and the tone you use. To get you started, I've provided a short list of phrases you may consider (or already use) to access each of the two sides of self-compassion. Try them out, write them down, tattoo them on your forearm — whatever works for you to be able to access them when you need them most. (And if you forget to use them when you could have used them, don't beat yourself up; just recognize that even that oversight is just another opportunity to be self-compassionate.)

(continued)

(continued)

Yang self-talk:

- "You've got this, big guy."

- "This crappy situation doesn't define you."

- "Your voice matters here; speak your truth."

- "You've faced hard times before, and you can do it again."

- "You belong. You matter. You have something to contribute."

- "How great would it feel to get a little exercise right now?"

- "WWJD: What would Jesus do?"

- "Remember: Discretion is the better part of valor."

- "Let's do this!"

- "Ahhhhhhhh."

Yin self-talk:

- "Oh man, this is *so* hard right now."

- "There's nothing to change, sweetheart. It's okay for now."

- "I'm here for you. You're not alone."

- "Awwwwwww."

- "This is big. It's okay to go slow."

- "You're doing the best you can, darling."

- "Right now, it's like this. And that's okay."

- "What do you need right now, my friend?"

- "What do you need to hear?"

"Yang-sights"

One of the most common hesitations that people have about practicing self-compassion is their sense that it is a kind of passive, "it's all good" kind of response to every situation. Nothing could be further from the truth when you look a bit closer, but it's worth exploring a bit more deeply to fully grasp the potential strength, power, and resolve that is inherent in self-compassion.

It can be helpful to differentiate between feelings and our responses to those feelings, because this is where the rubber meets the road in self-compassion. Have you ever tried to change an emotion that you were experiencing? We often do, but we rarely succeed. Perhaps you are angry because someone disrespected you, and you are fuming and ruminating over this injustice and telling a friend all about it. Think about how it would feel if your friend told you, "Just stop being so angry. Get over it!" My guess is that this would just intensify your anger, now including your friend for telling you not to be angry! I talk more in Chapter 3 about the consequences of resisting the reality of feelings and facts, but just now we can suffice to say that trying not to feel a feeling is nearly impossible, despite how often we try to do it. Take even the old example of inadvertently getting the giggles in a funeral service or some other serious gathering. Have you ever tried to stop the giggles in that moment? How did *that* work out?

Self-compassion teaches us to simply meet ourselves with kindness *because* we are having difficult feelings, without the agenda to make them go away (which is usually impossible anyway). But the key to yang compassion in particular is to know that simply comforting and soothing ourselves because we feel badly may be only half of the equation. Once we can fully acknowledge simply the *presence* of a feeling or a problem of some kind, we can also potentially chart a course of wise action in response.

Sometimes the wise "action" that is called for is actually to choose inaction. Perhaps, in a situation where someone has done something hurtful to you and is still angry and may continue to do harm, the wisest way forward is to move backward in that moment and wait to advocate for yourself in more supportive circumstances. But sometimes you need to step up and speak your truth, say "no" to things that you truly see as clearly wrong or hurtful, or make changes that need to be made. In each of these cases, a conscious choice to act (through speaking up when you might have stayed quiet, saying "no" when you mean it, changing your behavior because you see that it is not in your best interest, or simply *not* acting because action would not serve you in the long run) is a true act of self-compassion. When you access the yang side of compassion, you hold the truth of your feelings but let them inform and energize you for action, so that you focus on the things that need to be done. This is very far from passivity and looks a lot more like wisdom: seeing the whole situation from the larger perspective and choosing a response that best suits it.

As you have been practicing thus far, the next time you face a challenging situation where you feel overwhelmed, powerless, or helpless in the face of it, see if you can maintain some patience and curiosity to explore it a bit further than usual. You might temporarily soothe yourself with some yin compassion by resting a hand on your body or even giving yourself a brief inner pep talk along the lines of "you've got this" to just cultivate a bit of clarity and ease within you. With a little space and time to allow the adrenaline to loosen its grip on your nervous system, see if there is any indication of something that needs to be done or something you really need in this moment. Whether you provide for your needs simply by validating your emotions and not acting, or stand up to someone who is causing harm, or simply resolve to make change in the future, these can all be important expressions of yang (active) self-compassion.

Balancing soothing and strong

As you have probably already discovered, self-compassion is not really yin *or* yang but yin *and* yang. Just like the light and dark sides of the moon, these are part and parcel of each other, and one does not exist without the other. So self-compassion is neither all soft, warm, and fuzzy nor all strong, bold, and active. It is a complementary blend of these qualities that balance out each other and support us in navigating life in a wise and balanced way. If we are too yin, we become too passive, accepting, and wishy-washy and we are vulnerable to being taken advantage of, mistreated, or simply self-absorbed. When we have all yang with no yin, we risk reacting without wisdom because our emotions are not acknowledged and held so that they can truly inform and guide us in the actions we choose; instead, they lead us to impulsive actions that have negative consequences.

Finding a balance between yin and yang is not an easy task, but it is well worth the effort. I find it particularly helpful to really tune in to how my body feels when I'm practicing self-compassion and to fine-tune my practice to find a kind of balanced inner state that is somewhere between soothing and strong. That balance point is different in different situations, so it all comes down to the fundamental question of self-compassion: What do I need?

REMEMBER

If you can become aware of your inner state in a given moment, you may notice a feeling of passivity or helplessness that can be balanced by some validation or accessing of a protective yang energy. On the other hand, if you feel a sense of ferocity that is like unleashing a slightly unpredictable inner tiger, you may warm up the inner environment with some soothing words (I'm partial to "Whoa, big guy! Hold on there!" as one example). These two complementary forces combine to help you find the wise way through the tough spots, holding you when you need to be held, propelling you when you need to take action — always with that little dot from the yin-yang diagram of warmth in the yang and action in the yin to hold it all together.

Asking the Fundamental Question of Self-Compassion

In the end, for all the components and facets and considerations about self-compassion, it boils down to developing our capacity to ask and respond to a very simple question:

What do I need?

That's it. It's no more complex than simply stopping in a moment (or a whole stream of moments) and checking to respond to what is present for you and to see what you need. The act of stopping itself is an act of kindness, and it creates a space for you to step out of the stream (or raging river!) of life and to see with clarity and kindness what you may need.

Okay, although it is simple, I'm not suggesting that it's easy; otherwise, Kristin Neff and Chris Germer would not have dedicated their entire professional careers to understanding, exploring, and sharing the practice (and I wouldn't have taken the time to write this book!). But at its core, it comes down to this simple question and how we answer it. As I note earlier, this is generally easy enough for most of us to do for our friends and loved ones when *they* struggle, face failure, or have a hard time, but so often we look past our own struggles and pain, ignore them, deny them or push them aside for whatever reason (all to be explored in the pages ahead).

REMEMBER

But there is profound truth in the statement (sometimes attributed to the Buddha): "You, yourself, as much as anybody in the entire universe, deserve your love and affection."

Why not? Who are you *not* to deserve your own kindness, patience, and care?

Introducing the Mindful Self-Compassion Program

In 2009, Chris Germer published *The Mindful Path to Self-Compassion*, which was the culmination of many years of contemplative practice, clinical experience, and training. Chris's personal journey (much like Kristin's, which was detailed in her own book, *Self-Compassion*) had led him to his life's work of teaching and speaking about integrating self-compassion practice into daily life and into psychotherapy to support people in feeling happier, more fulfilled, and able to overcome challenging histories. In 2008 Chris and Kristin (at the time, mere distant colleagues) were invited to participate in an important meeting of the Mind and Life Institute in upstate New York and Chris offered to give Kristin a ride to that conference. On the auspicious journey back to the airport after the conference, the Mindful Self-Compassion (MSC) program was born.

I like to joke that the two of them were like those old commercials for Reese's Peanut Butter Cups. Kristin was the social psychologist who had done significant research on self-compassion but never considered herself someone who could teach the practice to others. Chris was a well-respected clinical psychologist with years of experience, study, and teaching of the practical application of self-compassion with a relatively modest research background. Chris and Kristin each started out suggesting the other was the perfect person to create a self-compassion training program and ultimately decided that they were better together than apart. In the commercials, one person enjoying peanut butter accidentally bumps into someone eating chocolate and their foodstuffs intermingle. "Hey, you got peanut butter on my chocolate!" says one. The other indignantly retorts, "Hey, you got chocolate in my peanut butter!" They each taste the magical combination, and the rest is history. Such was the case with Mindful Self-Compassion as well.

Working together and drawing on their respective experience and study, Chris and Kristin developed the program that they first offered at a workshop in 2010 at the fabled Esalen Institute on the central California coast. Despite the later success, it was an inauspicious beginning, as 12 people had signed up for the course and 3 dropped out within a day or so. (These days, their programs draw huge crowds.) Kristin and Chris later conducted a randomized controlled trial of the MSC program with very promising results, pointing to increased self-compassion as a result of the training (an important first point to establish — that one can actually learn to be more self-compassionate), as well as improved mood and greater quality of life, among other findings.

The MSC program has since grown and improved year by year, with the help and support of the nonprofit Center for Mindful Self-Compassion (the organization for which I work as the executive director), and over 2,700 people are now trained to teach the program worldwide. Research on MSC continues, and it is estimated that over 100,000 people worldwide have experienced the program in one form or another. The teachers continue to report remarkable impact on the participants in their courses.

This book and the vast majority of meditations, exercises, and topics in it are largely inspired by and drawn from the MSC program and my experience of learning and teaching it. It is a powerful and empirically supported way of systematically developing greater self-compassion. I highly recommend MSC for those who find the material in this book to be helpful. The opportunity to discover and practice self-compassion in the context of a group (whether in-person or online) is tremendously valuable because of the greater sense of common humanity, among many other reasons.

Practice: The Self-Compassion Break

PLAY

This is the quintessential practice taken directly from the Mindful Self-Compassion program and is perfectly suited to support you in deploying the three components of self-compassion in a moment of difficulty. I present it here like a formal meditation, but this is only to help you become familiar with the practice. The real value is in practicing it when you face a difficult moment or a time when you are feeling distressed or upset in some way. But for now, give yourself this opportunity to become familiar with the practice. Follow these steps:

1. **Begin by taking some time to relax.**

   Allow your gaze to soften and your face to relax. Notice your body sitting here. Perhaps take note of your breath moving in and out, over and over, as it does whether we are attending to it or not.

2. **Call to mind a situation in your life that is difficult right now and causing you stress.**

   It may be a health issue, a challenging relationship, a work problem, or perhaps stress related to one of your identities, such as your gender, race, ethnicity, age, or ability. Do your best to choose a problem in the mild to moderate range, not a big problem. Remember, this time through you are just learning this skill of self-compassion, perhaps for the first time.

3. **Give yourself time to really bring the situation to mind, to see, hear, and feel your way into the problem, perhaps enough so that you notice some uneasiness or discomfort in your body associated with it.**

   Where do you happen to feel it the most just now? See if you can have a sense of where it is in the body and simply open up to noticing it as it is.

4. **As you sense the discomfort in your awareness, note to yourself, slowly and clearly, "This is a moment of suffering."**

   This is *mindfulness*, simply opening awareness to what is present. Other words you might use are "Ouch!" or "This hurts," or "This is painful." Take your time and acknowledge what is here for you.

5. **Say to yourself, slowly and clearly, "Suffering is a part of living."**

This is *common humanity* as you note that all humans have moments like this. You may say instead, "I'm not alone," or "Me too," or "Others in my community would feel a lot like me in a situation like this." Remember that suffering is a universal experience, even though it is not equal across individuals or groups. Maybe you can have a sense of at least one person similar to yourself who may feel this like you do.

6. **Place your open palms over your heart or wherever it may feel supportive to you, feeling the warmth and tenderness of your touch.**

You might say to yourself, "May I be kind to myself," or "May I give myself what I need." This is the self-kindness that we often long for but may not receive from ourselves.

You can even explore just what kind of self-compassion you need just now, whether it is yin compassion or yang compassion. Yin might be "May I accept myself as I am" or "May I bring tenderness to myself just now." If you feel that yang is more appropriate, you might say, "No. I will not allow this to continue," or perhaps "May I have the courage and strength to make a change when I can."

TIP

If you find it hard to locate just the right words for yourself at any point in this Self-Compassion Break, you might consider imagining what would flow from your heart and mouth if a dear friend were facing a similar situation. What would you say to them, heart to heart, if they were feeling this discomfort? Once you've identified some words, can you offer those same words to yourself as well?

7. **Whenever you are ready and you feel you've given yourself what you need, allow your gaze to raise and your eyes to take in your surroundings.**

Take some time to settle, reflect, and perhaps take notes.

Inquiring: What arose for you when you took a Self-Compassion Break?

Notice that the Self-Compassion Break incorporates the three components of self-compassion (mindfulness, common humanity, and self-kindness) as well as the two sides of self-compassion (yin and yang), all wrapped up in a fairly straightforward practice. As I note in the preceding section, this practice is intended for you to deploy at a moment's notice when you become aware of struggle, pain, or stress in a moment. It can be as simple and brief as stepping through the three components in a cascade for a few seconds or creating some time and space to linger with each element of the break, whatever is needed and possible in a moment.

Reflect on the break afterward by considering the following questions:

>> When you called to mind the difficult situation, how was that for you? What was most noticeable when you imagined the difficult situation?

>> What was your experience in each of the three steps of the Self-Compassion Break? What was it like to acknowledge mindfulness, common humanity, and self-kindness?

>> Do you think you could use this practice in the future, the next time you face a challenge or difficulty?

Give it a try and see if you can do a Self-Compassion Break a time or two in the next day or so and see what happens and what you notice. Let go of needing anything to change just yet, and be patient with yourself as you slowly develop this capacity to respond differently in challenging situations. This will all take time, and we are only just beginning!

By the way, it is possible that you found placing your hands over your heart not particularly supportive or pleasant. A certain percentage of people find this to be the case. For now, be willing to experiment and see if there are other places on the body that may be better for you. Chapter 2 gives you an opportunity to explore other options for this soothing and supportive touch.

One last note: In this practice run, I invited you to call to mind a difficult situation in order to have a problem to work with as you begin to practice the process. I am absolutely *not* suggesting that you continue to do this, pausing now and then to call to mind a challenging situation to practice. Trust me, life will do quite a good job of handing you all the difficulties you need to master the practice; there's no need for you to open yourself to additional, unnecessary suffering. Just be patient and begin to notice when it happens. And it will.

Chapter **2**

Enjoying the Benefits of Self-Compassion

et's face it: Nobody buys a book like this because everything is feeling just peachy in their life. Whether it's *Calculus For Dummies* or *Cooking For Dummies* or *Self-Compassion For Dummies*, we buy these books because we're not satisfied with our current state of affairs relative to the topic (calculus, cooking, or self-compassion) and want to make a change. It all starts with a seed of discontent, a tug of self-doubt, or even a sharp hot jab of emotional pain or suffering. Think about it; as you're reading this book, you're probably focused on how bad it feels to criticize yourself, or how hard it is when you expect perfection, or the dark rabbit hole you retreat into when things go badly for you. In broad terms, you're coming here to get away from your suffering and your pain. Indeed, you've come to the right place.

But discomfort only gets the ball rolling, and the good news is that we can overcome this preoccupation with the negative and the hurtful and instead find what is possible when we treat ourselves as kindly as we typically treat others. So even if pain brought you to the dance, so to speak, it doesn't have to be your primary dance partner. In fact, you may be shocked to find out that you can become more self-compassionate without ditching your inner critic by the punch bowl!

The promise and power of self-compassion is that when we begin to treat ourselves with warmth, patience, and encouragement, we open up a whole new way of living and being in the world. The science is clear that when we are more self-compassionate, we are more able to bounce back in the face of life's challenges, our relationships are more rewarding, we are willing to take risks and try harder to achieve our goals, and we are able to navigate our lives in more satisfying and fruitful ways. And it all begins with how we treat ourselves.

In this chapter you discover the tremendous benefits of becoming more self-compassionate that extend well beyond relief of emotional pain. You see that you already have this capacity within you, and it is an innate capacity that science shows you can cultivate over time. You find out how accessing the self-compassionate part of you affects your body, your mind, and your emotions. I also explore with you some of the most common misconceptions about self-compassion and the doubts that you probably have right now about what it would mean for you if you became more self-compassionate.

What Science Says about Self-Compassion

Over 2,000 research studies have been conducted to study self-compassion in one way or another, and the body of research is growing exponentially, suggesting that we may be on to something here with this new way of being with ourselves.

In the following section, you discover, using scientifically solid data, just how self-compassionate you are (whether you really want to know or not!) and then explore what researchers have found out about how this way of being with yourself actually plays out in your daily life.

Measuring how compassionate you really are toward yourself

Dr. Kristin Neff's research has led the way in this important area of study, and she is the developer of the Self-Compassion Scale (SCS), which is a quick way of measuring just how self-compassionate you are. The SCS is by far the most-used measure of self-compassion by researchers around the globe.

TIP

As a step on your self-compassion journey, you may want to consider making an objective assessment of just how self-compassionate you are by completing the following adapted version of the short form of the SCS. The SCS measures

>> How mindful people are (versus how over-identified they get with their own struggles)

>> How deeply they feel a sense of common humanity (versus feeling isolated by their own imperfection)

>> The degree to which people are routinely kind to themselves (versus unkind)

(If you would like to complete the full Self-Compassion Scale and have your results calculated automatically, go to www.self-compassion.org/test-how-self-compassionate-you-are.)

The following statements describe how you act toward yourself in difficult times. Read each statement carefully before answering, and to the left of each item indicate how often you behave in the stated manner on a scale of 1 to 5 (note that the meaning of your rating varies with each group of items as shown).

Almost Never				Almost Always
1	2	3	4	5

___ I try to be understanding and patient toward those aspects of my personality I don't like.

___ When something painful happens, I try to take a balanced view of the situation.

___ I try to see my failings as part of the human condition.

___ When I'm going through a very hard time, I give myself the caring and tenderness I need.

___ When something upsets me, I try to keep my emotions in balance.

___ When I feel inadequate in some way, I try to remind myself that feelings of inadequacy are shared by most people.

For the next set of items, use the following scale (notice that the endpoints of the scale are reversed from those above):

Almost Always				Almost Never
1	2	3	4	5

___ When I fail at something important to me, I become consumed by feelings of inadequacy.

___ When I'm feeling down, I tend to feel like most other people are probably happier than I am.

___ When I fail at something that's important to me, I tend to feel alone in my failure.

___ When I'm feeling down, I tend to obsess and fixate on everything that's wrong.

___ I'm disapproving and judgmental about my own flaws and inadequacies.

___ I'm intolerant and impatient toward those aspects of my personality I don't like.

How to score your test:

Total (sum of all 12 items): _____

Mean score = (Total/12): _____

ADSCO

Regardless of the score you achieved on the Self-Compassion Scale, there's no need to be concerned and certainly no reason to begin criticizing yourself for not being kinder (perhaps the most ironic form of self-compassion). Instead, see if you can let this be ADSCO: Another Damned Self-Compassion Opportunity. We include the expletive because what we really want is to be free of the self-criticism and keep hoping that the next time something hard happens to us, we will *finally* be rid of the old way of being. But think about this: You've had a lifetime to build up a mental and emotional habit of responding to adversity with perfectionism, self-criticism, and shame. Why would you expect that a few weeks into trying something different, all that mental training will simply dissolve in a moment of rapture? This is a process that takes time, and each time we face an ADSCO, perhaps it gets a tiny bit easier to shift our old patterns.

We can think of these ADSCOs as tiny shifts in course by an ocean liner. When the ship leaving San Francisco turns half a degree farther south than it usually does, it's barely noticeable at first. But played out over thousands of miles, it can mean the difference between arriving in Japan and arriving in Fiji. We can celebrate the ADSCOs as little moments of tiny course adjustments that, over time, make a big difference in our lives.

As you explore self-compassion for yourself, you are likely to find no end to the ADSCOs as you tune in to the inner dialogue of your inner critic, a virtual inner radio station that is often playing in the background of your life, serving up pokes and prods and unwanted color commentary on your behavior (more on the critic in Chapter 9).

When you are practicing a new skill or developing a new resource like self-compassion, it's much like exercising: The more opportunities you have to practice (exercise), the stronger and more self-compassionate you get. When you're out on a walk with your cocker spaniel and you accidentally step in Fido's poop and begin to berate yourself for your mindlessness: ADSCO! When you get that panicked sinking feeling because you accidentally included your boss on an email you didn't want them to see, and you are already considering clearing out your desk: ADSCO!

The more you practice, the more you grow. Bring on the ADSCOs and watch your SCS score rise!

Average overall self-compassion scores tend to be around 3.0 on the 1–5 scale, so you can interpret your overall score accordingly. As a rough guide, a score of 1–2.5 for your overall self-compassion score indicates you are low in self-compassion, 2.5–3.5 indicates you are moderate, and 3.5–5.0 means you are high in self-compassion.

The SCS is a valuable measure of just how self-compassionate a person is, and it forms the heart of a remarkable body of research that I refer to from time to time in this chapter and throughout the book. But it's important to appreciate that no amount of science by itself can make you more self-compassionate. I share this important information to reassure you that what you are considering here has science behind it and that there is strong evidence for its contribution to a life well lived.

The research (much of it done by Kristin Neff) is clear in pointing to the tight linkage between self-compassion and a number of important life dimensions, including emotional well-being.

Emotional well-being

Speaking generally, studies have shown that self-compassion is linked to less depression, anxiety, and stress. Other studies that look at collections of similar kinds of research have shown quite clearly that as self-compassion increases, psychological distress decreases. (This is referred to as an inverse correlation. For example, the more money you have in the bank, the less anxiety you have about paying your bills.)

Of course, a key feature of self-compassion is that you don't criticize yourself as much, and the research is clear that self-criticism contributes to anxiety and depression. But even more than that, self-compassion turns out to actually protect us *against* these same difficulties. Self-compassion makes us more immune to life's trials that could otherwise send us into bouts of intense panic or deep sadness. People who are more self-compassionate are less susceptible to the harmful impact of stress because they take stressful events in stride as simply a part of life rather than a catastrophe to be avoided or resisted. Self-compassion becomes a kind of shock absorber on the car of life and allows us to navigate our way more smoothly along all of life's bumpy roads.

You may have heard the term *emotional intelligence*, which is really a fancy way of referring to how well you cope with the reality of being a human who has emotions. Are you able to be informed and guided by your emotions (both pleasant and unpleasant) without being overwhelmed or carried away by them? The degree to which you can navigate the territory of emotions reflects how emotionally intelligent you are.

REMEMBER

In general, self-compassion is associated with greater emotional intelligence, which means that people who are more self-compassionate are able to deal with their emotions in wiser and more productive ways. This means that if you are more self-compassionate, you are less likely to ruminate (literally to chew over) your negative thoughts and emotions, like a cow chews her cud. With self-compassion you can avoid the emotional quagmire of negative thinking and self-blame, and instead see emotions as helpful guideposts and experiences to be savored or appreciated when they arise.

In a number of interesting studies designed to elicit feelings of shame or deep embarrassment (sign me up!), researchers found that people who are more self-compassionate tended to feel less shame. When people were prompted to be more self-compassionate, they also felt less shame in similar situations than those who were not prompted to be kind to themselves.

It's worthwhile to note that, in keeping with the focus in this chapter on the particular benefits of self-compassion, this practice also appears to bolster feelings of well-being, life satisfaction, hope, happiness, optimism, gratitude, curiosity, vitality, and positive emotion. In fact, researchers have found that self-compassion bolsters the very pillars of well-being: autonomy, competence, and relatedness. So, practicing self-compassion can support you in feeling your own power and ability to make things happen, your confidence in your own abilities, and your sense of connection to others. Not a bad combination at all to set one up for facing the world.

The self-compassion trap

You may be surprised to learn that self-esteem is a bit of a sneaky character. The importance of fostering high self-esteem in our children to protect them against the thorny challenges of life has become conventional wisdom, and we still see the effects of that "movement" in many areas of education and society.

I like to call it the "Every Child Gets a Trophy Movement" wherein well-meaning parents, teachers, and coaches celebrate every child (as they should) and then recognize them with awards, certificates, trophies, and so forth regardless of how they perform or whether they actually earned them. And to add insult to injury, even the heroes, the best athletes, the most accomplished students and musicians, are not singled out for recognition for their outstanding performances out of concern that such accolades will lower the self-esteem of the other kids, making them feel bad.

It is indeed true that research has revealed that high self-esteem is definitely related to many positive things in life, such as successful relationships, improved work satisfaction, and better health. Furthermore, we know that people with low self-esteem are more susceptible to things like anxiety, depression, and even the likelihood to attempt suicide. And all of this would lead one to think that we should do whatever we can to increase self-esteem in our children. That's exactly what researchers thought late in the 20th century and how we came to be handing out trophies like candy on Halloween.

The trouble with self-esteem

"So, what's wrong with high self-esteem?" you ask. Nothing, really, if it arises naturally. But the way you go about achieving high self-esteem is the real test. Self-esteem is a way of viewing ourselves that is conditional, meaning that we look at ourselves (or a particular feature of ourselves, such as how we look or what we have accomplished) and compare that feature to others to decide how good we are. As a result, we gain self-esteem if we look around and decide that we are better-looking than our friends, or if the boss says more nice things about our project than a co-worker's.

We comfort ourselves by believing that we are above average at nearly everything. Studies have shown that all people tend to believe that they are above-average drivers, parents, and dancers. But you don't have to be a statistician to know that *everyone* cannot be above average. The concept of average doesn't work like that. In truth, most of us are average drivers, parents, and dancers because that's how average works. In normal situations, about 68 percent of us fall in the normal range on nearly everything. But think about this: Imagine you just came off the dance floor with your sweetheart, out of breath and beaming about your rendition of the Electric Slide as the last disco notes fade into the crowd noise. How would you feel if a friend sidled up next to you at the bar and enthusiastically said, "That was a really average set of dance moves you just demonstrated!"

I imagine you would be devastated to hear these words from a dear friend, even though they very well may be true. We operate in the world believing that we are above average because it helps us feel good about ourselves. This view helps us maintain our self-esteem, but then when we are confronted with reality, we are in serious trouble. We lose the dance contest, or we fail a test, or we drop a platter of dishes in the restaurant and our self-esteem plummets. We berate ourselves for being so inept, so stupid, so fallible, so . . . human, and we struggle to find our way back to some sense of ease about ourselves. Some of us spend our lives trying to claw our way back to feeling above average in *something, anything,* and suffer mightily in the effort because we need to feel or look or dance better than someone else. We can be totally dependent on our environment for our sense of self-worth, meaning that our whole lives become conditional upon conditions that are often outside of our control.

The conditional nature of self-esteem

When we have high self-esteem, we feel great, when we have low self-esteem, we feel terrible, and everything hinges on where we are and with whom we compare ourselves. The darkest side of this needing to feel better or more worthy than others is that it can also lead us to put others down, dismiss them, or even bully them to make us feel better about ourselves. The unfortunate slippery slope of this approach is that when we do this, we often feel worse about ourselves for having done it, berate ourselves further, and dig ourselves deeper in a low-self-esteem pit that can be associated with further bullying, deeper depression, and deeper shame.

As you may imagine, self-esteem is a bit of a roller-coaster ride at times and can be as elusive and changeable as the weather. The research supports this view in many ways, and also highlights how self-compassion is so much more stable, supportive, and reliable for people and avoids the pitfalls of self-esteem. For example, studies have shown that people who are more self-compassionate have more stable feelings of self-worth than those who simply have high self-esteem. (Interestingly, high self-esteem is closely associated with narcissism, which is rampant in our society today. *Narcissism* is an inflated and unrealistically positive view of ourselves.) All in all, the research suggests that, in contrast with those who have high self-esteem, self-compassionate people are less likely to be constantly evaluating themselves, feeling superior to others, defending their viewpoints, or angrily reacting against people who disagree with them. These sound like the kind of people I'd like to hang out with. How about you?

How self-compassion beats self-esteem

From another perspective, self-compassion is more helpful to us in coping with stress than self-esteem is and equips us to handle all types of feedback (positive, neutral, negative) from others better than self-esteem does, especially when that feedback is neutral or negative.

The good news here is that self-compassion is a better way of navigating life's challenges that is not at all conditional in any way, can be relied upon in any circumstance, and is always available to us whenever we need it. Not only is it powerful and present to us, but it also supports us to grow and to take in new information and constructive feedback so that we can improve our performance, consider our options, and learn from our experience.

REMEMBER

Self-compassion is not sugar-coating our view of the world or shielding us from challenges; it actually allows us to take it all in and meet life head-on with inner strength and resilience. Self-esteem is a positive evaluation of your own self-worth, whereas self-compassion is not an evaluation at all, but a way of relating kindly to who we are, especially when we feel inadequate or have suffered a misfortune.

Exploring the Physiology of Self-Criticism and Self-Compassion

Have you ever been physically harmed by a nasty email you received? Were you ever actually in danger when a zombie popped up out of nowhere in a movie? Of course not! We don't think twice about these instances and others where we find that we are alerted to some form of "threat" in our vicinity, real or imagined. But they explain a lot about how and why we have stress in our lives and also provide us some clues for how to deal with this stress.

Our bodies have been intricately designed to perpetuate our existence. We are physiologically "wired" to keep ourselves alive and procreating. If you're reading these lines, then this evolutionary process has been successful regarding the former, and you may even enjoy the latter from time to time as well. Our physiology has been working efficiently for millennia, such that it has allowed us to survive and thrive as a species. But the challenge is that we are now carrying the ancient day-to-day survival baggage of our ancestors into a life that rarely directly threatens our physical safety or our life. Imagine showing up with a wooden spear to play NFL football, for example. There's no doubt that your weapon might deter the opposition, but it is far outside the rules of modern sport to carry one.

You could say that we are the victims of our own success as a species. After generations of scrambling to survive, avoiding danger, outsmarting predators, conquering most disease and hunger, and generally building a lifestyle of comfort and ease, we can finally relax and appreciate it all and count our remarkable blessings, right? Not so much. Perhaps now and then we stop and smell the flowers of our lives and appreciate what we have. In the United States we have one day a year devoted to pausing and giving thanks for all that we have been given by life, and then we spend most of the other 364 days clambering to get the things we don't have, to do things that we believe will make us feel more secure, more safe, and more complete. We can't seem to help ourselves, and it's largely because of this ancient brain that we have inherited that is always on the lookout for danger, threat, or problems. But, as Paul Gilbert, the noted British psychologist, is fond of saying, "It's not our fault, but it *is* our responsibility."

REMEMBER

In other words, just because we have inherited this hunter-gatherer brain, we are still not doomed to live the life of our cave-dwelling ancestors. We've got options.

But first we need to appreciate just how that ancient brain influences us in our daily lives and exactly how the practice of compassion and self-compassion can help us access other human systems to overcome those roots and become fully modern humans who are satisfied, fulfilled, and happy, even while possessing seemingly outdated "hardware" between our ears.

The brain we share with our ancestors

At the most basic, reptilian level, humans have had to find a way to avoid pain and danger. Like the lowest forms of life, amoebas and plankton, we humans are equipped with systems that propel us toward what we need and want, and away from things that we don't need or would be harmful to us. Our reflexes make us recoil from a hot pan on the stove and also cause our mouths to water at the delicious soup inside. Thankfully, we are built in more complex ways than amoeba and plankton, largely because those organisms are not good at soup-making and have no opposable thumbs, among other, more noteworthy shortcomings as life forms (no offense, my little friends).

Our human auto-piloting system

What humans are blessed with is a system called the *autonomic nervous system* (ANS) that tends to all our bodily processes, maintains our temperature, is the caretaker of our internal organs, makes sure we are able to digest our food and expel waste, and oversees all the other multiple functions that keep us alive. Within the ANS are two complementary subsystems that dance together to make sure that the body responds appropriately, depending on the situation. When the body needs to be prepared for a threatening or dangerous situation (for example, a leopard pouncing on you from a tree), the *sympathetic nervous system* (SNS) kicks into gear with what is referred to as the "fight-or-flight" response. Under ordinary situations (seeing a sleeping leopard at the zoo), the *parasympathetic nervous system* (PNS) takes care of us by calming us and helping our body conserve and restore resources.

When our SNS (or Threat Defense System) is activated, it starts with the triggering of the *amygdala,* a brain structure designed specifically to sound the alarm and prepare us to fight, flee, or freeze (your three options when under attack). The SNS then uses chemical messengers (neurotransmitters, like acetylcholine and norephinephrine) to bring about certain reactions in the body. These reactions include elevating your heart rate (to prepare you to fight), slowing down digestion (to prioritize quick metabolism of fat and sugar for a sudden flight), constriction of blood vessels in some parts of the body (in arms and legs to prevent bleeding out if you are injured), dilation of blood vessels in other parts (for muscle activation), and "tunnel vision" that facilitates you being laser-focused on the threat ahead of you.

You know the feeling of SNS activation, because it's what hits you when you get that nasty email, when someone cuts you off in traffic, or when you hear a loud crash in the other room in the middle of the night. Eventually, if there is no actual threat to your survival or safety, the neurotransmitters begin to be broken down by the body (metabolized) and the PNS can begin to do its work of calming and soothing your body to bring it back down to baseline.

It may be helpful to see how the components of the stress response of the SNS unfold within us and how the three components of self-compassion can be the antidote to this process. Check out Table 2-1.

TABLE 2-1   ## Self-Compassion and the Stress Response

Stress Response	Stress Response Turned Inward	Self-Compassionate Response
Fight	Self-Criticism	Self-Kindness
Flight	Isolation	Common Humanity
Freeze	Rumination	Mindfulness

The cost of constantly sounding the danger alarm

Sounding the danger alarm may seem quite logical on the one hand, but this process of activating your SNS and the cascade of bodily functions that are affected, followed by the calming of the PNS, takes a toll on your body. The alerting function of the SNS is intended for the relatively infrequent (but very dangerous) situations where our ancestors had to deal with attacks. For short, intense bursts, the body can handle these periodic alarms and respond appropriately. In between, we are well-equipped to live in relative parasympathetic peace.

The problem in this situation is that, as modern *homo sapiens* (translated as "wise men") with brains that can also plan, anticipate, remember, and imagine, we can create so many more mental catastrophes than we will ever actually experience in real life. As the French philosopher Michel de Montaigne once said, "My life has been full of terrible misfortunes, most of which never happened." This is the same wise man who said, "He who fears he shall suffer, already suffers what he fears." And this, you see, is the rub.

We have these amazing human brains that can do many things, including conjuring up thoughts of misfortune and anticipating suffering well before it may ever happen. What really becomes difficult is that our ever-faithful SNS gets activated as easily over the *idea* of threat or danger as it does over the *reality* of it. And you know well that our brains can be incredibly productive idea machines. They make them faster than we can even think them, meaning that one bad moment (like a hurtful comment from a friend) can lead to a whole cascade of further thoughts, emotions, and resulting bodily reactions that can extend for minutes, hours, days, or sometimes even years. When we begin to ruminate over a single fact, what it means, how it was intended, and where it came from, each new catastrophic thought can trigger an additional burst of neurotransmitters into our bloodstream.

WALKING DOWN THE STREET

A little thought experiment can help you explore your own autonomic nervous system and how simple fleeting things like thoughts can lead to emotions and bodily sessions not that different from what you feel when you need to actually fight or flee.

Take a moment to pause from your reading and settle your mind. You may even take a deep breath or two and let yourself become present and focused upon your body and your breath.

When you're ready, imagine the following scene: You are walking down the street in your neighborhood and as you walk along, you look up and happen to notice a dear friend and valued colleague walking the opposite direction on the other side of the street. You're pleased to see this friend, so you smile and wave cheerily to them as you walk.

And they continue walking, not responding at all to your friendly greeting.

Take a moment to pause and notice what comes up for you as you imagine yourself in this scenario. Ask yourself these questions:

- What thoughts went through your mind when you realized the person was not responding?
- What feelings came up for you in this situation?
- Were you aware of any sensations in your body associated with encountering this situation?

I often describe this scenario for people in a mindfulness course and then ask people to share what their immediate thoughts may be, and these are the kinds of responses I hear:

- "He must not have seen me."
- "I wonder if she's angry at me for some reason. What did I do?"
- "I hope they're okay. I wonder if something is wrong."
- "What a jerk! How rude can you be?"
- "Was she embarrassed to potentially be seen talking to me?"

Each of these thoughts is very different, and as you can imagine, they leave people feeling very different emotionally. From indifferent, to fearful, to concerned, to offended, to shame. And each of these emotions may feel very different in the body as well.

But the really important question to ponder here is this: Which thought was right?

Of course, the answer is that we have no way of knowing, because all of this is based on a simple fact that you greeted a person who didn't respond. There's not enough data to make a determination, but our very busy idea machines in our heads are happy to serve up all kinds of options (often influenced by our existing mood or our way of seeing the world in general) and then play them out as if we actually *know*. And of course, this means that when we think these things, our body reacts as if these things are real and dangerous, our SNS kicks in, and a simple, random, meaningless encounter becomes a fight-or-flight moment.

The long-term impact of a chronically overstimulated SNS can be devastating, and you can think of it as the well-known effects of chronic stress. In the short term you can notice irritability, fatigue, headaches, difficulty concentrating and focusing, sleep disruption, digestive problems, and loss (or increase) in appetite. The unfortunate downward spiral of chronic stress is that when we feel stressed out, we often rely on comforting but unhealthy coping strategies to deal with it. We drink, we smoke, we use other drugs, we eat poorly or too much, and we tend to act out hurtfully to those around us. These poor coping skills (and frankly, we all have them to some degree, right?) then lead to further complications. Over months and years and decades, this pattern leads to heart attacks, strokes, ulcers, and other health problems.

This all sounds pretty ghastly and more than a little discouraging for us mere humans to contemplate. But you can take heart that simply understanding this process and taking the mystery out of it is actually the first great step that your amazing human brain can take to shaking loose the bonds of the ancient brain and coming into the modern world.

REMEMBER

Just as it's said that we study history so we are not doomed to repeat it, we study our neurophysiology so that we are not destined to be dominated by it. There is a saying: "What we name, we can tame," and thankfully, self-compassion is just the thing to tame the wild beast inside.

Being a mammal and "the cuddle hormone"

Besides being warm-blooded and having the capacity to feed our young through the secretion of milk, another feature of being mammals (which we humans are) is that our babies are born alive . . . and completely dependent upon us. At first blush you may just experience a little pulse of your threat defense system kicking in at the thought of having a human being fully dependent upon you. And of course, being a parent or a caregiver is stressful, but this miracle of mammalian life holds within it the key to what really raises us above our lower, ancient brain and its focus on friend or foe.

How our nervous system draws us together

In order for us to survive as a species, we mammals have to stick together, and not just for barhopping and barn-raisings. From our first moments on earth, we need care and attention in the form of food, clothing, and shelter, and we are, again, wired to get what we need. The infant instinctively knows to turn toward the nipple and suck (called the *rooting reflex*) and to cry when it is uncomfortable or needs a diaper change.

And more than pure instincts, we have another built-in system referred to as the *mammalian caregiving system* that operates by releasing the hormone oxytocin into our bloodstream when we are in certain caregiving situations. Called "the cuddle hormone," oxytocin strongly increases feelings of trust, calm, safety, generosity, and connectedness. Research shows that when a mother breastfeeds her infant; when parents interact warmly with their young children; when someone offers or receives a tender, affectionate caress, the body (both bodies, actually) releases oxytocin.

This all means that at a very profound and basic level, our body subtly but powerfully nudges us in the direction of connection to others: to get our basic needs met and to keep us safe. It actually feels good to connect, inside our bodies. We feel safe, calm, and trusting when we make contact, and this encourages us to continue to do this in various ways over a lifetime. Without really being aware of it, our nervous systems are parenting us and trying to keep us safe and secure by motivating us toward receiving what we need most: the love of another being. At the heart of this is the simple human desire to be loved, because when we are loved, we get what we need: food, clothing, shelter, and more.

You may have noticed in your experience that you don't always feel so warm and fuzzy (or loved) on a daily basis, as loneliness and disconnection are sad and ironic symptoms of our otherwise hyper-connected modern lives. The topic of the impact of smart devices, the internet, and social media is well beyond the bounds of this book (although self-compassion may play a role in contending with all of this), so next we focus on a very real human tendency and how it may play out to leave you feeling disconnected from those around you.

We humans like to compare ourselves

Humans have been shown to have a natural propensity to compare themselves to others. You come to know yourself by evaluating your own attitudes, abilities, and traits relative to others and coming to some conclusions about yourself as a result.

There is a whole theory called Social Comparison Theory, developed by social psychologist Leon Festinger in the '50s, that suggests that there is a drive within us to try to get an accurate self-evaluation in this way.

The key word in the previous sentence is "accurate," because being able to form an accurate sense of ourselves requires us to have good data to rely upon. More traditionally, we have made these comparisons in the places where we've encountered other people: our immediate families, our schoolmates, our colleagues, our neighbors. As we go about our lives and watch the other kids on the playground play tetherball better or worse than us, or when we pass a demonstration on our college campus and find ourselves drawn to it or offended by it, or even when we have a heated conversation about politics at a neighborhood barbecue, we are gathering data like scientists (usually without the white lab coats and clipboards).

All this data goes into evaluating and positioning our view of ourselves relative to others in the space of our own minds. Not a perfect science by any stretch (science is inherently imperfect in some ways), but a passable approach to developing a view of ourselves relative to others.

Where it really gets tricky: The harsh inner critic

But consider the scenario where there is a perfect storm of an inner critic that harshly evaluates everything about us and faulty data from our environment that may make everyone else look like they have things *way* more put together than they actually do.

We have already mentioned it previously — and we return to the inner critic in greater depth in Chapter 9 — but suffice it to say that many of us live our lives with ongoing inner critical commentary from a voice that is predisposed to see us as "less than" others in many different ways. This is the voice that may say, "You're not going out dressed like *that*, are you?" Or more painfully, it can be a harsh, hurtful voice echoing from an earlier time in your life that snarls, "Don't even think about saying that out loud. Your opinion isn't worthy of discussion." (It hurts me just a little bit to write this down, but I have heard similar things spoken by many real people in my courses.)

If you have a harsh inner critic (and many people do), you know how it evaluates your performance on a daily basis, and you usually come up with the short end of the stick, so to speak. Now, imagine hearing that nasty inner voice while you casually scroll through your Facebook or Instagram feed. You see the seemingly perfect lives of your friends with their impeccable wardrobes, their shiny well-behaved children, the gourmet meals, and the charming dachshund they rescued from certain death in a shelter. It's easy to mistake this "highlight reel" of their lives for their *actual* lives. We don't post the day we spent in sweats on the couch, the sullen teen at mealtime, the burnt pot roast, or the 3 a.m. dog vomiting episode. Life is not all of either of these — perfection or disaster — but instead a mix of all sorts of experiences.

Coming up short in our own lives

The thing is, when we see those carefully curated moments from social media and compare them to our actual lives, how could we not come up wanting? And when we've got the ever-present voice of an inner critic that is primed and ready to talk trash to us anyway, it lands us in a place of feeling unworthy or even unlovable. Not a pretty place to be, and one that flies in the face of our very human desire to be loved. The combination of poor social comparison and harsh self-criticism has been shown to activate the amygdala again and stimulate the SNS in its cascade of arousal. Thus, even a relatively benign activity like checking Facebook can leave us feeling on edge, attacked, and isolated.

Thankfully, there is solid evidence that self-compassion can not only decrease levels of troublesome hormones like cortisol that are released as a part of SNS activation, but also activate that mammalian caregiving system to comfort and soothe ourselves like we would a small child or a beloved pet. In this way, self-compassion can be seen as essentially jump-starting the system in our bodies designed to calm, strengthen, and nurture us in moments of difficulty.

Activating our instincts with soothing touch

Fortunately for us, science has shown us that we don't have to be a baby or give birth to one to activate our mammalian caregiving system. We all possess the necessary neural and biochemical circuitry to access our innate instincts to foster safety, warmth, and connection. You can think of it as your "mammalian secret weapon" that's always at the ready and always available to you in all situations, not just to connect with others but to feel safe and secure in your own skin too.

You may be wondering about how to access your secret weapon, and there, the science is quite clear. The mammalian caregiving system is triggered by two primary means that are both relatively easy for us to engage: soothing touch and gentle vocalization. Think about how you may soothe a screaming child, and it becomes quite obvious how you can meet yourself in the same way. You reach out to caress or reassure the child with your kind and gentle touch, and you may coo or whisper or hum a lullaby in the child's ear with the sweetest of tones. Together, these simple things release the cuddle hormone and the body's built-in opiates to foster a tiny little cocoon of safety and security around you. The same things happen to your adult self when you meet yourself with your own touch and compassionate self-talk.

Discover which form of touch works for you

TIP

In order to develop a practice of offering yourself compassion when you struggle and suffer to engage the mammalian caregiving system, you can begin by experimenting with what sort of soothing touch *you* can offer yourself. It can be your go-to recipe for self-kindness in a difficult moment. Here are some tips:

>> You may want to stand up for this little experiment or at least take a short stretch break so you can fully tune in to how your body feels. Allow your eyes to close if you like, in order to focus more specifically on the senses you feel during this exercise.

>> Begin by gently pressing your palms against one another and just notice whatever sensations you feel. Continue to do this with each subsequent instruction, pausing for a few seconds between each.

>> Try cupping one hand in the other or grasping one hand with the other so that you are effectively holding your own hand.

>> Gently place the open palm of one hand over your heart and then place the other open palm over the first.

>> Try forming a fist with one hand over your heart and placing an open palm over the fist.

>> Try placing just one palm over the heart.

>> Place one hand over the heart and the other over the belly.

>> Try placing both hands over the belly.

>> Experiment with placing one hand on one cheek.

>> Try placing one hand on each cheek, cradling your face in your hands.

>> Try crossing your arms across your torso and giving yourself a gentle hug (I like to refer to this as the surreptitious self-hug).

>> Gently stroke one arm with the hand of the other arm.

Take some time to go back and linger among these various forms of soothing and supportive touch to find which one "clicks" for you and perhaps unlocks a little cuddle hormone in *your* body when you offer it to yourself. Some of these gestures are likely to be more pleasant than others, and some may actually be unpleasant (more on that later). Remember that there is no one right way or one right form of touch. What works for you?

Sometimes it's all in the tone

Most of us have had the experience (especially when we were teenagers) of having had someone (usually a parent) say, "Don't use that tone with me!" Whether you were the parent or the teen (or both) in that scenario, you know the bottom line: Tone matters.

So it's not surprising that the way in which we speak to ourselves in our own head also matters. I discuss this further throughout the book, but in this context, we don't have to think about words just yet, but just gentle, soothing vocalizations like what we might offer the upset child. And these sounds just ooze compassion and kindness.

TIP

Pause for a moment and take a deep breath or two. Then, at the end of a nice deep in-breath, let yourself vocalize the natural sound of a nice, long, delicious out-breath as you release it. The sound is "Ahhhhhhhhh." Let it extend as long as it feels comfortable. Notice how you feel in your body in the aftermath of this soothing sound of letting go and becoming present. In other words, this is the sound (and the feel) of mindfulness.

Now, when you're ready, take another deep breath and maybe imagine you just saw the cutest baby photo of a beloved friend or a basset puppy trip over his long ears. Let your exhale be one of warmth and tenderness, sounding something like "Awwwwwww" and extending again as long as you like. Let this feeling of affection and compassion linger and notice how it feels as the oxytocin floods your system.

REMEMBER

By offering yourself soothing touch and warm, gentle vocalizations (our Mammalian Secret Weapon), you activate your innate mammalian caregiving system, counteract the fight-or-flight you may be experiencing, and ultimately reclaim your place as a mindful, compassionate, evolved being. For now.

Addressing Your Doubts about Self-Compassion

Earlier in this chapter I discuss the science and benefits of self-compassion, but maybe you're still not ready to board the Self-Compassion Train just yet. What's holding you back?

I would be willing to venture a guess and say that you are cautiously curious but still harboring some hesitation or doubts. You are not alone in your hesitation, and in the end, it won't be me or this book that will coax you into becoming more compassionate with yourself. But my hope is that what you read and practice here will lead you to explore further, and you'll decide for yourself based on how trying it feels. I understand that, in order for you to practice self-compassion, you have to at least be somewhat convinced that it's worth your effort and you have to have an open, if slightly questioning, mind.

The following is compelling information that may help you to slowly open up more fully to the possibility that this practice of self-compassion may be for you. The more you are really committed to giving this practice a try, the more likely you are to find it beneficial. But I get that I owe you some good, solid justification for why you ought to, and it would help if I could address the specific concerns you may have with some evidence, some facts, and some things to consider.

TIP

You are invited to take a moment to pause and get clear on where you stand relative to this whole idea of being more self-compassionate, and explore any doubts, hesitations, or misgivings you may have about it. You may want to have a pen and paper nearby to take note of what you come up with.

» Start by taking a moment to shift your attention (mostly) inside yourself while keeping these instructions within sight.

» Notice how your body feels just now and how your breath continues to flow in and out. Let any thoughts that were with you begin to settle like the sediment in a small pond that has been stirred up.

» Be patient and ask yourself the question: "What gets in the way of me being more self-compassionate?"

Give yourself time to answer. Don't censor yourself or ignore whatever comes up spontaneously.

» Ask yourself this question a few times and take note of the answers.

A few obstacles or hesitations are likely to come up, and all are worthy of your attention. You may even want to write them down to consider later.

» Another option is to ask yourself to finish the following sentence: "I'm concerned that if I get more self-compassionate, then I will _____."

Your response to these reflective questions doesn't have to be perfect, reasonable, or even rational. Give yourself permission to simply make room for whatever arises, and you can sort through it later.

» A further option is to think of what other people might say about self-compassion. Imagine telling a friend that you bought a book on self-compassion or that you decided to attend a Mindful Self-Compassion course. What would they say? What do you think others would be thinking? If you were reading this book over a cup of coffee in a busy coffee shop, what do you fear other people might think about you if they saw the title of this book?

(Full disclosure: I once read a book on self-esteem when I was a graduate student in psychology, and I always felt the need to hold it so that others couldn't read the cover. If anyone saw it, I felt the need to clarify: "Oh, this isn't for *me*, I'm just reading it for professional purposes because I'm studying to be a psychologist . . . really. No, *really*." I think I inadvertently said more about myself and my own self-esteem by this behavior than I intended!)

Review what you came up with and let go of judging yourself or your answers just now. Some ideas may be surprising to you, or a little bit embarrassing, but remember that they are just thoughts and may or may not have substance to them. You may notice a theme (or a few themes). Keep your list with you as you read further. And remember that you have come by these beliefs and ideas honestly, and there is no need to reject them just now. See if you can simply take note of them and be willing to test them out as you go.

The five most common misgivings

As I discuss in Chapter 1, one of the three components of self-compassion is the sense of common humanity, that we are not alone and that we share our joys and challenges and imperfections with the entire human family. The same is true of our doubts and hesitations about self-compassion itself. You may be surprised to find that whatever concerns you came up with in the previous reflection are likely to be found in the following list of the most common misgivings we encounter when we ask people about them in the Mindful Self-Compassion program.

Many of the doubts and hesitations that people have stem from not fully appreciating the yin-yang aspect of self-compassion that I share in Chapter 1. The majority of people tend to see the practice as primarily soft, comforting, soothing, and nurturing, and as a result tend to miss the powerful, energetic, and motivating aspect of self-compassion that goes with this softer side. You may even take a moment to return to the previous reflection and see whether this assumption underlies your particular doubts.

Thankfully, in virtually every case, solid research supports the opposite of these doubts and misgivings, and I mention this research briefly here (for an exhaustive compendium of self-compassion research, see Kristin Neff's website at self-compassion.org). Again, the purpose of citing the research is not to convince you of anything, but only to allow you to open yourself up to exploring this practice for yourself and making your own conclusions. I'm confident that, if you approach the balance of this book with an open mind and an open heart, you will discover the transformative power of self-compassion. But I don't hold the key to your heart and mind; you do, and only you can unlock it. I'm just here to coax you into feeling enough safety, ease, and curiosity to give it a try.

That said, the following sections address the most commonly heard objections.

"Self-compassion is really just a form of self-pity"

At first glance, some may come to the conclusion that self-compassion is an elaborate way of facilitating a "pity party" where you get to tell yourself "Oh, poor me, I'm suffering" and basically wallow in your misfortune and become mired in your own victimhood. "This always happens to me when I try something. I just can't get it right so what's the point of even trying? I'll just be self-compassionate and give up on my dreams."

The fact is that research uncovers a surprising thing about self-compassion: People who are more self-compassionate are actually much better than others at taking the perspective of *other people* and not over-focusing on their own distress. People higher in self-compassion tend to see the bigger picture and recognize the common humanity of suffering. In other words, they recognize that everyone faces hard times sometimes and that this is simply a part of life. They are also less likely to ruminate over misfortunes, a key protective factor in maintaining good mental health. These factors combine to protect them from exaggerating their own particular challenges over those of others, maintaining a healthy balance of awareness and perspective.

Self-pity says "Poor me" and gives up or retreats. Self-compassion says, "This is hard, but this is how it feels when people struggle in situations like this." Self-compassion takes stock of the situation and allows the person to assess what they need to navigate the situation wisely, even if it is very hard.

"Self-compassion is weak and wimpy"

It is adaptive for us as human animals to be alert for where we are vulnerable and to protect against potential threats, so it's not surprising that some people may see self-compassion as weak or wimpy in some way. Our gut reaction is to tense up and brace for impact (emotionally *or* physically) as a way of dealing with danger or threat, and anything that doesn't feel firm and solid can feel a bit disconcerting.

But think about what you *really* know about strength, or even more importantly, resilience, which is the quality that really makes us strong. In the physical world, resilience refers to the capacity of a substance or object to spring back into shape, and in a human capacity it refers similarly to our ability to recover quickly from a difficulty. Resilience is not solid and rigid, but strong and flexible, and this is what self-compassion supports. Think about how we build tall buildings these days. They are built to flex and sway with the occasional movement of the earth or wind, so that they bend but don't break, which is the essence of resilience. Research clearly shows that self-compassionate people are better able to cope with tough situations like divorce, trauma, and chronic pain or illness.

Self-compassion is a reliable and ever-present source of inner strength that confers courage and self-reliance for us to navigate difficult circumstances with purpose and resolve. Where weakness is passive or compliant to whatever comes along, and says, "Bring it on, it's all good, you win," self-compassion says, "I can meet this situation with bent knees and flexed muscles so that I can stay strong and present and keep my footing."

"Self-compassion will make me lazy"

Picture the scenario where you tell a friend you're learning to practice self-compassion and they nod their head, roll their eyes, and give you one of those "your secret is safe with me" looks implying that what you're really doing is going to the spa for a mani-pedi and a eucalyptus steam treatment. It can seem that self-compassion is about simply being nice to ourselves and giving ourselves what would make us happy in that moment.

But picture a different scenario. You're in the kitchen waiting impatiently and bleary-eyed for that first cup of coffee to drip-drip-drip its way out of the machine, and your 5-year-old in his red plaid jammies appears beside you demanding strawberry ice cream for breakfast. It may seem compassionate to just give in and say, "Sure, Jeremy, let me get you a bowl and spoon. Would you like chocolate sauce with that?" But is it *really* compassionate to give your kid whatever he wants whenever he wants it? Of course not, even if it would make him very happy just then.

This is because compassion (and self-compassion) are not feel-good practices, but ways of acting wisely, warmly, and firmly under challenging circumstances (and sometimes, this *does* feel good, but sometimes not). You can say no to ice cream for breakfast (and withstand the ensuing storm of protest that may ensue) because you are strong in your belief that a healthy breakfast is actually the wiser, healthier, ultimately compassionate way for Jeremy to start his day. And true to form, the research supports this notion, showing that self-compassionate people engage in healthier behaviors like exercise, eating well, drinking less alcohol, and going to the doctor more regularly.

One study of the Mindful Self-Compassion program showed that people with diabetes who were taught self-compassion practices actually had better HbA1c (average blood sugar levels over time) than those who did not learn the practices.

Putting your hand on your heart and being kind to yourself when you suffer does not automatically lower your blood glucose, but self-compassion practice does very clearly support you in making better choices that improve your physical health.

REMEMBER

Self-compassion is a deep well of strength and inner wisdom to draw upon and a way of maintaining the bigger picture of your hopes, dreams, goals, and values. Self-indulgence says, "Do what makes you happy now, no matter what, because you deserve it" while self-compassion says, "Give yourself what you truly need in this moment to fulfill what is most important to you in life, because you deserve it." And you do deserve to have what you most value in life.

"Self-compassion is really just self-centered and narcissistic"

Similar to self-indulgence, the practice of self-compassion can seem to some to be rather self-centered and self-focused, as if we are prioritizing ourselves over all others. This goes against all the messages we get growing up about helping others, putting others before ourselves, and generally focusing our compassion on those who have greater need. Nobody wants to be told that they are being selfish, and everyone knows that it is good to share.

But think back to a childhood example when you got the message that it was good to share. Imagine that you've come home with a bag of jelly beans that you purchased with your weekly allowance, your siblings are eyeing those colorful morsels with the look of ravenous wolves, and your mom is giving you "the eye" that says, "You know what I'm thinking, young man." You *very* reluctantly dole out a few to your siblings and they are overjoyed, your mother is proud, and you're only a few jelly beans lighter than you were before. While you may still be pouting after this incident, the shared joy can be palpable in the room. Everybody wins and there is joy all around, and you, my little friend, have just learned a little lesson in how your own joy is intertwined with that of the people around you.

This is all to say that when you practice self-compassion, it isn't about directing compassion *only* to yourself, but simply *including* yourself in the circle of goodwill that you already cultivate so easily for others. Why would you be any less deserving of compassion than any other human being? The research demonstrates that self-compassionate people actually tend to be more caring and supportive in romantic relationships, less jealous, and more likely to make compromises as needed in relationship conflicts. In fact, self-compassion is highly related to how compassionate you are toward others, suggesting that they go together and are not at odds with each other.

You may wonder how this works. Self-compassion seems to provide the sense of inner safety and the bravery to admit mistakes, to "own" our own emotions, and therefore not blame others. This helps us cultivate a kind of humility that makes for solid connections with others.

REMEMBER

Self-compassion is a means of giving ourselves a bit of what we offer to others, which means that we are filling our own gas tank while we help to fill the tanks of those around us. Self-centeredness says, "I matter more than you and you need to take care of yourself," while self-compassion says, "You and I both matter, and when we are both compassionate to ourselves, we are much better able to take care of each other too."

"I'll lose my edge if I'm more self-compassionate"

When I hear people say that they fear losing their edge or not reaching their full potential if they are self-compassionate, I always hear the lines of a country song in my head. (And no, it's not "My Achy Breaky Heart.") The line is "You got to dance with the one that brought you," and I think that this is what these people are trying to do. They have achieved a certain success through self-criticism, perfectionism, and putting aside their feelings when they arise, so they are hesitant to let go of this approach.

Think of the police officer who has a reputation for being a "cool customer" when things get real. Or the medical student who has relentlessly driven herself to achieve perfect grades and excellent test scores through relentless self-flagellation and withering self-criticism. It's hard to deny that these ways of being have helped get these people (and many others) to the heights they've achieved, and one can understand why they would be reluctant to stop. Why choose the carrot if the stick seems to have been working for you just fine?

Well, the sad thing is that while self-criticism can get us so far, self-compassion can take us much farther. Compare the motivational impact that a harsh, judgmental, punitive coach may have on your athletic performance to the impact of a kind and supportive coach with high standards for you and a wish for you to achieve your highest performance. The clever, popular saying is "the beatings will continue until morale improves," and this is the kind of approach that self-critical people take, believing that ultimately harsh treatment will lead them to the promised land of their desired goals. In reality, self-criticism turns out to undermine self-confidence and create a fear of failure instead.

And when you think about it, of course it does. If every time you failed, fell short, or made a mistake you suffered the wrath and disgust of your own inner critic, how motivated would *you* be to try again? Research is clear in demonstrating that self-compassionate people are no less likely to have high personal standards than those who are less self-compassionate. They just don't beat themselves up when they fail (as we all do) and are more likely to try again and persist in their efforts afterwards. The benefits are clear, and the penalties are not nearly as painful as those of their self-critical counterparts.

Imagine stepping out in front of an audience of a thousand colleagues at a professional conference to give an important speech. You may have rehearsed your speech a thousand times and edited and refined the words over and over again, but imagine having a voice in your head saying, "Well, you're about to blow it, dear. You have no business even being up here. What made you think you could do this?" Contrast this with "Wow, it's almost surreal to be able to give this speech and share what I've learned with so many of my trusted colleagues. I sure am nervous, and I can feel the butterflies, but I know this stuff and I've got this!"

REMEMBER

Far from undermining your motivation to achieve, self-compassion gives you the self-confidence and strength to follow up on and persist in pursuing what means the most to you, and actually supports you in having high standards for yourself. Where self-criticism and perfectionism say, "Your best isn't good enough, because you're nothing if you don't win," self-compassion says, "I know you have it in you to be the best. You're trying hard and I believe you have it in you to succeed."

Letting your experience be the deciding factor

As I say earlier, I don't actually expect you to suddenly be a true believer in self-compassion now that I have laid out some of the common misgivings and the findings of science that refute those doubts. My hope is that you now have a richer and deeper appreciation for what self-compassion actually is and what it is not, and perhaps you will be a little bit more inclined to try it out for yourself. I will always refrain from telling you what you should feel or how you should act, but instead invite you to try some things, give yourself some opportunities, and generally explore this practice for yourself. If you find that self-compassion works for you and brings you more ease, less distress, and a more fulfilling and satisfying life, you will keep it up. You won't need me for that.

Chapter **3**

The Self-Compassion Road Ahead

A s I highlight in the previous chapters, simply having enough information, science, or even inspiration won't necessarily turn you into a more self-compassionate human being. You can read a hundred books on swimming, watch dozens of YouTube videos of Olympic swimming competitions, and talk to all your friends who swim, but you're not a swimmer until you get into the water and do it. And the same is true of self-compassion.

Fortunately, with self-compassion, you don't have to just plunge into the deep end of the pool, so to speak, and flounder around until you either swim or drown. But you do need the willingness to change some old habits and patterns, to do some things that may not feel completely familiar or comfortable or even easy, and to have an open mind and patience about the whole process as you dip your toe in the waters of self-compassion practice. In this chapter I show you some ways to take care of yourself so that you can get the most out of this challenging practice.

Don't lose hope if you are thinking right now that your particular feelings are just too painful, too overwhelming, or too pervasive to be helped by self-compassion. Experience has taught me over the years that this is simply not the case. You have come to the right place, and the secret is all in how you pace yourself and take care of yourself while making this important change. This chapter prepares you well for the challenges ahead. You belong here, and if you remember that, even when the going gets tough, you will be glad you stayed.

REMEMBER

For ease of communication here and throughout the book, I use the umbrella term "suffering." Many of us equate the word "suffering" to the kind of intense unfortunate suffering that people experience in abuse, neglect, war, and other violence. This level of suffering is what I refer to as "Capital 'S' Suffering." Here, I use "suffering" to encompass any form of discomfort, stress, uneasiness, pain, or distress — it may be helpful to think of it as "lowercase 's' suffering." This is the kind of suffering that we all experience as humans in our everyday lives. Some call it "struggle" or "stress" instead.

Why Self-Compassion Isn't Always Easy

Perhaps the most difficult part of self-compassion is the fact that one needs to encounter and work with pain and suffering in order to practice it. The joke among Mindful Self-Compassion teachers is that the program is really more like the "Opening to Pain and Suffering Program," but if we actually called it that, nobody would sign up! Who wants to experience challenging emotions or difficult thoughts? Did you buy this book because you wanted to experience discomfort? Probably not. As a matter of fact, it may have been your suffering or discomfort that drove you to explore this practice in the first place. In other words, you came here to *get rid* of suffering and find more ease, and now you're finding out that in order to find ease, you may have to feel the things you least want to feel.

At this point, you may be feeling betrayed and disillusioned, and I wouldn't blame you for entertaining a few thoughts of quitting now and trying something else to control, avoid, or reduce the suffering in your life. But before you do this, I'd like to invite you on a little journey down memory lane to review your path to this particular moment. (This exercise is drawn from the innovative *Acceptance and Commitment Therapy* developed by Stephen Hayes and colleagues.) Carefully consider your answers to the following prompts:

>> Have there been times in your life when you found yourself suffering and wanting to somehow control these feelings through avoiding, suppressing, or ignoring them?

» What, specifically, did you do in response to those feelings to try to control them? (For example: Did you distract yourself; deny the feelings; do relaxation exercises or meditate; drink alcohol, eat, or take drugs; go to a therapist or doctor?)

» Whatever coping strategy you chose (and you may have chosen several over the years), how did each one work at first? Did you feel better or get some relief?

» What happened over time if you persisted with each of those same coping strategies? Did you continue to feel better or were there "diminishing returns" on your efforts? In other words, was the strategy less and less effective over time? And were there additional consequences to your coping strategy that may have made things worse? For example: Maybe you started drinking too much, over-relied upon anxiety medication, or got into trouble because you resisted or denied the feelings and actually worsened them by doing so.

» If you think about what motivated you to try these various things to control, avoid, or eliminate your difficult emotions, is it possible that the same motivation led you to pick up this book and explore self-compassion?

If you are like most people (and frankly, aren't we all?), then I would be willing to bet that the previous reflection led you to discover that you have been on a long (perhaps lifelong) quest to get rid of your suffering through various means of controlling, avoiding, or suppressing it. In the words of a certain famous TV psychologist: "How's that been working out for you so far?" I'm guessing it hasn't gone well in the long run.

So before deciding to make self-compassion your next thing in a long line of attempts to control these feelings, what would it be like to consider that perhaps the *real* problem here is not that you *have* suffering but actually the attempt to *control* these feelings in the first place? The common thread in your various attempts to contend with your suffering so far (without sustained effect) is that you have, in fact, been trying to control it. To put it another way, control is the problem.

If you instead consider self-compassion as a means of *encountering* these feelings, not to control them but to *change your relationship* with them, then there is some possibility of real, substantial change to happen. As I note in Chapter 1, one of the three components of self-compassion is common humanity, and it is reflected in the simple phrase from the Self-Compassion Break: "Suffering is a part of life." If you admit that these feelings are a part of the human experience, like gravity, imperfection, and death, you begin to slowly loosen the grip that they have on you because you recognize that they are experiences to be accommodated rather than problems to be solved.

Using gravity as one example, we all acknowledge that gravity exerts an influence on our lives (in practical terms, "gravity sucks," especially when we regard ourselves in the mirror periodically and see how things aren't quite where they used to be . . . thanks for that, gravity). However, despite the reality of gravity, nobody wakes up in the morning and gets out of bed, only to exclaim "Damn! I'm still stuck to the earth!" This is because we have come to terms with the reality of gravity and we work with it, rather than rail against it. The question is whether you can do the same with your very human emotions and suffering.

In the pages ahead I map out some ways you can begin to alter your relationship with suffering, but for now just pause and consider what it takes to do this. It means that when you feel pain or discomfort, you need to let go of trying to control it, push it away, or avoid it, and instead, to some extent, be willing to lean into it and see if there is something to be gained from doing so. The idea of leaning into pain that we would rather avoid may sound awful or even terrifying (like the idea of jumping into the pool when you can't swim), but even this can be done gradually, in line with what you can manage and nothing more.

This process takes no small measure of courage now and then, but the potential payoff can be tremendous. Take some time in the following pages to consider how to chart a course for relief of your suffering that is likely to take you on some bumpy roads and take some twists and turns. And know that, like life itself, this is where the really fruitful discoveries usually happen and where we truly grow as humans. I'm here to support you along the way, and I have no doubt that you've got this.

REMEMBER

A note of caution: While I speak about difficult emotions here in a somewhat light-hearted, breezy way, I know quite well that you may struggle mightily with incredibly painful, intense, pervasive, and debilitating emotions that are crippling at times and may seem just too overwhelming and powerful to work with in any meaningful way. This is true of large numbers of people who come to self-compassion and mindfulness courses. If this is true of you, you are not alone. Know that the guidance provided here still applies to you, but it is of paramount importance that you read this chapter carefully and follow my guidance to go slowly, allow yourself to ease into this approach, and know that balancing curiosity and self-care, safety and courage, will support you.

Getting the Most Out of This Practice

Have you considered what your relationship is to this practice of self-compassion? Probably not; it's not something that most of us do on a regular basis. But if you pause and consider it, you probably do actually have a relationship to this material and practice. Perhaps you are feeling intrigued or (dare I say it?) enthralled at what you have read so far, excited even. Or perhaps your relationship to all of this is a bit more cautious and skeptical. Maybe your attitude could be summed up in the body language of sitting back with arms crossed and saying (with your eyes and your posture): "Show me what you've got." Or maybe you're feeling relieved, as if this is the thing that will finally solve the problems you face in your life. Take a moment and check in with yourself to see what your relationship is just now with the idea of being kinder to yourself when you struggle.

There is room here for all attitudes. I'm not asking you to consider this to change you, but to make you're aware that your attitude makes a difference in how you experience something. I'm going to ask you to consider adopting certain attitudes toward the rest of this book and the practices I describe so that you can get the most out of them.

Think about the last time you had your favorite food. What was your attitude about that food? If you were ravenous and super-excited to be having your favorite pizza, you may have had a great deal of excitement, eaten quickly, and exclaimed loudly about how awesome it was. Or perhaps you had been anticipating it for many days and fantasizing about what it would be like, and when the day finally came, maybe you savored each bite, letting your eyes roll up in your head in delight (like they do on the TV commercials) as if the whole experience were one of pure ecstasy. Or perhaps the last time you had that favorite pizza you were engrossed in a Netflix binge-watching frenzy, and frankly, you don't really remember what the pizza tasted like. Attitudes are like that. They lead to different experiences.

And so, I invite you to have what experienced meditators call "beginner's mind" about self-compassion practice. This means letting go of your expectations and preconceived notions about self-compassion and seeing it with an open mind, like a beginner. Think of the first time you learned to do something that you now do relatively well. Everything is a discovery; there is curiosity, patience, maybe some confusion, a few missteps, but all in the service of opening up to a new experience, having a new adventure. This is your invitation to approach self-compassion practice with a sense of adventure and an open mind.

Having the spirit of an adventurer

Thus far I have spoken of your foray into self-compassion as a kind of personal journey. Notice how that notion feels in your body: You are on a journey. If you feel anything noteworthy, it may be a kind of heaviness or even fatigue in your body, as you contemplate putting one foot in front of the other for many, many steps. A journey is a task, a thing to be accomplished, a kind of solemn and noble obligation to get from here to there.

Now consider a different possibility: What if instead of a journey, you are on an adventure? Let that sink in and check in to see how that feels to you. Try it on and wear it around a little bit. It feels a bit different, right? There may be a spark of excitement, maybe a flareup of curiosity, a twinge of apprehension or even fear. I don't know about you, but when I contemplate going on an adventure, it gets my juices flowing and I have a sense of heightened awareness. My sympathetic nervous system just dumps a few drops of adrenaline into my system.

So I'd like to suggest that this journey is actually an adventure for you. See if you can approach it with the spirit of an adventurer, not only with a sense of beginner's mind, but also with a bit of anticipation of . . . something, though you don't yet know what. An adventure takes us into uncharted territory where we may very well encounter surprises, unanticipated obstacles, and glorious discoveries.

The obstacles in self-compassion practice may include strong emotions, hidden memories, or frustrating old patterns that try to keep us stuck in old, unworkable ways of being. Discovering these twists and turns on the adventure — the raging stream of pent-up, painful emotions; the deep ravine of untended shame; the perilous paths of persistent anxiety — is all part of the adventure of self-compassion.

Consider adopting the attitude of ancient explorers when all the maps of the earth still extended out to the distances that people had traveled, and then there were labels for the uncharted territories where it said "beyond there be dragons" to discourage future explorers from going into the unknown. I am inviting you to perhaps adventure into these regions of the unknown, acknowledging that there is not only some fear or apprehension, but also the promise of new discoveries. You can achieve a greater sense of mastery of the inner terrain and confidence in yourself for having gone there. I'm not asking you to be foolhardy, but I am asking you to be curious, patient, and willing to stretch yourself on an inner adventure.

Being a self-compassion scientist

While I provide a guide and a map for your adventure, and accompany you on this journey, it is up to you to explore the terrain and decide for yourself how it may suit you and what you may gain from becoming more self-compassionate. I suggest that you adopt the attitude of a researcher: Think of what I describe to you as your working hypothesis, use your own inner experience as your "laboratory," and observe your own "data" to come to your own conclusions.

The qualities of a good scientist include being open-minded about what you may discover (beginner's mind) and cultivating curiosity about whatever you witness. Recognizing that you are human, and as such, have various ideas (theories) about how things are or should be, can be a challenge to maintaining an open, curious mind. Our brains try to be efficient and like to create scripts for how things work (called *schemas*) and to summarize complex processes into simple labels (like "successful" or "easy" or "deserving"). But as a rigorous, objective scientist, you want to look a bit closer at these assumptions and test them out by studying them more closely.

For example, if you practice a meditation and find yourself characterizing it as "hard," don't settle for that label, but ask yourself, "What led me to call that meditation 'hard'? What was the *data* that led me to that conclusion?" Many times, things are not what our brain tells us they are, but we only know if we adopt the conservative approach of the researcher.

One last note about letting this process of self-compassion become a grand personal experiment: See if you can put aside the question of "why" and instead focus upon the "what" and the "how" instead. Ask yourself

>> *"What* am I aware of right now?"

>> *"What* did I notice when I was kind to myself?"

>> *"How* did I respond to a moment of struggle?"

These are the fruitful questions that researchers ask in order to gather good data.

You may wonder what's wrong with asking yourself "why" and that's a reasonable question to ask. In fact, even asking that question is actually a form of "why" question in itself ("Why can't I ask why?")! *Why* is a beautiful, deep, and thoughtful kind of question, and one that humans are uniquely able to ask and even answer sometimes. *Why* can bring some order and meaning to your experience, but when it comes to the complex world inside our hearts and minds, *why* becomes a bit of a rabbit hole down which you can easily disappear if you aren't careful. Wondering *why* you are having an emotion may lead you down a path of trying to eliminate or avoid the emotion, which we have already established is a nearly impossible thing to do. And even if we do know *why* we are feeling something, the question becomes what you can do about it if the *why* is in the past.

Sometimes the *why* question can also lead to trying to assign blame for a feeling or experience. While blame may be important in some circumstances, when speaking about our own internal experiences, it is not at all helpful. If someone else did something to lead to the feeling we have, we are still the ones having to contend with that feeling, regardless of blame. Blame leaves you stuck and powerless when you most need to access your own compassion to support and encourage yourself.

When you notice that you have an emotion, say shame, your natural human tendency is to wonder why you feel that shame and to try to ascribe a cause or a condition that led you to this feeling. But in your best scientific approach (picture yourself in the white coat of a lab researcher, looking through the microscope), your job is to simply observe what can be seen and described so that you can put this data with other data, to begin to understand your experience in a larger context. Give yourself permission to be free from the entanglement of *why* and explore the rich and fruitful world of *what* and *how* instead.

Being willing to be a slow learner and your own best teacher

In the pages ahead you will discover quite a number of different tips, tricks, meditations, exercises, and informal practices to help you develop your capacity to become more self-compassionate. As a package, it could seem impossibly hard to digest and integrate all of these different elements, but luckily, you don't have to (and most people don't). What I lay out ahead is a variety of options, a veritable self-compassion buffet, and your heart and mind (like your plate at a buffet) is only so big. Each of us has a different plate, so to speak, but the key is to not overload your plate and know that you can always come back for more, if you want. The self-compassion buffet is an all-you-can-eat affair, and fresh plates are always available. If you find a practice or way of thinking that suits you, come back for seconds and thirds. Feel free to skip other things that just don't inspire or move you. Of course, I hope you will try everything at least once (to have what my former in-laws called a "no thank you helping"), but don't feel obligated to embrace everything you find.

If you think of your introduction to self-compassion here as only the beginning of your adventure, then you can give yourself permission to go slowly and take it in at your own pace. In the Mindful Self-Compassion program, we encourage everyone to be a *slow learner* and to move, as the motivational speaker Stephen Covey likes to say, at the speed of trust. Specifically, the speed of trust is the speed that is *right for you*. Don't force yourself to move faster than you are able to assimilate the material. Just because you *can* move faster doesn't mean you *should*. You can easily defeat the whole purpose of self-compassion by flogging yourself to do more, to do better, and to do faster.

Let me share a personal example of what happens when you push yourself too fast. I once went downhill skiing with a dear friend named Fred. He and I were young and competitive, and on one particular steep run, I noticed Fred shoot out way ahead of me, going twice as fast as me and navigating beautifully. I told myself, "If Fred can do it, I can do it," so I let loose and sped up. I found myself going faster than I ever had, and it was exhilarating, but I was still losing ground to speedy Fred. I cranked out a little more speed, and sure enough I was holding my own and going even faster. But I wasn't quite catching up to Fred yet, and right in the middle of my next burst, still thinking "If Fred can do it, I can do it," I came to a sudden and frightening realization: "That's not Fred!"

Almost instantaneously I lost confidence, and right after that went control. I eventually ended up in a heap of snow, skis, poles, and my dignity. I glanced *way* up the hill and there was Fred, lazily sweeping down the hill, probably wondering what had possessed me to take off like that. I learned my lesson, to trust my own abilities and stay within myself. I encourage you to do the same and never say, "If Steve can do it, I can do it." Move at the speed of your own trust. That is just right.

Learning from your own experience, relying on your inner wisdom, and moving at the speed of trust are all powerful ways of letting you be your own teacher, if you are willing to do so. You may not be confident that you have anything to offer yourself, but trust me, you do. Take some time and listen, be curious, and be patient. Only take from the buffet the things that nourish and support you, and, voilà, you've just been both student and teacher!

If it's a struggle, it's not self-compassion

As you review the challenges of practicing self-compassion, you may be wondering just exactly what you've gotten yourself into. I hear you, but there's some good news in all of this that you ought to know. While this work can be occasionally challenging, the ultimate goal is to find a way to practice that is actually easy and pleasant. Moments of self-compassion are actually moments of ease, comfort, and encouragement, not striving, forcing, or berating. Your aim in this practice is to reduce stress and let go of your striving for something else and working so hard to find ease. More work is not the path to ease, just as more self-criticism does not lead to self-acceptance. The ironic pirate saying is that "the beatings will continue until morale improves." Struggling to practice self-compassion is likely to be just as fruitless.

In fact, as you make your way through this book and this practice, if you find yourself struggling, pushing yourself, or in some other way trying to make something happen, this is not actually self-compassion at all, and it's time to pause and take stock of the situation. You may wonder how to recognize and work with those moments of struggle, and I have a few tips:

1. **Notice your body.**

   If you find that your jaw is clenched, your brow is furrowed, your butt cheeks are clenched, or your shoulders are somewhere in the vicinity of your ears, you may just be trying a bit too hard. See what you can possibly let go of in the way of tension, clenching, or bracing, and see what unfolds.

2. **Listen for the sounds of resistance and forcing.**

   A moment of resistance or trying too hard can sound a bit like the sounds those Olympic weightlifters make when they thrust a barbell that weighs more than your sofa (with you on it) into the air. If the sound is something like "grrrrrr" or "aaarrrrrggggghhhh," then you are struggling and not practicing self-compassion.

3. **Take a moment to practice the sound of mindfulness.**

   The pause and letting go of needing things to be different can elicit a delicious exhale that sounds like "ahhhhhhhhh." Try it now: "ahhhhhhhhh." Notice how this feels in your body.

4. **Try a little tenderness.**

   If you're having a hard time, see if you can tap into your mammalian caregiving system (see Chapter 2) for a little warmth and soothing vocalization by offering yourself the quintessential sound of tender self-compassion: "awwwwwwww." Try it now: "awwwwwwww." Notice how that feels in your body. You can almost feel the endorphins flooding your bloodstream.

5. **Listen past your inner critic.**

   In Chapter 9 we spend a great deal of time and attention on how we can work with that annoying and hurtful inner voice. But for now, if you find the inner critic nattering on inside your head about what's wrong with you, see if you can simply listen *past* the critic for a few moments and listen to the other voice inside you that's been a bit quieter and wants the best for you. Maybe you can hear the whispers of self-compassion that can help you through the tough spots if you only listen.

Building Resilience Through Courageous Self-Compassion

The philosopher Friedrich Nietzsche famously said, "That which does not kill us makes us stronger." The implication here is that going through challenging experiences does not break us down but instead builds us up, and this is especially true for self-compassion. Self-compassion is not life-threatening (in fact, it's more life-affirming than anything), but it can be challenging. We also know that we grow through challenge, which is why when we go to the gym we don't immediately walk over to the smallest weights, but instead find our "challenge zone" so that we can build our strength and increase our ability to do what we want to do.

It's one thing to pick up a heavier weight at the gym (especially when nobody is looking and won't see you grimace when you choose one that's too heavy), but it's an entirely different thing when that "heavy weight" is actually a familiar but painful emotion like grief, fear, or shame. But think about this for a moment: You *already* experience these and many more emotions every day. They are coming and going with the twists and turns of your life journey anyway, and trying to change those emotions is fruitless. So why not see if you can come to terms with these feelings and slowly, over time, cultivate a more harmonious relationship with them?

In theory, cultivating a more harmonious relationship with your difficult feelings may seem like a good idea, and in Chapter 10 we discuss some particular ways to do that, but those are more advanced self-compassion skills to be built up to over time. For now, we need to "prepare the ground" for building our practice of self-compassion by creating an inner environment that supports us in making a significant change like this. This idea of staying present to unpleasantness and even pain is not our usual way of dealing with these feelings, and the ability to do it requires two very important ingredients. To begin to cultivate a different relationship with the difficult experiences that we are bound to encounter when practicing self-compassion, we need a winning combination of safety and courage.

Courage and safety: A winning combination

The greatest adventures in history all began with the same two important elements: safety and courage. Think of explorers like Marco Polo, Amelia Earhart, and Odysseus. We remember each as brave and intrepid individuals with a dream, a desire, and a passion for adventure as they indulged in grand escapades that still inspire us today. But each of these daring individuals also set off on their journeys from safe and supportive home bases, loaded up with adequate supplies, good maps, careful preparation, and an inner sense of confidence, support, and self-assuredness. There are also many historical examples of people setting off on ill-fated journeys that were certainly daring (like going over Niagara Falls in a barrel) but bereft of safety or even sanity. And of course, there are the "adventurers" who felt so incredibly safe and comfortable that they never left port, or even their homes, and we only know their names because they wrote about adventure rather than engaging in it. Safety without courage maintains the status quo. Courage without safety is just bold and impulsive risk-taking without regard for success and with a significant chance of spectacular failure.

The same is true of the inner journey of self-compassion. We need to feel safe and comfortable enough to try something that requires us to be courageous, and we're only able to act courageously if we feel safe and secure enough to do so. Safety and courage are complementary qualities that together make us resilient and strong in the face of the challenges of life. Thankfully, both can be cultivated and harnessed to support us on our self-compassion journey.

Try this reflection:

> Think back on your adult life and call to mind something you have done that was important or meaningful to you in some way — something that felt bold or risky at the time.
>
> It doesn't have to be anything huge, or anything anyone else was even aware of. Whatever it was, it may have represented a departure from your habitual way of doing things. Maybe it was asking someone out on a date, choosing to enroll in college courses, or volunteering to chair a food drive for your church.
>
> Putting aside the particular outcomes of your decision, see if you can recall what was going on for you right before you made the decision.
>
> There may have been a bit of internal debate prior to this decision, as if you had two little voices in your head (like the cliché angel and devil on each shoulder). One voice may have been urging you on, telling you to say "yes," and one voice may have been holding you back, reminding you of the risks, telling you "no" or just "not now." Courage and fear were dancing together in that moment. See if you can get in touch with both for a moment and make a little mental space for them to acknowledged.
>
> If you look a bit closer at this tug-of-war between courage and fear, you may detect another less obvious dialogue between the safety and danger. Safety may have been reminding you of how comfortable and lucky you were to be exactly where you were. Danger was saying "no guts, no glory" or "in order to make an omelet, you have to break a few eggs" (the clichés that we use to motivate ourselves are endless!). What were safety and danger each telling you in that moment?
>
> In this case, you didn't opt for the status quo or business as usual, but instead you made a valiant (for you) choice to shift and change. What made that possible for you? What was courageous in this choice? In what way did you feel safe and secure enough to take the calculated risk and be courageous? Can you feel how these two aspects of your experience, safety and courage, worked together to support you in taking action?

With this awareness of how safety and courage dance within you to help you make important changes, consider what may be possible in regard to self-compassion. Can you see how safety and courage play out when it comes to challenging emotions and pain of all sorts that we encounter in our daily lives as human beings?

What you resist, persists

I have often said that by far the worst advice anyone can give is "Don't worry." I mean, think about it. When, in the history of humankind, has that advice actually worked for literally *anyone*? And even though it has never worked for us when we've tried it, we continue to offer the same advice to everyone else nonetheless!

There is an element of wishful thinking in trying not to worry. When we worry, the thoughts we are having are uncomfortable, and of course we don't want to be uncomfortable, so we try to make the uncomfortable thoughts stop by wishing them away. But you know the old example: Try not to think about a pink elephant. Really try hard *not* to think about a pink elephant. Whatever you do, *don't* think about a pink elephant. Anyone who reads these words, whether they try to comply or not, has images of pink pachyderms floating in their head. It's how our human brains work.

This is all due to what psychologists refer to as the *ironic process theory* whereby deliberate attempts to suppress certain thoughts actually make them more likely to surface. In plain language, we say, "What you resist, persists." And not only does it apply to our thoughts, but it's also true of feelings and other phenomena. As one colleague says, if you resist your sleeplessness you get insomnia, if you resist your anxiety you get panic, and if you resist your daughter's lousy boy-friend, you get a lousy son-in-law. You get the picture. Resisting something doesn't make it go away.

Now take an example of difficult emotions and see how it often works. Consider the situation of the death of a loved one. Your beloved aunt, who largely raised you as a child, recently passed away after a long bout with cancer. Aunt Trudy has always been your rock, the one who could console you in your darkest moments and was there to celebrate you in your successes. And now she's gone and there is a feeling like a hole in your heart that feels impossible to fill. In fact, just noticing that hollow feeling in the middle of your chest triggers thoughts of overwhelm as you wonder how you will ever go on without her.

Many of us have had this sort of loss in our lives that leaves us feeling bewildered and incredibly alone, but that knowledge doesn't typically make us feel any better in the moment. In general, there are at least two forms that resistance can take: avoidance and immersion.

If you were to try to avoid the feelings of grief, you might try to distract yourself by putting all your energy into organizing a memorable funeral for Aunt Trudy and being the "hostess with the mostest" of a reception in her honor. You might establish the Aunt Trudy Foundation to raise money to continue her good works. You might take a long-postponed vacation because it's something that Aunt Trudy would have wanted for you. On the surface, nothing in these options is inherently bad or problematic, but if your primary motive in doing so is to avoid feeling the natural grief that arises in response to a loss of this depth, then you are actually resisting the reality of your legitimate feelings and trying to deny them in a certain way. The grief won't disappear just because you're not tending to it. As you and the rest of the world move on, the grief will linger in the shadows, and long after most people have adjusted to this terrible loss, you will still find yourself touching grief and reacting by distracting, throwing yourself back into whatever distracting activity you can. Thus, what you resisted truly persisted, and much longer than if you had been willing to confront it.

People have told me in therapy that they *really* wish that they could control the grieving or acceptance process because it is so painful and disruptive for them. I have, somewhat tongue in cheek, told them that I know only one way to control the process of healing. People sit up a bit straighter when they hear these words, and they lean in with questions in their eyes. I lean in too and say, "You *can* control the healing process, but only in one direction and not the other. That is, there's no way you can make it go faster, but if you continue to resist, deny, and avoid, you have the ability to make it go on indefinitely." Oddly, nobody likes to hear this so-called wisdom, but it's true. Think about a physical wound as an analogy. You can't rush the healing process like they did on *Star Trek* with the wave of some futuristic healing electronic device, but you can pick at scabs, not keep the wound clean, and generally futz around with it so that it takes seeming *forever* to heal.

On the other hand, maybe you become overwhelmed by the grief as you play out all the ways in which you feel you can't go on without Aunt Trudy. Seemingly in honor of the loss, you immerse yourself in the grief as if that will somehow transform it. You spend a lot of time watching videos of you and Aunt Trudy in happier times, or you reread the letters she wrote you when you were away at college, or you withdraw from most of your commitments "to grieve" when in fact you are just feeling more and more nostalgic for the past, feeling depressed and unable to continue. This is not grieving so much as it is wallowing and is actually a tricky form of resistance. On the surface it looks like you are "processing" your loss, but in fact you are stuck in over-identification with your pain, ruminating over what it means, and generally unable to gain enough distance from the situation to put it into perspective or to make meaning of it. And sadly, the more that you see that you are stuck, the more stuck you feel, and the grief spirals down into what psychologists call "complicated grief." Again, what one finds in this situation is that what was resisted (through immersion) has persisted, and if anything, was magnified.

What you feel, you can heal

In addition to avoidance and immersion, there is a third, middle pathway through the grief over the loss of Aunt Trudy that actually acknowledges the reality (including the pain and the sadness and the fear that comes with that reality) and supports you in coming to terms with the loss so that you can move forward. The distractions of avoidance and immersion keep you from being able to honor Aunt Trudy's tremendous contributions to your life and charting a course forward that is in line with what you learned from her and what she truly wanted for you.

The antidote to "What you resist, persists" is the saying, "What you feel, you can heal." The middle path for coming to terms with the reality of Aunt Trudy's death is to be willing to courageously find a way to acknowledge the pain that you feel, because it is absolutely, positively, 100 percent human of you to feel that loss. But rather than slipping away from this pain, the challenge is to see if you can allow yourself to experience it simply because it is here anyway. Once you realize how fruitless it is to try to avoid or immerse yourself in difficult feelings (again, the memory of *Star Trek* comes up: "resistance is futile"), it becomes a bit easier to instead try to find your way into some kind of tolerable and meaningful relationship with those feelings.

The key to what psychologists call "integrated grief" is to slowly let go of the initial resistance and denial and to instead integrate the thoughts, feelings, and behaviors associated with the loss, such that perfectly appropriate grief has a place in your life without dominating or distorting that life. Self-compassion can help you in this process, and this is explored in Chapters 10 and 11, but for now, my hope is that you see that there may be some wisdom (and healing) in being willing to encounter pain and suffering on its own terms, as a means of cultivating a more harmonious relationship with it. Even if you think of your suffering as an adversary or an enemy, you may be able to see the wisdom of knowing your adversary and appreciating its qualities as a means of conquering it. Michael Corleone in *The Godfather, Part II* shared the wise advice, "Keep your friends close, and your enemies closer." This gangster advice can apply to those difficult feelings, as long as you don't plan to try to "whack" those feelings when they arise.

Dancing with pain

No one wants to experience pain and suffering, but I believe I have established that this is actually a part of the human condition, and that perhaps our lives would be more fruitful if we could let go of the notion that suffering is actually a problem to be resisted, eliminated, or avoided. Instead, our challenge is to see if it may be possible for us to accommodate suffering the same way we accommodate gravity, because it's there, and then find a way to live alongside it in such a way that it doesn't derail or distract us from what is most important in our lives. That may sound good in theory, but you may also be wondering how in the world one actually *does* this in real life. A former client of mine named Dean provided a vivid and helpful example of one way of doing so.

Dean is a tough guy. He grew up in a rough neighborhood in Detroit, Michigan, and learned early how to get through life by fighting with whatever got in his way. He established his toughness by winning fights with neighborhood kids, climbing to the top of his weight class on the wrestling team at school, and learning to "be tough" and "play through the pain" as a football player. He went on to fight his way to the top of his professional field as a successful salesman. Then he had a couple of unfortunate accidents that led to multiple surgeries and implantation of various metal contraptions to stabilize his neck and spine, which gave him X-rays that looked a bit like Frankenstein's monster. But he was also left with debilitating chronic neck, shoulder, and back pain that led to severe depression and thoughts of suicide.

Thankfully, Dean's pain doctor referred him to me as a psychologist and he was receptive to taking a mindfulness course with me to try to help him cope more effectively with his medical condition. He was cautiously optimistic but very skeptical as well. He wondered if perhaps this was another in a long line of relaxation techniques that would barely touch his pain. He knew that his pain was chronic (meaning that it was ongoing and unlikely to go away), and he wondered how he could avoid or control or reduce his pain through simply becoming more aware of it. Indeed, the last thing he really wanted to do was become *more* aware of his pain.

But Dean's curiosity outweighed his skepticism, and he felt just safe enough with me to be brave and explore the practice of mindfulness. (*Note:* Mindfulness and self-compassion are intricately interwoven; I discuss the role of mindfulness in depth in the next chapter.) He enrolled in the course and diligently participated in every session, trying the home practices and doing his best to get the most out of the experience.

We had reached the midpoint of the mindfulness course when Dean arrived at class visibly excited and more upbeat than I had ever seen him. As we checked in with people about their week, his hand shot up immediately and he started by saying, "I finally figured out how meditating and paying attention can help me with this awful chronic pain." The room was captivated. "As you know, I've been a fighter and a tough guy all my life. It's what I do, or should I say, what I've done. And with this pain, you've heard me talk about it like it's a monster or an enemy, and how I fight with it every single day of my life, and most of the time I'm losing that fight. But this week it dawned on me that instead of fighting with my pain, or trying to pretend it isn't there, I could *dance with it instead!*"

Dean had discovered a different way of meeting his own suffering, thereby altering his relationship with his pain. Just stop for a moment and reflect on the difference between *fighting* and *dancing*, how it feels in your body to contemplate each of these and how they are associated with very different emotional states. Fighting may have a physical tension to it: gritting of the teeth or bracing for impact or curling of the fists. Dancing has a flow, a rhythm, and an ease that feels more relaxed, more purposeful, and sustainable. Both fighting and dancing are engaged with the pain; neither denies its existence nor tries to escape it (because it is inescapable) or surrender to it. There is a courage in choosing to engage and dance with pain and suffering that leads to harmony and a release of tension. Dancing with the pain has the feeling of saying "ahhhhhhh" rather than "grrrrrrrrr."

Another thing about Dean and his discovery: Imagine if, on his first visit to my office when he told me his story, I had said, "Ohhh, I know just what you need. You just need to learn to dance with your pain instead of fighting with it." How do you think that would have gone? I might very well have been yet one more victim of his tendency to punch his way through life! It would have sounded to him like I was telling him to "just get over it" or "suck it up, buttercup," and he would have (rightfully so) been insulted and angry and would have dismissed anything else I ever had to say to him. Some lessons are only learned in the living of them, and this is one.

I know that what I've written here points you in a certain direction and perhaps allows you to open up to the possibility that there is something important in what I am saying, but you will only know for sure if you take what I suggest and try it on for size for yourself. Dean got to where he did because he was willing to try what I was teaching and see how it landed *for him.* I urge you to follow Dean's example and see what you might gain from doing so.

Oh, and a note on this idea of *trying,* when it comes to self-compassion or mindfulness, or really anything else in life. This is a human capacity that every one of us possesses, which means that it's not really about trying, but simply doing. To quote the wisest Zen master who never actually existed, Yoda of *Star Wars* fame: "Do or do not, there is no try." It's up to you. I recommend that you do.

The Four Noble Truths: A Buddhist Perspective on Being Human

While compassion and mindfulness are universal aspects of being human, various spiritual traditions have examined these qualities of mind and heart and spoken about them in quite eloquent and helpful ways. Buddhism has perhaps explored these phenomena more than most, and while self-compassion is not a Buddhist practice per se, it may help you to shift your relationship with life's suffering by looking at how they speak of suffering.

Buddhism abounds with lists of things (for example, The Three Refuges, The Eightfold Path, The Four Foundations of Mindfulness, The Seven Dwarfs. Okay, not the last one, but you get what I mean.) We are not going to delve into most of these, as interesting and practical as they may be upon closer inspection, but there is one list that helps us see our own struggles in a larger context that can loosen the grip of suffering on our lives and make room for a more self-compassionate stance toward life.

The Four Noble Truths comprise the essence of the Buddha's teaching and lay out, in very concrete and concise terms, what he observed about life and suffering from being a keen observer of people and experience. Therefore, these are scientific observations made in the same spirit that I encourage you to be a scientific observer of your own experience so that you can draw your own conclusions. The Buddha came to the conclusion that if we are aware of these truths and accept or embrace them, we can find a way to liberate ourselves from suffering. I'm in; how about you?

TECHNICAL STUFF

A brief note on the label "The Four Noble Truths": The word "noble," in this case, refers to the discoveries made by people on the "noble path" or those who routinely embody admirable personal qualities like honesty, generosity, and courage. And the word "truth" refers to the predictability with which these things arise in daily life. So, The Four Noble Truths arise from direct observation of *the way things are for people* in the mental/emotional world, just as we know the truth of the laws of physics and thermodynamics by observing them in the physical world. These are not platitudes handed down from an ethereal or mythical being, but instead scientific observations made by wise and intentional humans who have sought to make sense of their experience.

First noble truth: Suffering exists

It seems simple enough, but this first truth is worth taking note of because it acknowledges that suffering is not something that intrudes into our lives or impedes our lives as humans, but is actually an integral *part of our lives*. When we can fully acknowledge that life *always* includes some suffering (in both obvious and subtle forms), it can begin to help us loosen our grip on trying to make it disappear. Like gravity mentioned earlier, when we acknowledge the reality of it, we can then find a way to live alongside it. It's also worth noting that even when things seem good to us, we feel some undercurrent of anxiety, dissatisfaction, or uncertainty. This is a part of being human. It is one aspect of our common humanity, and it binds us to each other because we all experience it.

Second noble truth: The cause of suffering

Seeing our suffering as having an explainable cause, rather than being random, chaotic, or inflicted by a source outside ourselves, is particularly helpful. The second truth says that the source of our suffering is desire (or craving) and the opposite of desire, which we could call aversion. Aversion is actually just craving in reverse, meaning that we are grasping for something other than what we already have. For example, "I ordered the fish, but I wish I'd ordered the chicken instead." Yes, we have to admit that, although we often like to blame things outside of ourselves for our suffering, such as circumstances, luck, or other people, the cause is actually us, or more accurately, our attitude toward the realities we face. This is not to say that we are to blame for the circumstances we find ourselves in, but it is in *wanting it to be different than it is* where our suffering arises. In a rather benign case that you are sitting in a boring lecture, wishing you were someplace else and feeling as if the boredom is unbearable and even painful, the suffering in this equation does not come from the lecture itself. The lecture is just the lecture. The degree to which you suffer during this lecture is the degree to which you are craving *the experience of not being there because of your boredom*. Suffering can actually be summed up as "the struggle with *what is*."

Third noble truth: The end of suffering

"Finally!" you are saying to yourself. "Enough with all the suffering and stress and pain, I want to know if it can end." The Buddha says that there is indeed an end of suffering because these ideas of deeply craving things and pushing things away that we are not willing to accept are just thoughts or ideas and not fixed realities. A thought that "this pain is unbearable" or "I don't deserve this kindness" is really only a brain secretion, a semi-random electrical firing of a few thousand neurons in your brain that is here one moment and gone the next. They have no palpable or persisting reality and are instead like clouds floating on the horizon or leaves on a stream. They come and they go, and they only influence us to the degree that we get caught up in them. Therefore, we can find a way out of our suffering by becoming aware of this, awakening to the actual reality of the workings of our minds, so that we are not enslaved by them.

"Don't believe everything you think," says a popular bumper sticker. The comedian Emo Philips famously said: "I used to think that the brain was the most wonderful organ in the body. Then I realized which organ was telling me this." Not falling for the tricky antics of our clever human brain is the essence of hope for the relief of our suffering.

Fourth noble truth: The path to relief of suffering

The Buddha didn't own a prescription pad to write it out for you, but thankfully he spelled out the path for all of us in his many talks to his followers over the years. Those steps have been laid out very clearly in something called The Eightfold Path (yes, another list). The important point for our purposes here is that he prescribed a simple path of living ethically, practicing mindfulness and compassion, and developing wisdom through doing exactly what I am proposing in these pages. In other words, not avoiding or denying the reality of suffering, but instead being willing to directly meet and get to know the suffering with clear eyes, steady concentration, a warm heart, and patient but persistent effort.

If you've been wondering as you read this whether we will *ever* dispense with all the preparations and get on to the *actual* practice of self-compassion in this book, perhaps now you can see why I have spent so much time on the preliminaries. My goal is to help you cultivate a certain attitude that will allow you to fully realize the potential of these Four Noble Truths and find a truly sustainable and effective way of alleviating your suffering. Thank you for being patient and bearing with me. It will be worth the wait.

Finding What You Need to Feel Safe and Courageous

Now is your big chance to try your hand (or maybe it's your heart?) at self-compassion. Yes, three chapters in and *finally* you get to unleash the power of your own kindness, albeit in the service of sorting out just what you need to proceed to the next chapters.

If you were planning on growing a beautiful garden, this would be the stage where you would be tilling the soil, fertilizing, and choosing exactly what seeds you will sow in your garden. It's not nearly as showy and fun as harvesting big juicy tomatoes or cauliflower as big as your head, but it's no less important (and perhaps even more so).

The process, not surprisingly, begins with that fundamental question of self-compassion: "What do I need?" If you're on board with the idea that this process will likely require you to be courageous and potentially lean into and encounter some of your more challenging emotions, then you should be well-prepared to do this to the extent that it feels right to you. In other words, you get to choose just exactly how much challenge you take on in order to explore the possibility of change while maintaining a sense of safety and internal support.

If you walk into the gym and head to the heaviest barbells, you won't be doing yourself any favors (unless, of course, you're one of those muscley gym rats who wears sweatshirts with the sleeves torn off because your biceps don't fit in regular sleeves). The same is true with self-compassion. Ambition is useful in some areas, but unbridled, unrealistic ambition simply doesn't work here because it just opens you up to too much emotional "weight" to manage as you ease into the practice. You won't be able to gain as much as you could if you took a more measured approach.

What I'm proposing here is the opportunity to *customize* your experience and exploration of self-compassion. By asking yourself "What do I need?" you are able to assess your readiness and capacity for this work and find just the right dosage for you. Make no mistake: Adjusting the dosage (either up or down) has absolutely nothing to do with the value of the practice. In other words, if you decide you need a lighter "dose" because you are feeling a bit depleted or overwhelmed or tentative, making that adjustment will actually make the practice *more* valuable because it will be matched to exactly what you need. In fact, even choosing to adjust your dosage is an act of self-compassion all by itself! And, sadly for you if you are the competitive type, upping the dosage of self-compassion beyond your capacity (like lifting the heaviest weights) earns you no extra credit in the self-compassion game and can have a downside. Find your own sweet spot by using some of the approaches that follow, and you'll be set up for success in this self-compassion adventure.

WHAT IF SAFETY ISN'T ENOUGH?

In Chapter 1 I use the example of a Coast Guardsman plucking drowning citizens out of the ocean as a great example of compassion that is not at all warm and fuzzy, but instead quite powerful, strong, and action-oriented. That example arose as a result of leading a two-day self-compassion workshop with a group of about 30 Coast Guardsmen a year ago here in the state of Oregon where I live. The workshop was both enjoyable and challenging, as this was not the typical group I encounter in such settings. It was predominantly male (a typical Mindful Self-Compassion course may have 10 percent men and often has none), younger than most, and certainly the motivation for attending was more about peak performance among some highly ambitious and heroic individuals than directly addressing suffering, but there was no question that there was a fair amount of suffering in the room as well (theirs is not an easy job). This was not going to be an easy job for me either, but the need for self-compassion was obviously great.

People were interested and engaged, but when I spent some time talking about this issue of cultivating a safe inner space or a kind of "safe harbor" to use Coast Guard terms, I saw some people struggling whereas usually I encounter a kind of relief or easing of tension in the group. I still remember one young man, who clearly was trying to make sense of the topic, finally raising his hand to challenge me a bit. (I love it when that happens because the honesty and openness is palpable, and the potential for growth and healing is huge in those situations.)

He said, somewhat tentatively at first, "I get that it's nice to create this safe harbor inside ourselves, but I'm having a hard time squaring that with the kind of situations we get into in our work. We are frequently not all that physically safe in our surroundings if we are on a little boat in a storm or if we are being lowered on a cable from a helicopter to try to retrieve a stranded boater or a drowning citizen. How can I feel safe inside when I'm not all that safe *outside?* That just doesn't seem possible. I can't be picturing bunnies and kittens and putting my hands on my heart when I have a dangerous job to do."

(continued)

(continued)

The group and I chuckled at that image for a moment, and then the room got quiet and they looked at me expectantly. Clearly, he had spoken something that several others were wrestling with as well.

What was unasked in his question was "What about the fear or anxiety that comes with dangerous situations or environments? Where does that fit into the equation?"

We ended up having a really fruitful dialogue as a group, and we sorted it out together because I didn't have an immediate answer. But having had a similar conversation with my two siblings, who are both in law enforcement, I knew that the answer would not include denial or avoidance of legitimate emotions like fear or uncertainty. I also knew that an element of this was a term that those in police work, the military, and other high-intensity professions call "situational awareness." To be effective at their work, they need to be alert to the environment, prepared, and able to respond quickly to fast-changing circumstances that can often be dangerous or turn dangerous in a moment. Not hyper-alert or totally on autopilot, but certainly aware and prepared.

Not surprisingly, we found that the space that we need to create inside ourselves in order to maintain some self-compassion and still do a stressful job in dangerous circumstances is more of a *brave space* than a *safe space*. These two things are intertwined in many ways, but in the situations where we may not feel fully safe for whatever reason, we can access the *yang* aspect of self-compassion to steel ourselves for challenges without checking out or resisting the reality of an unsafe situation. In essence we are telling ourselves in a confident voice, "This is really hard, but you've got this," or "You've got what it takes to handle this situation. Stay focused, stay aware, and act mindfully." There are no bunnies or kittens as far as the mind's eye can see in this scenario, but you can feel the flexible strength and the resilience in this approach. And the end result is, ironically enough, peak performance, compassion, and self-compassion all in one.

Just one final note on creating a brave space: This applies not only to physically dangerous situations but can also be useful in emotionally challenging circumstances or even when you're recalling (spontaneously or on purpose) a memory of past experiences where you felt unsafe or threatened. In those moments when you may have a memory of a traumatic event, the fear and uncertainty are no less real (your pounding heart and clammy skin can attest to that), even if the actual threat is not physically present. In these moments, if you are feeling able, you can still cultivate a brave inner space through patience, willingness to stay present, and self-talk like I suggest above.

This is not easy when you have experienced trauma, but it *is* possible and can be quite transformative if you go slow and don't push yourself harder than you are willing to go. Give yourself the opportunity to fully learn self-compassion practice in this book before trying too hard to work with traumatic memories. (You may want to work with a self-compassion-based psychotherapist in this process.) I mention this here to let you know that there is hope and potential in this practice when you have experienced trauma in your life. More on this in Chapter 11.

Opening and closing to adjust your "dosage"

We are all well aware of how our amazing human body tends to its needs through the process of self-regulation. The eyes dilate and constrict, our blood vessels do the same, our heart valves open and close, our lungs expand and contract; the examples are endless. This capacity to open and close in various ways is the key to maintaining the body at its optimal capacity. If you give it some thought, you will see that our hearts and minds do the same.

We are not "always on" just as we are not always "shut down," but we do have a sense of when we are "on" and when we are "off" — when we are receptive and when we can't take on any more challenge. We have a natural internal regulatory process for giving ourselves just the right amount of whatever we need, even if we don't always heed the inner signals about this process. It may be helpful to consider how we can tell when we are opening or closing so that we can use these signs to cue us to listen and respond to them when it comes to self-compassion practice.

Here are four indications that you may be opening:

>> **Your body feels relaxed but alert.** Your body has a way of letting go of tension so that you can focus and become receptive to new things. When you are open, you feel just the right amount of arousal in your body, like when you listen carefully to a new song or someone says something provocative and you tilt your head in interest.

>> **Thinking is vivid and clear.** The brain is able to engage and process information in efficient ways when you are opening, and you become more creative and inquisitive. When you are opening, there is a playful quality to your attention that facilitates savoring an experience, exploring an idea, or testing a hypothesis.

>> **Laughter happens.** When you are open, it means you have let go of tunnel vision. You can see the big picture and are willing to be surprised and delighted by the experience. Surprise is the essence of humor, so when you are open and willing to be surprised, you often find a smile on your lips and in your eyes.

>> **Tears may flow.** This one may surprise you, but crying is really the body's way of letting go of stress. In a moment of fear, for example, you are hyper-focused on the task at hand, like finding the lost child at the amusement park, and nothing can deter you in your efforts. But when the child is finally found safe, it is then that the tears can flow (for both parent and child!) because you are letting go of the fear and stress.

So when your heart is open to your feelings (including the sad ones) your tears can naturally flow. A Buddhist teacher, Lama Yeshe, says "The way to practice compassion is with wet eyes." And never fear — if you are not so much of a "leaky person," that's okay too. We are all different in our tendency toward tears, and it's not a problem if your eyes are dry.

Following are four indications that you may be closing:

>> **Huh? Distraction.** Our brains have an amazing capacity to "titrate" their dosage and to disengage from challenging tasks when they have had enough. The mind begins to wander in these moments and suddenly the tiniest thing seemingly becomes the most fascinating thing in the world. The stray dog hair on your pant leg or the amazing resemblance between the speaker and your Uncle Isaac suddenly swells up to fill your awareness, and you lose track of whatever you started attending to.

>> **Anger and irritation arise.** You know the drill. You've had an especially hard day at work, and you come home to your loving partner only to have them greet you at the door with a request to take out the trash and "speak to *your* son about his room." You're a responsible spouse and parent, but today this is more than you can manage. You feel the irritation rise up and you may or may not give vent to the hurtful comments that your mind offers up. You are closed (or closing), and this is your mind's way of fending off one more demand that it can't adequately process at this time.

>> **The inner critic chimes in.** When you have some awareness that you should be open (say to listening to an important talk by your supervisor) and you're simply struggling to focus and process what is being said, you may find yourself further compounding the situation by criticizing yourself for not being able to concentrate. "You're just not smart enough for this job," your ever-present, ever-nasty inner critic whispers in your ear. "You have no business even being here if you can't grasp what she's saying to you." Your inner critic likes to take a natural process (like closing when you reach capacity) and turn it into a character flaw or weakness that needs fixing.

>> **Boredom and sleepiness arise.** Sleepiness is your body's last-ditch effort to get you to close, by essentially beginning to shut down the attentional processes and force you to close. A close cousin to sleepiness is boredom, of course, and they often co-exist. While you can't always do something about a feeling of boredom or sleepiness (indulging in a nap by placing your head down on the conference table during a meeting is generally frowned upon in modern corporate culture), you can see it as a sign that you are naturally closing.

Once we recognize that our body and mind naturally give us cues when they are opening and closing, we can then take a more proactive role in both responding to these cues and managing the process to our best advantage. If you are naturally closing, then perhaps the self-compassionate thing to do would be to allow yourself to close. In the context of this book, if you have been voraciously consuming page after page of this material and trying all the practices, and now you are feeling "full," then maybe it would be kind to pause and put the book aside to give yourself time to digest what you've taken in. Or maybe you will want to honor when you are opening and set aside some time to delve back into the material or the practice with a renewed sense of adventure. There is no reward for "pushing through" the opening or closing process and forcing yourself to open or close. As the poet Daniel F. Mead said in his poem "If You Would Grow," ". . . accept, respect, and attend your sensitivity. A flower cannot be opened with a hammer."

It may be helpful to think of this process of opening and closing as a continuous range and not a binary choice. In other words, instead of thinking of opening and closing like flipping a light switch on the wall, think of it as turning on the faucet, or better yet, adjusting the temperature of the water to just the right balance of hot and cold to suit the situation. We can adjust our degree of openness to match our needs in any given moment (and believe me, it changes constantly). Sometimes the circumstances call for a deep and steamy soak in the tub, sometimes you want an icy drink of water, and still other times a warm flow is just the right thing for washing the mutt after a romp in the mud. Customize your degree of openness and you will be able to explore the practice of self-compassion in a meaningful and sustainable way.

Finding your sweet spot of tolerance

When Goldilocks of fairy-tale fame tried out the different beds belonging to the three bears, one was found to be "too hard," one was "too soft," and the final one was "just right." When we ask ourselves what we need in the practice of self-compassion, we need to feel our way into the "just right" zone, the "sweet spot" that best suits us. You can adjust the degree of opening and closing as we've just explored, but how do you end up knowing just what is the right temperature for healing and growth? If it's bathwater, you dip your toes in the water, and frankly, the same is true of self-compassion. But we do have some rough parameters for what is likely to work best.

Specifically, there is an optimal place, a sweet spot of learning and growth that comes somewhere between total safety and maximum risk. Scientists refer to this phenomenon as the Yerkes-Dodson Law, which states that there is a relationship between pressure and performance, such that performance increases with physiological or mental arousal, but only up to a point. When arousal becomes too high, performance then decreases. Think of the athlete who needs a certain amount of stimulation to approach peak performance, but at a certain point if they bear down too much or try too hard, their performance actually decreases. When it comes to self-compassion, we need to challenge ourselves but not overwhelm ourselves.

If you think in terms of Figure 3-1, you can begin to feel your way into your particular sweet spot.

© John Wiley & Sons, Inc.

FIGURE 3-1:
Zones of Emotional Tolerance.

The middle circle is the Safety Zone and reflects the place where you can stay all day without any danger of feeling pushed or pulled in any direction. A participant in one of the courses we taught in the United Kingdom several years ago said, "Oh, I know that place. I call it a 'duvet day' when I don't even want to get out of bed and do anything; I just want to curl up under the duvet and be safe and comfy." It's a sweet place to be, under that duvet, but one doesn't grow or change or move in valued directions from that safe space.

When you begin to edge out of that safe space and put yourself into the tug of war of life as it is, where there are unexpected things and delightful things and opportunities to make choices and pursue goals, you begin to find yourself in the fruitful sweet spot of life that is the Challenge Zone. Extending the tug-of-war analogy, the Safety Zone is where the rope is coiled at your feet, limp and unthreatening. In the Challenge Zone you are feeling a tug but holding your own, engaged in the struggle and finding your strengths but not outmatched.

If the force on the other end of the rope begins to tug you farther than you are willing to go and the imbalance is too strong, then you are in the Overwhelm Zone, and nothing fruitful can happen here. If you are the ambitious sort, you may think that you can multiply the impact of your practice by recklessly putting yourself into overwhelm. You will quickly realize that Dr. Yerkes and Dr. Dodson were onto something with their law, and your performance will suffer tremendously.

Inevitably, because self-compassion is an ongoing and varied human process, like all human processes, you will find yourself constantly treading and retreading this same journey out from Safe, into Challenge for a while, accidentally falling into Overwhelm, and then catching yourself and wending your way back to the platform of Safety so you can catch your breath, find your feet, and explore Challenge again. And what allows you to move back and forth between these zones? You guessed it, opening and closing! The two processes work hand in glove to help us find our optimal dosage, our sweet spot.

You may find it helpful to consider taking a few notes about how to recognize when you are in each zone, especially the Overwhelm Zone, so that when it happens (and believe me, it will) you will catch yourself sooner, spare yourself a lot of difficulty, and get yourself back to safety so you can regroup and move forward. Maybe you will find yourself unable to focus, or feel emotionally numb or disconnected, or possibly feel a rising sense of panic as if you want to run out of the room. Make a note for yourself. You'll be glad you did.

REMEMBER

Along the way I offer suggestions or moments to reflect on whether you are opening or closing and whether you are in the Challenge Zone or somewhere else to assure that you get the most out of each practice and exercise. Those are times when you can check in with yourself and customize your experience to suit where you are at that exact moment, taking stock of your available resources and your capacity to be challenged. Over time you will become adept at taking care of yourself in this way without my help, and you already have everything you need to do so. I just provide some helpful reminder nudges here and there to help you discover and develop this innate human capacity within yourself. As they say, "You've got this," and I have every confidence in that statement. Trust me. I'm a professional.

The experience of belonging and deserving

Thus far I have talked about safety as a kind of simple state of feeling sheltered and secure, but there are many dimensions of safety when I speak of it in the context of self-compassion. For those who are seeking to become more self-compassionate, it is especially important to look a bit closer at the feeling of safety to explore two related qualities: a sense of belonging and a sense of deserving.

In order for you to feel safe to practice self-compassion, you must feel as if you have come to the right place to do so. What that means in this context is that you may need to feel that you and I share something in common as humans, such that you feel welcomed and embraced, as if you, specifically, were invited. This may sound quite obvious to you, especially if you are a member of the dominant culture and hold identities that are largely privileged, embraced by society, and in the majority, but that is not the case for so many who have identities or histories that have caused them to be (or feel) marginalized, excluded, discriminated against, or mistreated.

My hope for you, if you hold one or more of these identities or experiences, is that you can look back on the pages you have read so far to see if you see yourself in the descriptions and the experiences I have described. When I teach Mindful Self-Compassion, which is a group-based program, it is especially crucial that we talk about this sense of belonging because people can easily look around the room and perhaps not see anyone who looks like them, or assume that nobody else in the room feels the way that they do. In this case, you are engaging in a more solitary endeavor that is less likely to cause you to feel a lack of belonging or acceptance, but these feelings are deep and long-held, and I don't want to overlook or dismiss them.

All I can say is that if you have any concerns about belonging here, I want you to know that, from the point of view of self-compassion practice, everybody who wants to become more self-compassionate belongs. Everyone has a voice; everyone is valued and appreciated. We are all humans, but we are all different, and yet we all are much more alike than different when you look past the superficial differences between us. We all just want to be happy and free from suffering, and at our very foundations, we all simply want to be loved.

There are those among us who have been the victim of terrible treatment in various forms and who emerged from those experiences with a deep sense of inadequacy, self-doubt, shame and self-hatred. If you, in your life, faced anything like this, I can tell you right now that I am overjoyed that you are here and so excited for you in making this difficult journey to healing and growth. But for now, you may be plagued by feelings of not deserving. This may be a sense of not deserving to have access to this practice, or not deserving of being free from your suffering, or simply not deserving of anything good. My heart aches for you if you feel that you don't deserve ease and peace and joy in your life, and again, I am so glad you are here.

But in the meantime, you need to contend with this nagging fear that you do not deserve this practice. As I have noted before, arguing with this insidious inner voice is fruitless and may actually take away from your potential to grow and change. However, I urge you to consider that your inner critic only gets one voice in your own inner poll of what is right for you. Consider what your heart whispers about what you *really* deserve. Think about the child version of you and what it wishes for you. What do the people who love and care about you most believe about what you deserve? Those are all votes that sway the results of your poll in favor of you belonging here and being deserving of your own good wishes and kind intentions.

If you struggle, you deserve to be free of struggle sometimes. If you hurt, you deserve to be free of hurt sometimes. If you have unease, you are worthy of peace. If you have sadness, you deserve joy. If you are imperfect, you deserve to feel perfectly imperfect. You deserve your own kindness, even if there is a voice to the contrary. See what you can do to acknowledge that nagging, irritating voice that has been with you for years, and simply let it natter on while you tend to the task at hand.

The Compassionate Friend Meditation

Note: Throughout this book I offer some meditations and exercises that are based upon similar practices in the Mindful Self-Compassion program to give you practical ways of learning to be more self-compassionate. Please be patient with these practices and know that the first few times are really about getting to know how the practice works and gently opening up to what it offers. Don't expect spontaneous healing of old wounds or tremendous insights or breakthroughs when you are first familiarizing yourself with these practices. Keep your expectations low and feel your way into them and see what you notice. The real power in these practices is making them just that, a practice that you engage on a regular basis in your life. Like physical exercise, you don't get into shape after one workout, even if it feels good. It takes time, patience, and persistence.

Whenever you embark on a journey or an adventure, it can be reassuring to have a sense that you will be escorted by a warm and supportive companion. Whether it's a cross-country road trip or a more contemplative exploration of your sometimes-challenging inner world, it's always better with a fellow traveler. For this journey you don't need someone to pay for half the gas or buy salty snacks, but you might like to feel accompanied and encouraged, nonetheless. This practice helps you find a compassionate presence, a Compassionate Friend if you will, within yourself for your self-compassion adventure.

As you embark on this Compassionate Friend Meditation, please know that it involves the use of visual imagery, and we all vary in the degree to which we find imagery accessible and useful. If imagery comes easily to you, then great. If not, don't feel like you have to force it. Just go along and see what arises within you as you hear the words, even if images don't arise.

In this practice, as in all the practices I introduce, it is important that you let go of *trying* and see if you can practice in a relaxed and open manner, letting things unfold and come to you rather than having to mentally reach for them in some way. And if you encounter moments of particular challenge, this is an opportunity to possibly practice a bit of strategic closing, by disengaging from the meditation and choosing to direct your attention to the soles of your feet, your surroundings, or your shopping list. Let each practice be easy and remember, "If it's a struggle, it's not self-compassion."

Practicing the meditation

Here are the steps to follow in the Compassionate Friend Meditation:

1. **Take a few moments to find a comfortable place for your body, either sitting or lying down, and take a few slow deep breaths to settle into being here.**

You might like to place a hand on your heart or some other soothing or supportive place on your body to remind yourself to give yourself *loving* attention in this practice.

2. **Now imagine a place that is as safe and comfortable as possible.**

See yourself in this place. It might be a forest clearing, a warm sunny beach, a cozy room with a crackling fire, or even an imaginary place like floating in clouds. Take a few moments to imagine being in this reasonably peaceful and safe space.

3. **As you have a sense of settling into your safe place, begin to consider receiving a visitor, a warm and compassionate presence.**

Think of this visitor as a compassionate friend — a being who embodies the qualities of wisdom, strength, and unconditional love.

Your compassionate friend might be an ancestor, a teacher who inspired you, a person from your past like a grandparent, or a spiritual figure whose being inspires warmth. It may actually manifest as a being with no particular form, but more like a light, warm presence.

Your compassionate friend cares deeply about you and would like you to be as happy and free from unnecessary struggle as possible.

4. **Take the time to greet your visitor, your compassionate friend, and either invite them into your safe space or meet them just outside, whatever feels right to you.**

Find just the right position for the two of you to be together and take a little time to appreciate the good company, imagining your friend in some detail. Savor the moment.

Your compassionate friend is wise and all-knowing, and understands exactly where you are in your life journey. Perhaps there is something your friend would like to say to you, something that is just what you need to hear right now. Take a moment to listen. And if no words come, that's okay too; just continue to enjoy being with your compassionate friend. Sometimes words are not as important as warmth.

5. **If you have something you would like to say to your friend, you can offer that knowing that your friend understands you and will listen deeply to what you have to share.**

6. **As visitors often do, your compassionate friend may want to offer you a gift of some kind, a material object that may have special meaning to you.**

   You can put out your hands and see if something appears. What is it?

7. **Take a few more moments to simply enjoy the company of your compassionate friend here in this comfortable place, pausing to appreciate a simple thing: Your compassionate friend is actually *a part of yourself*.**

   All the compassionate feelings, images, and words that you are experiencing actually flow from your own inner wisdom and compassion.

8. **Finally, as you begin to let the images gradually dissolve in your mind's eye, take a moment to remember that compassion and wisdom are always within you, especially when you need them the most.**

   You can call on your compassionate friend anytime you like on the adventure ahead.

9. **Give yourself some time to savor and reflect on this experience that you just had with your compassionate friend.**

   Consider any words that were said or gifts that were given. And ponder what it might be like to have this compassionate friend available to you at any time by simply going inside.

Inquiring: What was it like to find your compassionate part?

After each reflection, meditation, or exercise in this book, I invite you to pause and look inside before moving on. This pause and reflection is a process of self-inquiry where you have an opportunity to gain greater insight into the experience, to solidify any skills or resources you deployed, and to foster a habit of curiosity, kindness, and compassion. Think of it like an athlete reviewing the tape of a competition, or debriefing a big project at work to prepare for the next one. This is not an evaluation or a final exam, but an opportunity to revisit what happened and consider what you might take forward from the experience.

For the Compassionate Friend Meditation, ask yourself the following questions, giving yourself plenty of time to consider them and letting them soak in before responding. There are no wrong answers, but you may find answers underneath the answers that are worth waiting for. Let yourself linger with these questions awhile, like the last morsel of a delicious dessert.

>> Did a compassionate friend come to mind for you?

>> How did it feel to be in the presence of the compassionate friend?

>> Were words exchanged or a gift offered that had special meaning?

>> How was it to discover that this warm, compassionate friend is actually *a part of yourself*, accessible whenever you need it?

Please take an especially long time to ponder that last question. What you have done in this practice is to slowly reintroduce yourself to yourself, to reconnect with the compassionate part of you that may or may not have been that present to you lately. It has been a whisper in the background or a voice that had been possibly drowned out by other, louder, more hurtful voices, but it is there, and it will be with you all along the way.

Chapter **4**

Discovering Mindfulness in Self-Compassion

F ew words or concepts have gotten more popular press in the past several years than "mindfulness." A casual observer sees the word on magazine covers at the grocery store checkout lane and in titles on the shelves of bookstores (including *Mindfulness For Dummies!*) and hears it bandied about on talk shows and in popular movies. Images of tanned, fit, overly smug millennials sitting blissed out and cross-legged on cushions in pricey yoga clothes may come to mind, and you may begin to believe that mindfulness is the latest fad or craze and that "only the cool kids" practice it.

There has certainly been a meteoric rise in awareness of mindfulness in recent years, especially as a result of the pioneering work of Jon Kabat-Zinn, who brought contemplative practices that were born in Asia to the western medical establishment in the late '70s. Kabat-Zinn and his colleagues developed the much-researched and transformative Mindfulness-Based Stress Reduction (MBSR) program, which has brought relief and ease to millions of suffering people around the globe. So if you think of the "cool kids" as millions of people with stress, pain, and illness who have discovered the potential of present-moment focus (in other words, meditation or contemplation) to bring them relief, then yes, indeed, the "cool kids" *do* practice mindfulness — along with Buddhist monks, Christian contemplatives, Hindu gurus, and Quakers worldwide. That's quite a collection of cool kids that you may want to consider hanging out with if you're interested in relieving your suffering and struggles.

But it's important to differentiate the essence of mindfulness from the cultivation of it. In other words, it's important to explore and understand the difference between mindfulness and mindfulness meditation. Consider what you know about exercise and physical fitness. Physical fitness is the quality that we want to cultivate, and specific forms of exercise are the means of doing so. Mindfulness is the human capacity to be present and aware (as I discuss briefly in Chapter 1 as a component of self-compassion), and meditation or meditative practices are the means by which this quality is cultivated or developed.

In this chapter I unpack mindfulness a bit further and give you several opportunities to practice it on your own to familiarize yourself with this ability that you already have, whether you are aware (mindful) of this or not. The purpose here is to make mindfulness more intentional and available to you because self-compassion is embedded within it. Further cultivating mindfulness can help you really extract all the benefits of self-compassion practice.

Minding the Facets of Mindfulness

Jon Kabat-Zinn defines mindfulness as "paying attention, in a particular way, on purpose, in the present moment and non-judgmentally." That's a pretty tall order if you've ever tried it. In fact, you may want to take a moment to set down this book and give mindfulness practice a try.

There's no need to adopt any particular posture. Simply pay attention to the position of your body and see if you can find one that gives you a sense of stillness and dignity in your body, one you may be able to maintain for two minutes or so. Allow your eyes to close and let your attention rest lightly on your breath wherever you happen to notice it most vividly. Maybe at the nostrils as cool air moves in, maybe in the chest as the lungs fill with air and then empty, or maybe in the rise and fall of the belly where you notice the diaphragm drawing the air in and pressing it back out. Just let your attention rest on the gentle flow of breathing, like a butterfly on a flower, and nothing else.

After two minutes, take some time to settle and reflect on the experience. You were blissed out, right? Your mind was like an open plain, clear and calm as far as the mind's eye could see. You felt a kind of incredible relaxation and insight about the meaning of life and focused on the source of all happiness, correct?

Wait, no? This wasn't your experience? I'm shocked! Shocked, I tell you!

Okay, I'm messing with you now, but you probably figured that out. You will be pleased to know that if you had none of these experiences, you are entirely normal and human, and I would bet that your experience was virtually the same as that of everyone else who has ever tried this practice for the first (or the hundredth) time.

Mindfulness is actually not defined by the experience you happened to have, but whether you were actually present and *noticed* it. This means that if you can describe the experience you had (of a distracted, impatient, preoccupied, worried, confused, or active mind), then you were successful. As I like to say in classes, it's not *what* you notice, but *that* you notice. It is the attentional and intentional process of *being aware* that we are tending to here, not the *objects* of that attention (the things that come into our field of awareness when we are practicing). That's different from how we normally pay attention, but it's at the heart of mindfulness.

Why, you may ask, is it even important or valuable to practice mindfulness at all? So what if you notice that your mind is preoccupied, or bored, or focused? You already know how to pay attention when you need to. What's so special about mindfulness, and why is it worthy of all this hoopla?

Good question. If earlier in this book you've considered the things I've asked you to reflect upon or invited you to notice, you will realize that you have already been accessing your innate capacity to pay attention to your own experience. That is, I have been asking you to *be mindful* as a means of helping you get to know how your mind works and how you can navigate the twists and turns of self-compassion through becoming more aware.

REMEMBER

Mindfulness is not some rarified new skill, like learning to make Facebook videos or paint watercolor landscapes; it is your innate capacity to be present and aware. You have been tapping into and utilizing this ability all your life.

What I am suggesting is that, as long as you are going to be using this resource you possess, why not hone and refine it so that it is even more helpful? Think of the chef who sharpens their knives before cooking a meal or the juggler who practices for hours on end to prepare for their big performance.

As I note in Chapter 1, mindfulness is one of the three components that we tap into and cultivate as a part of self-compassion. Along with common humanity and self-kindness, mindfulness is the foundation of being able to bring compassion to ourselves. In order to practice self-compassion, we have to actually *notice* first, as well as have the skills to direct attention, remain present, and ground ourselves. The more we refine our capacity to be present and aware, to calibrate our instrument so to speak, to take stock of each moment and remain steady in moments of challenge, the more we are able to build on that platform to formulate a self-compassionate response to the situations of our lives.

In the following sections, we briefly explore the various things that we can be mindful of, as a means of untangling the threads of our experience and better harnessing the tremendous power of the human mind to be present, aware, and self-compassionate. Buddhists refer to these various aspects of experience as the Four Foundations of Mindfulness (body, feelings, consciousness, and mind objects), but you will see that there is nothing inherently Buddhist or spiritual about them. You will know these things from your own experience, and as such, they are simply observations about the human mind and how it works.

The Body: Your Constant Companion

Among the various things that we can be mindful of, perhaps the most immediate and tangible is the body itself. Take a moment right now to shift your attention from what you are reading to what you can notice in your body. You might even consider closing your eyes (right after you read this paragraph!) and just sweep your attention across your body from head to toe. See what there is to notice just now in your body — pleasant, unpleasant, neutral, hot, cold, tense, relaxed, tingling, numb, or even the absence of sensation where you thought you might sense something. Take a quick inventory of your bodily sensations in this moment. Sweep your attention from top to bottom and see what is "feelable" in your body.

What did you notice? Can you still notice any of these sensations as you read these words? Our body is literally a sensation generator. Nerve endings throughout this amazing organism are working constantly, sending signals to the brain like a vast fiber optic network of microprocessors, busily tending to whatever needs tending and dutifully transmitting bits of data. Most of this takes place well outside our routine awareness, but you do have the capacity (as you just did) to tune in to the activity and observe it.

Mostly we don't need to be conscious of all this information all the time. In fact, if we had to be that aware of all the signals that our body sends, our brains, as amazing as they are, would be overloaded trying to make sense of them all. And so, our body takes care of itself in most ways and, like a good executive assistant, only alerts us when something is important for us to know. This might be pain in our toe when we stub it on the foot of the bed in the night, or a racing heartbeat when we see our beloved coming up the front walk at the end of the day. Having this capacity to be aware of our bodies is how we have maintained our survival as a species all these millennia, because it provides valuable information essential to our day-to-day functioning.

Considering how you treat your body

So how do we honor this amazing, mostly self-sustaining human contraption most of the time? Sadly, most of us ignore or discount it and try to avoid what it tells us, usually to our detriment. We strive to push past pain to achieve an athletic goal or to "act like a man," we are rewarded for working through lunch, and we treat our woes with substances like alcohol and drugs that briefly anesthetize us but also harm our brains and organs. We have been entrusted with a remarkable piece of equipment and, in the words of the singer Jimmy Buffett, "I treat my body like a temple, you treat yours like a tent."

I bring this up not to shame you into feeling bad about your body, but instead to make you aware of your relationship with your own body. Jon Kabat-Zinn has famously quoted James Joyce from his collection of short stories entitled *Dubliners*, where he says, "Mr. Duffy lived a short distance from his body." We humans sometimes begin to think of our bodies as an impediment to our goals in some way and overlook, avoid, mistreat, and resist the reality of them. But where (and who) would you be without your body?

This may sound like a philosophical rumination of sorts, but think of the costs of not being aware of your body. Beyond the obvious abuse and neglect that I mention earlier, remember that your body tries to speak to you by giving you sensations. Think of the last time you had a headache. Maybe at your first opportunity, you popped a couple of ibuprofen pills to get rid of it. That's a pretty routine thing to do, but would there have been some advantage to actually stopping long enough to hear what your body was telling you? Maybe it was saying that it was dehydrated, or that it was suffering from muscle tension due to stress. Perhaps you were fatigued or strained your eyes too long at the computer, or maybe the headache had a hormonal source. One thing is for sure, I'm no physician, but I would bet money that it was not telling you "Hey sweetheart, I'm getting low on ibuprofen! Stock up!"

Anchoring your attention

In addition to the benefits of simply listening to your body, you can think of your body as a kind of anchor or tether to the present moment. As you begin to become aware that your body is always present for your attention, you can use it as a means of steadying your attention in moments when you're feeling unsteady, confused, distracted, preoccupied, or just plain distressed. Because physical sensations are always in the present moment only, focusing on them brings us automatically into the present moment. It grounds our attention in something immediate, real, and present, and helps us drop out of struggle, resistance, avoidance, and control.

ONE QUESTION THAT MAKES YOU MORE MINDFUL

The image that may come to mind when you contemplate contemplation is likely to be some form of formal meditation practice, such as sitting cross-legged on a cushion. That is, of course, one way to practice mindfulness, but practicing mindfulness can take many forms, and some of them are quite easily accessed on the fly, when you need them most.

I worked as a psychologist assessing patients in our hospital's emergency room when there were concerns about their mental health, and the vast majority of those patients had a great deal of anxiety. In some cases, anxiety was their *only* problem. (Studies have shown that about 80 percent of people who come to the emergency room with chest pain do not have any true cardiopulmonary emergency.) The prevalence of anxiety in the ER is quite striking.

My role was to sit with the patients and listen to their stories, direct their attention to their current symptoms and situation, and ground them in the questions and process of my examination. Inevitably, the most anxious patients tended to become less anxious over the course of my interview, and this was without me ever asking them to *not* be anxious or doing any sort of explicit relaxation exercises with them. Instead, what I was really doing was actually embodying mindfulness: staying grounded in the moment and returning to the present moment whenever they or I wandered into the past or future.

I would comment on this to the patients many times and point out that their anxiety receded as they focused upon the present moment. You may think I was distracting them, but I was doing just the opposite of distracting by asking them about what they were thinking and feeling and noticing in their bodies as I interviewed them. If there was any "distraction" going on, it was that I was distracting them from their preoccupation with an imagined future situation, which caused their anxiety, and focusing on what was *actually* there.

In a moment of inspiration with one of these patients, I suggested that, since coming into the present moment seemed to free him of some of his anxiety and give him a sense of presence and focus, perhaps the next time he found himself distressed in some way, he could ask himself a very simple and almost silly question: "Where are my feet?"

They are, of course, always right there with you. In a moment you can tune in to the sensations of your feet and you are suddenly back in the present moment. No special equipment or years of meditation needed. Just a simple intention to become present in a moment of difficulty.

Try it for yourself. The next time you find yourself upset, anxious, sad, or angry, see if you can ask yourself that little question and notice what happens when you do. "Where are my feet?" is the shortest, most portable, and most effective mindfulness practice I can imagine. To this day I still periodically encounter people in the hospital who say, "Hey! You're that 'Where are my feet?' guy! I'm still using that!"

You may be tempted, in a moment of distress, to try to anchor your attention in an emotion or even try to respond to thoughts that come up in your mind. For example, if you notice some internal dialogue after you have made a very public mistake at work, you may tend to want to silence your inner critic by arguing or disputing what it says. When the critic says, "This is what you always do, because you're just not smart enough for the job," you may respond by saying, "I am indeed smart enough for this job. You're wrong. I'm good enough, and I just made a simple mistake that anyone could make." You may have found, if you have ever tried arguing with an inner critical voice, that you never win. Never. Because the mind is tricky; basically, it always knows what you are going to say next and has a clever response already queued up before you've even articulated your point. It's like trying to chase a fly that is always one step ahead of your swatter and quicker than you could ever be. While there are empirically supported ways of responding to difficult thoughts that creates a kind of "psychological immunity" to them, I am suggesting a slightly different pathway toward relief.

The good news is that the body is much slower than the mind. If you have a sensation in your body, even if it is a relatively fleeting one like tension in your neck or a rapid heartbeat, you can settle your attention upon it like a bee alighting on a flower and let your mind rest. It's almost like being able to reach out and grab a railing on a steep and rickety staircase. The sensation of the body can be a solid place to temporarily rest your attention and regain a sense of balance and presence, to find your way into the present moment (like locating the "You are here" point on a map), and to then proceed forward with clarity and calm.

Practice: Compassionate mindfulness of the body

The body scan was popularized by Jon Kabat-Zinn in the Mindfulness-Based Stress Reduction (MBSR) program and forms one of the foundational practices of that highly effective program. Here is an abbreviated version of that practice from the Mindful Self-Compassion (MSC) program called the Compassionate Body Scan that beautifully integrates the kindness of self-compassion and demonstrates how mindfulness and self-compassion work together, and how simply attending to the body can help us cultivate both qualities.

You may have a somewhat conflicted relationship with your body, as many people do. Perhaps you don't like how a particular part looks or how it functions, or some areas of your body may hold a connection to a previous traumatic event. This is not at all uncommon. What we are doing here is simply acknowledging the truth of the body as it is in each moment. See if you can engage in this body scan with a sense of cautious curiosity and see whether you can be warmly present to whatever may come up as you move to these different parts of the body. Notice that you may be inclined toward some areas and repelled by others, and just see whether you can notice these preferences (we will return to them in the next section on mindfulness of feelings) and remain present, nonetheless. Go slow and give yourself permission to move attention away from parts of the body if being with them in this way is just too challenging for now. If you choose to mindfully redirect your attention to something else because it's too painful to stay where you are, you're already demonstrating your capacity to practice self-compassion!

In this Compassionate Body Scan, we bring warmhearted attention to various parts of the body, inclining our awareness toward each part with curiosity and tenderness, the way we might attend to a sleeping child or beloved pet. As you move your attention through your body you may find that the mind will wander or become impatient or distracted in some way. When this happens, and it will from time to time, just gently and warmly but firmly direct it back, like a wayward puppy that has wandered off: "Over here! Over here!"

1. **Begin by finding a comfortable position for your body.**

   If you are going to read along with this practice, you may just want to find a comfortable place to sit where you can view the script but have some degree of stillness and ease in your body. Listening to a body scan is probably the best way to fully experience it.

2. **Direct your attention down the body to the left foot and rest it there gently.**

   Narrow the beam of your attention as if it is a floodlight and you are transforming it into a spotlight. Begin to notice if there are any sensations here — coolness, warmth, ease, discomfort — letting each sensation be just as it is. Simply notice.

   Maybe acknowledge how this one foot helps to hold you up and move you around, how the sole of the foot bears the weight of your entire body every day, and how it serves you dutifully and consistently, the best that it can.

3. **Allow your attention to shift from the left foot slowly up the left leg: the ankle, the shin and calf, the knee, the thigh.**

   Pause in each area to take note of what is present, including even the possibility of the *absence of sensation* in some areas. Can you simply take note of whatever you encounter and be kindly present to *that*?

4. **When you are ready, repeat this process through the right foot and leg.**

   Really take note of whatever you encounter, but also appreciate the work that each part of the body has performed for you throughout a lifetime.

   Along the way you may encounter tension or holding in the body. Your assignment here is to simply notice what tension *feels like* in the body. You are not required to release the tension or relax, but you may choose to do so if you like. This is not a relaxation practice, but an awareness practice. Simply noticing is all that is required.

5. **Allow your attention to approach the torso, continuing the process of moving up the body.**

   Move with patience, pausing to take stock of what is present, redirecting attention if it has wandered, and letting the experience just be as it is.

6. **If you find areas of discomfort or pain, see if you can possibly just observe the sensation of discomfort arising.**

   See what you notice about *this* sensation too. Does it stay steady, or does it change? What is the quality of the sensation you are experiencing? Can you describe it?

7. **You may begin to become more aware of the flow of breathing happening in your body and the subtle effects that this movement has on how your body feels.**

   Let your body continue to breathe as it needs to while you train your attention on the process without needing to change it in any way. If you notice that your mind has wandered or drifted, take this time to gently redirect it back to the breath.

8. **Taking some time to move your attentional spotlight up each arm, and into the neck, the head, the face, the ears and even the top of the head.**

   Don't strain to feel anything in particular; just direct the spotlight of attention on each area to illuminate whatever happens to be there. Perhaps you might even direct attention to the brain inside, not to necessarily feel something, but to simply attend with kindness and appreciation for what it does.

9. **When you are ready, widen the beam of the spotlight out to a floodlight again to encompass the whole body as it is in this moment.**

   Take some time to just dwell in this moment, in the presence of this amazing human body that sometimes poses some challenges, but nevertheless has been there for us our whole lives, trying to do its best.

   Appreciate yourself for having taken this time to truly dwell within this magnificent package and to feel what it feels like to be a living, breathing human being.

Give yourself some time to allow this Compassionate Body Scan practice to sink in. Take stock of what you notice as you come to the conclusion and allow whatever you to feel to be okay. It may be that you feel relaxed, but it may also be that this was challenging for you. Your body may have had pain, you may have felt restless and irritable, or you may have been bored and distracted. See if you can even notice what those things feel like and take heart that if you noticed *literally anything* during this practice, then you were actually practicing mindfulness! Remember, it's not *what* you notice, but *that* you notice.

The big deal about the breath

One feature of the body, or at least all living ones, is that it breathes. And that breath is worthy of your attention. I need to warn you now that I'm about to talk about the incredible value of attending to your breath. I really appreciate the wisdom and humor of the author Anne Lamott, and she comes to mind when I say this because in her book *Bird by Bird* she speaks of the value of getting quiet and says, "You might also consider trying to breathe. This is not something that I remember to do very often, and I do not normally like to hang around people who talk about slow conscious breathing; I start to worry that a nice long discussion of aromatherapy is right around the corner. But these slow conscious breathers are on to something . . ." Rest assured, you won't see the word "aromatherapy" again in this book, but I will talk repeatedly about returning to the breath.

Breathing is a fascinating phenomenon. It is the one human process that I am aware of that happens automatically, whether we are aware of it or not, but that we can also choose to control for short periods of time. The good news here is that no control is required to tap into the power of breathing as a steadying force, and all I ask is that you consider being a watcher of your own process of breathing. The favorite piece of advice I ever got from my mom was a colorful and memorable pronouncement on breathing: "Breathe in, breathe out, and don't (mess) with the sequence." (Mom used a more "colorful" word than "mess," which made the whole thing even more memorable). Nonetheless, you may be thinking about how boring attending to the breath sounds, but if you think the breath is boring, try doing without it for a minute or two. It will suddenly become the most important thing you've ever encountered.

If the body itself is the most basic object of our attention, then awareness of breathing (which of course happens in the body) is a slightly more advanced practice because it is a bit more dynamic and ephemeral. "Where exactly *is* the breath?" you may ask. We know that we are breathing because we feel the sensations of breathing in our bodies, but the location of the breath is hard to determine. Nonetheless, we can track the various sensations of breathing by noticing movement of cool air past the nostrils, or the filling of the chest as the lungs expand, or the rise and fall of the belly when the diaphragm draws air in and presses it back out.

What makes the breath helpful to continue this process of training and refining the mind is that it helps us to be able to stay present under continually changing circumstances, like life itself. While the body and its sensations do change slightly over time, the breath is always moving and fluid, and by beginning to tune in to this ever-changing process, we develop the capacity and steadiness to track the cascading sensations of the breath. It's one thing to be able to strap on ice skates and find your way to a standing position on the ice (not the easiest process for a beginner), but it is an entirely different feat to begin to move across the ice with a sense of purpose, intention, and grace.

It takes one type of mental capacity to be able to direct the attention to a single point of focus and cultivate a steadiness of mind that allows us to maintain that focus. This is obviously a helpful skill when we have tasks to accomplish or things that we need to study. But we also need the capacity to track a moving target, so to speak, because much of life is like that. Certainly, tracking the highly dynamic and changeable landscape of human emotions and interactions can be a highly adaptive capacity to develop.

Practice: Affectionate breathing

PLAY

Awareness of breath meditation is the core form of formal mindfulness meditation that is practiced in the West. Simply attending to the flow of breathing turns out to be not that simple, but a worthwhile endeavor nonetheless, as a means of exercising our attention muscles, so to speak. Again, like any mindfulness practice, this can be done with kindness and warmth. In fact, you may recall Jon Kabat-Zinn's definition of mindfulness at the beginning of this chapter, where one element of the definition is ". . . paying attention *in a particular way* . . ." In this case, the "particular way" is with warmth, patience, kindness, and curiosity. The following short practice drawn from Mindful Self-Compassion, called Affectionate Breathing, is aimed at cultivating this particular way of attending to the fascinating and ever-present process of breathing.

As you begin this practice, remember that attending to the breath can be a bit more challenging than attending to the body, so be patient with yourself as you ease into it. If you find that you have a hard time fixing your attention on breathing, or if doing so actually causes you some additional distress, know that you are not alone in this and that the key to making the exercise fruitful is to listen to what you need and respond to it. So, if you need to take it slow; or to only periodically tune into breathing, to feel your entire body as it breathes; or to just take a break for now if you need to close, then let yourself make this self-compassionate choice (and congratulate yourself for giving yourself what you really needed in this moment). The breath is powerful, but it can take some time for people to feel as though it's an ally in their mindfulness practice.

1. **Take a few moments to find a posture for your body that is comfortable and allows you to feel supported.**

   If you are listening to this meditation, you may want to allow your eyes to gently close, or you can simply direct attention inward as you soften your gaze and look toward the floor or your lap.

2. **If you are inclined, you can offer yourself some form of supportive physical touch as a reminder that you are not only bringing awareness to your breath, but also loving, tender awareness to the experience and to yourself having that experience.**

3. **If it feels right to continue, begin to notice the simple sensation of breathing within your body.**

   Notice how the body is going about its daily business of breathing in and breathing out.

4. **You may take a moment to recognize how your body is nourished on each in-breath and cleansed and relaxed on each out-breath, breath after breath, in a steady rhythm and cadence.**

   When you let go of trying to control or direct your breath, you are, in a way, allowing your breath to *breathe you.*

5. **Consider inclining your attention warmly toward your breathing as you would toward a beloved child or dear friend, with appreciation and tenderness.**

6. **Allow yourself to feel your whole body breathing, the subtle movement of the body almost like the movement of the sea.**

7. **When you mind begins to wander from the breath and find other things to attend to, just gently nudge it back to the breath.**

   Think of the tenderness with which you might direct a curious child back on task.

8. **From time to time you may notice that you have a sense of *watching* your breath rather than simply *being* with your breath. See if you can let go of watching and *feel* it instead.**

   Try to feel the internal *caress* of the breath moving in and out.

9. **When you're ready, gently release your attention on your breathing and taking a few moments to sit quietly in the midst of your own experience.**

   Feel whatever you feel and be just as you are. If your eyes have been closed, wait until a time of your choosing to allow them to open.

After each meditation, including this one, it's worthwhile to give it time to settle, to rest in the presence of whatever has arisen and not be too quick to move on to the next thing. You may even ask yourself: "What did I notice in this meditation?" See if you can put aside judgment or interpretation or even labeling (like "good," "easy," or "relaxing") and instead simply take note of the actual moment-to-moment experience of being a breathing human.

Feelings: Love 'em or Hate 'em, We All Have Them

When I talk about mindfulness of feelings, I'm speaking not about emotions (which we often describe as "feelings") but more specifically about a nuanced aspect of our experience, which we might call the *quality* of the experience. In other words, when we encounter anything, from an erratic driver on the freeway to the best deep-dish pizza we've ever had, to the experience of slipping into a warm bubble bath at the end of a difficult day, we have a feeling about these experiences as well as emotions associated with them. The feeling of a thing is usually something along a continuum of pleasant, neutral, or unpleasant, and interestingly enough, all three can lead to suffering, which is why we want to practice mindfulness of them as a means of reducing our suffering.

Here's an example of how something like the feeling of pleasant can lead to suffering. I have often said that I am pathologically unable to say "no" to things when people ask me to do them. I realize that I *am* actually able to form the word "no" with my mouth and speak it, but sadly, I suffer from what I consider to be an addiction. When someone asks me to do something that I love to do, and they *really* want me to do it for them, I think I'm addicted to the little hit of dopamine that my brain gets when I say "yes" and I see their pleased and relieved expression. I have made someone happy in that moment, and it feels great. This is how addiction works, right?

And then the reality hits: For me it is often when I end up finding myself with a ridiculous travel schedule where I hop from country to country teaching mindfulness and self-compassion. Don't get me wrong; I'm not complaining about the opportunity to teach what I love and to see the world (all while getting paid to do so), but the problem comes when I over-commit, spend too many nights living out of a suitcase and far from my wife and home, and slowly get burned out. What began as a pleasurable burst of connection with someone whom I wanted to please slowly transforms into a burden that I am carrying. You may recognize this as the craving I mention in the previous chapter, and it is the source of most of our suffering.

This leads us to see how liking or not liking something is a powerful predictor of our suffering, *independent of* the emotions that may follow our initial feeling or inclination. If we find that something is unpleasant, we may want to push it away, and we've already established how fruitless that can be. And even finding something to be neutral can be a problem because it leads us to ignore feelings altogether, resulting in confusion and lack of clarity.

As I get older and my memory is not quite as sharp as it used to be, I have been particularly able to tune into these feelings of pleasant, neutral, and unpleasant when I can't quite remember the thing that I needed to do that day. I *know* that there's something that I intended to do, but I can't for the life of me remember exactly what it was. But in that moment of memory failure, I can generally get the felt sense of whether I was inclined toward or away from the thing I can't remember. I notice within me a kind of repulsion/aversion in some cases (like when I was supposed to take out the trash) or an inclination and excitement in other cases (when I had planned to devour the leftovers of a particularly wonderful meal my wife prepared the night before). It is that *felt sense* that I am referring to, and it's worthy of our attention.

Unpacking pleasant and unpleasant moments

Borrowing here from the Mindfulness-Based Stress Reduction (MBSR) and Mindfulness-Based Cognitive Therapy (MBCT) programs, I invite you to contemplate two different kinds of experiences that you have had in the last 24 hours, and to look at them in a particular way.

1. **Begin by calling to mind a moment you recently experienced that you consider pleasant.**

   It doesn't have to be anything transcendent or worthy of sharing on Instagram, but just a moment of pleasantness.

2. **Let yourself savor the moment and relive it in your mind's eye.**

3. **When you are ready, ask yourself the following questions:**

   - Were you aware of the pleasant feelings at the time?

   - How did your body feel at the time this moment occurred?

   - What moods, feelings, and thoughts accompanied the experience?

   - What thoughts, sensations, or emotions do you notice now as you recall the event?

4. Take a moment to consider how you came to define this particular experience as pleasant.

What were the exact elements of this event that led you to apply that label of pleasantness?

5. Let go of this pleasant experience and these questions and take a moment to take a few breaths and allow your mind to settle.

6. Now call to mind a moment you recently experienced that you consider unpleasant.

It doesn't have to be a catastrophe or a disaster, just a moment that was difficult or disagreeable in some way.

7. Let yourself return to that moment and relive it in your mind's eye.

8. When you are ready, ask yourself the following questions:

- Were you aware of the unpleasant feelings at the time?
- How did your body feel at the time this moment occurred?
- What moods, feelings, and thoughts accompanied the experience?
- What thoughts, sensations, or emotions do you notice now as you recall the event?

9. Take a moment to consider how you came to define this particular experience as unpleasant.

What did you observe in this experience that led you to apply the label of "unpleasant"?

10. Pause now and let your mind settle.

The purpose of this exercise is not to evoke pleasant or unpleasant feelings, but to give you an opportunity to look a bit closer (through the steady lens of mindfulness) at some experiences and begin to see how they are made up of multiple elements. You may have noticed that your pleasant event had some unpleasant aspects and vice versa. This is normal and is just one discovery that people make when they do this in the MBSR and MBCT programs. Others notice that the thoughts they have about something end up leading them to feel a certain way as well. I touch on the latter observation more directly in the section "Minding the 'Weather' of the Mind."

Developing the capacity to recognize feelings

One can learn a lot from looking more closely at events in this way and recognizing the reactivity of the mind to dart away or become absorbed in certain things. Specifically, in regard to feeling states, it helps us to catch the liking, the not liking, and the neutrality as a phenomenon that can alert us to the very first moment that clinging and aversion might arise and lead us down a path of suffering.

As you develop the capacity to recognize these sometimes feelings, you can acknowledge them without always falling victim to them. This capacity can then allow you to notice the arising of feelings but not to succumb to them, but instead to observe them as mental phenomena that have no actual substance.

We know this capacity and benefit from it already in some ways, but we aren't always able to deploy it. Think of what arises for you when you see the most delectable sweet morsel behind the glass in the bakery and a huge desire to devour it arises. The feeling of pleasant is arising, big time. And then maybe there is another feeling of revulsion as you remember the number from your bathroom scale this morning and you see how this éclair, however light it may appear, is *not* going to help you keep your weight down. You have that proverbial angel and devil on your shoulders in that moment, and listening to either one could lead you down a path of suffering, either through self-indulgence or self-recrimination.

But when you can see this whole process arising just as I am describing it for you here, there is another, larger awareness holding the whole scenario. This is your "bigger mind" or your "observing ego" or simply your mindfulness that sees all the factors involved, all the players in this little Dessert Drama, and has the perspective that those little creatures on your shoulders doesn't. It may whisper in your ear, "I know you love éclairs, but you love your health even more. You can say 'no' to this treat and you will feel good about taking care of yourself just now." This voice of mindfulness is also, as you can see, quite compassionate and wants you to be happy and free from suffering.

When we can wriggle out of the clutches of our feeling states, we find ourselves in a space of self-compassion, patience, and equanimity. Rumi, a 13th century Persian poet, once wrote: "Out beyond ideas of wrongdoing and rightdoing there is a field. I'll meet you there." This is the space that you cultivate when you practice mindfulness of feelings.

Minding the "Weather" of the Mind

Expanding upon the idea of feeling states of liking, not liking, and neutrality, one can also be aware of the overall state of the mind as well. I like to think of it as assessing the weather of the mind.

At different times we can be aware that our mind is scattered or focused, confused or resolved, or feeling lust or hatred, just to name a few "internal weather conditions" we may encounter when we check in with our amazing human minds. I use the concept of weather because of a couple of parallels to these mind states. First, they are not always predictable or within our control (like the weather, where the old saying goes, "Everybody complains about the weather, but nobody does anything about it"). Second (and most importantly), the weather obscures the actual landscape of the earth the way these mind states obscure the reality of each moment as they lead to us seeing these experiences through a lens or against the backdrop of our mental or emotional state. We see the sunrise as glorious when we are holding the hand of our beloved, and heartbreaking if we have just lost that same beloved. The sunrise remains the same, but our experience of it varies considerably based upon our mental and emotional state.

I spend a considerable portion of Chapter 3 exploring the world of difficult emotions and the rationale for being willing to explore and encounter them as a means of becoming more self-compassionate. Now we can look at emotions more broadly, as one manifestation of our "internal weather patterns" that play a role in how we experience our lives. Make no mistake, I am not suggesting that emotions don't serve a useful purpose in our lives at all, but it would be helpful to separate when they support and inform us from when they mislead and undermine us.

For example, if you find yourself struggling or suffering in some way, large or small, and feeling a lack of ease overall, it's worthwhile to not only ask yourself "Where are my feet?" as I suggest earlier, but also to see if you can take note of the state of your mind in that moment. Perhaps you are feeling confused or irritable. (The neuropsychologist and Buddhist scholar Dr. Rick Hanson once said the difference between irritable and irritated is that when we are just irritable, we are just *not yet* irritated. But we're willing.") When you can name the presence of a mind state like irritation or confusion, then you can begin to see how this state is separate from the reality of the situation you are in.

The power of language when working with the mind

One very important way that we can begin this decoupling of mind state from situation is in the language that we use. One unfortunate aspect of the English language is that when we speak about experience of emotions, we routinely use language that fuses us with the emotion (weather pattern) that we are experiencing. In other words, we say things like "I am angry" when in fact we are *not* the anger itself, but just experiencing anger or being visited by anger in that moment. Think about it: If you go out into a blizzard, you don't say "I am a blizzard." You say, "I am experiencing cold, blowing snow."

This may seem like a pointless foray into semantics, but it makes a significant difference over time. When we say "I am angry," we can easily forget that we *are not* our anger, and as such, we can forget that we do have a relationship *with* anger that allows us some freedom in the face of it. While we may not be free of anger itself, we can influence its impact upon us based upon whether we resist it, ignore it, try to control it, or dance with it.

Ultimately, what you may aspire to do is to free yourself from these mind states when facing circumstances that may stir them up so you can bring all your resources to bear on them. In other words, if you can see that a particular situation (for example, getting lost in the forest) fosters frustration and even fear in you, you would like to also be able to see this situation in such a way that you are less overtaken by those initial emotions and are able to think clearly and rationally enough to consider proven ways of becoming un-lost.

The Buddhist teacher U Pandita once said that this practice of becoming aware of our state of mind serves to "expand the range of experiences in which we are free." Freedom, in this case, refers to the state of having options and not being constricted by the narrow way of thinking that often characterizes an emotion-charged mind.

Is the dog walking *you?*

We often don't feel very free from the activity of our minds. In fact, we may feel as if we are hapless victims of a mind that won't sit still. This state of affairs is often referred to in meditation circles as "monkey mind." Teachers sometimes say that the mind can be like a monkey in a house with six windows, representing each of the senses: sight, sound, touch, smell, taste, and consciousness. The monkey of the mind dashes back and forth from window to window, grasping at this, pushing at that, and generally creating a lot of mental chaos that can be overpowering. Some have said that the experience is so strong that it's more like a gorilla than a monkey.

But I suggest we switch animals to something perhaps more mundane and see how we can cultivate a different relationship with the active mind. I once had a sweet, but huge, golden retriever named Cody. Walking Cody taught me something important about mindfulness, mainly because he was so big — we often went not where I wanted to go, but where he did.

Have you noticed that you seem to be at the mercy of your mind? You know the feeling; you're sitting there minding your own breath when the mind serves up a juicy thought. Perhaps you find yourself contemplating Tom Cruise's marital woes and your odds for stepping in as his next love. Maybe it's just the enticing smell of dinner simmering in the other room. In the Disney Pixar movie *Up*, there's a dog named Doug who wears a device that allows him to talk. Bright and cheerful, Doug can carry on quite a conversation, but let him catch sight of a bushy-tailed rodent and he immediately exclaims "Squirrel!!!!" and he's off on the chase. That's how our minds can be: doglike, reactive, and distractible.

We can't change the nature of our dogs, and the same is true of our minds. Their nature is to be caught up in various states and following various phenomena, especially if they are compelling, seductive, and promise an adventure of one sort or another!

Try cultivating the neural equivalent of a retractable leash. You know, those handy devices that are spring-loaded and allow your dog to go off on little mini adventures here and there, investigating fascinating smells, scurrying creatures, and the occasional impassive feline, while you blithely continue down the path you have already chosen. You stay on track, and your dog has their own adventure.

How do you do this with your mind? Practice mindfulness in the form of meditation. Notice your mind doing what it does with playful curiosity, tolerance of its tendencies, and still with a sense of intention to stay where you are. Little by little, when we let go of needing our mind/dog to go exactly where we intend to go, we find that we stay on our path and the mind follows dutifully (or at least it hovers somewhere in the vicinity). So mindfulness cultivates an allowing of the peccadilloes and idiosyncrasies of our mental activity, all the while staying on task, which is to notice. Just notice!

If you practice meditation and your mind finds its latest squirrel, see if you can watch the chase with calm abiding amusement. Trust that if you stay here, it will return eventually, and sooner than if you had chased after it and tried to subdue it.

THE BRAIN IS A WANDERER

Perhaps the most common observation that people make when they begin to practice mindfulness meditation in any form is that their mind wanders. This is often brought up in meditation courses as if it is a problem that the new meditator has discovered and is hoping to solve with the help of the teacher. There is a (mistaken) assumption on the part of many people that the "goal" of meditation is to have a mind that sits patiently like a well-trained pet, never wandering off or getting distracted. The truth is that the mind simply wanders; it is the nature of the mind to do this, and there are some good neurophysiological and evolutionary explanations for why this happens. But for our purposes here, it's worth looking at an interesting study of the wandering mind.

In 2010, Matthew Killingsworth and Daniel Gilbert published a study entitled "A Wandering Mind Is an Unhappy Mind" in the journal *Science*. The study was rather unique in that it utilized technology to try to sort out just how much the mind wanders and what the impact of all that wandering may be. The researchers sampled data from 2,250 adults who carried smartphones with them for a period of time and agreed to respond periodically to three questions that would be sent to them by text message at random times. The questions were a happiness question, "How are you feeling right now?"; an activity question, "What are you doing right now?"; and a mind-wandering question, "Are you thinking about something other than what you are doing?"

The study revealed two very important findings:

- People's minds wander frequently: 46.9 percent of the time to be exact. So if you feel like you are lost in thought with your mind wandering all over the place much of the time, you are in good company and probably not that different from anyone else. The mind wanders close to half the time we are conscious. Oddly, it didn't seem to matter what sort of activity people were engaged in (pleasant, unpleasant, or neutral), the mind wandered about the same for all activities. In fact, there was only one human activity in which many more people reported that their attention was much more present than any other: making love. (This of course prompts one to wonder about who those people were, and why they were answering text messages in the middle of sexual activity!)

- Most importantly, statistical analysis of the data revealed that people were significantly less happy when their mind was wandering than when they were attentive to their experiences. In fact, even when people's minds wandered to pleasant topics, they were still less happy than those who were able to stay focused on what they were actually doing in the moment (regardless of how pleasant or unpleasant that activity was).

Taken together, this study demonstrates strong evidence for why there is a benefit in cultivating mindfulness, simply from the standpoint that we are happier and more satisfied with our lives when we are present to them, even though we have amazing human brains that allow us to think about things that are not here in the present moment. In other words, our tremendous thinking apparatus comes at an emotional cost that can be a real burden in our daily life. And we might as well give up on trying to make the mind sit still and instead install an inner retractable leash!

Mental Objects: Often Arising, Sometimes Helpful

You may have found yourself marveling at just how many things you can be mindful of. Whether it's the body or the breath, the feeling tone of your experience (pleasant, unpleasant, or neutral), or the state of the mind (the emotional "weather" inside), there's a lot going on inside and available to your awareness. And you aren't done yet! The final area for you to notice and investigate is that of the actual objects of your attention, or the things that you notice when you pay attention. Previously I said that our focus in mindfulness is not so much upon *what* we notice but *that* we notice. But there is still value in knowing the inner terrain of our attention and the kinds of things we tend to become aware of and how some of them can lead us astray while others can bring us back to the present moment.

For the purposes of cultivating a solid mindfulness foundation for practicing self-compassion, I focus here on the two most common and challenging mind objects you may encounter along the way. My hope is that by becoming intimately familiar with these mental objects, you will recognize them and respond to them in ways that support your intention to be more self-compassionate, even when that path is somewhat challenging.

The two mental objects that you are mostly likely to encounter are

>> **Inner dialogue:** The voice (or voices) that tend to comment on every experience and can often lead you astray

>> **"The Five Hindrances":** Common obstacles that meditators face when they practice

Consistent with the philosophy that "an ounce of prevention is worth a pound of cure," my aim is to prepare you for these two challenges ahead of encountering them in the practice of self-compassion. Forewarned is forearmed, as they say. The clichés are endless when it comes to human experience.

A little less color and a little more play-by-play

I have been a sports fan for as long as I can remember, and I have many fond memories of listening to Oakland Raiders football games or San Francisco Giants baseball games as a kid. These warm memories are as much of the voices of the sportscasters as they are of the actual athletes and teams. When you think about it, most sports come to us via the conduit of these silver-tongued professionals who describe and elaborate on the actual event.

Our minds can be said to be the "sportscasters" of our direct experience. What happens to us and around us (and even within us) just happens. And then our minds try to make something meaningful of those experiences. It's not a bad thing, really. As a matter of fact, it is this process that makes us uniquely human. But it does have some pitfalls, mainly because we have at least two sportscaster voices in our heads most of the time. The first is the steady, factual, even-handed play-by-play announcer, and the other is the bombastic, reactive, intense and enthusiastic color commentator. (For those of a certain age, think of Pat Summerall and John Madden in these respective roles.)

While the stalwart play-by-play announcer dutifully (and mellifluously) provides a moment-by-moment account of what unfolds in the game (in other words, our lived experience), the color commentator pontificates, judges, explains, extrapolates, and speculates in a way that creates our suffering.

While this applies to all experiences, consider how it manifests in the laboratory of your mind when you meditate. You ride the flow of the breath into your body, you feel the rise of your belly as your diaphragm draws the air in, and then the settling of the belly as the air leaves. Woo-hoo! You just managed to be mindful of *one whole breath!* "I did it!" you proclaim to yourself with some sense of self-satisfaction and pride. "I usually have more trouble than this! I think I'm getting better at meditating," you note analytically. And that's when your trouble begins because you went from the moment-to-moment observation of what happened to the color commentary on *how you were doing* and *judging* your experience as better or worse than another.

My sense is that we are practicing the art of "Intrapersonal Play-by-Play," noticing the unfolding of experience as an impartial witness to what happens as we sit, as we work, as we go about our daily lives and contend with all that we are faced with every day. We notice what there is to notice, in the external environment, this body of ours, and the vast mindscape within us. But a part of us wants to provide context, story arc, suspense, drama, anticipation. That is our own private color commentary.

And imagine the worst-case scenario: We are used to having our color commentators chosen for us by media executives because of how they might enhance our experience or engage us positively in the game. But you and I don't get to choose our color commentators for our intrapersonal play-by-play. They are assigned by history, experience, and random forces beyond our comprehension. What if your color commentary is provided by, say, Eeyore or Chicken Little or Dr. Phil, for heaven's sake? What then? Are you doomed?

I don't think so. Those commentators can't easily be silenced. In fact the more we start to argue with them, the louder they get, and while we are arguing we are actually missing the game/our life. What are we to do?

Perhaps we can simply and self-compassionately go back to the play-by-play. Drop into the breath, notice that while our own color commentator yammers on and on . . . and on, we can simply comfort ourselves for how hard it is to hear this commentary and turn our attention to the game itself. Notice the action, check the score, feel the familiar tension in the pit of our stomach at the critical junctures, and appreciate the beauty and brilliance of the game unfolding. All while holding ourselves and our experience with the same warmth and kindness that a tight end uses to pluck a floating screen pass out of the air at the goal line.

And when the color commentator comments colorfully (or critically) on you or your experience, thank it for trying to help you and return to the fullness of this precious moment that blooms on its own, with or without commentary, analysis, or clever metaphors. It just is what it is.

Five obstacles and how to RAIN on their parade

When you form an intention to be mindful and perhaps commit to formally practicing it in meditation, it won't take long on your journey until you encounter one or more of a family of five potential colorful characters that loom large in the path toward mindfulness. In fact, it is pretty certain that you have already encountered some of these mental factors as you have dabbled in mindfulness practice while reading this book. See if you recognize this rogues' gallery of hindrances:

>> **Samantha Sense Desire:** Samantha is a seductive traveler who cozies up to you very gently as you sit and meditate. At first she sits next to you, and you can feel her warm presence and get a gentle whiff of her intoxicating perfume. So far so good, but as time goes on, she leans over and whispers breathily into your ear: "This meditation is nice, but it would be even nicer if you had a fancier cushion, or maybe if you laid down instead of sitting. Or maybe you deserve a little break, and you could come back later when you're

more comfortable and meditate then instead." Samantha is that part of ourselves that just wants pleasure in any sensory form. This isn't necessarily a bad thing, but if it leads us to want to replace an irritating or uncomfortable feeling with its opposite, it is a form of clinging that leads us to a path of struggle. Samantha says "if only . . ." and takes us from the present moment.

» **Angry Andrew:** Andrew harbors ill will and is something of the opposite of Samantha. He challenges you and intrudes on your tranquility with hostility, rejection, and aversion to the present moment. Andrew is critical and quick to find fault with the present moment, your practice, your teacher, and even yourself. His ill will infects you, and your view is clouded by anger and hostility as you practice. Andrew says, "It should not be this way," and you resist your experience.

» **Sluggish Sally:** Often referred to as sloth and torpor, Sally is listless, lazy, drowsy, and apathetic. She curls up at your feet and yawns loudly like an indifferent housecat who longs for another nap, a little sunlight, and perhaps a few sips of milk. Sally invites you with her soft ways to slip into dreamland and to let go of your attentional energy. Sally says "mmmmmmm, it's nice and warm and cozy here" and saps your vitality and inclination to practice.

» **Restless Reshmi:** That tap, tap, tap on your shoulder is Reshmi, reminding you that she can't sit still, and you can't either. There is a worried quality to her restless presence, and you can feel it as you sit, as if there is something else that needs doing . . . now. Simply being here is almost intolerable. Reshmi convinces you that the thought of moving is actually a fact and she says to you, "Come on, don't just sit there, *do* something," and the tension rises in your body.

» **Doubting David:** David has always lacked confidence: in himself, in the value of meditation, in his commitment to becoming more self-compassionate. He sits down behind you and periodically whispers his doubts to you. Everything is a question with an answer that is pessimistic, unfortunate, and skeptical. David says, "Are you *sure* this is a good idea for me? What if it doesn't work?" And you let go of the practice to explain and argue.

Sound familiar? Which of these hindrances has visited you along this journey/ adventure of self-compassion already? How have you responded to them? What happened when you did whatever it was that you did in response to them? Are they still hanging around, ready to impede your path as you go forward?

Here is a simple four-step approach to the hindrances (called RAIN, developed by meditation teacher Tara Brach) that hinges upon the same old practice of mindfulness: being willing to simply turn toward and acknowledge their presence in the moment and meet them with calm awareness, acceptance that they are present, and maybe even kindness because they are old familiar companions on the journey of your life.

1. **Recognize:** Simply putting a name or a label to the hindrance that is present is perhaps the most powerful thing you can do to lessen its impact. Being able to say "I see you, Sluggish Sally" allows you some immunity from the spell that the hindrance can cast on your awareness. By naming the presence of a hindrance, you create a little space between you and it, and in that space is freedom. The psychiatrist and Holocaust survivor Victor Frankl famously said, "Between stimulus and response there is a space. In that space is our power to choose our response. In our response lies our growth and our freedom."

2. **Allow:** Once you note the presence of something and can recognize it, you have the option in that precious space between you and it to simply let go of resistance and instead allow it to be here, because it already is. You know how fruitless it can be to resist an experience, so the alternative to resistance is allowing. In a way, you are saying "Ahhh yes, Samantha, here you are again, my old friend," with no agenda to push her away or to pull her in, but simply *allowing* her to dwell uncontested in the background.

3. **Investigate:** Your natural, kindly curiosity will be aroused when you begin to see the hindrances not as fixed obstacles but simply visitors to your experience that come and go, and actually have no real objective substance to them. As you watch them arise, you can be a little bit curious by asking yourself, "What is happening inside me here? What am I believing in this moment? What does Doubting David want from me?" You have the option to act on the answers to these questions or simply let them linger and be attentive to what comes up.

4. **Natural Loving Awareness:** By following the first three steps of RAIN, you begin to loosen the grip that any particular hindrance has on your psyche and your experience. You are not on the defensive or on the offensive, you are simply present to what is here. When you are not fused with any particular limiting emotions, you have a kind of openness that allows experiences like this to come and go like clouds on the horizon or leaves on a stream. You can say, "Oh, Andrew, I see your anger and the pain underneath. Let's sit together nonetheless."

Being able to cultivate this attitude of RAIN, as you can see, is not a sneaky form of eradication of the hindrances, but instead it is a way of coming into alignment with the reality that they will be visiting you. You are finding a way to work with them that is actually productive and allows you, once again, to cultivate an inner safe and supportive space of warmth, strength, and self-compassion toward yourself in any situation or with any difficult or challenging experience. You may even find yourself dancing in the RAIN the next time you intend to practice mindfulness and self-compassion.

A word about practicing mindfulness

The practice of mindfulness is foundational to being able to meet ourselves with kindness when we suffer or fail or fall short, and my hope is that you have discovered some different ways of harnessing your own natural capacity to be present and aware in a way that supports your commitment to self-compassion. You can continue this practice through a variety of means, but the most traditional way of looking at mindfulness practice comes in two general forms: formal and informal practice.

>> **Formal practice** is what we most often associate with mindfulness, in that it is setting aside the time and honoring an intention to systematically sit and meditate, the same way we might set aside a period of time to go to the gym. We practice formally for its own sake, regardless of whether it is pleasant, unpleasant, or neutral, and without becoming attached to a specific outcome or emotional state. Therefore, we don't meditate to become relaxed, or happy, or even self-compassionate, but to become present to where we actually are.

>> **Informal practice** is what we can do in our daily lives. When we choose to ride the bus mindfully or eat a meal mindfully, or when we have a difficult conversation at work with a degree of mindfulness or self-compassion, we are deploying our resources of mindfulness and self-compassion and thereby strengthening and reinforcing the practice.

We can have an informal practice without having a formal practice, but they dance best together. We practice formally so that the informal practice is easier and more accessible when we really need it in our lives. We practice informally to weave the practice into our routine and to make it a part of who we are and not just something we do. Plus, the more that we find the informal practice to be helpful to us, the more inclined we are to practice formally to develop the capacity more fully. When you win a race, you want to go back to train harder to win more races.

Formal or informal, when we practice, we are tapping into our own inner wisdom and capacity to be mindful and compassionate.

2

Traveling on the Self-Compassion Journey

Explore how mindfulness of body, mind, and emotions can support you in becoming more self-compassionate.

Discover how appreciating your common humanity reduces feelings of isolation and supports you in self-compassion.

Find your inner inclination toward self-compassion, give it space to thrive, and find your own language for speaking kindly to yourself.

Chapter **5**

Common Humanity: Connection and Belonging

"

'm only human."

How often have we heard this statement (or said it) and not given it much thought? Usually, we say this when people or circumstances are demanding that we be much more than human. In other words, when we are being asked to *do* more than we reasonably can, to *be* more than is within our grasp, or to simply be perfect. We offer the statement as a kind of apology or excuse for being what we are: human. Perhaps the origin is from the days when many humans believed in a pantheon of gods and amidst those exalted beings we were "mere mortals."

But as Marianne Williamson has said, "Your playing small does not serve the world." Not only that, but your playing small doesn't even serve you! We humans spend a remarkable amount of emotional and cognitive energy denying and avoiding the miracle of our existence as human beings. But "only" human? Are you kidding me? With all that our human minds and hearts can accomplish; all that we have built, created, discovered, harnessed, and celebrated through our collective efforts as social and creative beings, how can we disown that heritage through apology for not being better or more or perfect? Just the simple fact that we have the capacity to think ahead and plan and execute that plan (like making breakfast) is a uniquely human capability that can be celebrated.

REMEMBER

We don't need to excel or achieve great things to be a part of the human race. Sometimes simply surviving life's challenges is an incredible accomplishment. For now, just let that sink in.

If you ever feel particularly isolated or different from other people, then you have yet another reminder of our common humanity, and you've come to the right place. As another component of self-compassion, this awareness is a powerful force for healing and growth because it dispels the illusion of isolation from each other and from our common human existence, and instead reminds us of our shared experience so that we feel less alone and more connected to each other.

In fact, the road to joy and understanding is paved with recognizing and embracing our common humanity and finding the common ground upon which we all stand. The pages ahead allow you to explore and experience our common humanity as an important element of a more self-compassionate you.

The Inescapable Truth: We Need Each Other

The image of the rugged individualist is embedded in our Western culture and is often a point of pride for those who have achieved greatness in various ways. Certainly, nothing is wrong with being bold, charting your own path, or overcoming peer pressure to strike out in a new direction. Self-reliance and independence are admirable traits and much of what we aim to instill in our offspring as dutiful parents (so that our children aren't still asking us to make them peanut butter and jelly sandwiches at the age of 30).

But the truth is that, however independent and self-reliant we may be or become, we are social beings who need each other for our very survival. As mammals, we are born helpless and dependent upon our parents or other caregivers to make sure that we have food, clothing, and shelter. And this reliance on others is only the beginning, as we continue to exist in community and connection. We collaborate to accomplish many of the great things that mankind has created (from the banking system to bridges to sliced bread). As John Donne famously said:

> "No man is an island entire of itself; every man is a piece of the continent, a part of the main; if a clod be washed away by the sea, Europe is the less, as well as if a promontory were, as well as any manner of thy friends or of thine own were; any man's death diminishes me, because I am involved in mankind. And therefore never send to know for whom the bell tolls; it tolls for thee."

We are all "involved in mankind," which is to say that we are actually all engaged together in this business of being members of the human race, and we are interconnected in this way. I know the hesitation that arises when people like me start saying "We are all connected," because it sounds a bit New Agey to some. In the words of my beloved brother the police officer, it may sound like "that weird California hippie shit that you do" when referring to my teaching of mindfulness and self-compassion. But this reality of interconnection is nothing weird or metaphysical or theoretical. It is observable, irrefutable fact that we are *inter*dependent beings who can't survive or thrive without each other. But we like to tell ourselves that we can. We can say "I am independent because I make my own cheese." But if someone else milked the cow, another person transported the milk, and someone else sold you the milk, then the illusion of your independence begins to fade. And this doesn't even take into account how the cow got there in the first place, where its food came from, and who made the container that you carried home to "independently" make your own cheese.

I remember getting angry at my parents when I was a youngster and vowing to run away from home and assert my independence to protest whatever unholy injustice I felt was being visited upon me at the time. It was probably an early bedtime or having to clean my room, but nonetheless, it was both inconceivable and tragically unfair in my mind. I would grab a few prized possessions (all given to me by my parents), empty my piggy bank (which had also been both given and filled by my parents), and hit the road. I was going to show them and go my own way. Needless to say, I was always back by the next mealtime, but I had made my case. I was independent!

The absurdity of this scenario (although admittedly charming in its own way) is less obvious when we act similarly as adults. When we see ourselves as wholly independent beings not reliant on others or subject to the same conditions as all other human beings, it gives us a sense of self-efficacy and self-determination that can motivate us to persist against the odds or in difficult circumstances, and potentially triumph in whatever we aim to accomplish. This is quite powerful if all our ideas are flawless, all our efforts succeed, and we never make mistakes. But here in the real world, human activities don't go like that. The smartest scientists form hypotheses and test them out, with a humble willingness to refine those ideas if the data doesn't support the original hypothesis. These same scientists know that they stand on the shoulders of those scientists who came before them, and most scientists do not resemble the movie characterizations of them as crazed and passionate loners in the attics of castles with burbling test tubes. (Even the fictional Dr. Frankenstein had his faithful assistant, Igor.) Imperfection and interconnection are accounted for in every successful human endeavor, even something as seemingly tangible and concrete as science.

REMEMBER

The point is that we are fooling ourselves if we think that we are truly independent of our larger human condition. Even more relevant to the practice of self-compassion, we are setting ourselves up to amplify our suffering when we perpetuate this fantasy that we are not a part of a larger "tribe" or collective.

If the previously mentioned scientist discovers that their hypothesis was flawed or their experiment was based on a miscalculation, she has two options. If she is enlightened and recognizes that one of her human inheritances is fallibility (in other words, she knows she is human and therefore subject to making mistakes), she will correct the error, inform her team, learn from it, and move on. If the same scientist is a perfectionist (overlooking the human impossibility of perfection), a similar error could lead to a spiral of self-critical thoughts (such as "I'm a terrible scientist," "My colleagues will now find out that I'm not as smart as they thought," or "I should just quit my job and get work flipping burgers instead") that descend into shame and a lifetime of suffering.

Awareness of our common humanity, as you can see in these examples, allows for us to see past our "small selves" and into the larger perspective of ourselves as fallible but talented human beings with incredible strengths and capacities along with inevitable weaknesses and shortcomings, all just seeking to be happy and free from suffering. But in order to change our perspective on the fact of being human, it may be helpful to explore our tendency to overlook the fact that we do, in fact, need each other.

Albert Einstein described humankind's tendency toward separateness in this way: "He experiences himself, his thoughts and feelings, as something separate from the rest — a kind of optical delusion of consciousness."

REMEMBER

When we shake that optical delusion and see ourselves as fully connected to all our human counterparts, we begin to be able to tolerate and even embrace the reality of our lives, including the moments of imperfection, failure, and falling short.

In other words, we become more able to have compassion for ourselves in these moments because of the reality that they happen to *all* humans, rather than seeing them as evidence of something fatally flawed about just us.

HOW YOU DENY YOUR HUMANITY

What are some ways that you deny your humanity? How do you routinely overlook the fact that you share your human nature with every other human who has ever lived or will ever live? Here are a few ways that you may recognize:

- You observe the fact that human beings come in separate envelopes of flesh (also known as "bodies") and mistake this for a kind of separate existence that causes you to believe that you don't need anyone else to survive. And then, when you feel the need to connect with other people (and to be seen and heard), you see it as some sort of unique weakness in your character rather than a feature of your birthright as a human.

- You (gasp!) make a mistake and immediately enter a downward spiral of self-recrimination and self-criticism. You convince yourself that you are uniquely flawed and imperfect and "less than" everyone else, whom you are convinced would *never* make such a mistake.

- You find out you weren't invited to a party to which several of your friends were invited. Although you act outwardly as if you are cool with that, inside it feels like your world is collapsing into a deep, dark hole, and you feel your heart pounding in panic over the slight.

- You find yourself having dark, shameful feelings toward your boss over a work con-flict. You find yourself so mired in hurt, anger, and resentment toward them that you can't even empathically acknowledge that, just like you, they are going through life with a desire to be happy and free from suffering. Your boss is actually a fellow traveler on the human highway, but you want nothing to do with this acknowledge-ment. It feels better to see them as motivated by some sort of evil or destructive force that is foreign to you and needs to be defeated. As a result you harbor resent-ment and fear, and feel stuck and powerless in this conflict.

- You decided you need some expert help with your lack of self-compassion and decide to pick up a book about the topic. But as you read it, you find that the author (me) is someone who is also a "hot mess" sometimes and recently beat himself up for failing his first try at a written driver's license test in a new state. Reading this, you start to feel hopeless, as if you will never get it right because even the experts aren't perfect. (I must confess that I, too, am human.)

Acknowledging Our Universal Human Need

I find myself intrigued by why we invest so much time and energy keeping up that optical delusion of separateness. Einstein went on to call this state "a kind of prison for us, restricting us to our personal desires and to affection for a few persons nearest to us." So for me, the question becomes, why have we checked ourselves into this very human prison and just exactly how long is our sentence? The answer, not surprisingly, is that we get sprung from this particular joint whenever we are able to embrace our common humanity and see ourselves as part of something bigger than ourselves. Some would call this spirituality, but you can use whatever word works for you. I think of it as taking the wide view and seeing the whole picture of our existence.

But that still begs the question of how we have come to be imprisoned to begin with. I think it has to do with the fact that we do literally need each other to survive. Starting with infancy, as I mention earlier, we are completely reliant on the kindness and care of others. Our offspring come out with certain survival needs and few rudimentary tools at their disposal to get those needs met. Mainly those tools are confined to crying . . . and crying louder, but over time babies expand their repertoire to facial expressions and more nuanced verbalizations. Our children are not like those sea turtle babies you see hatching on nature shows, where they burst out of their little eggs in the sand, waddle on down to the water, and swim off into the sunset. Our little "hatchlings" are far more helpless, and as a result, nature (in its infinite wisdom) has endowed humans with a deep and instinctive drive to connect, to seek out sources of vitality and safety, and also, to be on alert to any threats to that short but vital food chain of survival.

It is this last bit, the fear of being cut off from others and therefore vulnerable and at risk of not surviving, that is underneath most of our illusion of separateness. Think of astronauts in the early days of the space program. These brave souls donned big shiny spacesuits with bulbous helmets and an all-important, ever-present lifeline to explore space outside the ship. The lifeline is essentially a hose that attaches them to the spacecraft and provides the oxygen (and other vital elements) they need to survive in the vacuum of space. Now imagine that you were one of these astronauts and how extremely vulnerable you would feel, how careful and alert you would be to anything threatening that lifeline, and how *mindful* you would be to make sure that the lifeline was intact and functioning.

As an astronaut, you would have learned about the importance of your lifeline, but as a human being, you are already innately hardwired to treat your own "lifeline," your connection to your caregiver, as the key to your very survival. The infant cries not because he is inconvenienced or uncomfortable; he cries because his survival literally depends upon someone providing sustenance. And this system, however crude it may seem, has worked for our entire existence on this planet.

As we grow older, we begin to engage other means to be attuned to others, including some fascinating structures in the brain referred to as *mirror neurons* that allow us to feel the feelings of others. More on that in Chapter 12.

Survival equals love

But it's a bit more complex than this, because the baby isn't like the hungry plant Audrey in *A Little Shop of Horrors* insisting "Feed me, Seymour. Feed me!" The infant is charged with causing a broader bond to be created, a lifeline to be installed, that assures his continued existence by getting all his complex needs met (food, clothing, and shelter being only the beginning). This bond is the deeper, broader bond of love itself.

When the infant can manage to be loved by an adult, all of their needs can be met, and they can not only survive but grow and thrive. At the very foundation of our human bond, at an instinctive level, the thing that binds us together is love. Love equals survival for us, and so anything that may put that love in jeopardy is to be avoided at all costs. We want nobody to stand on our lifeline, our universal human need for love.

The poet Hafiz (loosely translated by Daniel Ladinsky) once wrote about this "great pull in us to connect" in a poem called *With that Moon Language*: "Everyone you see, you say to them, 'Love me.'" Let that sink in for a minute. Can you feel the truth of this down deep in a metaphorical sense? As Chris Germer says, "We wake up every morning with the wish to be loved and go through the entire day with the wish, although we may never realize or admit it." (What is even more intriguing is the fact that, when we can recognize and acknowledge this wish, we can more easily see the same wish in others, and suddenly we can feel less alone and afraid. More on this in the later section "Practice: Just Like Me.")

So as human beings, we need love. It's just that simple, but it's not so easy sometimes. Usually, we think of being loved as a kind of privilege or happy circumstance that may or may not happen to us and may be fleeting. But we rarely think of love as a survival need.

Perhaps it would be helpful to think more broadly about love as encompassing all the different forms of love that the ancient Greeks studied and articulated. They identified eight different forms of love: *philia*, or affectionate love; *philautia*, or self-love; *pragma*, or enduring love; *eros*, or romantic love; *ludus*, or playful love; *storge*, or familiar love; *agape*, or selfless love; and *mania*, or obsessive love. Love obviously comes in many forms and from many sources, but the point here is that we need it (in its varied forms) for our physical as well as our emotional survival. We are happiest when we feel loved and saddest when we do not. If we feel isolated or tragically different or separate from others, then we have a deep-seated feeling that our lifeline has a fatal kink in it and that we are unloved. The feeling that arises in us is akin to having your oxygen supply threatened in the vastness of the vacuum of space.

What arises if we feel unloved . . . or unlovable?

With our very survival feeling as if it is riding on feeling loved, or at least lov*able*, one can see that the stakes are high when these possibilities are threatened. In fact, the primal nature of this fear is actually the source of the most troubling of human emotional experiences: shame. I talk further about the experience of shame in Chapter 10, but here you can explore how shame is bound up with your sense of common humanity in so many ways.

To appreciate this relationship, you need only look at one definition of shame, by W.K. Hahn (italics added): "a complex combination of emotions, physiological responses, and imagery associated with the *real or imagined rupture of relational ties*." That sounds a lot like "Excuse me, but your foot is on my lifeline." This "real or imagined rupture of relational ties" can, as you have seen, be much more than just an inconvenience because they tear at the very fabric of our existence and survival as humans.

But let's look beyond humans for a moment and consider the antelope. These beautiful creatures of the plains live in community and travel as a herd from place to place to eat and procreate (and to play with the deer if the old song "Home on the Range" is accurate). They don't just travel in herds because they enjoy each other's company, but because there is safety in numbers. Being in a herd protects them, to some degree, from predators like wolves, cougars, bears, and even eagles.

It is a dangerous thing to be a lone antelope with those treacherous creatures lurking all around, so you stick to your herd and try to blend in. And when your herd is spooked by something that you don't notice and they scurry off to escape the perceived threat while you are obliviously munching on green grass, you are suddenly exposed and in potential danger. This unfortunate situation is a major rupture in your relational tie to the herd, and you may not survive it if a wolf is prowling nearby.

Take a moment to imagine how this would feel and consider that the feeling is not that different from how you might feel if you were shunned or disowned by your family when you were young, or how you might feel if you were fired from your job. In our own way, we humans are no different from herd animals like the antelope in our need to feel connected to feel safe. But antelope are concerned only with physical survival, whereas our human sympathetic nervous system does not differentiate between real and imagined threats. So these hazards can potentially come from being physically attacked, from imagining a potential injury, or even from receiving a nasty and hurtful email or phone message.

This interdependence that I am speaking about goes two ways, of course, but mainly I've been exploring why you need everyone else. However, it's worth exploring the other direction too, because it also has some important pitfalls that are worth appreciating.

REMEMBER

Your human herd or tribe needs *you*, as it needs all its members, and this can put you in an awkward position if you don't feel as if you belong or you don't feel worthy of being a part of the collective.

In moments when we fail, fall short, or make a mistake, we can tend to attribute these unfortunate events to our flaws as individuals. We feel as if we alone have these feelings, that somehow, we are uniquely bad or stupid or ill-equipped, and that these are enduring features of ourselves and not fleeting experiences that all humans have at times. When we lack the sense of common humanity, every unfortunate experience becomes another brick in the wall of our isolation from others because we feel, at some deep, cellular level, that this flaw makes us uniquely unlovable and therefore separate from everyone.

Our relentlessly comparing minds then see us as *less than* others in a fundamental way, not measuring up and simply not worthy of the crucial love of our human clan. This is the painful experience of shame, where you feel as if you carry around a shameful and malignant truth about yourself which, if discovered by the people you need (and who need you), would cause them to reject and abandon you. The feeling of shame is that you will be left on your own in dangerous territory, vulnerable to your predators, whatever they may be.

In this case, you can feel like you alone could potentially be the cause of this rupture in your relational ties to others (you are standing on your *own* lifeline, so to speak), so you do everything in your power to hide this terrible, fatal flaw as if your life depends on it. Literally. And of course, if you fear being "found out" for the shameful "fact" of your imperfection, you hunker down to hide that flaw or run away from others. This, of course, leads you to feeling even more isolated from them and even farther from a sense of common humanity.

This scenario paints a rather dark picture of the cost of not appreciating our common humanity, but it also begins to map a course toward a way out of the clutches of Einstein's "optical delusion" and into the light of embracing our humanity as a great gift of safety, security, and strength for finding happiness and freedom from suffering. Self-compassion invites us back to humanity. As Mary Oliver says in her poem "Wild Geese":

> Whoever you are, no matter how lonely,
>
> the world offers itself to your imagination,
>
> calls to you like the wild geese, harsh and exciting
>
> over and over announcing your place
>
> in the family of things.

THE FEAR OF BEING FOUND TO BE A FRAUD

Have you ever had a moment of relative success or paused to reflect on how fortunate you are to be doing something that you had always hoped to do? Perhaps you have been invited to give an important commencement speech at your alma mater or you've been promoted within your company to a coveted new role. You feel some gratification, you bask in the compliment that has been extended to you, and then you start to feel doubt and uncertainty tap you on the shoulder. You start to worry that you aren't up to the task, that someone (or multiple someones) has vastly overestimated your skill or talent or ability, and that when you begin to fulfil your new role, this terrible oversight will become visible. People will find out that you really don't know what you are doing and have just been a successful faker and fraud so far. And then the proverbial stuff will hit the proverbial fan.

My moment was the day that my wife and I walked out of the hospital with our one and only child. Baby Ben was a treasure, and we were so excited to welcome him into our lives. When the day came for mother and baby to come home, we were escorted to the entrance of the hospital. As my wife handed Ben to me to buckle him into the infant car seat, I had a moment of panic. "Wait. You mean we get to just take this human home with us? Don't you want to check our qualifications first?" I had led what I thought was a good life and had thought I was well-qualified to be a parent (I'd read the books, taken the classes, paid attention to my own parents) . . . but was I, *really?* Maybe I was not at all cut out to do this important job. What if I turned out to be a really terrible parent? Then what?

I muddled through, but you know that moment of panic, of being found out to not be what people think you are? That, my friend, is a flavor of shame that many of us have experienced, and it is referred to as "impostor syndrome." At its root, it still goes back to the fear of being unloved or unlovable. "What if people find out who I *really* am?" you say to yourself, and you think, "If they knew, they would reject me. I would not be loved. I would be unlovable if people really knew me." So again, the survival instinct powers the illusion of unlovability, and we quake in our boots.

The fact that there is a name for this phenomenon should be some indication that it may be more widespread than you may have thought. In other words, most of us have some sort of self-doubt (which can be healthy to make sure we do our best), but that self-doubt can easily tip over into feeling separate, alone, and isolated from others if we lack self-compassion. So, take heart! You are among fellow imposters (also known as humans) and it's a part of our simple desire to be accepted, appreciated, acknowledged . . . and loved. When we wake up to this, we are like the two wolves dressed in sheep's clothing in a Gary Larson *Far Side* cartoon. They are standing up and have taken off their fake sheep's heads, standing amidst a whole flock of what look like "sheep" in similar makeshift costumes, with no actual sheep in sight. One is saying to the other, "Wait a minute! Isn't anyone here a real sheep?" The humor is that we are all "real sheep," which is to say that part of our reality is that we just want to be loved and accepted, and fear being found to be unworthy of love for some reason. Could you be just a little bit kind to yourself for having that fear, the way you would comfort a dear friend who was feeling unlovable?

Three common blocks to embracing your common humanity

Seeing ourselves in the larger context of our human condition perhaps sounds admirable and worth exploring, but when people actually explore this possibility, many encounter some challenges. Here are three of the most common obstacles that can arise, along with some guidance to support you in overcoming them and finding your way toward feeling your deep connection to other humans as a means of becoming more self-compassionate. You will see that the thread running through all three of these blocks is the strong tendency of our mind to compare and contrast everything. We find that we often learn about things by contrasting them with others. We might say "it tastes like chicken," or ask, "Is it as funny as *Caddyshack*?" (Just to be clear, nothing is as funny as *Caddyshack*.)

Our human brains are efficient at this process and serve us well in many ways, but when we slip over into comparing the *facts* of things into comparing the *value* of things, we begin to get into trouble. When we decide that our own suffering is better or worse than anyone else's, or that someone else is more worthy of an experience than we are, we deny the reality of our own humanity. The goal with embracing common humanity is to stick to the *fact* of it and to let go of comparing one person's particular experience to another's.

The following sections describe those obstacles you're most likely to encounter.

Feeling unimportant

"It makes me feel like my problems are trivial compared to others'."

When we remind ourselves that other people have similar problems, we can feel as if we are dismissing our own problems as inconsequential. I once attended a meeting in which an important authority listened to the complaints of one of my colleagues, paused, and then responded, "and other people have other problems," and moved on. This was an unfortunate way of discounting this person's concerns by somehow suggesting that they weren't worthy of attention. When we are already inclined to feel unworthy (due to a lack of self-compassion), we are easily triggered to feel this way about our own struggles.

The key to overcoming this obstacle is to bring our practice of mindfulness to the experience and realize that acknowledging the *presence* of our problems is the point. We need to notice how the mind habitually wants to compare our experience to others, and to coax it back each time that it wanders off to comparing. We are just *making room* for our own suffering alongside that of our human brethren, acknowledging that we experience pain just as all humans do, and that this experience (regardless of the specifics) is a human one that binds us together rather than separating us.

A recent meme making the rounds in response to the COVID-19 pandemic has been, "We are not all in the same boat. But we are in the same storm, and with the support and understanding of our fellow humans, we can all come through the other side a little kinder, a little gentler, a little more human." Common humanity simply acknowledges and validates our suffering as a shared human experience, even if it manifests differently in each of us.

Feeling overwhelmed

"Even thinking about my suffering just becomes too much when I think about the enormity of it."

Often what keeps us in denial is that we build up our fear of the thing were avoiding such that it becomes much bigger in our minds than it actually is (this is the opposite of denial). I once found myself playing golf and chasing an errant ball into the woods. As I picked up my ball to head back to the fairway, I heard rustling in the bushes. With each step I took, faster and faster, the sound continued in my direction and my fear and anxiety mounted. I imagined mountain lions, bears, and alligators chasing after me to eat me. When I finally got to "safety," breathless and sweaty, I had enough presence of mind to turn and look . . . and to see the cutest little bunny rabbit come hopping out of the shrubbery. There was indeed something alive behind me, but the rest was a construction in my imagination.

Not all our pain is the equivalent of a bunny rabbit, but when we see it for what it is and not what our brain tells us it is, that is often the first powerful step to coming to terms with it. When we can let go of resistance to a feeling and simply recognize it as part of our human experience, we are taking an important step toward coming to terms with our life (including our suffering) as it actually is, rather than what we fear it may be. As I note in Chapter 2, this is not necessarily an easy thing and takes some courage to do, but you can do this with small steps. Be willing to simply begin by touching the suffering that you carry, be patient, and always respond to what you need to embark on this exploration with attention to what you are ready to encounter. You do not have to embrace anything, but simply, slowly, kindly open up to it as you can.

Understanding that everyone suffers

"Realizing that everyone is as much of a hot mess as I am kind of freaks me out."

Far from being comforting, this awareness that everybody suffers can at first be a painful reality check, but perhaps a necessary one. At the beginning of a recent Mindful Self-Compassion course, after everyone had arrived and taken their seats in a circle, quietly whisper-chatting with people nearby, not making eye contact across the circle and generally feeling a bit self-conscious, the course began. People introduced themselves briefly one by one and made reference to what kinds of challenges and issues had brought them to the class.

The last woman to speak had the most memorable observation of all. She lit up as she said, "When I came into the room tonight I looked around and everyone looked so *normal!*" There were a few self-conscious giggles in the room, and she realized that what she'd said could have been misunderstood as unkind. "I don't mean it that way. I just felt so different from everyone else because I have always had this dark feeling inside like there's something terribly wrong with me as a person. But when you all shared some of your stories, I realized that we *all* have these feelings and we're actually more alike *because of this* and not *in spite of it.* I was doubting whether I belonged here, and now I know I do."

This is the essence of common humanity and, by extension, self-compassion. As the meditation teacher Rob Nairn has said: "The goal of practice is to become a compassionate mess. This means fully human — often struggling, uncertain, confused — with great compassion."

Starting small with common humanity

Each of us has a variety of different identities that help to determine our sense of self. These identities include race, ethnicity, gender, sexual orientation, religious preference, physical ability, and any one of literally millions of other dimensions upon which we align with certain people more than with other people. We may think of these as simply features of who we are that we happen to share with other *homo sapiens*.

This concept of the things we share with all humans is actually pretty huge when you delve into it. Genetically speaking, we are more than 99.9 percent the same, which is what the Black poet Maya Angelou was referring to when she said, "We are more alike, my friends, than we are unalike." One of the more subtle stumbling blocks that people encounter when acknowledging common humanity is that, based upon their experience of particular identities that they hold, and the degree to which holding those identities has led to disenfranchisement, discrimination, marginalization, or mistreatment, people do not feel that connected to the entire human race.

If you recognize this experience, you may feel that your views, beliefs, practices, or features are not held by the larger society and as such, you may feel isolated from the rest of humanity to some degree. If that's the case, it's a pretty tall order to consider embracing all the commonality that you share with every human being who ever lived or ever will live.

People of some diverse backgrounds (especially those who identify as BIPOC: Black, Indigenous, and People of Color) struggle with the concept of common humanity because they feel as if society has constructed their particular identity as *un*common and separate from the dominant culture, and therefore somehow lower on some imagined hierarchy of humanity. So, people with these identities feel as if the talk of common humanity discounts their lived experience of society's injustice.

This is obviously a huge topic, but for our purposes here, if these ideas resonate with your lived experience, then I admire your willingness to dig in and explore this more deeply. Perhaps despite these cultural constrictions, you may begin to build and grow some common ground at the more basic level of the mere fact that each of us is human, imperfect, and subject to suffering. (And if you are someone who holds identities that have been traditionally more privileged or valued by society, it may be an opportunity to see where your own privilege may have led you to feel more separated or different from those who have not had that opportunity.)

TIP

Consistent with grasping self-compassion in the first place, you can give yourself the gift of being a brave, patient, and steady learner regarding common humanity. Think of yourself as being at the center of various concentric circles of identity and see if you can slowly find common ground and comfort in the common humanity of that circle. For example, if you are a Latinx, heterosexual, Catholic, cisgender female (to choose just a few identities) and are struggling with feelings of isolation and having difficulty fully appreciating common humanity, what if you choose to focus on one of those identities (say being Latinx) and see if you can sense whether even one other Latinx person may understand how you feel (it may or may not be a specific person you know). If you can make that connection, then you might widen the circle to include other people, for example, people who share your identities of being Latinx and Catholic. Be willing to experiment, to go slow, and to feel your way into Mary Oliver's "family of things."

Common humanity does not have to be an all-or-nothing proposition. The overarching principle, the guiding intention, is to see ourselves as a part of all humanity, but we can begin with one little piece of territory that we feel we can reclaim and go from there. "Walk slowly, go farther" as someone once said.

Two Tasks to Embrace Common Humanity

Circling back to Mary Oliver's poem, the practical question for you becomes "How do I answer the call and claim my place in the family of things?" You may face some challenging obstacles to embracing the reality of our shared common humanity, but perhaps you are now more open to considering it. You may need to undertake a couple of important tasks to fully open yourself to your humanity and thus lead you to a more self-compassionate way of being. There is one thing you need to embrace and one thing that you need to release, and both require you to be patient with yourself and be willing to be a slow learner once again. But if you begin to travel down the road of embracing your human inheritance and releasing any tendency toward perfectionism, you will find that you can easily find "your place in the family of things."

Claiming your human birthrights

At times the term "common humanity" has been misunderstood by people as implying that everyone's experience is the same or that everyone's suffering is equal in some way. By now I hope you see that we are not speaking in terms of the quality of suffering or the intensity of it, but just the mere fact that we all experience it. No matter who we are, we can always identify someone else who has suffered more, or more acutely, just as we can identify others who have suffered less.

The common thread between us is that suffering itself is part of our makeup as humans, and it is part of our legacy.

But being human is more than just suffering, it comes with an inheritance of intrinsic value and worthiness. You are here because you belong. You are worthy, loved, needed, and have value. These are not just lofty platitudes but real truths of our existence that are easily overlooked, especially by those who have inner critical voices that speak to the contrary and may have spoken in those terms for a lifetime. I don't expect you to simply accept these things about yourself because I said them, but it is worth considering the possibility of beginning the process of exploring what it means to belong to the human race.

What I'm suggesting here is that you look at your own good qualities and abilities as a human (and there are many) and consider making a little room for them in your heart. Take the time to actually appreciate and acknowledge the things that you bring to the table as a person, not because you are better than anyone else or the best at something, but just because you recognize that you have certain unique or admirable capabilities and talents. Start small. The fact that you are reading this book (even the fact that you *are able* to read this book) is a reflection of your deep and abiding desire to be kinder to yourself, that you seek to be happy and free from suffering, just like every human being on the planet. This is enough, but you don't have to stop there.

TIP

Make a list of ten things that you appreciate about yourself, however seemingly small and insignificant, and don't stop until you have at least ten. A hundred would be better, but you don't have to put a lot of pressure on yourself. You won't have to share this list with anyone, so you can be totally honest. If it helps, you can even take a moment to reflect on whether someone was instrumental in developing or nurturing a particular quality. A mentor, a parent, a coach or teacher, even a spiritual figure or author may have helped you unlock a natural tendency or talent that you may not have known you had. By adding that quality to your list, you are honoring that person and their contribution to your life.

This can often be a challenging exercise for people, so it's okay to go slow. Strangely enough, some people find that accepting their own flaws and inadequacies is doable, yet they find it incredibly hard to acknowledge their own strengths and accomplishments. If this is you, then this is a practice you may want to cultivate intentionally on a regular basis.

Avoiding the perils of perfection

We have spent a great deal of time in this chapter focusing on how much we actually depend upon each other for our survival, safety, and well-being. We have explored how we fear being shunned from our "herd" or "pack" and how that can cause us to feel unloved or unlovable. I have painted a rather bleak picture of our deep-seated insecurity as human beings who simply seek to be loved and accepted, but constantly fear being rejected and isolated from others. This is a challenge of being human, but not an insurmountable challenge, and most of us do not give up in the face of it. We simply plod along as best we can, wishing we felt more connected than we do and wondering what is wrong with us that we don't.

Cassius proclaims in Shakespeare's *Julius Caesar:* "The fault, dear Brutus, is not in our stars, but in ourselves, that we are underlings." What Cassius is pointing to is what Marianne Williamson was also suggesting when she said, "Your playing small does not serve the world." We do not do ourselves any favors by placing ourselves one down from everyone else and seeing ourselves as underlings. It is not fate that we see ourselves as less valuable or deserving than any other human being, but simply the result of our own belief that we are not. When we see that this belief is simply an idea — another brain secretion or random neuron firing — and not a fact or immutable truth, then we can begin to loosen its hold on us.

One way that you may find yourself putting yourself down compared to others is by making the observation that you are actually not perfect. You make an error, you fall short at something you attempt, or you fail at something and immediately you are shame-stricken because you are reminded that you have imperfections. The resulting shame-spiral may even be familiar to you. The feeling of being isolated, separate, and different from everyone else begins to envelop you as you sink deeper in the mire and muck of imperfection. You may go so far as to feel as if you are uniquely flawed, tragically doomed to a life of failure, and completely unworthy of anyone's love or affection.

REMEMBER

All of this downward spiral unfolds because you were imperfect. All because you exhibited a trait that is true of every human being who has ever lived and ever will live on the face of the planet. In other words, in that moment of wallowing in your "unique" imperfection, you are experiencing the pain that every human feels when they make a mistake, fall short, or fail. Every single human. Ever.

In the Native American Navajo tradition (and in many other ethnic and cultural customs), rug weavers leave little imperfections in their beautiful creations to reinforce the understanding that only God is perfect and that humans should not pretend to be perfect as well. These little imperfections, called "spirit lines," are subtle reminders of the common humanity of imperfection. Taken together, this deliberate imperfection is a nod to acknowledging and embracing our shared imperfection as humans.

TIP

If you simply *must* feel perfect, then my invitation to you is to see if you can turn this around 180 degrees and consider your own imperfections as a human being to be absolutely perfect. Could you be perfectly imperfect as you are?

Practice: Just Like Me

PLAY

The invitation here is to put aside all of these ideas and concepts about common humanity, perfection, shame, survival and the rest, and to simply see if you can begin to develop a felt sense of common humanity through a simple practice that I will guide you through. What you are tapping into here is the awareness that all of us wish for happiness and freedom from suffering, that this too is a part of our common humanity.

Just Like Me meditation

This meditation is inspired by the writing and teaching of Thupten Jinpa in his book *A Fearless Heart: How the courage to be compassionate can transform our lives.*

Take some time to settle into your body for a few minutes, allowing your attention to drop inside. Take note of whatever is present in the way of sensation inside your body. You may notice the touch of clothing, the pressure of the supporting surface on certain parts of your body, or just sensations of coolness or warmth, relaxation or tension, ease or discomfort. Just take note of where and how you are in this moment. You may notice the movement of breath into and out of the body as well, recognizing that the breath has continued to breathe itself since you last attended to it.

Imagine someone whom you hold dear, someone who brings a smile to your face when you think of them, someone with whom you have a relatively easy and uncomplicated relationship. This may be a family member like a child, a grand-parent, or even a pet. Try to go beyond the *idea* of this being and see if you can actually feel what it feels like to be in their presence.

Notice any pleasant feelings that may arise as you hold this beloved being in your awareness and see how easy it is to acknowledge that this one too, has the same aspiration for genuine happiness that you have.

Now call to mind someone else, someone that you recognize but don't have much meaningful interaction with and don't feel any particular closeness to. This may be a person whom you see quite often, in the hallway at work, behind the counter at your favorite coffee shop, or driving the bus you take regularly. Notice what feelings arise for you as you picture this person and how these feelings may be different from what you felt in regard to the loved one you imagined first.

Usually, we don't give much thought to the happiness of people in neutral roles in our lives like this. But see if this time you can imagine what it might be like to be this person. Imagine their life, their hopes and fears, which are every bit as real, complex, and challenging as yours. You may even recognize a certain similarity between yourself and this other person at the level of your common humanity. "Just like me, she wishes to be happy and to avoid even the slightest suffering."

Next, bring to mind a person with whom you may have some difficulty, someone who irritates or annoys you, someone who may have done you harm, or someone you think might even take satisfaction in your misfortune. If you can, picture this person in front of you. If uncomfortable or painful feelings arise as you do this, maybe place a hand somewhere on your body that is comforting, soothing, or reassuring to simply acknowledge that this is difficult. See if you can acknowledge the difficult feelings, even if you find yourself recalling painful interactions with them in the past. Don't suppress the feelings, but also don't reinforce them by trying too hard to accurately recall those exchanges.

Now see if you can put yourself in this person's shoes for a moment, recognizing that he is an object of deep concern to someone, a parent or a spouse, a child or a dear friend of someone. Begin to acknowledge that even this person with whom you have challenges has the same fundamental aspiration for happiness that you have. Allow your attention to stay with this awareness for some period of time (say 20 to 30 seconds). Allow thoughts and feelings to come and go as they will, as you remain present to whatever arises, with no other agenda but to observe and be kind to yourself in that presence.

Finally, see if you can bring together these three people in one mental picture in front of you. Take some time to reflect on the fact that they all share a basic yearning to be happy and free from suffering. At this dimension, there is no difference between these three people. In this fundamental aspect, they are exactly the same. Just take the time to relate to these three beings from that perspective, from the point of view that they share the aspiration for happiness and a kind of perfect imperfection.

And be sure now to include yourself in this circle of awareness, reminding yourself that

>> These people have feelings, thoughts, and emotions, just like me.

>> These people, during their lives, have experienced physical and emotional pain and suffering, just like me.

>> These people have been sad, disappointed, angry or worried, just like me.

>> These people have felt unworthy or inadequate at times, just like me.

>> These people have longed for connection, purpose, and belonging, just like me.

>> These people want to be happy and free from pain and suffering, just like me.

>> These people want to be loved, just like me.

With this deep recognition that the desires to be happy and to overcome suffering are common to all, silently repeat this phrase: "Just like me, all others aspire to happiness and want to overcome suffering."

Take some time to sit with whatever wishes or feelings arise from this practice, allowing them to arise and fall away. Your only agenda is to notice and take note of their arising.

Inquiring: What was it like to see how others are just like you?

Take some time to settle in and reflect on your experience of the preceding meditation. See if you can adopt an open, nonjudgmental stance toward whatever comes up for you in the way of thoughts, emotions, or anything else. This is not always an easy practice, and the key to success is to be open and curious to the process and let go of specific expectations.

Consider the following questions as guides to your exploration of your own experience of the Just Like Me meditation:

>> How was it to imagine a beloved being and to acknowledge their desire to simply be happy and free from suffering?

>> When you turned your attention to a relatively neutral person, could you call them to mind? Were you able to get some sense of what it is like to be in their shoes and to live their lives? Did you sense any similarity between you and that person?

>> What came up for you when you called to mind the difficult person? Were you able to stay present and compassionate even with that person in mind and your history with that person?

>> What was it like to call this difficult person to mind and stay present with them?

>> Were you able to sense any way in which you and the difficult person have in common the simple desire to be happy and free from suffering?

>> What was your experience of holding all three people in awareness and considering how they were more alike than different?

>> How was it to contemplate the various "just like me" observations?

>> What is your relationship at this moment to the truth of common humanity?

If you found this practice fruitful in any way, I invite you to consider practicing it throughout your day, especially when you encounter people from whom you feel different or separate in some way. See if, by pausing and warming up the conversation with compassion, you can see some ways in which this person shares some common humanity with you. You'll be glad you did.

Chapter **6**

Cultivating Your Innate Kindness

As you continue on this adventure of self-compassion, it's worthwhile to pause and take an inventory of your journey to date. After briefly defining and exploring the basics of self-compassion, I share the benefits of practicing it, as well as dispelling some of the most common misgivings. This sets the stage for you to really commence the adventure by becoming intimately familiar (both conceptually and experientially) with each of the three essential components of self-compassion, because they form the foundation of the practice and are common threads through the rest of the book.

The journey begins where such journeys need to begin, with awareness, which we define as mindfulness. This basic human ability to be aware of each moment as it arises in all its fullness is an incredibly powerful capacity. It supports you in disengaging from a discursive, resistant, and wandering mind that prefers to go into the past and future rather than stay present. Mindfulness is your anchor and lifeline to the present moment, which is the only place where anything can actually be accomplished.

I then introduce common humanity as the second component of self-compassion. This deep awareness of our shared humanity and all that it entails is the broad and supportive base for self-compassion practice because it reminds us that we are not alone and have a shared inheritance with the entire human family. Fully embracing our common humanity allows us to see our missteps, foibles, and errors as stemming from the common imperfection of humanity.

It may seem now like you have everything you need to become more self-compassionate, and indeed you do have it within you, but I would like to help you connect more fully and directly in this chapter with the third and final component of self-compassion identified by Kristin Neff: self-kindness. Speaking more generally, lovingkindness or "boundless friendliness" is what we explore here.

This natural human tendency toward happiness and satisfaction tends to be either overlooked as just a given or overemphasized as if it is all that is required for self-compassion: to simply be nice to yourself. However, in the larger context, trying to practice self-compassion without the warmth of kindness (just relying on mindfulness and common humanity) leads to a kind of stark view of the human condition where we are acutely aware of each moment and how difficult it is for all of us, without any sense of comfort or soothing for that difficulty.

On the other hand, confusing self-kindness for the larger practice of self-compassion leaves out the grounding of mindfulness or the reality check of common humanity. What you are left with if you try to meet your suffering with just self-kindness is a kind of warm, moist, sickly sweet sentimentality that is ineffective because it is clueless (un-mindful) and ungrounded (disconnected with the human reality of suffering and imperfection).

Therefore, it's important that you tap into all three components of self-compassion to really unlock its true potential, and that includes tapping into your own natural tendency toward kindness, joy, and well-being.

We All Just Want to Be Happy

Following on from the Just Like Me meditation in the preceding chapter, it is incredibly valuable to operate from a place of awareness that, regardless of how people behave or what we think of what other people think, say, or do, they are just like us in that they simply want to be happy and free from suffering. Other people may very well go about trying to be happy in ways that are sadly unfortunate, sometimes hurtful, and occasionally hard to fathom, but when we see it all in the light of this universal human desire to have joy and satisfaction, we begin to see ourselves (and others) in a new light. That new light is the light of lovingkindness, or our innate inclination of the heart toward joy and satisfaction.

A note on what we do to be happy: It's important to note that I am not suggesting that this motivation gets people off the hook for truly hurtful or dangerous behavior, just because they are seeking happiness in doing it. I am only speaking to their motivation for doing it and am not excusing the behavior itself by any means. And please keep in mind that these choices that people make are in the service of *seeking* happiness — it doesn't mean that they find it in these behaviors or activities. "Seek and ye shall find" does not apply when it comes to happiness, and sometimes poor choices lead to the opposite of happiness. Remember that the U.S. Declaration of Independence only grants the right to "the pursuit of happiness" and not happiness itself.

When you look at another person and scratch your head over their choices — of boyfriends, hobbies, or hairstyles — these choices take on a new dimension when you see them as expressions of that person's inclination toward happiness. You may see a tragic pattern in your sister's choice of partners because they tend to be charming guys who are incredibly insecure and narcissistic, and ultimately end up treating her badly. But when you see that this is just her unmindful seeking of happiness that leads her to make these choices because of how these men make her feel when she first encounters them, it changes how you view your sister. You begin to see that she is not masochistically choosing men that she knows are bad for her or seeking out men that she knows you won't approve of, just because she has a beef with you. She is just charting her own idiosyncratic course toward happiness, as she knows it, with the best of intentions, but perhaps a little too much naïveté or lack of awareness that could be more protective of her tender heart.

Take a moment to call to mind someone whose behavior, attitudes, or choices are hard for you to fathom. Maybe it's the woman on Facebook who posts nothing but videos of cats in costumes, or the guy behind the meat counter with the incredibly detailed face tattoos, or maybe it's someone who supports a different political candidate than you. You may find any of these to be offensive, disturbing, or confusing and something you would never choose, but is it possible for you to not take any of these things personally?

In other words, the butcher did not choose that image of a snake wrapping around his neck to offend you personally, but because he liked how it made him look. It made him happy in some way, even if you happen to cringe inside every time you see it. This is a benign example, but even in the most challenging of cases, seeing the underlying motives of another as being essentially guided by goodness and the pursuit of happiness, and nothing intentionally hurtful to you or anyone, can change your experience.

The key to being able to have this attitude is not just having the belief that all people simply want to be happy and free from suffering, but cultivating the open heart and kind intention to accept the presence of whatever is here (mindfulness) and the awareness that we share these deep motivations (if not the penchant for serpentine tattoos). This practice asks us to watch our reactivity and initial impressions and be willing to go a little deeper to tap into our *own* natural capacity for kindness and our *own* desire to be happy so that we can cultivate an inner landscape of good will. The more that we tend that inner garden of goodwill, the more our heart opens, and the more our heart opens, the more seeds of benevolence can be sown for others and for ourselves.

An alternative metaphor you could consider comes from a dear friend with whom I was teaching a workshop on self-compassion for men a few years ago. We practiced the lovingkindness meditation I present later in this chapter, and in the post-meditation discussion, someone asked why we would even be doing this. My colleague used the analogy that it's like going to the gym to exercise your muscles, but then in an unfortunate act of improvisation in a room full of men (who easily descend into being a room of preadolescents with the slightest prompting), he said, "Except in this case, the muscle you are exercising is your love muscle." Saying "love muscle" in front of a group of men, however enlightened and open-hearted, is like throwing raw meat to hungry lions. My friend may still shudder when he thinks of that unfortunate detour. But all questionable references aside, this is actually an apt description of what we are doing in practicing lovingkindness.

Investing in Your Capacity to Be Kind

Whether you are planting a garden or exercising a muscle, the key is that you are investing the effort now, not because you expect immediate results (however much any of us might like that instant gratification), but because you have some faith that it will pay off over time to cultivate lovingkindness (or "boundless friendliness") in this way. This is the essence of why we practice lovingkindness meditation: to tap into and develop a deep inclination of the heart toward kindness, joy, and satisfaction.

Lovingkindness meditation has a long and rich history and was mainly brought from Asia to the West by meditation teacher Sharon Salzberg. The practice is a way of training the mind to be more loving and compassionate through a variety of means, especially the use of language, as the "vehicle" of the meditation. Words have particular power over us and our way of thinking about and being with our experiences.

We all learned to respond to people who said mean things (in a sing-song voice): "Sticks and stones will break my bones, but words can never hurt me." Sadly, as is the case with many platitudes, it sounds good but is entirely wrong. Think about it. Have you ever experienced a broken bone in your life? Has it healed? Now think about times when you have been deeply hurt by words that were spoken by someone else. Do you still feel the sting of that injury? Words matter. There is a saying, "Be careful what you say to yourself because you're listening." Words can often hurt us, which is why schoolyard bullies are often so skilled in finding just the right thing to say to push your buttons.

If words can leave lingering pain and distress, then the good news in this is that we can use other words to promote healing and ease. We can bring words over from the dark side to the light side and gently but firmly cultivate an attitude of kindness and warmth if we are consistent and persistent in our practice.

Mixing together the power of words plus a dollop of imagery (for those among us who are visual learners), a sprinkling of concentration, a pinch of connection, and a dash of good old-fashioned human caring, lovingkindness meditation manages to become a rich stew for us to marinate in and coax out our natural juices of goodwill. I'm getting hungry just thinking about this practice. Time to give it a try.

Practice: Lovingkindness for a Loved One

PLAY

This practice is drawn directly from the Mindful Self-Compassion program and is called Lovingkindness for a Loved One.

Begin by settling yourself into a comfortable position for your body, either sitting or lying down. You may even set the stage for this practice by offering yourself some soothing or supportive touch and allow yourself to really feel the kindness in the warmth of your hand touching your body. Let yourself feel supported and soothed by yourself.

When you are ready, call to mind a person or other living being who naturally makes you smile when you think of them. Choose someone with whom you have an easy, uncomplicated relationship, like a child, a grandparent, perhaps your pet — any being that naturally brings happiness to your heart. See if you can settle on just one if more than one appears.

With some patience, allow yourself to pause and feel what it is actually like to be in the presence of this beloved being. Allow yourself to enjoy the good company by creating a vivid image of this being in your mind's eye.

After a few moments, reflect on the fact that this being wishes to be happy and free from suffering, just like you and every other living being. Repeat softly, slowly, and gently, feeling the importance of your words:

> May you be happy.
>
> May you be peaceful.
>
> May you be healthy.
>
> May you live with ease.

You may even want to repeat these phrases again. If at any point you notice your mind wandering, you can simply return to the words and the image of the loved one that you have in mind. Take the time to appreciate any warm feelings that may have arisen. Linger and savor this precious being.

Now, when you are ready, gently usher yourself into your circle of goodwill and create an image of yourself in the presence of your loved one, visualizing the two of you together. Feel your way into this connection and take your time. Eventually offer these phrases:

> May you and I be happy.
>
> May you and I be peaceful.
>
> May you and I be healthy.
>
> May you and I live with ease.

Again, take your time and possibly repeat the phrases.

Now, when it feels right, let go of the image of the other, maybe even briefly thanking your loved one before moving on. Then let the full focus of your loving attention rest upon yourself, just for now. You may want to again offer yourself some form of soothing or supportive touch. Take the time to visualize your whole body and scan from head to toe, noticing any stress or uneasiness that may be lingering within you at this time, and offer yourself the phrases:

> May I be happy.
>
> May I be peaceful.
>
> May I be healthy.
>
> May I live with ease.

Let the words and the kind intention wash across and through you, possibly repeating them again and again and feeling them land in your experience.

And, when you are ready, just take a few breaths and rest quietly in your own experience, allowing yourself to feel whatever you are feeling without needing anything to change. Meet yourself just as you are in this moment, with kindness, warmth, courage, and affection.

Take some time after concluding this practice to simply settle, reflect, and perhaps take a few notes about your experience, what you noticed, and how things unfolded for you. Don't be too quick to judge your experience, but take note of it and let it settle.

Inquiring: What was it like to cultivate kindness?

After having reflected a bit, consider what you noticed in your practice of loving-kindness. Whether it was the first time you've tried this or if it is a part of your regular meditation routine, what came up in *this* meditation today?

It may be helpful to consider what you noticed in each of the three components of the practice:

>> What was it like to call to mind a beloved being and to wish them these good wishes?

>> What was it like to include yourself alongside your loved one and to wish both of you good wishes?

>> How did it feel to let go of the other and let your "circle of goodwill" rest solely on yourself?

After people encounter this meditation, it is not unusual for them to enjoy the first part of it, be a little uncomfortable when they slip themselves into the mix, and have a harder time when the spotlight of lovingkindness rests solely on them. If this approximates your experience, you're not alone. We are not accustomed to being kind to ourselves (for a variety of reasons that I will explore later) and we get twitchy when we're in the spotlight — even our *own* spotlight.

In general, people have one or more of three different experiences with this practice: They enjoy it, they feel neutral about it, or they find it uncomfortable. None of them is a reflection on you or your ability to practice lovingkindness, and each is explored briefly below. I can virtually guarantee that each time you practice this meditation your experience will vary, sometimes a little bit and sometimes a lot.

Just like working out at the gym, you have good workouts, you have neutral workouts, and sometimes you have unpleasant workouts. But in the end, the important thing is that you *worked out*, and you kind of knew that working out was not necessarily going to be consistently enjoyable anyway.

Backdraft: When you experience the unexpected

Perhaps the most disconcerting experience when we begin to practice directing kindness to ourselves is that sometimes the feelings that result from doing this are far from what we expect. In fact, some people find that they feel just the opposite of compassion when they practice. A whole variety of feelings may arise at first when we embark on this practice, many of which could be unpleasant. If this is the case for you at any time in the course of this book, it's very important for you to know that your experience is not uncommon, and although painful, it is actually a promising sign that you are on the right track of healing. Let me explain with a brief but colorful analogy.

When firefighters enter a burning building and come upon a door to a room, they check the temperature of that door before opening it. They do this because if there is a fire behind the door, there is a high likelihood that the fire has consumed much of the oxygen in the room, and if the firefighter flings open the door, the fire will rush out to consume the flow of oxygen coming in. This puts the firefighter in extreme danger. This very hazardous phenomenon is called *backdraft* and is well known to firefighters. In fact, there was a popular movie in 1991 called *Backdraft* based on this principle.

How the firefighter analogy relates to you

The analogy is to our own tender hearts that may have endured a lifetime of emotional fires and either the absence of compassion in our lives, or tragically, even the opposite of it when we needed it most. In order for us to function in life, we may very well have learned to simply store away this pain so that we can protect ourselves and not be overcome by it.

We have done what needed to be done over a lifetime to survive, an amazing testament to our strength as humans, but it has left us with a heart that is hot with suffering. Most of us simply go about our business with this internal furnace smoldering away, but when we begin to swing open the door to our hearts and let the fresh air of compassion in, a lifetime of old pain and fear is likely to come whooshing out. This is the phenomenon of backdraft, and it can be quite painful or confusing.

Backdraft can manifest in a variety of ways that may or may not be easy to spot. Emotionally, backdraft can arise as waves of shame, grief, fear, or sadness. The mental manifestation of backdraft can come in thoughts of "I'm all alone," or "I'm a complete failure," or "This practice is not for me. I can't even do this right." Backdraft can also reveal itself in physical sensations like body memories, aches, pains, and muscle tension. Sometimes when you direct kindness and compassion toward yourself, you experience an overall uneasiness that comes out of nowhere, or you can find yourself weeping for no apparent reason or subject to intense feelings of anger, resentment, or resistance.

What you can do when you notice backdraft arising

Recognize that these uncomfortable feelings may very well be backdraft and don't let yourself become overwhelmed by them. A few ideas follow for how to facilitate this, but first I need to point out something extremely important before you go any further.

When backdraft arises, however painful or uncomfortable it may be, it is *actually* a sign that you are moving in an important direction and it is a sign of healing. You may be inclined or conditioned to think that this is actually a sign that you have done something wrong or that you aren't able to be self-compassionate, but nothing could be further from the truth.

If you suffer an internal injury and you go to the emergency room for care, the doctor is likely to palpate your body and ask you some version of "Where does it hurt?" When the doctor pokes you in one particular spot and you react in pain, they now know the location of the pain so they can begin to sort out how to treat your condition.

Feeling backdraft is very similar. If directing compassion and kindness to yourself provokes backdraft, then you know you've delivered the kindness to the ailing part: your own tender beating heart. So backdraft is not *created* by self-compassion practice, but it is *revealed* by it. You may think of it as an emotional X-ray that highlights what you probably already suspected: Self-compassion has been lacking in your life, and your heart is hurting as a result.

TIP

Therefore, if backdraft arises and you think you're doing it wrong, you are actually doing it just right because you are beginning to open the door of your ailing heart. You are simply releasing old pain when you do this, which is a natural healing process and nothing to be concerned about.

Practical tools for managing backdraft

You may be thinking, "Well, that's all well and good for you to say, but how do I actually *do this* when it's so hard and so painful?" I'm glad you asked. The first key to navigating through backdraft may be to just acknowledge it and the fact that it is painful. Simply saying to yourself, "Ahh. I'll bet this is backdraft. This sucks! Ouch!" can begin to loosen the grip of backdraft in the moment. "Name it and you can tame it," as someone said. And then considering the fundamental question of self-compassion: "What do I need in this moment?"

After identifying and acknowledging it, you can consider continuing to adjust your dosage, as you did to some degree by simply naming it. Just as with medications, each person's tolerance for the strength of the drug is different, so sometimes the doctor overshoots your tolerance and needs to back down on your dosage.

Remember when I introduced the idea of opening and closing? This is an opportunity to practice the refined art of closing. Not closing entirely, but slowly and firmly swinging the furnace door in the direction of being closed and stopping when the "heat" is tolerable. We can do this via a variety of means, including:

>> Check in with the body to see if the feeling is registering somewhere, as tension in your neck, a hollow feeling in the pit of your stomach, or a headache, and give yourself a bit of soothing or supporting touch in that area.

>> Redirect your attention to a neutral focus inside your body (like the soles of your feet or your breath) or outside (like sounds in the room or the view out a window).

>> Find an everyday activity that either captures your attention (a mindful activity like gardening, sewing, walking, or art) or something that comforts and soothes you (self-compassionate activities like making a cup of tea, sinking into a warm bath, listening to music, or petting your dog).

>> If you still find yourself struggling, you may want to reach out to your own personal support system of friends, family, a therapist, or teachers who know you and support you.

REMEMBER

Whatever you do when or if backdraft arises, it's important to remember that if you are responding to your question of "What do I need?" then you are actually practicing self-compassion in that moment, meaning that you are accessing the exact resource that you have come here to discover.

When things don't go the way you expect them to, you may be inclined to blame or criticize yourself for somehow not being up to the task or doing it wrong, but the more you can notice the situation (mindfulness), see that these things happen to people sometimes (common humanity), and respond with warmth, tolerance, and patience (self–kindness), the more you are practicing powerful self–compassion when you need it the most. Challenging though it may be, backdraft can be an amazing self–compassion teacher. Even better than me!

LIFTING THE HEAVIEST WEIGHTS IN THE GYM

Traditionally, the lovingkindness meditation is practiced with a large cast of mental characters that customarily begin with those who are presumed to be the easiest and proceed to more challenging ones, almost like you might begin at the gym with the lightest weights you can lift and, as you get stronger, you move on to the heavier ones. Interestingly, the sequence that evolved in Asia from the Buddha's teachings tended to begin with directing the wishes to oneself, which was presumed to be the easiest starting place. What teachers like Sharon Salzberg and others discovered in the early days of presenting the practice in the West was that many people really struggled with directing these wishes inward toward themselves, mainly because so many people felt undeserving of this kindness and very uncomfortable wishing it for themselves. Thus, the practice in the West tends to start with a beloved being to kind of "jump-start" the process or warm up the heart so that you can move on to yourself and then others. If you struggled a bit in the Lovingkindness for a Loved One practice here, that may have been a manifestation of this phenomenon.

For our purposes here (and in the Mindful Self-Compassion program), we confine our focus to just two beings: the beloved other and ourselves, as a preparation for more focused practice related to self-compassion and being able to direct this goodwill toward ourselves specifically. But as I note earlier, typically lovingkindness meditation is practiced with a variety of beings. The whole idea, consistent with this parallel of working out in the gym, is that you are "trying out" a variety of different "weights" to slowly build strength or capacity to access your lovingkindness. The sequence is often something like this: beloved being, self, friend, neutral person, difficult person, all beings. (You can find quite a number of lovingkindness meditations, referred to as *metta* in the Pali language, online and in books. And if you are interested in pursuing this as a regular practice, I highly recommend it.)

You may be an ambitious person (dare I say "perfectionistic"?) and you may wonder about the potential value of challenging yourself even more by trying to direct lovingkindness wishes to neutral people, difficult people, or whole groups of people. I admire your ambition and enthusiasm, and want to support you in your continued cultivation of this important quality of mind and heart. In the spirit of self-compassion, if you decide to explore this further, be willing to cut yourself some slack and meet yourself in the practice with kindness.

(continued)

(continued)

Especially when you begin to direct lovingkindness wishes toward a difficult or challenging person in your life, it will be like walking over to the heaviest barbell in the gym. This being is included in the practice precisely because they are challenging, and you might even question why you would want to wish goodwill for someone you dislike or may even hate. The rationale is embedded in the common humanity practice of Just Like Me from the preceding chapter. This is an opportunity to see that, below the ill will and bad feelings, you can still recognize that this other person wishes to be happy and free from suffering, just like you. This person suffers at times, is afraid at times, has had hard times and joyful times, has succeeded and failed at times, and through it all they are genetically 99.9 percent the same as you. When you can see through your feelings to this essential reality, and your heart can remain warm and open in the practice, you are truly practicing lovingkindness in its most transformative form.

But please be willing to go slow. Perhaps if you are going to identify a difficult person to work with (a heavy weight to start with), you may want to choose one at first that is less challenging and easier to work with and then work your way forward to the more challenging ones as you feel more adept at meeting this challenging practice and remaining kind.

What if you practiced and felt absolutely nothing?

Good for you in noticing your experience, even though nothing stood out or seemed noteworthy. It's not easy to notice the absence of thoughts, feelings, or emotions. You may be thinking of this as a failure, but in fact it is a glorious success of mindfulness. Take a moment to take that in. You noticed the absence of something, which is equally noteworthy and important as noticing the presence of something.

Think of all the times you have felt sick and thought to yourself, "I don't appreciate being well often enough, because this is terrible." Does this sound familiar? We so often overlook feeling well because we expect things to be that way, and then we kick ourselves when we realize how good we had it when we weren't sick. So, noticing the absence of something is a great skill akin to acknowledging when we are feeling well.

But perhaps your observation comes with a concern that perhaps you did something wrong or that you were *supposed to* feel something. Perhaps you thought if you did a lovingkindness meditation, you would actually *feel* lovingkindness. A reasonable and logical expectation to have, but look back and reread what I say earlier about the practice. Did I ever promise you that you would *feel* lovingkindness? I actually didn't, because this practice is not about cultivating *good feelings* but instead about cultivating *good intentions*, a warm inclination of the heart toward kindness.

When we exercise, we are cultivating physical fitness, but often when we exercise (or shortly thereafter) we don't feel physically fit at all. We continue because we know that persistence and consistency will lead to our desired goal of fitness. It is the same with lovingkindness, and perhaps why we call it "practice."

We practice and practice and practice lovingkindness (using various images of beings in our lives like weights at the gym), and ultimately, we incline our hearts and tap into our natural leanings toward kindness and warmth. Jon Kabat-Zinn refers to mindfulness practice as akin to weaving a parachute, and this applies to lovingkindness as well.

TIP

The time to start weaving your parachute is not right before you have to jump out of the plane. You begin early and often, weaving your parachute (practicing lovingkindness), over and over, day after day, week after week, so that when you need it, it is there for you. In a moment when you want to tap into your natural loving human heart qualities, if you've been practicing, kindness is more readily available to you and it becomes more often your default stance toward experience.

What if you practiced lovingkindness and felt great?

You probably don't see this outcome as a problem, and neither do I, but it is important to be clear on what feeling something positive or pleasant or enjoyable in some way means. I hate to be a buzzkill here, but don't get your heart set on having this experience all the time. It doesn't mean you've mastered lovingkindness (or failed at it, for that matter), and having a good feeling wasn't really the point of the practice. But that doesn't mean you can't take a moment to simply revel in the warm feelings of lovingkindness, to savor them and to let them register in your mind ("taking in the good" as Rick Hanson likes to say). Just don't get attached.

What I mean by that last snide comment is that one of the sneakier aspects of pleasant experiences is that they can be seductive. We do something like practicing lovingkindness, and a pleasant feeling arises while we are doing it or shortly thereafter. We pat ourselves on the back for having conjured up such a nice feeling, and then we're off in the pursuit of the next pleasant experience. When I put it like that, it's almost like an addiction, which it probably is, as we go about our days craving the pleasant, trying to avoid the unpleasant, and even seeing the neutral experiences as unpleasant because they are boring. On the latter point, I think we are finding boredom to be particularly uncomfortable these days, and we carry around an easy distraction to these moments: a smartphone. This accounts for why so many of us find ourselves checking our phones while we are sitting in the bathroom. But I digress.

So when we meditate and then have a pleasant experience, our amazing human brains begin to wire those two experiences together and very subtly, over time, we begin to act as if doing one (meditation) will bring the other one (bliss). But remember that we are not meditating to conjure up a feeling but to practice being present to whatever comes up, and the same is true for lovingkindness. We are inclining the heart so we can access our loving intentions more readily, regardless of the situation.

Encountering the felt sense of lovingkindness as a result of the practice is a welcome but seductive and unpredictable outcome. Enjoy it for what it is . . . and let go when it passes.

Oh, the Places You'll Go with Lovingkindness!

I'm paraphrasing Dr Seuss with the headline above, but there is some reason for a little glee and anticipation about where you can go when you open up to your tenderheartedness and wish to be happy. This inclination of the heart toward a natural state of kindness, warmth, and well-wishing can be a powerful and skillful antidote over time to our own mind states like anger, fear, resentment, and shame.

The systematic cultivation of boundless friendliness toward ourselves and our experiences in life leads us to develop new neural pathways and to overcome old habits and conditioning developed over a lifetime that previously took us down dark roads to fear, shame, isolation, and rumination. Although this is not necessarily an easy practice (the best things never are), it is not an unattainable one either. All we are really doing is intentionally tapping into our own good nature and natural tendency toward kindness and freedom from strife, and making room for these other, more wholesome qualities to grow.

One struggle that many people face at first is when they feel that they or the person who is the object of their practice do not currently possess what they are wishing for. For example, we say, "May I be healthy" and we happen to have diabetes or chronic pain or some other medical affliction that makes us less than healthy. The key here is remembering that what we are cultivating is *the wish* to be healthy and not health *itself*. This is not like the genie granting us three lovingkindness wishes to come true in the world, but instead about giving a respectful nod to the deep wish inside each of us to *be* healthy or to *want* health for our loved ones and fellow humans.

When we practice lovingkindness, we put aside circumstances and situations that are constantly changing and instead connect to the abiding inclination of our hearts toward health, safety, joy, and ease. If we were on a journey in the wilderness with our compass and our map, we would encounter specific obstacles (boulders, streams, snow banks), but because we'd be clear on where we were going, we could navigate safely around or through these objects to get where we were going, nonetheless. Similarly, when we connect with our inclination toward happiness and freedom from suffering, we can feel supported and have a sense of intention that will guide us through the times when we struggle, feel lost, or face misfortune.

Think about it: When you are at peace, you can wish to be at peace, and when you are feeling unsettled and in turmoil, you can wish to be at peace too. In fact, the wish to be at peace can guide you *through* that turmoil. The wish persists unconditionally and separate from your specific circumstances, and it is this that we are fostering with our practice. The wish to be healthy supports us in getting healthy when we are ill. It nudges us to take our medicine, call our doctor, and do what needs to be done to treat our malady or injury. The wish to be healthy also guides us in our daily choices when we are, indeed, healthy, so that we stay healthy. The wish to be healthy is quite powerful, and when we practice lovingkindness, we make it even more powerful in our lives by giving voice to it and acknowledging it. The same is true of happiness, peace, and ease (and many other inclinations of the heart that we may have).

You may be like other people I have met in that you doubt that you have this quality of kindness within you. Maybe you don't even feel worthy of having or fostering goodwill, especially toward yourself. Don't worry; you are not alone in this at all. This can be a huge block for people beginning to practice lovingkindness meditation, and if this is the case for you, I ask you to see if you can be just a little bit kind with yourself, a little bit patient, even a little bit skeptical but willing to explore it tenderly and in small steps.

TIP

If you are struggling with this practice, try returning to the idea of dosage and see if maybe when you offer yourself or someone else these wishes, it may feel like just too much to take in or give out all at once. Maybe when you say to yourself, "May I be happy," it just feels too far removed from your present experience, as if this is asking *way* too much of yourself for whatever reason. Even uttering these words and intentions for yourself may just feel like too heavy of a lift, so to speak, and you are not inclined to continue the practice as a result. If you're willing, see if you can add some qualifiers to your wishes that lower the dosage or lighten its weight (to mix metaphors), by seeing it as a progressive process. What that means in practical terms is that instead of "May I be happy," you might consider something like "May I begin to consider the possibility that at some point in the near future I could perhaps know a bit of happiness." You can find your own dosage between these two extremes and continue to increase as needed, take it regularly, and call me in the morning.

If you are human, and virtually everyone who purchased this book is likely to be, then you have within you the wellspring of kindness, goodwill, and a wish to be happy. I'm relatively certain that you may doubt this from time to time or find it hard to access on a regular basis, especially when it comes to directing it to yourself, but you can trust me in my confidence that you have it.

Think of your kindness as the tenderest little tendril of a new flower poking out of the fertile ground in a garden overgrown with weeds. We can't make the flower grow faster, but we can improve its conditions by tending to the garden, pulling the weeds, tilling the soil, and making sure the plant is watered and gets sunlight. This is the practice of lovingkindness: simply making space for your own light to shine, for your tender heart to open and radiate the love that you already feel somewhere within.

This may sound too poetic and flowery for you, but somewhere down deep you feel the truth of it. You wouldn't have picked up this book or read this far if some part of you didn't believe that you have it in you to be kinder, warmer, and more patient, with others and especially with yourself. Take some time to listen to this tiny voice inside, and as you listen to it and quiet your doubts, it will slowly grow louder and accompany you on this adventurous journey of self-compassion.

Chapter **7**

How Kindness Transforms in the Fire of Life

The preceding chapters begin to explore each of the three components of self-compassion (mindfulness, common humanity, and self-kindness), and perhaps you are beginning to have a sense of your own inner landscape from this perspective. What I suggest here is that, just like violin virtuosos and their instruments, trustworthy surgeons with their scalpels, or top-notch chefs with their knives, you are becoming more and more intimately familiar with your primary "instruments" for the practice of self-compassion. You may have noticed yourself becoming impatient to "get on to the good stuff" and to tackle self-compassion head on, but getting familiar with your instruments and appreciating their contributions to your practice will pay off in the long run.

In this chapter we begin to make the transition into where, as they say, "the rubber meets the road." This means that you will have the opportunity to try out bringing these three qualities (mindfulness, common humanity, and self-kindness) to address the fundamental question of self-compassion: What do

I need? By all means, I hope you will be patient and curious with this process, remembering my early guidance about being willing to be a slow and patient learner. I encourage you to be open to difficulty when it may arise, and to respond to your own needs with opening and closing as needed so that you can find just the right dosage of self-compassion for where you are at any particular moment (and this will vary from moment to moment).

REMEMBER

There is nothing to be gained by rushing in and trying too hard, but invariably you will. It seems to be a feature of our human DNA that when we decide we want something, we will stop at nothing to get it. I only ask that you catch yourself from time to time and remember that self-compassion is not "out there" to be achieved, but inside you, to be fostered and cultivated through patient and affectionate practice.

Specifically, we are going to explore the subtle but important difference between lovingkindness and compassion. Many people confuse or conflate the two, and they are certainly closely related, but knowing the difference is vitally important to becoming more adept at being self-compassionate. And when I say "knowing the difference," I don't mean "knowing" in the traditional sense of mental understanding or grasping the *idea* of lovingkindness or compassion, but instead *knowing* with a truly felt sense, the experience inside of you of each of these.

By knowing these heart qualities from the inside out, you can actually recognize them in a way that makes them less mysterious and more available to you when you need them. Consider the difference between reading about how to ride a bicycle and actually *knowing*, experientially, how to do it. The same principles apply to lovingkindness and compassion, but the danger of falling and skinning your knee is considerably less . . . and no helmet is required.

Awakening Your Heart and Opening Your Eyes

I'd like to invite you to try a short exercise that will give you a felt sense, from the inside, of what lovingkindness and compassion feel like, both when directed at another person and when directed at yourself. I will share some of the theory and ideas related to these topics after you have done the exercise, but it would be nice for you to go into this experiment without much more than the usual clutter of thoughts and emotions that we all carry around with us most of the time. (This exercise is a modification of an exercise in the Mindful Self-Compassion program that is called "Awakening Our Hearts," and that exercise was drawn from a similar one first used widely by Buddhist teachers Jack Kornfield and Joanna Macy.)

You will see some similarities between this practice and the *Just Like Me* practice in the previous chapter, and there is indeed some overlap. I encourage you, however, to primarily focus upon your own felt sense of each step of the exercise and the experience of the different parts, even though you will certainly encounter aspects of the feeling of common humanity as you explored it in the last chapter.

For the purposes of parts of this practice, you will need to have a photograph of the face of another person. The practice is typically done in live groups and people pair up with another person, but since you will be reading this exercise, it is probably best to simply use a photograph. It can be a photograph of a loved one or a stranger. In the MSC course the partner is often a stranger and it can be quite powerful, nonetheless. Once you have a photograph available in some form, you can begin the exercise.

Beginning the exercise

As you begin to settle in to engage in this exercise, it's important to note that this exercise can actually be quite moving for some people and you are encouraged, as always, to take care of yourself and honor your own process of opening or closing as needed. If you find a point where you need to set the exercise aside for another time, you can congratulate yourself for practicing self-compassion. There is nothing gained by ambition when it comes to learning self-compassion. A gentle inclination is all that is required, and carefully responding to what you need is what it's all about.

After reading each paragraph of instructions, please take the time to follow those instructions in your own experience. Then, after some period of time (it may be several minutes), you can come back and move on to the next step.

When you are ready, take a few moments to settle and ease yourself into the present moment, perhaps finding an especially comfortable position for your body and allowing your attention to turn inward, perhaps with closed eyes (although of course you will need to open them to read each instruction). You may offer yourself some tender touch to remind you of the feeling of kindness and warmth that you intend to bring to this practice.

Next, direct your attention to the person in the photograph. Imagine the unique gifts and strengths that lie within this person. Know there are gifts and strengths that are already realized and those that are still seeds of potential. Like in every human life, there are wonderful moments of strength, courage, humor, creativity, generosity, and tenderness. Your heart and the heart of this person, like all human hearts, are capable of more love and kindness than you ever dreamed possible.

As you continue to look at the photograph, imagine the person as a child. Recognize that there is still a child that lies within all of us. Let yourself feel how much you want this child to be nurtured, to be able to grow into their full potential. Recognize how much you want this child to stay well, safe from harm, peaceful, and happy. Consider how much you naturally want to bring forth and celebrate what is beautiful in this child.

If you are seeing this person's potential, and a wish is arising to cherish and honor this person, know that you are experiencing your innate capacity for *lovingkindness*, and this capacity is there in you, always. Take some time to let this experience register in your own body, heart, and mind. Take note of how it feels to contact this wish within yourself.

Turning your kindness inward

Now imagine the unique gifts and strengths that lie within you. Know there are gifts and strengths that are already realized and those that are still seeds of potential. Like in every human life, there are wonderful moments of strength, courage, humor, creativity, generosity, and tenderness. Your heart, like all human hearts, is capable of more love and kindness than you ever dreamed possible.

Now, if it feels right, imagine yourself as a child, or just keep imagining your adult self. Recognize that there is still a child that lies within all of us. Let yourself feel how you may want this child to be nurtured, to be able to grow into their full potential. How you may wish for this child to stay well, safe from harm, peaceful, and happy. How much you may want to bring forth and celebrate what is beautiful in this child.

If you are seeing your potential, and the wish is arising to cherish and honor that potential, know that you are experiencing your innate capacity for *lovingkindness* toward yourself (self-kindness). And it's worth noting that this capacity is there in you, always.

Directing compassion toward the other

You may pause and offer yourself a soothing gesture as you now direct your attention to the other person again, letting yourself reflect on a measure of sorrow that lies within this person right now. The burdens that are carried, the suffering and pain accumulated over a lifetime, as in every human life.

Depending on the conditions of our lives, we carry different types of disappointments, failures, loneliness, loss, and hurts — things that may have seemed impossible to bear at the time, yet somehow were borne. Let yourself open to this pain, turn toward it, acknowledge it. You can't fix the pain or make it go away, but you can be with it, with a spirit of courage and an open heart.

Now, imagine the other person as a child, recognizing that there is still a child that lives within this person, sometimes frightened, hurt, confused, struggling. Let yourself feel how much you may want that child to know that they can lean on you for support, for understanding, for love and respect.

If you are seeing this human vulnerability, and a wish is arising to honor, to protect, to comfort, and to support this person in the midst of their suffering, know that what you are experiencing is *compassion*. And this capacity is there in you, always.

Making a compassionate U-turn

As you turn your attention from the other person toward yourself, take another moment to give yourself a warm gesture of support and comfort, with a hand on your body or an inner warm smile. Slowly let yourself become aware of a measure of sorrow that lies within you right now. The burdens that are carried, the suffering and pain accumulated over a lifetime, as in every human life.

Depending on the conditions of our lives, we carry different types of disappointments, failures, loneliness, loss, and hurts — things that may have seemed impossible to bear at the time, yet somehow were borne. Let yourself open to this pain, turn toward it, acknowledge it. You can't fix the pain or make it go away, but you can be with it, with a spirit of courage and an open heart.

Now, if it feels right to you, imagine yourself as a child. Recognize that there is still a child that lives in each of us, sometimes frightened, hurt, confused, struggling. Let yourself feel how you may naturally want to reach out, to soothe, to reassure. How much you may want that child to know that they can lean on you for support, for understanding, for love and respect.

If you are seeing this human vulnerability, and a wish is arising to honor, to protect, to comfort, and to support yourself in the midst of your suffering, know that what you are experiencing is *compassion*. If you were directing the words toward yourself, that would be *self-compassion*. And this capacity is there in you, always.

Inquiring into the exercise and being patient

Take some time to reflect on the experience of this exercise, giving yourself time and space to have whatever feelings may have been stirred up by this contemplation. Specifically, were you able to notice a subtle (or not-so-subtle) difference between lovingkindness and self-kindness, or between compassion for others and self-compassion? Or perhaps you noticed a difference between compassion and lovingkindness? And if you didn't notice any particular difference, what *did* you notice in this exercise? It's all useful data for your self-compassion experiment/adventure. Just take note.

Perhaps you found one of these four experiences (lovingkindness, self-kindness, compassion, self-compassion) easier than the others, or maybe they were all equally challenging . . . or easy. What were the obstacles you faced as you tried these experiences on for size?

Before moving on, please know that if your experience of this exercise was challenging or if you felt something other than what I described, that is totally okay and not surprising. You are still relatively new to self-compassion practice, and if it were easy, you wouldn't have purchased this book and read this far, so please consider being patient, curious, kind to yourself, and willing to let whatever your experience was simply be what it was. Pay attention to what you experienced and try not to make too much out of it just now.

Remembering that goodwill serves as the common thread

You may have noticed as you did the preceding exercise that there was a consistent tone of goodwill, patience, kindness, and warmth that ran throughout the four elements of the exercise. This tone begins to give you an idea of the foundation of both lovingkindness and compassion. Indeed, they both spring from the same source when you look deeply (as we did in the exercise), and this may be why people commonly use the terms interchangeably, even if they are qualitatively different from each other.

TIP

I find it easiest to look at this topic by thinking of lovingkindness as the built-in inclination of our hearts toward happiness. We all just want to be happy, and we go about this endeavor (as I discuss in the previous chapter) in various ways, but all with the same motivation. You may find your joy in volunteering at the local food bank, and I may find it in teaching mindfulness and self-compassion, but down deep we are both following the same human inclination of the heart. This is lovingkindness, and this deep motivation can be cultivated through practice and intention.

EMPATHY VERSUS COMPASSION

A popular misconception is that empathy and compassion are equivalent human experiences, when in fact they are quite different. You can think of empathy as one component of compassion, but not the whole package. Empathy is the capacity that we have, as humans, to understand and share the feelings of another person. But empathy is only half of the journey to compassion. We can easily be attuned to the feelings of another person, but if that awareness isn't held within the larger space of the desire to relieve that suffering, it is simply a steady flow of suffering coming at you with no means to work with it. Empathy alone leads to burnout.

As a clinical psychologist, I have often had conversations with non-psychologists who say things to me like, "I don't know how you do it, man. There's no way I could sit and listen to people share their problems all day long, hour after hour, day after day. That sounds horrendous to me. More power to you, but that has to be *so* hard!" When you put it like that, it sounds absolutely awful, demoralizing, and overwhelming. If that were what clinical psychology was about, I wouldn't have gone anywhere near the field, and anyone in it would burn out incredibly quickly.

The key to appreciating this is that being a psychotherapist of any sort is not *just* about passively being empathic and feeling the pain of another person, like a 50-minute dousing with a firehose of agony. True, therapists do encourage people to share their struggles within the safety of the therapy room, but we do so in the larger context of therapy itself, which has as its compassionate intention the relief of that suffering as well as the means to do so (via various means). This means that when we feel and hear the suffering and struggles of our patients, we maintain a calm and abiding awareness that there is a larger context that can support that person to make their way through the suffering and to find ease and joy in their lives. We are willing to walk that path alongside our patients or clients with an eye toward an end to their suffering. This isn't to say it is always easy, but from a compassionate stance, one can hold any human suffering with warmth, kindness, and presence, and this instills hope and healing all by itself.

The intention of this book is to help you explore how this can be true for you and your own suffering, which works the same way as it can for others. You will slowly develop greater capacity to be your own loving companion on the journey of life, especially when you hit the rough patches and you encounter the inevitable challenges of human life.

Compassion, on the other hand is what arises when this warm intention encounters struggle and suffering and remains warm. The Dalai Lama (2003) has said that lovingkindness is "the wish that all . . . beings may be happy" and compassion is "the wish that all . . . beings may be free from suffering." The journal article "Compassion: An Evolutionary Analysis and Empirical Review" provides a more contemporary definition of compassion: "the feeling that arises when witnessing another's suffering and that motivates a subsequent desire to help" (Goetz, Keltner, Simon-Thomas). A simpler definition would be that compassion is the deep awareness of suffering coupled with the desire to relieve that suffering.

Personally, I am fond of the more colorful description once offered by a meditation teacher from Myanmar: "When the sunshine of lovingkindness meets the tears of suffering, the rainbow of compassion arises." Who doesn't love a rainbow, right? I also appreciate this description because it captures the ever-present quality of the sun (goodwill) even if it is occasionally obscured by clouds and storms (suffering). For myself, when I feel that the good will of lovingkindness is always shining within me, regardless of circumstances and unconditionally, it is easier to tap into it when I am struggling or suffering. In these moments that inclination toward goodwill, even in a storm of suffering, becomes the rainbow of compassion.

Weathering Our Own "Storms" of Suffering

So here we are, once again talking about suffering, when the last thing you (or anyone) wants to do is to suffer. The important point of course is that I'm not really introducing you to suffering in this book, as you already know it quite well from the experience of your life on this earth. What I am suggesting is that, given the ubiquity of suffering (it's one of our shared experiences as *homo sapiens*), we have two options available to us. One is to avoid, resist, and attempt to control our suffering, which we have pretty thoroughly explored in previous chapters and roundly dismissed as fruitless and even counterproductive. The other option is to acknowledge and open up to this reality and discover how to meet it — and more importantly, ourselves — with compassion just because it is a part of life. I'm guessing this is why you are still here reading along with me, and if you're like most people, you're still not quite sure what this may look like or feel like. Excellent. You're right where you ought to be (curious, hopeful, and skeptical) and you will continue to develop this practice in the pages ahead.

First, it is important that you appreciate that compassion is compassion is compassion, regardless of its object. In other words, self-compassion is no different from the larger experience of compassion for others. In fact, self-compassion is simply including oneself in the circle of compassion that we already maintain. As we establish early in the book, most of us find it relatively easy to direct the bright spotlight of our loving hearts onto others, especially our dear friends and family when they have a hard time. We are happy to let them be the stars of the show in those moments when they struggle and suffer, but when *we* are the ones enduring difficulty, we are like camera-shy celebrities who shun the spotlight and prefer to be anonymous. Old habits die hard, but the practice of self-compassion includes gently but firmly coaxing our spotlight-averse selves into the light of our own love — where we rightfully belong, alongside all the other beings in our lives.

As you have probably already discovered, this coaxing ourselves into the light of our own compassion is not an easy task. If it were, you might already be doing it regularly, but instead, you (like many of us) look past your own suffering to that of others and end up prioritizing others and leaving yourself for last. Or sadly, you feel as if you somehow don't deserve your own kindness, or even worse, believe that you deserve the suffering you are experiencing. This is what makes self-compassion so challenging for so many. But trust me when I say that you are already making progress toward beginning to change these old patterns of self-criticism and self-abuse. Like a sea captain, you are charting a course toward more ease and freedom from suffering in your life, and you are steering the ship called *You* toward new, warmer, and more inviting waters, but the journey has only just begun.

Knowing that we are suffering

Strangely enough, I have found that people coming to therapy or self-compassion courses are remarkably terrible at recognizing their own suffering when it arises. If I ask people if they suffer, they often respond in the affirmative (sometimes they respond not just with "yes" but with "hell yes!"), but they are hard-pressed to identify moments of actual suffering. What people often point to are difficult circumstances that they face and not their own suffering. In other words, their attention is outward toward what they face in the world rather than inward to their own experience of these situations. People say, "Of course I suffer, I have cancer, for God's sake!" or "My soulmate just left me and you're asking me if I suffer? Are you sure you're a real psychologist?" The thing is, the suffering itself is not in the circumstances, but in the way that people meet those circumstances.

Try a short thought experiment with me here. Imagine that you have met ten men with prostate cancer. They are all about the same age; each has the same type and stage of cancer and the same poor prognosis and difficult treatment ahead. And then you interview each of them to see how he is coping with his circumstances. I'm sure you can imagine that you would have ten different impressions of these ten men after speaking with each one and exploring how each is holding up emotionally under the strain of cancer. One will be withdrawn, one will be sad and depressed, another will laugh it off, still another will be overwrought and tearful, another one angry, and so on. This is the nature of humans; many factors predict how we will respond to situations when we face them.

The point is that in this small thought experiment you have revealed something important about suffering. Even though every single person in your "study" had the same medical condition and prognosis, their emotional state varied considerably. This means, apropos of my earlier point, that the suffering itself does not reside in the circumstances but in the way the person responds to them. In the situation of this experiment, you could certainly make a case that some of these responses are more or less helpful or adaptive, but right now what you've learned is the lesson I raise back in Chapter 4: that suffering (also known as stress) results from the *struggle with what is*.

When you can peel your attention off your circumstances (which you most often cannot change in any appreciable way in the short term), the only object of your attention left is yourself and how these circumstances are being met within your own psyche. And here is a place where you have some ability to adjust your stance, change your attitude, begin to dance with what you previously fought against, and *bring about* some degree of ease, not by getting rid of the immovable circumstances but instead by shifting your (movable) relationship with them. What is most remarkable about this important shift is that you go from powerlessness to freedom, which is pretty amazing if you think about it. This is not denying things that are difficult or sugarcoating very hard things, or discounting deeply painful past experiences for that matter, but simply acknowledging that these things exist and then formulating a mindful and compassionate response to them. Big difference.

It all begins with being able to retrace your attentional steps from the circumstances of your life to how they land within you, which is where the practice of mindfulness can serve you so incredibly well. When you have the literal presence of mind to notice distressing circumstances or upsetting people that capture your attention, and then can redirect your attention inwardly, you can see how you are actually experiencing them as a first step toward being kind to yourself, for the sole reason that these feelings are painful or difficult. Rather than being entangled by context, you are able to drop inside and find your own inner resources for contending with that context.

It all begins with mindfulness

Ironically, we very often miss the fact that we are suffering, mainly because we are actually so caught up in the experience of our suffering. For example, I once was in a therapy session with a patient (I will call her Angelica) who had had long-standing difficulties relating comfortably and sustainably with friends or colleagues. She could form rewarding relationships at first, but they inevitably unraveled over time and the same pattern repeated frequently. She often came to sessions complaining about how this person or that person treated her unfairly, or was selfish, unavailable, or had betrayed her in some way. As a therapist, perhaps the most frustrating sessions are those that end up being all about people who aren't actually in the room with you. This was one of those sessions, and I could feel my frustration arising over my own powerlessness to be of help . . . until I had a moment of revelation.

I paused Angelica as she reached a peak of outrage at the latest friend who had turned on her. In that moment her face was getting a bit red, I could see that her fists were clenched, and her voice was getting higher and higher the longer she went on about her former friend. I said, "Angelica. Could we just pause for a moment?"

She nodded hesitantly and I went on, "If it's okay with you, could we just pause and take a few breaths together?" and we did.

After perhaps 30 seconds, I said, "It strikes me that as you have described this situation to me in session, all the things that your friend did and said, and all the unacceptable behavior that she engaged in, someone was overlooked."

She looked back at me quizzically and said, "Who?"

"Could you just put your hand on your heart right now and feel the warmth of your touch on your body? Right now, in this moment here, who in this relationship between you two is suffering? Who is distressed and upset and in pain right now?"

I briefly noted, "And as I sit here with you, I can feel the weight of your struggle in me as well. I can't know how you feel, but I do know what it feels like to suffer in this way."

She looked at me like I was crazy for a moment, and then she took a deep breath and began to sob as she realized the truth of her own suffering in that moment (and perhaps over a lifetime).

This moment did not "cure" her problems or relieve all her suffering, but simple acknowledgement of her own pain in her situation opened the door to working with what was possible in the therapy relationship (her own feelings and reactions) rather than what was not possible (changing other people in her life). This was a moment of noticing her suffering (mindfulness), realizing that we all suffer sometimes (common humanity), and bringing the tiniest bit of kindness to herself (self-kindness in the form of gentle touch). This was self-compassion, and most importantly, it all hinged on her first becoming mindfully aware of her own suffering.

Common humanity: What to do with awareness

Once you become aware that suffering is present (notice how I did not say "you are suffering" because this fuses you with your feelings, which is a setup for even more suffering as I discuss in Chapter 4), you are really standing at a fork in the road like the one described by Robert Frost in his poem "The Road Not Taken": "Two roads diverged in a wood, and I — I took the one less traveled by, And that has made all the difference."

If you have a history of feeling isolated, self-critical, and ashamed (also known as not self-compassionate), when you notice suffering you may tend to prefer the more familiar and well-worn path of withdrawal, feeling uniquely bad, flawed, or unworthy because you are experiencing difficult feelings. However, to whatever degree possible, if you can see your suffering in the larger context of human life always including some suffering ("into each life, some rain must fall"), your awareness of common humanity allows you to weather this particular "suffering storm" with some degree of willingness to allow it to be here when it arises. This is the "road less traveled" that is available to you when you recognize it and choose to walk down it.

When we can see that this particular pain is not unique to us, nor indicative of anything other than the fact that we are human and this is what humans experience sometimes, then we are beginning to adopt the stance of learning to meet ourselves in these moments with kindness rather than criticism, with warmth rather than cold rejection, and slowly but surely, we can begin to shift those old patterns toward relief of the suffering rather than being overcome by it.

When we notice these moments of suffering and can stay present to them as a reality of life, rather than an unfortunate feature of *us*, then we are poised and ready to ask ourselves that all-important central question of self-compassion: "What do I need in this moment?"

Exploring What We Need in a Moment of Suffering

You find yourself here, poised at the precipice of self-compassion practice, with that tantalizing but slightly mysterious question on your lips: What do I need? On the surface it seems like such a simple question, but in reality, it turns out to have many layers and also is quite unfamiliar to many of us. Most of us rarely ask ourselves this question, although we do respond to some of our needs quite readily without much thought. When we are hungry, we grab a bite; when we are tired, we crawl into bed; when we need to pee, we head to the bathroom. It's what we do, and no elaborate reflective process is required to tend to the basic human biological needs. But when we broaden our focus out to ourselves as humans more broadly, knowing what we truly need can be much more difficult to sort out.

"What do you need?"

It's a tricky question because we are often unsure of what we need under normal circumstances. And when our sympathetic nervous system is activated because of some situation or another, we can't really think as clearly as we usually do. So a fair amount of frustration can arise in those tense moments if someone asks us what we need. "I don't know what I need! I guess basically what I need is for you to stop being annoying by asking me what I need!" Can you relate to this? I have uttered those words on more than one occasion over the years. But I probably used to struggle with answering the question because I hadn't ever developed the capacity to stop and check in with myself to actually be able to answer it when I needed to. It was a skill or a resource that took time to develop more fully.

We are often pretty good (or at least we think we are) at deciding what *other people* need, and sometimes that ability to empathize and offer something to those people hits the mark and is well-received. Other times, we are way off base, but we have good intentions, and our friends appreciate that more than anything. But if you think about it, if your friend is facing some sort of challenge, perhaps she has just learned that her boyfriend has been unfaithful, how do you decide what to offer her? One way is to just outright ask her what she needs, and that's not a bad option. But another, more heartfelt and thoughtful way to go is to imagine that you were facing that same situation. What would *you* want or need if it was you whose heart was broken?

Including ourselves in the circle of our compassion

Throughout this book I suggest periodically to consider how you would respond to someone else facing a similar situation or what other people might think to offer you under similar circumstances as a way of jump-starting your own capacity to provide these things for yourself. The best news about this is that you aren't learning some new skill or talent in these situations, you are simply learning (little by little) how to actually include yourself in the warm circle of your own compassion by tapping into your existing capacity to direct these intentions toward others. You are learning to orchestrate a U-turn of your own natural compassion.

Cultivating the capacity to identify what you need in a moment and to find a way to offer it to yourself turns out to be a key ability for practicing self-compassion, and I invite you to engage in a practice shortly that can help you do just that. This practice is somewhat similar to the Lovingkindness for a Loved One practice from the previous chapter, in that it involves offering up wishes in the form of phrases, as a means of tapping into our own natural capacity for goodwill. But the brilliance of this particular practice (conceived of and developed by Chris Germer in the Mindful Self-Compassion program) is that it gives you an opportunity to respond to the question "What do I need?" through a careful process of customizing wishes specific to you.

Once again, you can see the overlap between the practices of lovingkindness and compassion in that we are still practicing tapping into our natural tendency for goodwill, and the wishes are unconditional. So they apply whether we are feeling fine or we are struggling or suffering in some way. The only real difference is that lovingkindness becomes compassion when you are inclining your heart toward areas of difficulty, stress, pain, or suffering. The goodwill remains the same; the only thing that is different is that the sunshine of lovingkindness is generating a rainbow of compassion.

Traditionally, as I note earlier, lovingkindness phrases were offered to a whole variety of different people in the course of one meditation, but there is a unique opportunity inherent in taking the time to direct the goodwill only toward yourself. Instead of needing to formulate generic wishes that can apply to a number of different people, you can instead find just the right words and phrasing and tone *for you* that is just what you need to hear. In order to support you in this process, I list a few helpful hints:

>> Approach this practice with an air of curiosity, exploration, and a soft touch, almost as if you were creating an art form of some sort. If you are working too hard, it's not self-compassion; it becomes drudgery, and you lose the whole warm quality of the practice. You may already have lovingkindness phrases of your own that you prefer, and you can continue to use those, but I invite you to stretch yourself a bit and see what may come up if you try this practice.

>> Any phrases that you craft should be simple, clear, authentic, and kind. One great guideline is that when you offer them to yourself, they should not provoke any argument in the mind. Instead, the phrases should evoke a sense of gratitude or release when you receive them. It's also very important to tend to the tone of your inner voice because you can feel the difference between a warm, affectionate tone and a harsh one. You know what happens if you shout at a small child to calm down, and the same can happen inside of you if you snidely snarl, "May you know your own goodness" at yourself.

» In keeping with the preceding bullet, these wishes are absolutely not affirma-tions. Some may remember the character Stuart Smalley on *Saturday Night Live* whose affirmation was "I'm good enough, I'm smart enough, and doggone it, people like me!" Affirmations are statements of certainty that we want to be true but are not true in the moment. That means that when we say to ourselves, "I'm becoming better every day," we provoke our brain to point out when that isn't true or how it's never true. A wish like "May I learn to accept myself as I am" is indeed an unconditional wish and not a statement. The focus in this practice is on our direction and not our destination, so to speak.

Interestingly, research suggests that affirmations (although quite popular in self-help circles) make people with high self-esteem feel happier and people with low self-esteem feel worse. If there is too much difference between the affirmation and the reality, we simply feel discouraged and self-critical.

» I have known people who are put off by the wishes beginning with "May I . . ." because it sounds a bit like begging (for example, Oliver Twist asking, "Please, sir, may I have some more?"). There is nothing magic about these particular words and the intention is closer to something like, "May it be so," but you can drop them if they get in the way for you. Simply stating the word or wish, like "happy" or "accepting" is good enough.

» It seems that how we address ourselves makes a difference. For some, saying "May I be happy" works quite well, but for others, it lands more fully when they say "May you be happy" when referring to themselves. Research also suggests that our self-talk makes more of an impact if we use our own names, so even saying "May Steve be happy" could work, as long as your name is Steve (although I appreciate the kind wishes nonetheless!).

» It's always best if your lovingkindness is fairly general and not too specific. Saying "May I be healthy" is preferable to "May I be free of my heart disease" because the latter focuses your attention too closely on the circumstance rather than the wish, and you are better off focusing primarily on the "wish side" of the phrases you use.

» Finally, some people find that when they really carefully consider what they need, it may feel as if it is something that they need from someone else, and thus they feel powerless to make it happen. For example, perhaps you find yourself realizing that you need to feel respect from your partner. If your wish relies on someone else, consider the scenario where you *finally* get all of whatever it is you desire from that other person. In that situation of getting what you need, what then? Perhaps you would feel your own value, or you could finally cease your endless pursuit of validation and know ease. So in these cases, your wishes could come down to something like "May I truly know my own value."

Practice: Finding lovingkindness phrases

As I mention earlier, this practice called Finding Lovingkindness Phrases is largely based upon the informal practice of the same name from the Mindful Self-Compassion program. It is specifically designed to help you discover what you truly need and what you need to hear from others and can be done over and over again to refine and update these wishes over time. Most people's needs tend to shift and change over time, and so it is worthwhile to revisit the practice from time to time. It can also be helpful to settle on some phrases that work for you and then give yourself plenty of time and frequent opportunities to offer them to yourself and cultivate the practice of giving yourself what you need. Again, returning to the example of exercise, the more you lift the weights, the more you build the muscle. Even the love muscle.

You may want to use a paper and pencil or electronic device during this exercise to make notes of the ideas and wishes that occur to you along the way, so make sure you have them handy before you start. Give yourself as much time as you need to make your way through this exercise. When we share it in the Mindful Self-Compassion program, we allot 20 minutes because we have a lot to cover in each session, but taking an hour or more could really be a leisurely and compassionate way of exploring what we truly need and need to hear. Let this be like a brainstorming session, where no idea or phrase or feeling is off the table or unworthy. Let go of judgment to the extent that you can, and be adventurous in exploring things with an open, curious mind.

What do I need?

When you are ready, take a moment to pause, to settle your body and allow your mind and heart to relax and open and to become receptive (a bit like a flower opening to the sun). Maybe place a hand on your body in some place that is supportive and encouraging for you, just to remind yourself that you intend to be kind, patient, and affectionate with yourself in this process.

As you are ready, offer yourself the following question and allow the answer the time and space to arise in your awareness: *What do I need? What do I truly need?* (If this need has not been fulfilled in a given day, your day does not feel complete. Think in terms of universal human needs like the need to be loved, connected, healthy, peaceful, safe, valued, and so on.) When you identify something, take the time to write it down, and perhaps go back inside and see if other things arise.

You can form these needs into wishes or leave them as they are. In other words, if "belonging" is a need, you can simply leave that as a phrase to offer yourself, or you can frame it as a wish like "May I know that I truly belong."

What do I need to hear?

PLAY

When you are ready to move on, perhaps close your eyes again and consider a second question from a different perspective: *If I could, what do I need to hear from others?* These are words that, as a feeling human being, you really need to hear on a regular basis. These may be phrases like "I love you," or "I believe in you," or "You're a good person."

If you could, what words would you like to have whispered into your ear every day for the rest of your life — words that might make you say, "Oh, thank you, thank you," every time you hear them?

As words arise (if they do, because sometimes they take some time), take a moment to jot them down and go back to reflect further. Take your time and be patient with yourself. If lots of words come, take a little time to form them into a short phrase that could be a kind of brief message to yourself.

Often what we need to hear from others are the things that we easily forget, so these phrases can help us stay on track toward our intention to be more self-compassionate. For example, needing to hear "I love you" may mean that we simply wish to know that we are lovable, so we might form a phrase like "May I know that I am truly lovable." *What do you want to know for sure?*

Here are a few examples:

>> The phrase "I'm here for you" could become the wish "May I know that I belong."

>> The phrase "You're a good person" could become the wish "May I know my own goodness."

>> The phrase "I want you to be treated fairly" can become the wish "May I be strong and stand up for justice."

Take some time now to linger with what you have come up with so far and see if you can formulate these words and wishes into two to four offerings that will be gifts you can give yourself. Keep in mind the guidance to keep your wishes simple, clear, authentic, and kind. If it would be helpful for you, write down your latest draft of these words and phrases to help cement them in your mind for the meditation ahead.

Giving yourself the gift of what you need

When you have the wishes settled in your mind, allow yourself to let go of the focus upon thinking and reflecting, and instead take some time to settle into your own skin as you sit here and tune into the flow of your breathing. There is nothing else to do, no place else to go; just allow yourself to slip into this process like slipping into a warm bath. You can let the words do all the work.

Begin by saying the words or phrases slowly and gently (paying attention to the tone, assuring that it conveys warmth, patience, and a loving intention). You may consider whispering them into your own ear the way you would whisper into the ear of a loved one. Take your time, offering up the precious gift of your own intentions and wishes without an agenda or a timeline. Savor them as they echo in your mind. Pause. Repeat the wishes as it feels right and savor them again. Let it be a kind of marination in your own lovingkindness — luxurious, languorous, relaxed, and easy. Let the words and the intentions behind them wash over you as you receive the words that you most need to hear.

When your mind wanders (and you know it will!), just refresh your focus by perhaps offering yourself soothing or supportive touch, or just tuning in to the sensations arising in your body in the moment, grounding your attention in this body and breath, in this very moment. And then return to offering yourself the good wishes. Consider keeping this up for as long as you have time.

When you are ready to move on from this practice, gently release the phrases and give yourself some time to simply rest in the experience of having offered yourself what you needed. Know that you can return to this practice anytime, perhaps refining or modifying the words until they are just the right fit for you.

Inquiring: What was it like to offer yourself what you truly need?

Without having to rush to make sense of this practice or analyze it in any way, take some time to reflect on what this was like. Ask yourself some of the following questions:

>> What was it like to ask yourself, "What do I need?"

>> Was something different uncovered when you asked, "What do I need to hear from others?"

>> If you found a word or phrase that was just right, how did you know that this was so? Was there something you noticed in your mind, in your heart, or in your body? Was there a release, a letting go, a warm resonance of some sort? Listen carefully to what your experience tells you.

>> Regardless of what words or phrases you settled upon, what was it like to offer yourself these precious gifts? What was it like to receive them from yourself in this way?

>> Did you find any difficulties or struggles in the process?

TIP

You will find it fruitful to consider the process of identifying just what you need and what you need to hear, as a gradual process of exploration and discovery. Give yourself permission, once again, to go slowly, to be patient, and to not draw any conclusions too soon. If parts of this process were difficult, try to see those difficulties as areas worth inquiring into.

For example, if you found it uncomfortable to offer yourself just what you felt you needed, perhaps it is an indication of backdraft arising for you, and a slower, more measured pace may be called for. Or, as I note in the previous chapter, maybe a lower dosage would help you to slowly develop the capacity to receive the gifts. So "May I know my own goodness" can become "May I consider the possibility that one day I will have a sense of some part of my own goodness." Whatever allows you to engage in the process in a way that suits where you are at the time is a small step in the direction of self -compassion.

3

The Heartfelt Power of Self-Compassion

Reflect upon and identify your core values as a compass to follow in your self-compassion journey.

Find ways of working with your inner critical voice that help you make change and move in valued directions in life.

Discover powerful new ways to work with your challenging emotions when they arise . . . and they will.

Transform your way of being in relation to others, whether they trigger anger or threaten to drain you.

IN THIS CHAPTER

» Finding core values as a support to determining what you need

» Discovering how core values are like an inner compass

» Identifying our core values and aligning with them

» Exploring how we can learn from our failures and misfortunes

» Reflecting on our silver linings with compassion

Chapter **8**

Discovering Core Values: Your Inner Compass

Well, if you've read this book up to this point, you now know pretty much everything anyone ever needed to know about self-compassion. Practice mindfulness, embrace and appreciate your common humanity, and offer yourself kindness when you struggle or suffer. Simply treat yourself the way you would treat a dear friend when *they* have a hard time, and you're good to go. I have helped you load up on all the necessary supplies for the self-compassion adventure and I'm dropping you off at the trailhead. *Adios* and *vaya con dios*, my friend! Happy trails and best of luck!

"Wait!" you may be thinking. "That's it? But just because I know all this stuff and I've dabbled in accessing my inclination for goodwill doesn't mean I know what to do with it, where I'm actually headed, or really why I want to embark on this journey at all. What about practical skills and applications of what I've been learning?"

Ahhh, you are beginning to see the challenge to this work. Knowing it and doing it are two entirely different things. Okay, you've talked me into sticking around and walking you through the tricky territory of self-compassion in daily life that lies ahead. I can guide you as you navigate the terrain, and over time you will get accustomed to becoming your *own* best guide, because I can't be there for you forever.

No good journey begins without a clear map of the landscape ahead, and that is what I provide you in the preceding chapters. But even with a map in hand, you still need a good compass and a healthy dose of motivation to propel you out on the trail and to sustain you when you hit the inevitable rough spots. This sense of tuning into your guiding intentions and finding a deeper purpose in this work is what we explore in this chapter.

Most importantly to your point of not *really* knowing what to do with the knowledge you've gained so far, it's important to emphasize here that self-compassion is a practice or a way of being and not an intellectual pursuit. Up until this point my emphasis has been on teaching *about* self-compassion, but as you proceed forward, you will be focusing much more on *learning* self-compassion itself, from the inside. Imagine the difference between reading a travel book on Morocco and actually being there, tasting the food, seeing the views, meeting the people. The actual practice of self-compassion will come alive as you explore how to make changes in your life, how to work with challenging emotions and people, and all sorts of other human endeavors that are better when we are kinder to ourselves. Time to get moving and see where this trail leads and why you may want to explore it with self-compassion.

Core Values Guide Us and "Re-Mind" Us

As I establish in Chapter 1, the quintessential question of self-compassion is, "What do I need?" The thing is, this is a pretty deep question with a lot of layers when you consider it, and you may have discovered just that in the section at the end Chapter 7 entitled "Practice: Finding lovingkindness phrases." If I were to strike up a conversation with you at a party and ask you, "What do you need?" you might be at a loss to answer it. You would most likely respond by saying something like, "What do you mean? Like what do I need right now? Like would I like another beer, or do I have another party to go to?" Another possibility would be that you would take it as a deeply philosophical question: "Do you mean, what do I, as a human, really *need* in life?" And of course, there all the other layers of "need" in between these two extremes.

There is also the issue of deciding what "need" actually means relative to wants. If you are a parent, you have undoubtedly had this discussion with an insistent child at some point, perhaps many times. You find yourself explaining that your child does not *need* the latest toy or version of the video game, but instead he actually really *wants* it. Tuning in to the fundamental role of needs in your life allows you to disentangle them from your more fleeting and insubstantial wants. In fact, you might say that wants come from the neck up and needs come from the neck down.

Finding meaning through core values

As you begin to plumb the depths of the layers of need, you encounter not only basic human needs but also core values. Human needs are most commonly associated with physical and emotional survival, like the need for security, connection, or health. In most cases, we share a fairly similar set of human needs with all our fellow humans. We all need food, clothing, and shelter, for example.

Core values, on the other hand, relate more directly to meaning in life and tend to vary a bit more from person to person. For example, I might enjoy creative pursuits more than you, but you may find social connection and friendship to be more important than I do. Each value (creativity or social connection) may exist for each of us, but to differing degrees. Your values inform your sense of meaning in your life. This variation has a lot to do with how you choose to spend your time, who you are drawn to, and what you may seek out in a career or hobby. And of course, values and human needs do overlap to some degree. A life devoid of meaning may not feel worth living, so meaning is no less crucial to our survival than are food, clothing, and shelter.

Because core values vary from person to person, they are big factors in what makes each of us unique and special in spite of our similarity to each other. When we say, "He marches to the beat of a different drummer," we are often just saying, "He's kinda weird." But really what we mean is that something different motivates him, that he has different core values from ours, and we just acknowledge it by naming it in this way. We recognize that, despite our common humanity, we also each possess a relatively unique set of core values that determines how we show up in the world.

This is all well and good, but it also suggests that perhaps we can all hear our own "inner drummer" and are largely going about our lives fully in sync to that drumbeat in a world that is a kind of chaotic cacophony of various core values and different drumbeats. To some extent this may be true (although the mental image is pretty jarring), but nobody was ever handed a list of their core values and a set of instructions about how to align with them. Most of us operate on a felt sense of what moves us combined with life circumstances that may or may not facilitate us living in alignment with those values.

We muddle along, like a paramecium under the microscope, drawn in by some things and repelled by others and just trying our best to find our way in the world with some degree of ease and peace. Paramecia probably don't have core values, but like you and me, they "know" in their core what they like. Our human needs and abilities are more complex, and that is why we are exploring this topic here.

You see, core values are a bit like an internal compass. A real-world compass is attuned to the earth's magnetic poles and gives the adventurer a constant guide as to which way is north, and therefore, which direction to walk if one wants to go in a particular direction. Our core values are like our own unique inner compass that is attuned to what is most important to us (instead of to the North Pole).

REMEMBER

The challenge for us is to find a way to tune into our core values and to be able to sense the position of the needle on our inner compass, to detect when it is aligned with our core values and when it is not. Bluntly speaking, when we are living in alignment with our values, we are happier than when we are not.

What this means is that our core values are intimately intertwined not only with our life satisfaction but also with our suffering. In fact, one could say that our suffering largely arises out of a conflict between our actual life circumstances and our deeply held core values. If you deeply value human connection, then you will be disappointed when a friend cancels a visit, but if you really value your "me time," then the same cancellation could be an unforeseen gift instead.

Your core values determine your experience

The view of core values I describe in the preceding section also helps explain why things that seem objectively to be good things may not be seen so by some people. For example, if you are a social worker who values making a difference for individuals in their lives, then your recent promotion to agency manager may not make you that happy. Perhaps the promotion means more money or prestige or freedom (all of which may be valuable to you too), but if this takes you away from the joy you derive from working one-on-one with people, the new role may be a hollow achievement in some ways. Another social worker, with a desire to bring about system-wide changes and transformation in the community may find the same promotion from the one-on-one work to be a dream come true. How the promotion is experienced is driven by the core values of the one who has been promoted. Being laid off from your job may be a disaster if you value security and supporting your family, but it may be a godsend if you really treasure adventure and new horizons.

I am speaking specifically about core values here, and not goals. In other words, core values speak to valued *directions* whereas goals speak to valued *destinations*. Other ways in which these two concepts are different include the following:

>> Goals can be achieved, but core values guide us even after we achieve our goals.

>> Goals are something we do, but core values are something we are.

>> Goals are set by us, while core values are discovered.

>> Goals can be visualized, while core values are more often felt.

A few examples of core values are more stable across human beings and are related to how we treat other people, such as compassion, generosity, honesty, and loyalty. At the same time, many of our core values tend more to our own personal needs and desires that are deeply relevant to us but may not have the same importance to others. Some examples of personal core values are personal growth, creativity, tranquility, nature, and busyness.

The relationship between core values and suffering

Because we are not routinely aware of exactly what our core values are, we can often find ourselves in situations (relationships, jobs, geographical locations) that do not support us in fulfilling those values, and thus lead to us feeling dissatisfied, unfulfilled, unhappy, or even anxious or depressed. Complicating matters further, we have a tendency to see the blame for our discomfort or dissatisfaction as due to the circumstances (an insensitive boyfriend or a crummy job) rather than the mismatch between those circumstances and our core values.

This unfortunate situation often leads us to re-create these unsatisfactory situations over and over again. If you decide that you are unhappy in your factory assembly job, so you quit and then go find another factory assembly job, you may be overlooking the very real possibility that your original dissatisfaction had to do with the type of job it was and not the specific one you had.

This is not to say that you may not have a lousy boyfriend (or job), for example, but rather than pinning everything specifically on him, you might consider what you value in relationships that is not being honored in this particular one. This way you can come away from the relationship with a better sense of what is meaningful and important to you, and seek out that quality in your next boyfriend. And if you reverse this situation and have a partner you love and enjoy very much and that relationship ends, you may be heartbroken. But if you can identify what you loved about your ex-partner, it can help you find someone new who makes you happy.

Some who wander are, indeed, lost

When I think of how discovering your core values can transform a difficult experience into one of clarity and purpose, I often think of Brian (not his real name). Brian was referred to me by our hospital's chronic pain clinic. Brian was referred to me because he was severely depressed related to his chronic pain condition. Brian was a third-generation roofer in his family's business. He had always seen himself as a roofer and happily presumed he would live his entire life in that role.

But one day, Brian fell off of the roof of a building he was working on. He suffered a massive break to his right arm (he is right-handed), and even after multiple surgeries to repair the damage and some return of functioning, he was unable to lift the tools of his trade and had a tremendous amount of lingering persistent chronic pain. Brian's life as a roofer — as he had envisioned it — was gone, and he was lost and distraught. Brian couldn't imagine life being anything but a roofer, and now that that possibility was gone, he really couldn't imagine life itself. He was depressed and suicidal.

Brian and I only worked together for a few sessions, but they were deep and meaningful sessions. Once he had a chance to verbalize his frustration and deep devastation over his situation, we began to explore the deeper layers of his vision for himself. I asked him, "What is it *about* your job that brings you joy and satisfaction?" In other words, rather than getting tangled in the specifics of his particular job (putting roofs on buildings), I was trying to help him tap into his core values that were fulfilled by doing it. My hypothesis at the time was that if he could identify how that particular job aligned with his core values, then he could identify those core values and "shop them around" to other work that might be physically possible for him.

Our work together ended sooner than I had hoped because of other circumstances, but before we finished, he was able to list a few features of his work that were particularly meaningful. These features included being outdoors in nature, mentoring and training others, teamwork, creativity, and being a leader. This was a solid list of qualities that could easily be seen as core values, and I was disappointed that we couldn't work together on the next steps.

But then Brian surprised me. I had not seen him for about three months when I ran into him in the clinic one day. He was positively beaming and not looking the least bit depressed, especially compared to when he and I had worked together. I was happy to see him happy, but I was particularly curious about what had changed.

I asked him what he was up to and he replied, "I found myself the perfect job!"

I could hardly contain my curiosity because I had racked my brain for jobs that fit the profile of the values he had identified and come up empty.

"I got a great job as the director of a youth nature camp!" he exclaimed.

I wasn't quite sure what to say. It seemed so disconnected at first to what he had done before, but as we talked, I saw that when he was able to identify those core values, it led him to be able to see underneath the specific role (he had no prior training in that field) to what moved and inspired him. In this new role he was able to be outside in nature, he was helping troubled teens get their lives together, he worked in a team that he led as the director, and he was able to be creative in developing the program. A perfect match that neither he nor I could have imagined when we started working together.

Brian was able to locate his inner compass and pay very close attention to what it said to him about where his values lay, and then he followed it into his job as a camp director. While we didn't talk about it at the time in these terms, what this bold move required was his courage and openness to be able to admit that he was struggling and to meet himself and his suffering with patience and kindness nonetheless, so that he could see what was truly important and valuable in his life.

This capacity to acknowledge suffering and to meet himself with compassion (rather than to resist it and spiral into further depression and self-pity) was the key to his success in finding his way back to alignment with his core values and, as a result, to a life of greater joy and satisfaction.

The Christian theologian Thomas Merton once wrote: "If you want to identify me, ask me not where I live, or what I like to eat, or how I comb my hair, but ask me what I am living for, in detail, and ask me what I think is keeping me from living fully for the things I want to live for."

Practice: Uncovering your core values

If you are willing to explore self-compassionately within yourself to identify your inner compass and what *you* are living for and what is getting in the way, then the exercise in this section is for you.

Like many other such exercises in this book, this one is extensively drawn from an exercise called Discovering Our Core Values in the Mindful Self-Compassion program, and *that* exercise is adapted from Acceptance and Commitment Therapy and the work of Hayes, Strosahl, and Wilson (2003). The process is intended to take you a bit deeper to discover the core values that are already a part of who you are and see where you can better align with them, as well as how self-compassion may support you in that shift.

Even if you aren't a person inclined to follow and do multi-step exercises like this one, there is a "short form" that may be helpful. Take the time to look around at your particular situation (your home, your partner, your job, your hobbies and activities, your friends and family, your church, and your community). Take each one in turn and ask yourself, "What is it *about* this person or thing that brings up my joy and satisfaction, or my discomfort and dissatisfaction?" In other words, look below the particular features of meaningful things to the *essence* of what they bring (or don't bring) to your life. This will provide clues to your core values and a rudimentary map for the road ahead (and maybe inspire you to do this full exercise too!).

To prepare for this reflective exercise, it would be helpful to have paper and pencil nearby, or a keyboard to record your thoughts and observations. Once you have this, take a moment to "clear the decks," close your eyes, and settle yourself in to this moment. Maybe even give yourself a little warm inner smile of welcome to this moment and this exercise on what is most important to you. You might remember that this is just a continuation of your life, in which you have sought happiness, joy, and satisfaction all along, sometimes with more or less awareness of what brings that joy, but always with a good, warm heart that simply wants to be happy and free from suffering.

Looking back on a life well-lived

Take a few moments now to imagine yourself in your later years. You are in a comfortable place, feeling relaxed, safe, and content, and you are contemplating your life. As you look back on the period of time between that later date and now, you feel a deep sense of satisfaction, joy, and contentment. Even though life has not always been easy, you managed to chart a course for your life that kept you true to yourself and your values the best that you could.

What core values were expressed or followed in that life? These could be values like meaningful work, adventure, tranquility, loyalty, service, or compassion. Take some time to write down some of the core values that were represented in your life. You may also take the time to write down the activities that you engage in that align you with these core values, the things you do that bring you joy, contentment, and satisfaction in your daily life.

Considering where you are not aligned with your values

When you are ready and feel you have identified at least a few key core values for yourself, drop back inside and pause to settle and reflect on something different. Ask yourself whether there are any ways in which your life seems out of balance with your values, especially the more personal ones. Maybe your leisure time activities are too full of pressing demands for you to indulge in more creative pursuits, even though creativity is a great love in your life.

If you have more than one value that feels out of balance, for now just choose one that feels most important to focus upon and write it down. You can always come back to this exercise again and again and explore other values as well.

Identifying the obstacles you face

We all have obstacles that prevent us from living totally in alignment with our core values. Take a moment to consider first what *external obstacles* may be getting in the way. These obstacles may be not having enough money or time, or having other more pressing obligations or responsibilities to tend to. These are often the first things that come to mind when we realize we are out of accord with our values. Take some time to reflect on these obstacles that you face and write them down.

Also consider that, in addition to *external* obstacles that you may face, there may well be some *internal* obstacles as well. Often these are a bit less obvious and may take some time and patient reflection on what they are and how they are pulling you out of alignment with your core values. Maybe you have a fear of failure, or maybe you doubt your abilities, or perhaps you have a particularly vocal inner critic that gets in the way of you moving in valued directions.

Cultural obstacles are an insidious form of internal obstacle, where you may doubt your ability due to a prevailing cultural narrative about your identity that is limiting in some way. It is even possible, from a cultural perspective, to realize that your internal obstacle is sheer exhaustion from feeling pulled to stand up for yourself all the time. Whatever the obstacle, take your time and make note of any internal obstacles you face.

Finding a place for self-compassion

Give yourself some time now to consider whether self-compassion (in either its yin or yang form) may help you live more in accord with your deeply held core values. Following are some examples:

>> See if you can find a compassionate alternative to your inner critic, one that motivates you out of a desire to align with your values rather than out of a fear of failure.

>> Perhaps self-compassion may help you feel safe and confident enough to take new (maybe even bold) actions.

>> Tap into the yang energy of self-compassion to see if you can find enough inner safety and bravery to risk failing at something that is meaningful to you.

>> Pause to look around to see if you are clinging to anything that isn't serving you anymore, and if so, consider self-compassionately letting that thing go so you can move on.

Give yourself plenty of time to explore how self-compassion can support you in this inner work of connecting to your core values. Try things on for size, test them out, and be willing to be creative, patient, and kind with yourself in this process.

If you identify some obstacles that are truly insurmountable in this moment, can you give yourself compassion just for the fact of that particular hardship? Maybe just pause here, if this is the case for you, and give yourself a few words of appreciation for even doing this work and respecting your core values, even if your obstacles are just too big or imposing right now. You may even consider exploring *other* ways that you can express your values in some way, even if that expression feels somewhat incomplete. For example, if nature is a great value but your family responsibilities get in the way, perhaps you can find time to simply gaze at photographs or videos of nature in the meantime until other opportunities arise.

And finally, if the absolutely insurmountable problem is that you are imperfect, as all human beings are, can you forgive yourself for that fact as well?

Inquiring: What was it like to discover your core values?

Did you uncover any core values in this exercise? If you discovered a few, did one in particular rise to the top as you reflected upon it? If one did, how did it feel to name it and consider it? Were you aware of any feelings that arose as you did that?

Please note that sometimes people identify a core belief in this exercise that they feel has been overlooked or ignored for large portions of their life for a variety of reasons (both within and outside of their control).

REMEMBER

The purpose of this reflection is to identify these important values, not to assign blame for not living in alignment with them or to feel any amount of shame or embarrassment for losing track of them along the way.

If difficult feelings came up as you contemplated a core value, see if you can simply comfort yourself because sometimes discoveries can be painful at first. This is understandable, but see if you can be patient with yourself, as most of us live much of our lives without much conscious awareness of our values. The good news is that once these things are in your consciousness, then, and only then, can you begin to make changes, to make amends with yourself and to find your way into alignment with what is important to you deep down.

How did it feel to name the obstacles, both internal and external, that you face in trying to live in accord with your core values? Were there any surprises or any apparent obstacles that perhaps turned out to be less formidable than you had assumed? Sometimes an obstacle in one area can loom so large in a person's awareness that it seems like it prevents them from pursuing any of their values. Often people who have a physical disability let that challenge prevent them from engaging socially with others or finding meaningful work, but when they look a bit closer they realize that it need not be an obstacle to these activities.

Most relevant to our purpose here, did you find any way that being more self-compassionate could help you to align better with your core values?

TIP

I recognize that you are still pretty new to self-compassion practice, and I would strongly recommend that you return to this exercise after you've read a few more chapters and tried some of the other self-compassion practices. See what may change over time as the ability to be self-compassionate becomes more readily available to you.

This is not a "one and done" sort of exercise. Many people find that returning to this reflective process over and over can be very helpful to periodically "recalibrate" and focus on what is most important, as life can often cause us to drift off course. A patient of mine who was previously in the military referred to becoming "OBE." OBE stands for Overcome By Events, and I have always been struck by how life can feel like one incident of OBE after another. We can often feel like a ship being tossed about by stormy seas and can easily be blown off course through no fault of our own. The good news is that values work is like the North Pole or the stars above, always available to support us in navigating back to our intended course.

Translating values into action

Exploration of our core values is often a very fruitful exercise and stirs up a lot of feelings for people. We may feel bad for not having lived up to our core values in the past, but it's important to view this practice as a potential turning point instead. As I mention earlier, once you are more acutely aware of your core values, *then* you are actually able to do something about them.

Quite often, based on the experience of this exercise, I see people resolving to take action on what they discovered and trying to figure out ways to make the changes that they see as crucial for realignment with their values. The next chapter actually explores some of the challenges people face when seeking to make substantial changes like this, as well as some ways that self-compassion can actually help us make change in our lives. But for now it's good to really cement these values in your awareness so that you are more conscious of them and they're available to you when you make decisions in your life.

If life is like a long boat journey where you are the captain, each moment when you make a decision is like a tiny turn of the wheel on your boat. It may seem small at the time, but if you stay on course it can lead to a very different destination over time. Only when you have your direction firmly in mind can you steer the ship of your life in a steady, consistent direction, making course corrections now and then when you drift off course, and always keeping your eyes on the prize.

TIP

The following hints can help you stay aligned with your values and keep them in your awareness as you go about your life:

>> Write down your core values and post them someplace where you will see them daily, such as your bathroom mirror, the refrigerator door, or the wall of your cubicle at work. (Tattoos are good, but perhaps a bit too permanent and public for your taste. I understand.)

>> Create a little vow for yourself. A simple statement that is much like a lovingkindness wish can be quite powerful if you return to it on a regular basis, almost as a kind of small sacred ritual for yourself.

For example, turning a core value like social justice into a vow might look like "I vow to seek justice whenever the opportunity arises." Repeating it each morning, or lighting a candle and reciting it each evening, can slowly embed it in your consciousness and guide you like the north star.

Dark Nights and Dark Clouds: Wisdom Gleaned from Life's Challenges

Perhaps it has slowly dawned on you that much of the practice of self-compassion is focused on the benefits of being able to kindly accompany ourselves through the challenges of life and the suffering that each of us experiences as a human being. Maybe your initial motivation for exploring the practice and buying this book was to see if there was a way you could tiptoe around the suffering in your life (or possibly simply banish it) and simply be happy (or at least happier) all the time. Sorry about that, but you have probably begun to realize that this is not actually realistic, and frankly it would be a relatively dull life if everything always went smoothly.

I know, I know, you're probably rolling your eyes at that last statement and thinking, "I would be more than happy to have a nice long stretch of smooth sailing and happy feelings. That whole "suffering builds character" is highly overrated, and I already have more than enough character, thank you." Okay, I get it, but think of the richness of your life when you look at it in its entirety.

REMEMBER

The joys and sorrows, the pleasures and the pains all blend together into a complex stew of experience that makes up where you have been and partially determines who you have become (the nurture part of the age-old "nature versus nurture" discussion).

Seasoning in the stew

I am writing this chapter during the Christmas season, and right now I am in the process of making posole, which is a rich, flavorful Mexican stew often served at the holidays. I just started the process by pouring boiling water over a collection of intensely flavored dried chiles that will ultimately form the base of the stew alongside pork, hominy, herbs, onions, and other tasty ingredients. My point here is that each life is like this rich stew, with a variety of intense experiences (flavors) that all blend together to create the experience that you call "me." These experiences don't define you, but they do contribute to who you are. This may sound all poetic and flowery, but I doubt you would want to have a big bite of my soaking chiles. They are intense, and by themselves would be overpowering and downright painful to experience.

I'm not suggesting that you should necessarily love or treasure all the painful or challenging things you have experienced, but the experiences you have had all blend together to contribute to where and who you are. And of course, the past is behind you and your challenge is really to give up all hope of a different yesterday so that you can show up fully for today, where you *can* make a difference. This can take the form of realigning yourself to your core values, as we just explored, or seeing what deeper lesson can be learned from your past experiences to enrich your future.

REMEMBER

It's important to clarify that some painful and traumatic experiences are hard to acknowledge and embrace as ingredients in the stew of your life. If you have had this sort of experience, you may feel as though it has poisoned the stew or at least made it incredibly distasteful. I'm not discounting this possibility at all. Rather, I ask that you continue to go slow and explore how you can engage in what psychologists call *post-traumatic growth* to see if you can find a way forward that makes some meaning out of your terrible experiences and eventually transform your history into a foundation for some freedom from this particular suffering.

Quite often, the simple fact that you survived a terrible, painful, or traumatic experience is the most important takeaway message you can glean from these things, and that is more than enough. Again, please be kind to yourself, go slowly, and let your own experience be your guide as to what you need and what you may learn if you are gentle but brave in touching these experiences only as much as you are willing. Be curious and kind and see what you might discover when you listen in this self-compassionate way.

How failure and hardship teach us

None of us seeks to flop when we try things, and we don't usually seek out adversity to overcome, but nonetheless these things happen. The challenge to living our lives to the fullest is not figuring out how to eliminate these inevitable things from happening, but seeing if we can learn lessons from them when they do.

Often the lessons that you learn or the silver linings you discover inside the dark clouds of your hardships are things you never would have realized otherwise. Even infants and toddlers learn from unexpected and unfortunate experiences. When the toddler pushes his tippy cup off the edge of the table, he learns about gravity (and what not to do if you are thirsty). Often our hard lessons are much more painful than spilt milk, but they are nonetheless potential teachers. The poet Jane Hirschfield says, "Suffering leads us to beauty the way thirst leads to water."

I once was called away for work when my teenage son was going through a rough period in his life and our separation was painful for both of us. Our communications were tense, and he was full of adolescent angst and said some pretty harsh things to me that were hard for me to hear. My mind just wouldn't let go of my guilt and shame over every parenting move I had ever made, and it was distracting me from my job at the time, which was to teach a Mindful Self-Compassion course with Kristin Neff, one of the co-developers of the program. That was nerve-wracking enough because she and I had never taught together. (Imagine acting in your first movie across from Robert DeNiro or playing doubles tennis with Serena Williams, and you have some idea about how I felt.)

This all felt like a double-whammy of suffering, but in the midst of it as I meditated early one morning, I somehow discovered a calm place inside that helped me see my son's pain in the larger arc of a young person's life. I was able to see what he said as simply an expression of his pain. It didn't solve anything, but this momentary shift in perspective taught me the capacity to take the larger view and to feel less overwhelmed by life's twists and turns.

This is a lesson that I have tapped into numerous times since then, sometimes in regard to my son, but often in other situations. I found something inside me that I never knew I had, and it has been available to me ever since. (And incidentally, my son and I now look back on that situation ten years ago and laugh and tease each other about it.)

Challenges often force you to go deep inside and uncover resources or capacities that you never knew you possessed or never dreamed you would have to tap into. Self-compassion plays an important role here because it helps you to create that brave and safe inner space that gives you courage to turn toward this suffering and see what it may have to teach you.

Exercise: Silver linings and golden gifts

This reflective exercise is drawn from the Mindful Self-Compassion program and is intended to support you in discovering first-hand what is possible when you look at life's failures or hardships in a different light.

This reflection is best done with a way to make notes, either on pencil or paper or on a keyboard. Once you have prepared yourself to write down a few things, allow your eyes to close and your body and mind to settle. Perhaps take a few slow, deep, relaxing breaths to allow your attention to drop inside and out of your thinking mind.

When you are ready, call to mind a struggle in your life that seemed very difficult or even impossible to bear at the time, but that in retrospect, taught you something important. Be sure to choose a situation that is far enough in the past and has been *very clearly resolved* such that you have already learned whatever you needed to learn from it. Please, do not choose a traumatic event that could be re-traumatizing if you recall it now.

Please remember that not every dark cloud has a silver lining, and sometimes there is nothing to be learned from suffering, except that simply having returned (or tried to return) to ordinary life is a triumph in itself. But for *this* reflection, choose an event that did have a silver lining.

Call to mind the situation in question, what the challenge was, and how it felt to go through it at the time.

Pause to really take some time to honor yourself for the difficulty you endured and how you struggled with it at the time. This is not about reviewing how you handled the situation, per se, but how it was to be in it, doing your best to navigate through it.

Make a few notes about the situation for yourself, what the experience was like. Also, take some time to add some kind words to offer yourself that validate what you went through. These may be the kinds of words you would offer a friend telling you a similar story of their own struggles. You might have words like: "That was hard!"; "You were so brave to get through that!"; or "There was no way you could have anticipated that, but you got through it."

As you are ready, give yourself some time to reflect on what *deeper lesson* this challenging situation taught you that you may not have learned otherwise. Write that lesson (or lessons) down too. Consider how that lesson has resided within you ever since, perhaps guiding you through other difficult situations or helping you avoid some hardships as a result. This is the golden gift of the silver lining: a lasting legacy of wisdom gained in the midst of a challenging experience of suffering.

Inquiring: Were you able to identify a silver lining?

Like many of the reflective exercises that I introduce in this book, this is one that can be returned to over and over, and new discoveries can be made. Also as with the other exercises, you would be wise to take your time and let these practices, reflections, and ideas linger and mellow and transform over time. Don't be too quick to formulate a concrete lesson learned, but instead entertain possibilities, like a scientist entertains hypotheses. Hold it in mind, test it out, see how it withstands the test of your patient scrutiny, and see what emerges. As always, patience, persistence, kindness, and curiosity are the keys to discovering the transformative power of reflecting on silver linings.

REMEMBER

We don't have just one core value, but many of them, and they can be related to important dimensions of being human, like your relationships, your culture or community, your spiritual life, your work, your family, and so on.

IN THIS CHAPTER

» Discovering how self-monitoring becomes harsh

» Exploring why we even have an inner critic

» Seeing how our inner critic can be sneaky

» Finding a new relationship with our critic

» Applying self-compassion in the service of finding our compassionate part

Chapter **9**

Dancing with the Inner Critic and Making Change

I n Chapter 4, I suggest that we all have an inner experience akin to watching sports on television. We have an inner play-by-play announcer that simply watches and reports factually on what it observes moment by moment. And then we also have an inner color commentator who, with a flair for the histrionic, interprets what has happened, analyzes the experience, and breathes drama into the same experience. As I note, we are well served by focusing our attention primarily on the former and perhaps turning down the volume a bit on the latter.

This is all well and good if your particular color commentator is just a harmless and colorful character with a beguiling accent or an inclination for melodrama. However, for many of us this incessant inner voice is more sinister, dark, dismissive, and doubtful. The inner commentator is really an inner critic instead, providing consistently harsh, hurtful, and unsolicited criticism of virtually everything you think, say, or do. (Often it is the internalized voice of someone from your past, just to make matters more difficult.) Imagine being an actor on the stage and having a theater critic in the audience, not just taking notes on their experience of the play for a later review in the newspaper, but instead calling out their observations randomly *while* you are performing. This may not be hard for you to imagine if you have an inner critic, because you live with it all the time.

One of my favorite authors, Anne Lamott, wrote a brilliant book on the process of writing called *Bird by Bird* (Ancho Books) in which she details what writer's block is like for her. She describes an inner radio station "KFKD" that she interprets with an expletive that I won't repeat here. She goes on to say, "If you are not careful, station KFKD will play in your head twenty-four hours a day, nonstop, in stereo . . . Out of the left speaker will be the rap songs of self-loathing, the lists of all the things one doesn't do well, of all the mistakes one has made today and over an entire lifetime, the doubt, the assertion that . . . one is in every way a fraud, incapable of selfless love, that one has no talent or insight, and on and on and on." Does this sound familiar? For some, this account is mild by comparison, but the concept of an inner monologue of criticism is painfully recognizable.

Take a moment to consider how you respond to this inner critic and its constant barrage of disparagement. My guess is that, more often than not, you simply go about your business making no particular extra effort to cope, learning to live with its presence. And if you have chosen to try to do something about your hurtful inner critic, you've either tried to ignore it (you couldn't) or tried to argue with it (you lost). How did I do? Regardless of which approach you've taken, you may very well feel powerless over your inner critic and perhaps even feel a bit deflated and defeated by it, as if you are carrying a heavy weight around your neck all the time. This chapter is devoted to a viable option that you may not yet have considered for how to contend with the inner critic, so if you are feeling discouraged right now, wait until you've read this chapter and tried the practices, and see what your experience tells you about this new option.

REMEMBER

If all this talk of an inner critic doesn't really resonate with you and you are feeling as if this is one challenge that you don't happen to have, I suggest you read on, nonetheless. I describe some of the sneakier and more insidious ways that an inner dialogue may be playing out such that you aren't even aware that it is undermining and limiting you, especially when you seek to make noteworthy change in your life. The typical inner critic is harsh and judgmental when it shouts into the ears of some people, but the inner trickster is more subtle and may be whispering instead. I don't want to sound like a pessimist, but you may not be as free of crippling self-talk as you may think.

The Inner Critic: Self-Monitoring Gone Haywire

One of the unique human capacities that you possess is the ability to observe your own behavior (including your thoughts and emotions) and to take that information into account as you navigate through life. Imagine the situation where you approach someone to whom you are attracted and hope to cultivate a closer relationship. You see her across the room, laughing and chatting with friends, and feel something inside you that informs you that she is attractive to you. Maybe your heart flutters or you feel a warm flush in your face, or you think "Wow, something about her is special!" Some other part of your consciousness takes note of this and urges you to approach her. You start walking across the room toward the object of your future affection and a voice says, "Slow down. You're walking too fast and she's going to freak out if you seem too aggressive." You slow down and begin to saunter instead (who knew that a saunter was even in your repertoire!) and you make eye contact. She smiles and that same voice says, "Is she looking at you or over your shoulder at that big muscly guy at the bar behind you?" You decide it's you, and then your voice says, "Smile, dude. Hurry up or she's going to think you're weird." You dutifully smile and then you have the thought to say, "Oh my God, what's your name? My name's Lyle" (thanks to singer Lyle Lovett for the pickup line). You immediately hear a voice in your head saying, "Really? That's the best you could do? What if she thinks that's a ridiculous way of introducing yourself? You may have just blown your big chance with this woman. Retreat! Retreat!"

We've all been there in one form or another, where we have some idea that we are sailing along alone on the sea of life but find that we have one or a chorus of voices onboard our little ship accompanying us, guiding us, and narrating our lives for us. Like it or not, they are with us. Frankly, although they can be annoying at times, under normal circumstances having your own internal "navigator" can be a comfort and a guide and keep you on course. This self-monitoring is like having a good friend escorting us through the more challenging aspects of life so that we feel less alone and can avoid some of the potential pitfalls that we can't quite see along the way. Another analogy is a submarine with a radar system, gently feeding back "pings" (data) about what is ahead, what to avoid, and where the waters are clear — and generally keeping you out of trouble and on course.

The wisdom of our self-monitoring and self-talk is gleaned from a lifetime of experience, and much of it comes from our earliest experiences with our primary caregivers, parents, teachers, and other influential people in our lives. Little by little we learn lessons, whether we are trying to or not, that then live on within us for years to guide and inform us. Over time we learn how we should act in various social situations, what things are worthy endeavors, what to avoid, what is important, and what is unimportant.

In fact, many of our core values (explored in the previous chapter) are formed in the early years of our lives by observing our parents and other influential people and what appears to guide *them*. From these observations we infer certain things, and then we endeavor to follow (or avoid) that example with ongoing self-monitoring. In other words, we have a mental image of the desired behavior or attitude, and then we try it out in real life, course-correcting as needed and relying on constant self-monitoring to align ourselves with the values we have embraced.

For example, if you witnessed parents who were particularly involved in social activism, you may have incorporated their deep appreciation for justice and fairness. Then, as opportunities arise (say you witness a situation at work that is patently unfair to a colleague), you act in the way that seems consistent with what you learned to value earlier in your life. Your inner commentary guides you along, finding just the right path. When you are able to chart that course, you get a deep feeling of satisfaction that further strengthens that value within you for future situations.

REMEMBER

The challenge with this process comes when the messages you receive in your life about how to be, who you are, and what you are capable of accomplishing are negative, dysfunctional, or downright harsh or hurtful. The underlying process of having a constant, helpful self-monitoring companion then becomes subverted by these difficult messages and circumstances such that your companion becomes your nemesis. When the inner dialogue begins to sting and focus upon the negative, the inner critic is born.

Living with your own worst critic

So, the roots of the inner critic are in this powerful human capacity that you have to take note of your thoughts, emotions, and behavior and make use of them to navigate through life. In a way, it's like you're the pilot of an aircraft, and as you settle into your seat to prepare for takeoff, you find out that your co-pilot is The Joker from the *Batman* series. Except that this particular co-pilot is with you for every single flight you ever take. He goes home with you at night and whispers nasty comments in your ear every day. Not a pretty prospect, and not that funny either, especially if your inner critic is particularly adept at pushing your most sensitive buttons or uses intensely hurtful language, as many of them do.

In most cases, one does not simply wake up one morning and discover that one has an inner critic that has taken up residence in their brain overnight. This voice begins weaseling its way into your consciousness at an early age and becomes so constant and insidious that you almost don't recognize it as a presence in your awareness so much as simply a fact of your inner life. The inner critic can start to hide in plain sight because it is so ubiquitous.

I once lived across the street from a police firing range, and virtually every early evening, San Diego's finest would show up to practice their marksmanship there. At first, the barrage of gunfire was disconcerting, to say the least, but over time my wife and I came to not really notice it at all. In fact, we most often became aware of it when guests came for dinner and got this panic-stricken look in their eyes all of a sudden. We would chuckle as we realized what was happening and snap out of our "trance" and notice the sounds as well, reassuring them that it was friendly fire.

The message of the inner critic can range from the merely constructive to downright destructive in content, tone, and timing, but the experience is difficult, nonetheless. Whether the voice is literally that of an early caretaker or parent, or just a disembodied, unidentified voice, it is hard to hear things like "You are just a loser and will never achieve anything in your life," or "What makes you think you have any business trying *that* of all things? You're not nearly smart enough to be successful at it," or simply, "You aren't worthy of having friends." The inner critic whispers things in your ear that you wouldn't dare to speak out loud to any other person.

In fact, in a striking French commercial produced by the Dove soap company, this paradox is illustrated quite clearly. Some women are asked to write down the self-critical statements that they hear in their minds over the course of a day. Then two actresses are positioned in a Paris café as if they are two friends enjoying a coffee together, except that one of the women is saying things to her "friend" that were written down by the earlier women. You see the women saying things like "Don't you feel horrible right now? With those large thighs and your horse's hips?" and the cameras catch the faces of nearby diners overhearing the dialogue.

The bystanders are at first amused, then shocked, and even outraged at what they are hearing, even interrupting the two actresses to tell them how hurtful it is for them to be saying what they are saying. The irony is that the bystanders are actually the women who were originally interviewed, and they are hearing, in many cases, *their own self-critical words* being spoken out loud. One woman says "But yes, it's what I say to myself all day long. Now I get how violent it is!" and the commercial ends with these words: "If it's not acceptable to say it to someone else, why say it to ourselves?"

TIP

Later in this chapter you will engage in a reflective exercise to look more closely at the inner critic as a means of dampening its negative effects on you, but for now, perhaps take a few minutes to consider what kinds of things your inner critic says to you on a regular basis. You may even consider writing these things down so you can see them at a little distance, like the women in the commercial hearing other people uttering their own self-critical dialogue.

There's nothing to be done with these phrases just now, but it's good to acknowledge their presence. In much the same way that offering ourselves lovingkindness phrases over time can slowly "marinate" us and incline our hearts in a particular direction, the same can be true (in the opposite direction) of corrosive and belittling self-criticism. These are the long-term effects of self-criticism that we explore further in the sections that follow.

Exploring the function of an inner critic

It becomes quite interesting when you contemplate the question of what function the inner critic serves or whether there is any value to having one. After spending a lifetime with that voice droning on inside your head, you can imagine that it has planted some interesting justification for its existence in there, and some of it is right on target; even other aspects are a little twisted. Often, we see the inner critic as a huge source of pain and would like to get rid of it if we possibly could, but it's really not so simple for a variety of reasons.

For example, when we ask participants in the Mindful Self-Compassion course this question about the function of the self-critic, the typical responses include the following:

>> "Self-criticism motivates me to constantly improve."

>> "It keeps me on the straight and narrow, so I behave properly."

>> "It lowers my expectations, so I won't disappoint myself or others."

>> "I find that if I criticize myself, it makes others feel more comfortable around me, so they like me more."

There is a certain amount of sense in these statements, and it's worth recognizing these factors because they point to why, once again, we are not looking to eradicate this uncomfortable phenomenon in our lives but instead to cultivate a different, more fruitful, and less disruptive relationship with it. In other words, it may be possible to *dance* with the inner critic rather than *fight* with it.

The myth of motivation

The most common response people offer to the question regarding the function of the self-critic — that the inner critic motivates us to do better and achieve more — has some logic to it. If you try something and fail, it's worthwhile to critically review your performance and try to identify where you could improve and what mistakes you may have made. But here's where it gets tricky. If we were talking about an athletic competition, then our inner dialogue could be like our coach. If you make a crucial error in a bike race, which of the following two options is more likely to keep you trying hard to improve?

>> The coach berates you with a statement like "I can't believe you were so stupid to try that maneuver in that situation. You keep doing the same boneheaded thing over and over again and getting the same result. I'm beginning to wonder if you're smart enough to succeed in this sport."

>> The coach who has high standards for you says, "Man, what happened out there with that maneuver? How can you break out of that habit that keeps getting you in trouble? I know you have it in you to do better, and I want to support you in that."

This comparison is pretty obvious and is at the heart of why, as I describe in Chapter 2, people who are more self-compassionate tend to try harder and persist longer in pursuing their goals than those who are more self-critical. Most of us are much more inclined to try harder with a compassionate coach than with a belittling and critical coach.

The difference between criticism and discernment

It is important to note here that what I mean by self-criticism is different from what some people may call critical discernment. We have incredible human brains with sophisticated frontal lobes that help us make choices between things and critically evaluate our options as a means of anticipating the consequences of our decisions. Sometimes people call this discernment "judgment" or "being critical," but you can distinguish between this helpful internal process and the more damaging self-criticism I am discussing here. The way that you can distinguish them from each other is in the tone. The critical discernment is more calm, rational, and almost scientific in its manner, whereas self-criticism definitely has an edge or a grating, provocative, or dismissive quality to it.

Because the critic can be harsh at times, it's true that self-criticism can "punish" you when you do something wrong or improper, and this can certainly motivate you to behave better or more lawfully, but as a primary means of motivation, fear is a terrible teacher. And beating ourselves up just to put others at ease around us is just plain twisted and self-defeating, as well as kind of annoying for those other people. Sometimes we do this (criticize ourselves out loud) in order to gain praise from others, in an equally odd and distorted way.

I am willing to admit that on occasion I have said something self-deprecating so that someone else would dispute it. If I said "I wrote this book called *Self-Compassion For Dummies*, but it's not really very good. I could have done better," you may feel compelled to say something like "Oh, that's not true, Steve. It's really good and it helped me a lot! You're a great writer!" So, in a weird way, self-criticism can help me ultimately feel good in the end (and if you think I'm right about the book not being very good, please keep that opinion to yourself!).

Furthermore, if you think that self-criticism itself is bad, imagine the scenario where you engage in it to avoid feeling something even worse. Sometimes people criticize themselves to avoid deeper, more difficult feelings like guilt or shame. If you accuse yourself of being weak or stupid, in a way it kind of gets you off the hook from opening up to painful guilt or shame over things you have done in moments of weakness and stupidity. If you say, "I'm too weak to resist sweets," it's less painful than the feelings of remorse and shame that come from eating an entire quart of Ben & Jerry's Cherry Garcia ice cream in one sitting (although I, for one, would at least applaud your taste in ice cream!).

Also, if we fear that others will criticize us for the things we think, do, or say, we may find that berating ourselves for those things is more manageable than hearing it from others. In other words, we sometimes find that beating others to the punch is our best option in some situations. I have to say that I just feel a tremendous degree of sadness when I meet people who do this, and it inspires me to do this work to support them in changing that hurtful pattern.

A note on the malicious inner critic

You may have already discovered that the inner dialogue spans a spectrum from a strongly encouraging, compassionate inner coach or cheerleader; to a judgmental and critical judge; to a really nasty, undermining, and hurtful inner abuser. Thus far I have focused mainly on the lighter side of that spectrum, but it's important to touch on the darker end of this range because it is sadly all too common among those who seek to practice self-compassion. There are actually some redeeming aspects to the inner critics that many of us experience (which you are about to explore), but there are important exceptions as well.

As I note earlier, much of your inner dialogue and inner criticism results from things you have experienced in your past, how you were raised, how society has treated you, and who had some form of influence over you. In the very unfortunate situation where people have been influenced by early abusive caregivers or painful cultural oppression, the voice and intention of the inner critic can actually have no redeeming value at all. It is simply the residue of a system or a person that was discharging its pain without regard for us or our well-being. If this is the case in your situation, please, as always, be kind, patient, and curious as you proceed through this chapter and the reflective exercise ahead.

The exercise coming up encourages you to turn toward the inner critic and to work with it in a compassionate way, but for those with histories of trauma and abuse, this can be a bit tricky, to say the least. This can actually feel a bit like standing up to those abusive voices from the past, which is an option that may not have been available to you at the time. In fact, this new (somewhat counterintuitive) stance can feel like you are breaking an invisible contract that you essentially made with yourself to preserve your safety and help you survive at the time.

You may also experience backdraft when you begin to warm up your inner dialogue (see Chapter 6 for more on this phenomenon). You can meet this fear and reactivity with mindfulness and self-compassion, of course, but you may want to go slow and perhaps even seek out the support and guidance of a counselor or therapist if you haven't already done so.

I am not suggesting that anything discussed in this chapter may not be helpful to you if your inner critic is largely fueled by a traumatic or oppressive upbringing, only that your task is to treat yourself compassionately by letting go of being overly ambitious and "powering through." Instead, go slow and let yourself respond to the ever-present question of "What do I need just now?"

REMEMBER

The important thing is that you have overcome these past experiences and maintain a deep and strong intention to move beyond their constraints to greater ease and relief of your suffering. Allow yourself the opportunity to take your time and ease into a different relationship with your inner critic, and yourself.

The devious inner trickster

Perhaps you are thinking right about now that you are one of the lucky ones who has escaped the uncomfortable burden of a harsh inner critic. If that is the case, then I celebrate that happy circumstance with you, but I have to say that I once thought that this was the case for me as well, and I turned out to be wrong. I don't want to be a buzzkill here, but if you think you don't have a severe inner critic poking and berating you at every turn, there are at least three possible scenarios that may be going on with you:

» You may be right (the simplest scenario), which is great news, but there two other possibilities as well.

» Another likelihood is that you have never really explored this aspect of your experience, having kept your mind occupied in ways that distract you from the critic or generally avoid it somehow. However, if you begin to look a bit closer, you may find that your inner critic is still doing its work but in a more subtle and subversive way, more with a whisper than a shout. It's worth it to see if this may be the case for you, not because I am sadistically nudging you toward painful experiences (which may sometimes be what this process has felt like so far!) but because by tuning in to these inner dialogues you may discover how they may be undermining your efforts and holding you back from achieving greater satisfaction and joy.

>> The third possibility is the sneakiest one of all and happens to be the one that applies to me. I call mine the inner seductress, although I realize that is a rather sexist term, and others refer to it as the inner trickster. (Mine actually has a name, Angelica, as a matter of fact, and I can picture her as I write this. Picturing your inner critic or your inner trickster can sometimes help you maintain a bit of distance between you and it.) The way this devious inner voice can work to undermine you is that it first cozies up to you like a good spy would infiltrate the enemy's team, making you think she is on your side.

For example, when I contemplate going to the gym to work out, Angelica cozies up close and warm and whispers breathily in my ear, "Ohhhh, you don't need to go to the gym today. You went *yesterday* and you work *so* hard. You deserve a little break. You'll be fine if you don't go today." If I listen to her, it feels good for a little while and I feel gratitude to Angelica for her warmth. But the clue that she has seduced me away from my core value of wellness and fitness is in the sinking, demoralized feeling that hits me very soon after. I feel disappointed in myself; I question my resolve, and a bit of shame arises as I realize what I've done (or haven't done), and I hear echoes of the word "lazy" rebound in my mind. This is the clue that you may have an inner trickster: that you feel a kind of "morning-after shame" or deflation over your inability to accomplish things that are important to you or your inability to stop yourself from doing things that get in the way of important valued principles.

The motives of the inner trickster or the whispering critic are the same as those of the more traditional harsh inner critic, and we explore those in the next section. But as you proceed through the rest of this chapter, see how you can customize what you discover to your particular type of undermining inner companion. You may not be feeling particularly burdened or restrained by this inner dialogue right now, but you may be surprised to discover that loosening its grip can help you achieve peak performance in ways you may not have thought were possible. Like the Olympic swimmer who shaves off every bit of body hair to potentially trim milliseconds off his time, you may find that when you are free of this inner dialogue, you too can move more swiftly and aligned with your core values (with no actual shaving required!).

Changing Your Relationship with Your Inner Critic

As you have seen, there are some marginal benefits to having an inner critical dialogue, but the predominant impact is really quite negative, limiting, painful, and counter to your values overall. As a permutation of our very valuable human capacity for self-monitoring, it is not something that we can simply excise or eliminate from our consciousness, any more than we can eliminate sadness or fear from our lives. These are all essential elements of being human and serve a useful purpose, even if they are painful at times. What we *can* do is to shift our relationship with the inner critical voice, much as we discuss doing something similar in regard to other challenging experiences in Chapter 4.

What is your relationship with your inner critic these days? Take a moment to check in with yourself and see just how you relate to this entity within you, that is *not* you on the one hand, but is intimately a part of your life and outlook on a regular basis. I suspect that you have what some people euphemistically refer to as a "conflicted relationship" with your inner critic, because most of us do. Like how you feel toward a recalcitrant child or irritating colleague, you probably maintain some ongoing internal struggle or angst over the presence of the critic and have attempted over the years to eliminate or avoid it without success.

How our attempts to manage the critic are doomed

The thing is, our inner critic has a powerful secret weapon that those other challenging people in your life don't have: It knows *exactly* what your particular "hot buttons" are and knows all your deepest, darkest fears and insecurities because it lives in the space of your own mind. For example, Angelica (my inner seductress) knows that being called "lazy" has deep roots in my psyche that can rattle my cage like no other adjective. I can't hide from Angelica and her taunts, and you can't hide from your cruel inner critic either.

REMEMBER

If you attempt to outsmart your critic, you're doomed from the start. It's like playing chess against an opponent who can read your mind and knows exactly what you are attempting before you make a move and has formulated the perfect countermove every time.

When you tangle with your inner critic, you feel powerless to overcome it or subdue it because it always seems to have the upper hand and just the right thing to say to hook you into the web of doubt and self-criticism. When you say to your inner critic, "I am *not* stupid! I'm smart enough to go for that promotion and I'm going to do it," your inner critic knows that even though you believe you are smart enough, there was *that one* time when you got negative feedback from your boss for not doing a good enough job on an important project, and it was really painful. You've since come a long way, but that nagging doubt is there, down deep in your mind. Your inner critic has no hesitation in responding with "You think you're smart enough to do that new job, but remember how you failed miserably at that project that time? You'll never change." And then, there you are, back at square one feeling discouraged, powerless, and incompetent.

Even when you try to avoid or deny the comments of the critic, it has its tricks because it knows just the thing that will prod you out of denial and back into the fray. It's a bit like your annoying little sister who knows just the right kind of escalating and annoying tone (or well-timed threats) to *finally* coax you into having a tea party with her. It starts sweet and continues to ramp up until you simply cannot resist any longer.

As I discuss earlier, the saying "what you resist, persists" is quite true of our thoughts and feelings, and that includes your inner critic as well. When you say to your critic, "I am going to be optimistic and think of the times when I succeeded at this," your critic inevitably says, "You mean there were times when you failed instead? What were those times? Tell me about them." It goes on to offer up possibilities like "What about that time in high school? And remember the time on that date with Frank? That did not go well at all." In other words, your inner critic can spot denial a mile away and will attempt to foil your attempts at every turn.

Thoughts are not facts, and our critic is not us

Returning to the earlier chess analogy, we are easily sucked into the idea that our critic is our adversary. Therefore, the objective is to somehow triumph over the critic and wrestle it into submission. But we've already seen that as an adversary, our inner critic will outwit and outflank us every single time, and you may be feeling a bit hopeless and helpless at this point. Bear with me, the solution is coming soon (and you may be shocked to find out that self-compassion is a key component of that solution).

In order to begin to shift our relationship with the inner critic, we must first shift our perspective on the whole process. Rather than seeing ourselves as a combatant in a chess match, pitted against a wily opponent (black versus white), we can borrow a metaphor from Stephen Hayes's Acceptance and Commitment Therapy and *be the board* instead. Take a moment to consider the situation in which you are locked in a death-match with your inner critic.

The inner critic represents one part of you and can cite real examples from your life that point to certain of your tendencies, your foibles and your weaknesses, but these things alone do not define who you are, they just contribute to the whole you. At the same time, the part of you that is striving to move in valued directions also believes certain things about you and can point to other aspects of your patterns and strengths that are also factual and real. But these positive aspects don't solely define who you are, either. In other words, neither the white pieces nor the black pieces are actually "you" but instead simply different aspects of your experience. And all of this leads to the conclusion that if you try to eliminate the inner critic, you are really trying to set up a situation where, in order to get on with life, large parts of your actual life experience must disappear forever. Good luck with that.

If instead you become the board on which all of this drama and *mishigas* (a delightful Yiddish term meaning craziness, silliness, tomfoolery, and nonsense — not so different from Anne Lamott's radio station KFKD) plays out, you remain present, unscathed, and ready for whatever comes next. As a human chess board, you are free to observe all the tomfoolery in your mind and heart and still move in valued directions toward the things that have meaning for you.

This may sound quite good in theory, but the key ingredient to being able to make this whole process happen is to understand how to disentangle from the critic's hurtful and undermining monologue. How do we view the critic and what it says to us such that it feels less malignant, and we feel worthy of our efforts to squash or eliminate it? Like when you are at a party and out of the cacophony of voices you happen to hear someone mention your name, when the inner dialogue is *about you* and emotionally charged because the source is your own collection of insecurities, fears, and doubts, it's nearly impossible to let go of it. It feels too hard to see it as just so much mental activity, like Shakespeare's *Macbeth*'s speech "a tale, told by an idiot, full of sound and fury, signifying nothing." In order to make this shift, it can be eye-opening to explore and discover the real and perhaps surprising motive behind our inner critical dialogue, because it can help us see it in a brand-new light.

The surprising motive of your inner critic

An interesting thing happens when you disengage from the chess match with your inner monologue and stop trying to dispute each utterance of the critic, and instead look at its motives. When you ask the question that we did earlier, of "What purpose does the critic serve?" and look more deeply at the theme that runs through all that hurtful and painful criticism, you may find the last thing you expected.

REMEMBER

It may be hard to believe at first, given the outright nastiness and hurtfulness of the critic, but it is actually *trying to protect you and keep you safe!*

You may be shocked to read that last line, but you may want to pause before you dismiss it. When you see how the critic likes to tell you not to attempt things, or risk things, or make changes, or explore new things, it uses your hot buttons to keep you from trying them. When you consider taking a risk to start a business, for example, and your critic begins to point out all the times you failed at other, similar things, or tells you how you are poorly suited to be an entrepreneur, it is using the most painful method possible to make sure you don't take the risk. Not because it isn't a good idea, but because it doesn't want you to feel the pain of potential failure or struggle.

I find it easiest to grasp this concept by thinking of our inner critic as a completely inept and overwhelmed parent who has few skills to manage the incredible stresses of parenting. Picture a young, single, first-time mom whose husband has left her and who is struggling financially, having to live in a rough neighborhood, with little other support to raise her daughter. Parenting is a huge challenge for those with ample resources, but in this case, she's barely hanging on. She wants the best for her daughter but has no time for lofty aspirations or dreams because she is busy trying to protect the two of them and provide for their daily needs. When her daughter wanders out the front door, she screams to get her back inside because she fears for her daughter's safety. When her daughter brings home a poor math test score, her intense desire for her daughter's success to transcend her meager existence outweighs her greater wisdom, and she demands to know why she "only" got a B on her test instead of an A.

You can picture the scenario. The mother is deeply motivated by her desire to keep her daughter safe and to assure her success in life, but the way she ends up going about it can be painful in the short term. Your critic is like that mom, simply trying to prevent you from having pain, from experiencing the sting of failure or making mistakes that will make life hard for you in some way. The inner critic is actually like an over-protective parent who would rather have you not try to walk than to experience what it is like to fall down and pick yourself up. If your father told you not to try out for the football team because you're "not nearly strong enough to make the team," he was trying to help you avoid the disappointment of not being picked, or of playing and failing in some way. The motive is compassionate and kind, but the means turns out to be hurtful and limiting.

As I mention earlier, for some people who have had particularly difficult early life experiences or traumatic childhoods, their inner critic may not be similarly motivated by their safety, but instead simply be a result of an abusive caregiver acting out their pain and shame. If this applies to you, your inner critic may not have any redeeming value whatsoever, and you may want to tread lightly in the exercise ahead.

When you look at the inner critic in this new light (and the whispering critic and the inner trickster are doing the same, just using less harsh and obvious means), you can begin to see the experience of inner criticism differently. It also allows you to begin to open up space for another inner dialogue from another part of yourself.

Specifically, in addition to an inner critic, we also have an inner compassionate self that also wants us to be safe and to thrive but operates via very different means. This compassionate voice provides unconditional self-acceptance and would like to support us in making change or moving in new directions, not because there is something wrong with us as we are (which is where the critic may focus), but because it wants the best for us.

If we want to make a change in a behavior that is not in our best interest in the long term such as smoking or overeating, instead of berating us for doing it, it urges us to make change because it wants us to be healthy and to avoid harming ourselves. Like a dear friend who wants us to be healthy and vibrant and happy, this inner compassionate part of ourselves is motivated by a positive intention, rather than the fear tactics and intimidation of the inner critic. (Richard Schwartz has developed Internal Family Systems Therapy around the idea that we are made up of a variety of parts like this, and his work has inspired this approach to working with the critic.)

This all leads to the inevitable conclusion that the inner critic, like the overwhelmed parent, actually has a good intention but really terrible technique. When we begin to see the critic as our inept but well-meaning guardian, we can alter our stance toward its presence and its words. The old saying "love the sinner but hate the sin" may apply here. Would it be possible for you to actually acknowledge and thank the inner critic for trying to keep you safe, even though its methods were hurtful and actually inhibited your ability to make change? The following exercise begins to explore this territory within by looking at behavioral change and seeing how this new approach may open up new possibilities for you to make such change happen in your life.

Practice: Compassionate motivation for making change

This reflective exercise explores the difference between motivating a behavioral change using self-criticism versus self-compassion and is largely based on the exercise entitled Motivating Ourselves with Compassion from the Mindful Self-Compassion program. As an exercise in an eight-week course, it necessarily has to be kept relatively short, but as you embark upon this exercise in this book, you are encouraged to take your time and pause along the way to allow yourself adequate time to reflect on the prompts and to be willing to explore what comes up.

Working with the inner critic can be emotionally challenging for a lot of people, especially those with histories of trauma or mistreatment. As always, give yourself permission to move slowly and patiently through the steps, taking breaks as needed. Even disengaging entirely from the exercise, if that is called for, is totally appropriate and a reflection of your capacity to be self-compassionate. I strongly encourage you to exercise that capacity whenever you need it. And if your inner critic is the harsh, internalized voice of someone who traumatized you in the past or meant you harm, you may even want to consider skipping this exercise altogether. It is entirely up to you to decide what you need.

If you are choosing to proceed through the exercise, then gather a pen and paper (or keyboard and screen) to make some notes along the way.

When you are ready, take some time to settle into your experience of this moment just as it is, and into your body and mind just as they are. Give yourself a little time to simply *be* and invite yourself to be patient and kind toward yourself in this process.

Identifying a behavior to change

Now call to mind some behavior that you would like to change, perhaps choosing something that you routinely beat yourself up about. Try to come up with a behavior that is actually causing problems (or *could* cause problems in the future) but is mildly or moderately problematic, as opposed to something that is extremely harmful.

Keep in mind that a behavior is something that is within your grasp to change, so don't choose a characteristic or feature, like big feet or a speech impediment, that is difficult or impossible to change. Some examples of behaviors you may consider include not exercising enough, eating junk food, being quick to lose patience, not meditating enough, or not saving money the way you would like.

Write down a behavior that you would like to change and that you typically try to change through self-criticism. You may also make note of the problems that the behavior is causing you (aside from the self-criticism that it may provoke).

Finding the self-critical voice

Once you have noted the problematic behavior, write down how you typically react when you find yourself doing the behavior. How does your inner critic chime in at these moments? What *words* does the critic use? Can you hear or feel the *tone* of the inner critic at these times? There may not even be words but just an overall sense of coldness or disappointment when you find yourself behaving this way. How does a critical attitude express itself in you? Do you have a felt sense in your body of how it feels to disappoint or anger your inner critic in this way?

Taking a moment to switch your perspective, see if you can get in touch with the part of you that *feels criticized*. What does it feel like inside of you to receive this harsh message or messages?

If you'd like to at this time, give yourself some compassion for how hard it is to be the recipient of such unkind treatment. You could simply verbally acknowledge this hardship by validating the pain, saying, "This is hard," or "This sucks!"

Turning toward your inner critic

As you feel ready, see if you can figuratively turn toward your inner critic with some degree of interest and curiosity. Pause for a few moments and reflect on *why* the criticism may have gone on for so long. Is your inner critic trying to keep you safe from harm in some way? Is it trying to spare you some pain or discomfort, or even trying to *help* you in some way that wasn't obvious before? If so, write down what motivates your harsh inner critic to say what it says to you.

If you can't find any way that your inner critic is trying to help you (sometimes self-criticism has no obvious redeeming value, or is really just the internalized voice of an abuser or a culture that abused or oppressed you), just give yourself some time and space to give yourself compassion for how much you've suffered at the hands of the critic over the years.

But if you were able to identify some way your inner critic was attempting to keep you safe, see if you can acknowledge its efforts. Consider writing down a few words of thanks, a kind of thank-you note to your critic, acknowledging that you realize that its intentions were good. Even though the way the critic has acted is not serving you well anymore, you know it was doing its best.

Finding your compassionate voice

Now that you have given some "airtime" to the self-critical voice, the time has come to make room for a different voice, your compassionate voice, to be heard. You may find it helpful to punctuate this shift by taking a big inhalation, holding it for a moment, and then releasing the breath in a long exhale.

Pause and close your eyes, perhaps placing your hands over your heart or in another soothing or supportive place on your body, feeling the warmth of your own touch. Allow the compassionate side of you to emerge slowly, perhaps in the form of an image, a posture, or simply a warm felt sense of your own kind presence. Take a moment to appreciate this kind part of you.

As you make room for the compassionate voice inside you, recognize that this part of yourself loves and accepts you unconditionally. It is wise and can see you clearly and warmly, recognizing how the behavior that you criticize yourself for is creating problems for you and may be causing you outright harm. This compassionate part of you wants you to make a change, but for very different reasons.

Calling to mind the behavior that you are struggling with, consider how this compassionate side of you views the situation. Your inner compassionate self would like you to try to make a change not because you're unacceptable as you are, but because it wants the best for you. See if you can come up with a phrase that captures the spirit of your compassionate self, or perhaps resembles what a dearly beloved friend or admired confidante might say to you right now. It could be something like: "I love you and I don't want you to suffer," or "I know how much this change means to you and I want you to know I support you. You've got this," or "I see how this hurts you, and I want to help you make a change because I care about you."

Give yourself plenty of time to find just the right phrase, to offer it to yourself with warmth, patience, and understanding, and to let it fully land in your own heart. Receive the gift of your own kindness and take the time to savor and appreciate this heartfelt gift.

Putting the voice into words

Set aside a little time, perhaps 20 to 30 minutes if you have it, to begin to write a short, heartfelt letter to yourself in a compassionate voice that expands upon the sentiments and intention of the phrase you came up with in the preceding section. What emerges from the wish and words "I love you and I don't want you to suffer"? What are the words that *you* need to hear that will support you in making a meaningful change in your own behavior . . . your own life?

Sometimes finding words for a letter like this can be difficult at first. You may find that you can jump-start the process by beginning to imagine the words that would naturally flow from your own heart if you were encouraging and supporting a dear friend who was facing a similar challenge. Once you get started, let the words flow. Don't worry about perfect grammar, sentence construction, or spelling; just let the words and the wishes come. You can always refine it later or even rewrite the compassionate letter to yourself again and again.

As a final step, find a point where you can let go of the search and reflection and give yourself the heartfelt gift of your own wishes by reading what you wrote and really taking it all in. Even if you had difficulty finding just the right words, offer yourself what you came up with and honor your intention in starting this process. As with all the rest of the practice of self-compassion, give yourself permission to walk slowly so you go farther. When you set an intention to make change and point yourself in that valued direction, over time new habits will form, words will flow, and you will notice change little by little.

Inquiring: What did you discover?

As always, please don't feel pressure to come to any quick conclusions or pronouncements about this exercise. Let it settle, let it work within you, and see what emerges over time. But for now, consider what you discovered in doing this exercise. For example, consider asking yourself the following questions:

>> Were you able to identify how your inner critic expresses itself?

>> What was it like to give compassion to the part of you that feels criticized?

>> Were you able to identify any way at all that your critical inner voice was trying to keep you safe or help you in some way?

>> How was it to thank your inner critic for trying to help?

>> Were you able to contact the inner compassionate part of yourself?

>> What did you notice about the impact of saying compassionate wishes to yourself about making the change?

This process of turning toward, acknowledging, and even thanking the inner critic for its service can sound both simple and silly at the same time, but it also has the potential to be profoundly transformative. In other words, you may have found it actually quite difficult to do, and it may have stirred up some strong emotions.

Besides the coincidence that the next chapters focus upon encountering and working with difficult emotions, the point here is that you have the luxury of time to explore exercises like this at your own pace and as shallowly or deeply as you choose, based upon what you need. Please don't rush and don't feel like any of this needs to be "mastered" (whatever that means anyway); instead, continue with your sense of adventure and curiosity and give it all time to play out. Remember you have had a lifetime to develop into the person you are, with the habits you have and the preferences and tastes that you possess.

REMEMBER

Don't expect everything to fall into place in one pass, and don't assume that a habit of a lifetime will change in a day. The important thing is that you are beginning to chart a new course, and the rest will follow with time, patience, and a lot of kindness and compassion.

Chapter **10**

Encountering Difficult Emotions

S ometimes during the Mindful Self-Compassion course, I let people know that the next session is focused on difficult emotions and then say, "You're in luck because if you don't have any of these, you can skip that session!" The same is true for you and these next two chapters, but something tells me you will still be sticking around.

The joke, of course, is that difficult emotions like sadness, anger, anxiety, grief, loneliness, and jealousy are simply a part of being human. By now, if you've been following along over the previous chapters, you can see a recurring theme of self-compassion being primarily a practice of learning to fully embrace all of what it means to be human, as opposed to eliminating or avoiding certain parts of your human experience. Self-compassion invites you to embrace your human imperfection, your moments of suffering, your deep connection to all other humans, and the challenges you feel in contact with others, just to name a few aspects of our common humanity. If you are still on a mission to find out how to eliminate these things from your life and unwilling to explore the possibility of accepting them as part of the richness of being you, you may have a hard time with the chapters ahead. If you are cautiously skeptical and considering the possibility that embracing yourself, warts and all, might be worth a try, then you're right where you ought to be.

This willingness to encounter and explore difficult emotions is not easy work and not always pleasant, but virtually always fruitful. As I note in Chapter 2, you are best equipped to engage in this work if you have created a safe and brave inner space from which to operate. In the pages ahead, you explore the nature of these emotions and have an opportunity to discover the different ways in which it is possible for you to encounter, observe, and navigate the arising of emotions in a more satisfying and fruitful way.

REMEMBER

You are making a bold and brave step by being willing to wade into these waters. (It's all part of the "adventure" of self-compassion, remember?) It may feel unfamiliar and even a little scary, but little by little you will be developing the capacity within you to travel in this emotional environment with a greater sense of purpose, harmony, and maybe even ease. Some would call this developing emotional intelligence, resilience, affect tolerance, or even equanimity, but as Shakespeare said: "A rose by any other name would smell as sweet."

Where Are You Now? Stages of Self-Compassion Progress

In order to proceed into the territory of difficult emotions, it's worthwhile to know exactly where you are in this process of learning self-compassion. I know from experience that the way you approach these feelings determines your likelihood of success in finding new ways of being with them. Think about the ways in which you learn new things, especially multifaceted and challenging things, and you begin to see that your attitude makes all the difference.

For example, many years ago as a young adult, newly in love with my fiancé at the time, I was coaxed into a vacation with her family at a beautiful lake in Montana (where I had lived). I say "coaxed" because camping is not my favorite thing, and waterskiing was to be one of the activities. I was never a thrill-seeker as a youngster (the Ferris wheel scared me to death, and I always chose the horses on a merry-go-round that were fixed and didn't go up and down), so the prospect of whizzing across the lake being towed by a motorboat was not intriguing to me. However, I was in love and wanting to please, so when the time came to try waterskiing, I agreed. "What could go wrong?" I thought (which are famous last words, right up there with "Watch this. Here, hold my beer").

I was given more advice than I could really process before being unceremoniously dumped into the lake and left to scramble to grab the rope and get myself maneuvered into the skis and into position. Everyone said, "Whatever you do, do *not* pull on the rope but let it pull you, instead!" So I perched in the water, ski tips up, tense, nervous but a bit excited too. I heard the engine rev up and saw the boat begin to gain speed and felt my heart rate increase as the rope tightened. I was ready and excited by this point, certain that I would be a terrific water-skier in no time. It was exhilarating to be in that place, so as I felt the tug of the boat, what did I do? Well of course, I pulled back to get up on top of the water and show my stuff!

Big mistake, as this prompted a ridiculous show of awkwardness and incompetence as I tumbled head over heels back into the lake, let go of the rope, and flailed about with the skis still on my feet and my pride slowly sinking to the bottom of the lake. In my resulting embarrassment, I resolved never to try this again, certain that I was a failure and incapable of learning to waterski. I was dejected and disillusioned and ready to quit.

I did quit for a while and spent time in the boat watching others having a great time. Finally, I tried it again, but this time I listened to the advice, let the boat do the work, and immediately was gliding across the water with great abandon and the biggest smile you ever saw plastered across my face.

The reason for sharing this embarrassing experience is to highlight that it parallels how most people find grasping a complex new skill or ability. Three typical stages of this process are evident in my story in regard to learning self-compassion: striving, disillusionment, and radical acceptance. These are natural processes that have to do with exploring new emotional territory, finding the edges or boundaries of that territory (which is likely to involve missteps and stumbles), and then discovering just the right pace and space to suit your needs and achieve your objective. I discuss each stage in the following sections.

The early stage: Striving

It is only natural to approach new things with enthusiasm, optimism, and a fair amount of anticipation, and such is the experience of most people who pursue training in self-compassion. Think about it: It took some of these qualities (or at least a healthy amount of curiosity) to get you to purchase this book and read this far. This is a very good thing because when we are excited and curious, our minds and hearts are open, and we are receptive to new things. This is the excitement (with some trepidation) that I was experiencing prior to my first go-round with waterskiing.

Whatever your pathway to this point, you may have found that something you have discovered in the realm of self-compassion has been helpful, and you may have even had enthusiastic thoughts like "This is it! I have finally found the solution to all my problems!" or similar sentiments. Maybe you put your hands on your heart in the Self-Compassion Break (covered in Chapter 1) and felt a rush of ease and relief that you had never felt before. Perhaps you had trouble sleeping one night and decided to do a short self-compassion practice and next thing you knew, it was morning. So far, so good. You're happy and content, and you feel you've found the answer to the question you have been asking forever: "How do I feel better?" You are in love with self-compassion, and like any new love, the feelings are pretty darn good.

And then the next night comes and you are tossing and turning, and the thought occurs to you to try the same meditation as a new technique to help you fall asleep . . . and nothing happens. Nothing. You're still lying there wide-eyed and sleepless. Or you practice a Self-Compassion Break in a tough situation when you want to feel better, but when you put your hands on your heart you feel . . . nothing. No rush of joy or ease or anything much at all. "What's up? What's wrong?" you think. "It worked yesterday for some reason, but it's not working today." This is the experience of striving, that it "works" right up until it doesn't, and then you are left feeling disillusioned.

The "muddy middle" of disillusionment

When we begin to strive and rush and try to identify the "secret weapon" or the "perfect technique," a strange and frustrating thing happens: It dissolves like cotton candy (much like my vision of being a masterful water-skier by pulling myself to the lake's surface). Just as you think you've found "the thing," you lose it again. This is understandable in the case of self-compassion. I share more about that in a moment, but for now let it sink in.

A meditation teacher once said, "All techniques are destined to fail." What he was referring to is that a *technique* is defined as "an efficient way of doing or achieving something." Just fine if you are a surgeon, but not so helpful with something more ephemeral like self-compassion. This is because "techniques" are just (seemingly) clever ways that we think we've developed to alter or manipulate our actual experience in the moment, to make pain go away or to help ourselves feel better. I believe I have previously established that changing our moment-to-moment experience is fruitless and impossible.

What we are really doing with our "clever techniques" is a really slick, slightly subversive new form of resistance, which of course just gives us more of the same (remember "what you resist, persists?"). We find ourselves stuck in a mire of our own making, getting more and more frustrated and disillusioned at this practice that seemed so promising only moments before. We are wielding self-compassion like a sword to slay the dragon of our particular difficult experience, and by now you know how battling that particular dragon is a fool's gambit. In other words, you don't want to go there.

The really challenging part of the disillusionment phase is that it very easily ensnares those of us who are very self-critical, perfectionistic, and harboring a lot of shame and self-doubt. In other words, confident people who are learning to dance (for example) can tolerate some instances of stepping on their partner's toes or stumbling on the dance floor by seeing it as all part of the learning process and inevitable as they grow and develop as dancers. But the sort of people drawn to learning to be self-compassionate (in other words, people who are lacking in self-compassion) are particularly vulnerable to moments of perceived failure like this phase of disillusionment, because they are much quicker to spiral down into shame and overwhelm.

If this applies to you, then it may be helpful for you to simply know that the potholes on your journey are deeper and more treacherous than the ones that others face, and if you fall into them, they still are not bottomless pits, so you can step back out of them with experience and a lot of self-compassion. You may begin to have thoughts like "I'm just not cut out for self-compassion," or "This is just another example of what's wrong with me, because I can't even do *this*."

This is not unusual, and if you are feeling disillusionment, it is a direct result of your initial striving and wanting to be more kind to yourself. When disillusionment brings you to your knees in despair and hopelessness, this is, paradoxically, when progress toward more self-compassion *actually* begins.

The bearable lightness of radical acceptance

The ironic truth of self-compassion is that progress really begins when we let go of the concept of making progress. When we let go of striving to get somewhere or to achieve mastery of self-compassion or to change our experience, we are beginning to refine and correct our intention for practicing it in the first place. I achieved a moment of radical acceptance when I let go of needing to get myself to the surface of the water and instead let the boat, physics, and the skis do the work (which is counterintuitive, to be sure). Rather than becoming fixated on the *outcome* of self-compassion practice, we instead just simply engage in the practice for its own sake without regard for achieving anything in particular beyond a routinely warm, supportive, and strong inner support for ourselves and our experience.

To enter into the stage of Radical Acceptance, we often let go of old habits of "doing" and engage in simply "being" instead, a shift that is hard for us busy, hardworking, goal-oriented humans. We rarely do things for their own sake because we are instrumental beings, meaning that we are always doing something to achieve something or get somewhere or improve ourselves. But when we give up on what meditation teacher Rob Sharples says is "the subtle aggression of self-improvement" and realize that we do not need to be fixed or improved, possibility arises. Just as I noted early on, if it's a struggle, it's not self-compassion. Trying to change our experience is a struggle, trying to make unpleasant feelings go away is a struggle, and avoiding pain is a struggle.

REMEMBER

In self-compassion practice, we are guided by a simple yet radical principle: When we struggle, we give ourselves compassion not to feel better but because we feel bad. I invite you to pause and take this statement in, as it will guide and support you the rest of the way in this journey. It bears repeating: *When we struggle, we give ourselves compassion not to feel better but because we feel bad.* In other words, we don't practice self-compassion to get rid of our pain but simply because it is hard to feel the pain, which of course is part of being human.

I have always appreciated the analogy of caring for a child with the flu. We bring the child more blankets, apply a cool washcloth to their feverish forehead, and cuddle with them not because we believe we are treating the influenza virus, but simply because it is uncomfortable to have the flu. We have no illusions of making the flu go away, and this is the attitude that we need to bring to self-compassion. Can we simply comfort, soothe, or encourage ourselves *simply because we are facing hardship,* and let go of needing to make the hardship go away? In these moments, we can feel the pain, but we also feel the love *holding* the pain, and that makes it more bearable.

As another meditation teacher, Rob Nairn, has put it: "The goal of practice is to become a compassionate mess." It means coming to terms with being fully human, often struggling, uncertain, confused, and fearful at times, with great patience, curiosity and compassion. No matter how difficult our life circumstances become, or how lost or overwhelmed or imperfect we may feel, we can still be mindful of what is arising, remember our shared common humanity, and give ourselves what we need. This is the essence of self-compassion, and it is always within our grasp, including when we fear that we have drifted very far from it in a moment of suffering.

A brief reflection to find where you are

Take a few moments to reflect on the following three prompts before moving forward in this chapter:

1. **Consider what stage of the cycle you may be in right now (striving, disillusionment, or radical acceptance).**

   Keep in mind that you will cycle through these three stages in your self-compassion practice.

2. **If you are struggling in certain areas of your practice, is there by any chance an opportunity to reduce that struggle?**

   Maybe there is something you could let go of, or allow, to give a little more space and time to your practice to unfold in its own way, without needing to force it or make something happen.

3. **In the midst of whatever stage you are in, can you possibly bring a bit more kindness and compassion to yourself in this adventure?**

   Maybe there are some words of encouragement, support, or understanding that you may need to hear just now or at some future point if you face some difficulty. Consider writing them down for yourself to refer to later.

These three stages of progress in self-compassion practice are not "one and done" stages, and the process is not always linear, although it can be at times. Most often, it is best to think of it as a circular process (like points on a bicycle wheel), which you cycle through over time. You find yourself striving, which leads you into disillusionment, and when you let go of the struggle, you find yourself in radical acceptance. But being human and fallible, you will inevitably find yourself slipping back into striving again when you have a pleasant experience and you forget the earlier lesson and try to prolong it, and the cycle continues. But like points on a bicycle wheel that go around and around, the wheel is also rolling forward at the same time, so you are always "here again in a different place." Your job is to do your best to go along for the ride and let the practice do the work, the way I let the boat, physics, and skis do the work for me way back on that lake.

The Practice of Meeting Your Emotions

When I first started teaching mindfulness, many of the participants in my courses were people with chronic pain. These were often desperate people who had tried many things to contend with their condition over the years, and to some extent, mindfulness was a last resort. If I could coax them into exploring mindfulness and the practice of actually opening up to the experience of their pain alongside their experience of all aspects of life, they were often incredibly grateful to have learned to practice mindfulness. The research data supports this finding in many ways as well.

But by far the most common sorts of comments I got from these individuals with chronic pain in the first weeks of the course were related to this novel idea of opening up to their experience of pain. They were skeptical, to say the least (much as you may be about opening up to difficult emotions), and many reported that when they did allow the pain to be present and they included it in the field of their awareness as they meditated, they were *absolutely certain* that the pain increased in these moments.

Physiologically speaking, simply paying attention to pain is not likely to impact the *sensation* of pain. But it most certainly can strengthen the overall *experience* of pain, because it now occupies center stage in your awareness — where you may very well have been working quite hard to avoid and deny the pain, in some cases for many years. The same is true of challenging emotions in that when we endeavor to turn toward them and gently, patiently encounter them after years of running away, avoiding, medicating, or otherwise resisting them, our emotional pain can initially increase. While I'm not a huge fan of the cliché, in this case it is accurate, if a bit harsh: "No pain, no gain."

But here's the good news: In order to begin to practice self-compassion and to begin to shift our relationship with our troubling and painful emotions, we do *not* need to face them in their full intensity like knights slaying fire-breathing dragons. Again, like the weights at the gym, we can begin by lifting the lightest weight and work with it until we aspire to the next one. We only have to *touch* painful emotions in order to slowly develop a practice of self-compassion to work with them.

But before I ask you to get on board and explore just *how* to do this, I'd like you to pause and consider *why* you may want to meet your emotions in this way and what the potential benefits may be for doing so. If you are going to embark on this particular adventure, you need to have a sense of what you may discover.

"This being human is a guest house"

The preceding section heading is the first line of the quintessential mindfulness poem "The Guest House" by Jalaluddin Rumi. He goes on to equate our human experience of emotions to being like visitors to our guest house, swooping in and out, disrupting our plans, and he suggests that we "meet them at the door laughing, and invite them in." How does that sound to you? I'm guessing you're not excited about that whole approach, but let's see if I can change your mind.

How do you feel about your feelings? Has anyone ever asked you that question? It's worth considering because it forms the foundation of how you meet your feelings when they arise. If you see them as annoying distractions from the business at hand of being a human, you will respond one way. If you find some feelings to be something like a tsunami rushing in to wash you away, your stance will necessarily be different. If you are confused by your feelings, or disgusted by or ashamed of some of them, all of this is important information that can inform and enlighten you in your quest to find a more harmonious relationship with yourself in experiencing the whole range of human emotion.

In most cases, our attitude toward our feelings varies by the feeling, so it may be instructive to you to go through the following list and write down what your attitude is toward each of these when or if you experience them. Imagine a scenario in which you felt each of these emotions and see if you can pinpoint how you responded to the arrival of this particular visitor to your guest house:

Feeling	Attitude
Frustration	
Anger	
Sadness	
Grief	
Disappointment	
Fear	
Confusion	
Guilt	
Shame	
(Add your own here)	

Your attitude matters

If your stance on any particular emotion is something other than simple calm abiding presence, equanimity, and willingness to meet it (and it usually isn't), you may actually consider whether the way you feel about that emotion actually magnifies or intensifies your experience of that emotion. For example, if you know the experience of anxiety and your response is to resist or battle it in some way that often leads to panic, then perhaps you are playing into the equation of "pain times resistance equals suffering." In this case, the "pain" is the initial emotion of anxiety, the resistance is your attitude, and the result is panic (an even more intense experience of anxiety). This is not intended to blame you for your panic (or other outcomes) but to help you see the chain of events that typically unfold when we are visited by strong difficult emotions, and to give a clue as to where we might intervene to break that chain for our own well-being.

Keep in mind that the problem here is not the emotions themselves, because they are a part of being human. Emotions have evolved for humans to help us rapidly reorganize our various resources to prepare for whatever life throws at us on a daily basis. In Chapter 2, we explore the function of anxiety or fear as a trigger to our sympathetic nervous system that alerts us to potential danger so that we can respond appropriately. But using that simple example, where anxiety is the equivalent of a car alarm going off when a thief breaks a window in your car, you would want to take some sort of action in that scenario. You might call the police, shout at the criminal, or run after him if you are particularly brave (or foolhardy).

But imagine feeling the wave of anxiety rise when your car alarm goes off and immediately scrambling to suppress and avoid it instead of responding. This could easily lead to a panic attack in which you are frozen in fear, unable to do anything productive, and feel overwhelmed by terror, frustration, and helplessness. Resistance of the feeling in this case (and really, all cases) is not only unhelpful, it is actually counterproductive because it also makes you feel terrible. The main function of the anxiety (to signal danger) is totally overridden by your resistance and the resulting panic, and having anxiety just feels like a cruel joke with no redeeming value.

Finding hidden value in difficult emotions

Beyond simply allowing emotions to function as they were originally intended — to prepare and alert us to situations in which we find ourselves — there are some additional benefits to being willing to explore our emotional reactions. Think of these as "bonus gifts" that you may not have anticipated in all of this (and for heaven's sake, with all this suffering I'm suggesting you endure, you could use a nice, pleasant discovery for a change!). Many discoveries can be made when we are willing to look beyond the fire and fury of strong emotions to their source.

This calls to mind the big scene in *The Wizard of Oz* when Dorothy and her companions are gathered in the chambers of the "Great and Powerful Oz." They are cowering at the booming voice and bursts of flames emanating from the "wizard" right up until Toto pulls back the curtain to reveal a sad little man pulling levers and speaking into a microphone. "Pay no attention to that man behind the curtain!" Oz says. But the ruse has been revealed, and this leads to an honest and fruitful revealing of good intention, faith in human nature, hope, self-confidence, and self-compassion that sends everyone on their way. You can think of me as Toto pulling back that curtain and consider at least two things you may discover there, which I cover in the next two sections.

A part of you needs your love and attention

Emotions are the body's way of alerting you to certain situations, challenges, or events that are worth your attention. Without emotions we would be relying solely upon logic and calculation (think of Mr. Spock of *Star Trek* fame). In this scenario, imagine that Mr. Spock's wife has just left him (presuming he would have even wanted to be in a relationship to begin with, but perhaps the pragmatic Mr. Spock could see that it would be helpful for procreation). In a situation that may be devastating for humans, Mr. Spock would note the change in status, file the divorce paperwork, and take her name off the mailbox, calmly and coolly. Now imagine how a human would respond in this situation. Much differently, I would assume.

Now, there are probably really difficult periods in your life when you would have preferred to be a bit more Spock-like to get through them, but then you realize that these hard times are the price we pay for the good ones. We grieve the loss of a partner because they meant something to us, they once brought us joy and we valued them, so it hurts when they are not there. When we recognize this, then we can see that in a situation like the loss of a loved one, there is a part of us that is in pain and needs empathy, comfort, and soothing.

The emotion of grief is your body's way of saying that part of you has been deeply wounded, the way physical pain can be the sign of an injury to your body. When you feel physical pain, you can choose to ignore it, push through it, and deny it, but that can have disastrous consequences. Running on an ankle that has been sprained can lead to further, and even permanent, injury. Resisting grief can complicate it and make it last far longer than the natural process of grieving typically takes.

People often want to find the shortcut to getting through the healing process as quickly as possible, but in the end, we only have one way of influencing the natural healing process, and we probably don't want to do that. We can either let it run its natural course, or we can fiddle with it and prolong and complicate it. Those are our only two options. It's hard to stomach sometimes, but with emotional healing (like physical healing), the only way out is through.

But before you grudgingly take this on as a burden or a necessary evil of having emotions, consider what "through" really means. Could you open up to the possibility that if you have suffered a loss (as one example), some part of you has been wounded? Perhaps you could respond to this wounding as you would to a sprained ankle, by pausing, noticing, and tending to the injury with an attitude of kindness and compassion. Maybe you could ask this part of you, like you might ask your ankle, "What do you need just now?" In the case of an ankle, you may need rest, ice, pain medicine, just a warm caress, or extra support; in the case of your wounded heart, you may need the emotional equivalents of these.

When you can see emotions not as an adversary but as your faithful alarm system letting you know that some part of you needs attention, you begin to alter your stance toward those emotions. To return to the car alarm analogy, imagine that rather than cursing the alarm when it goes off (the way you might dread the arising of a painful emotion), you respond to the break-in that the alarm is alerting you to. The challenge, when you feel the emotion arising, is to remain present and discover what needs your compassionate attention. I explore this practice further in Chapter 12 in talking about the "hard emotions" like anger, but even the "softer" ones like sadness, fear, or longing are signals that some part of us needs our loving attention.

TIP

The next time you notice a painful emotion arising, ask yourself, "What part of me is calling for my attention and what does it need?" It's important to note that some emotions call for soothing or comforting of ourselves, but others call for protecting, providing, or motivating some part of ourselves. If we are feeling oppressed or mistreated, then a part of ourselves needs our loving but firm support, encouragement, and even a friendly nudge toward action. Giving space to the parts of ourselves that need our attention is a deep and powerful way of gently becoming kinder and more compassionate with ourselves overall.

The treasure map of emotional pain

The alerting function of emotions, as I note earlier, can be very helpful if we actually heed that alert and look closer. There is actually much more to discover when we take this radical (and admittedly, sometimes difficult) attitude toward our emotional life. Beyond alerting us to a part of ourselves that needs our attention, if we are inclined, we can go a little bit deeper and find additional "treasure" to be considered.

One way that emotional pain is different from physical pain is that when we say our ankle is injured and acknowledge it and tend to it, that's it. There's nothing further to do. However, when a part of our emotional self is wounded, there are deeper roots that can be tended to.

Take the example of your boss overlooking you for a big promotion at work in favor of a co-worker who is newer and less experienced but tends to be quite visible and vocal in the office whenever the boss is paying attention. You may feel betrayed, disregarded, or unappreciated by this oversight. Regardless of the circumstances, you can offer yourself compassion for the way you are feeling in that moment, just because you are feeling it. This is the response you just explored, but there is also an opportunity to honor what is underneath your pain in this situation. What has happened is that your core values of hard work, dedication, perseverance, and loyalty have been violated by this move by your boss.

Often our suffering (as I discuss in Chapter 8) results from ways in which we are out of alignment with our core values, so when a situation (like this promotion) moves us away from our values, we feel the pain (or hear the emotional "alarm").

This is not just an interesting intellectual exercise. It also gives us some opportunities to respond to painful situations like this one with more than anger, outrage, and a desire to assign blame. It's also an opportunity to strengthen our resolve to follow our values and to celebrate these core aspects of our identity. In situations like the one I describe, it is easiest to focus all your wrath on the boss and their decision, blaming them for what you see as a bad move, and perhaps even speaking up or challenging them. There are indeed times when this sort of outward action may be called for and justified, but at the same time, you can honor your deeply held core values and even have some pride in your values and your commitment to them. If you truly appreciate your values of hard work, dedication, perseverance, and loyalty, then you may need to take action where you are or find a new job or situation that aligns with them. This is a constructive and self-compassionate approach to the problem versus either suffering passively in silence or lashing out impulsively and risking your job.

This response of recognizing and honoring your core values when you are feeling difficult emotions is especially helpful when you feel powerless over a situation. For example, if you are feeling outrage over a political leader's racist actions that violate your values of justice and equity, you may feel unable to change a big societal issue like this. You probably don't have direct contact with this leader or any influence over their choice of policies. But when you identify your deep commitment to justice and fairness, you can consider ways that you can renew that commitment with local action to align with those values. You can do your part in a larger cause because you are in tune with what is important to you. This is often expressed in the saying "Think globally, and act locally." So often we are so focused on the global (like focusing on the boss in the preceding example) that we feel overwhelmed and powerless, but when we affirmatively assert our commitment to our own core values, suddenly we have freedom, opportunity, and a chance to find some ease in the situation.

As you did earlier in this chapter, it is worthwhile for you to continue the process you may have started in Chapter 8 and look for the "buried treasure" of your core values in the moments of suffering and difficult emotions you encounter in your life. The next time you notice a difficult emotion rising up, you can tend to the part of you that is in pain but also ask yourself: "Which of my core values has been challenged or violated in this situation?" If you can identify a core value or two, give yourself some time to reflect on these core values, to appreciate yourself for holding them, and even to consider how you can better align with them going forward. Let the emotion be the X on the treasure map of your heart: There lies the fortune.

The Five Stages of Encountering Emotions

At this point, my hope is that you are at least a little more inclined to want to find your way into a different relationship with your emotions, especially the more challenging ones. As I note at the beginning, one piece of good news is that you don't have to rush in, embrace, and accept every emotion that arises. You don't necessarily have to "meet them at the door laughing and invite them in!" as Rumi would say, especially if they are "a crowd of sorrows." In order to begin to shift your response to these feelings, all you have to do is gently touch the suffering, the way you would touch a pan on the stove to see if it is hot — lightly and gingerly (at first) as you tend to your own sense of safety. The emotions show up out of the blue sometimes, like a big wave on the beach, but you still retain the capacity to meet them in a way that suits your needs.

One helpful way of thinking about your challenging emotions is to follow Rumi's example and imagine them like unwelcome visitors to your home. Perhaps your spouse has a family obligation to take care of a beloved uncle of his who is down on his luck. Uncle Seth is kind of unpleasant, if you really stop to think about it. He's got a drinking problem, personal hygiene is not a top priority for him, and he has a habit of spouting offensive opinions on the news, the state of affairs in the world, and virtually everything else that comes up in conversation. But Uncle Seth is a man with good intentions, and he's family, so your husband has agreed with his siblings to take him on for a short time. You don't like him, he's hard to handle, and you'd prefer that he was somewhere else, but there he is: on your living room couch and sleeping in your den. Uncle Seth is now the human equivalent to your feelings of shame. Unwelcome, unappreciated, painful, but here.

What are your options in this situation? Your husband is committed to doing the right thing by his uncle and his family, and you appreciate his good heart and commitment to family, but this is hard to take. You could argue and wheedle and cajole him into giving Uncle Seth the boot, but that is unlikely to result in a change, and it will antagonize your husband and make a difficult situation worse. You don't want to leave, either, but the thought has crossed your mind. The same is true of your shame: You can bargain, you can resist, or you can try to run away, but again, this will make the situation worse, as you already know from your experience of trying to control your emotions.

What about taking a revolutionary approach instead? What if you begin, in very small increments, to simply allow Uncle Seth to be there because he already is? In the immortal words of Rick to police boss Louis in the movie *Casablanca*, "I think this is the beginning of a beautiful friendship." It won't be a friendship at first, and it may never progress entirely to that level, but such is our experience of the people we meet. At first they are strangers, and later they become friends.

Now consider that the emotions are Uncle Seth and he is making his way up your front walkway. Chris Germer and Christine Brähler have identified five different stages of acceptance of emotions that correspond to different ways of greeting Uncle Seth when he arrives at your door. Each of these stages involves the application of a subtle and refined form of mindfulness and self-compassion. See if you can detect these at work as I lay them out here.

Resisting: Slamming the door

Slamming the door and shouting at Uncle Seth, "Go away! Nobody's home! We don't want you here!" is often our gut-level response to unpleasantness of any kind. We struggle against the feeling because, after all, who wants to feel uncomfortable? You know that having Uncle Seth in your house will be a trial of your patience and an offense to your sensibilities as well as your values of peace and tranquility. It is a natural response to want to resist what is obnoxious, and this is a natural human defense mechanism designed to prevent harm and to keep danger away — if it is really danger.

We are equipped to resist as part of our threat-defense system (it's the defense part), and we can appreciate this capacity, even if it doesn't always serve us when we're not mindful about it. At times our nervous system says "Danger!" when in fact the situation is not dangerous. In the classic example, if you peer into the shadows of your yard and see a long thin shape and your mind says "snake!" your heart will race, and you may step back hurriedly. It may very well *be* a snake, but then again if you pause and take a look, you might see that it is actually a garden hose. It's worth taking a closer look, which is what I have been saying all along.

Perhaps in this particular example with Uncle Seth, barring the door is not an option, but in other situations the best thing we can do is in fact to resist in the moment. Not as a long-term strategy but as a short-term coping mechanism to navigate or survive the situation. Imagine that you are a surgeon who is about to go into a very delicate and dangerous surgery on a patient and you are visited by a wave of anger over a new hospital policy that you believe is ill-conceived. You (and especially your patient) would do well to just keep that particular outrage standing outside your front door, at least until you have completed the surgery and can deal with it directly.

REMEMBER

Contrary to other *Star Trek* lore, resistance is not always futile; sometimes it serves and protects us. In the unfortunate situation when we are traumatized and victimized by someone with a great deal more power than we have, for example, the only way to protect our delicate psyche may be to resist and deny anything related to the assault. It is how we cope when we have no other means available to us, and it works to a point. These repressed memories that can surface later are locked away so we can continue to survive in difficult circumstances. They may have implications in the future if they are not tended to with the support of a mental health professional, but in the moment they are truly lifesaving. This is one of the many wonders of the human mind and brain.

Exploring: Peering through the peephole

Another tentative but fruitful alternative to slamming the door and pretending you are not home when Uncle Seth arrives is to *explore* from a safe distance in a controlled way, whatever (or whomever) presents itself. In the case of Uncle Seth at your door, you might silently creep up to the door and take a look through the peephole to see just exactly what you are facing. This is what I meant earlier by simply lightly touching the suffering just long enough to gauge its intensity and what it has to say for itself.

Although these stages are presented in order, there is no implication in any of them that you *must* progress through them or process the emotions through to the end. In other words, peering through a crack in the curtains to check out Uncle Seth does not obligate you to go further and let him in. You can give yourself permission not to commit to a full course of action in response to the emotion, and instead take it one step at a time. You always have the option to retreat a step or two if that is what you need.

Being able to gently contact the difficult emotion begins to inform you of what is actually here (garden hose or venomous snake) and can begin to dispel any accumulated emotional baggage that may accompany the emotion. If anxiety arises in a moment and you can briefly touch the anxiety by feeling it in your body, for example, you might disentangle this particular anxiety (perhaps about an upcoming difficult conversation) from the larger tangle of many other anxieties that you have experienced in your life. My own experience is that if I wake up early in the morning (as I am prone to doing sometimes) and find myself anxious over some upcoming responsibility, I will put my hand on my heart and say "just this" to remind me that this one thing is all that needs my attention now, and not all of the "what ifs" and "and thens" that naturally follow when I get anxious.

TIP

The next time you want to try simply touching an arising emotion and peering at it through your own internal peephole, consider taking a moment to settle and ground yourself. Take a few slow, rhythmic breaths and mentally turn toward your body to see if the emotion is manifesting there. This is often a great place to first encounter our emotions (more on this in the next chapter), but once you have contacted the emotion, you might say to yourself "just this," meaning that just noticing and touching it is all that is required. Just this. Let this be enough for now. Just this.

Tolerating: Setting your limits

Simply enduring the presence of an emotion is your next option, and that may very well be where you start with Uncle Seth. You open the door (grudgingly) and allow him into the entryway with his scarily stained knapsack, his muddy shoes, and his ridiculous knit cap with earflaps. You make it clear that he should just stay there, out of the rain for now, and he is not to wander around.

You have probably had that attitude toward some intrusive and persistent emotions that you could no longer resist. Maybe the rising resentment over the outcome of a legal dispute just will not dissipate no matter how much you ignore it, so you are forced to acknowledge its presence. You're not happy about it, but for now it's here. An extension of "just this" is "right now, it's like this." Perhaps that helps you tolerate the presence of this emotion.

I tend to think of tolerating as the tensest of the stages of acceptance of difficult emotions. My jaw clenches when I consider tolerating things, and this is no exception. An uneasy truce has been enacted between you and the unwelcome visitor, and the tension in the silence is so palpable you could cut it with a plastic knife. You try to maintain some steadiness or groundedness in these moments of tolerance. It's not a relaxed or grounded steadiness, but that's okay. The breath can support you in these moments to take the edge off your tension and resistance, as well as help you to maintain some degree of this stability.

The biggest challenge to tolerating is that your human mind can play little tricks on you by implying that there will be an endpoint to whatever you are tolerating. This is actually true of all that we face in life (including emotions), and you know this — that things come and go like the weather and are impermanent — but you have to be careful not to cling to this. Tolerating Uncle Seth in the moment is entirely possible, but if we let our minds creep in and tell us that if we tolerate him in this moment, then he will go away at some particular future moment, our mind has just served up a surreptitious portion of resistance and we may make the whole situation intolerable instead.

REMEMBER

In other words, what I am highlighting here is an important reminder of the message from earlier in this chapter: that we give ourselves compassion not to feel better, but because we feel better. We tolerate our emotions not to change or eliminate them, but to come into more harmonious alignment with them. As soon as we tolerate Uncle Seth solely in the hopes that he will leave soon, he gets the idea that he is welcome to stay as long as he likes. What has happened in this scenario is that toleration has become a form of resistance, and by now you know what happens to things when you resist them . . . they persist.

The fine art of toleration is to stay present in the moment and to practice it in small doses at first, not to get rid of the emotion but to develop the capacity to tolerate it over time. Think of it a little like slowly opening the door of a hot furnace, leaving it open as long as you can tolerate it, and knowing full well at every moment that you can close it again as you need to. Toleration is a kind of transitional way of coming to terms with your challenging emotions.

In the next chapter we put this into practice in a very specific way, but you can get yourself ready for that by experimenting with toleration. You should definitely choose a mild to moderate emotion that visits you periodically and one that you can easily access if you think of it. Maybe call to mind a situation that prompts the emotion and give yourself a window of tolerance (say, 10 seconds) during which you will choose to withstand the heat of that emotion, and then let go of it. Not pushing it away or stuffing it down, but just releasing your focus upon it and perhaps widening your awareness to the space around you, your sense of your body or the soles of your feet. The most important aspect of this brief exercise is to feel a growing confidence that you have the *ability* to shut the furnace door when you need to. You are not cultivating a way of coping with emotion here; you are cultivating a way to simply *start* the process of tolerance. Patience is the key.

Allowing: Letting go

I invite you to do a little experiment with me. If you're willing, slowly bring the teeth of your lower jaw in touch with the teeth of your upper jaw. Notice the subtle tension involved in this simple movement. Then, if you can, begin to squeeze the jaws together and feel the tension grow in the various muscles of your lower face. Hold that squeeze for at least a few seconds (you can use some other muscles in your body if the jaw is not a good choice for you). Hold the tension for as long as you can tolerate it, and then on the next available outbreath, release the tension and the breath and observe how that feels in your body. For me, I notice my shoulders drop, I feel some warmth in my face, and I feel my whole face relax. Your experience may be different, but see if you can let it register in your awareness.

This is the felt sense of allowing, the next stage of encountering our emotions, and the experience is worth taking note of. It is a natural sequel to tolerating, but again, just because you are willing to tolerate an emotion does *not* mean that you are then obligated to allow it. But oh, it has such potential for ease!

The thing is that, initially, allowing an emotion to meander through us, like letting Uncle Seth wander freely around our tidy house, can be an exercise in uneasiness. With Seth we find ourselves hovering behind him, darting ahead to grab that creepy knapsack before it knocks the treasured vase off the shelf, deftly slipping the coaster under his beer before it hits the antique coffee table. But little by little, as we release our clenched fist around the emotion, we can see it moving in us and not *always* "violently sweeping your house empty of its furniture" in Rumi's words. We feel the tension of toleration slowly dissolve and some degree of ease replace it as we come to terms with our emotional visitor. This, like everything else in this practice, takes time, but is well worth the gentle, kind persistence.

I find that sometimes the concept of "acceptance" is a challenging one for people, largely because it is misunderstood, but also because it is mistaken to be something easy, which it is definitely not. People hear "acceptance" but immediately translate it into their minds as "surrender" as if accepting something in the moment is the same as giving up all hope of anything ever being different. Or people say *"just accept it"* as if that is the easiest thing in the world. "*Just accept* that you were fired from your treasured job that supplied all your family's income," or "*Just accept* that you've been sexually harassed and there's nothing you can do about it."

That word "just" literally trivializes everything that comes after it, and in this case shows no respect to the incredible task of coming to terms with some things as they are. So, acceptance is not surrender and it certainly is not easy, but it is quite simple.

REMEMBER

Acceptance is the capacity to accept the reality of the present moment just as it is . . . and that's all, period, full stop. Because of the verbal and emotional baggage that the word "acceptance" carries, I have chosen to use the word "allow" here instead, but both imply the same thing: to simply allow the reality of the moment (and the presence of the emotion) to be what and where it is. In other words: just this.

TIP

A wine connoisseur will take a sip of a new wine and allow it to roll around in the mouth. They are practicing "beginner's mind" as much as possible in this moment by fully encountering the wine and curiously exploring it. This is not an exercise in savoring the wine or luxuriating in it just yet; they are just meeting it fully to see what it offers. There is no smile on their lips or excitement in their eyes; they are practicing equanimity and presence. If you think you may be able to bring this quality of presence to a difficult emotion that is present for you (especially if you can practice first with a milder, more familiar one), see if you can sample this feeling in the same way. You don't have to love it or even like it a little but see if you can simply allow it to present itself fully to the palate of your awareness. Taste the feeling, see how it strikes you and how it doesn't, get to know the quality of the feeling, and see how it is to sense it in this way. (And if you need to spit it out now, please feel free! For now.)

Befriending: Sitting down to tea

You have probably felt everything leading up to this particular stage for encountering difficult emotions. But make no mistake: This is not the holy grail of encountering emotions, and you need not always be on a quest to befriend every vagabond and sketchy friend of Uncle Seth who shows up at your door asking to come in. When we can sit down to tea with these difficult visitors and hear what they have to teach us and how they simply want to help us, it is a wonderful thing, but not every emotion will be a good and welcome guest in the home of your heart. Some visitors will still have you keeping an eye on your family silver and locking your jewelry drawer when you go out to buy groceries.

There is a certain wisdom perspective to befriending emotions, in that this process asks that we see the value in all of our human experience and not just the pleasant things. Being willing and able to sit down and look deep sadness in the eye, so to speak, takes wisdom and courage to do with any degree of grace.

TIP

Do not rush, and do not feel obligated to do this, but know that if you can, you can let the emotion be your teacher.

And this is not a passive process by any means, as you may want to sit with a strong feeling of injustice and outrage that may propel you to stand up and take action in a fiercely self-compassionate way. This is not a reactive act of vengeance, but a purposeful and principled stand for what is right and in alignment with your values. There is huge possibility in befriending your emotions and letting them be your teachers.

Being willing to befriend our most challenging emotions may be a little like the Silver Linings exercise in Chapter 8. When we are willing to sit down and learn from these visitors, one thing that they can teach us is that it's possible to even do this. It is often quite difficult to endure a feeling of guilt for having inadvertently offended a loved one, but if we can patiently look into the eyes of our guilty feelings, we may learn about how we came to do what we did or maybe where our blind spots may be so that we can attend to them in the future.

I very recently accidentally offended my beloved sister in a text message and felt terrible guilt for having been inadvertently insensitive. I spent some time sitting with my guilty feelings and learned some important things for myself. What I at first *wanted* to do was dismiss her reaction as simply being too sensitive and blame her for the misunderstanding to prevent myself from feeling what I felt: guilt. But when I let guilt into the house, so to speak, it taught me a lesson in humility, love, and appreciation. What can your feelings teach you if you sit down to tea with them?

Chapter **11**

Finding Tools for Working with Feelings

While I have tried to make each chapter of this book very concrete and practical, you may have found yourself wondering after the last chapter just how to manage the visitor metaphor in regard to your challenging emotions and just what it may feel like to do so. This chapter explores some very specific ways of bringing mindfulness and self-compassion to bear on these emotions and provides you with some very practical and useful means for doing what I describe.

A note to consider as you venture into this territory of strong emotions, especially, perhaps, if you have scanned the table of contents and jumped immediately to this chapter because it sounded "juicy" or like just what the doctor ordered. First of all, I applaud you for being able to recognize what you need most and for responding in the way you have, as this is truly the foundation of self-compassion. Responding to what you need is not always an easy thing to do, especially when it comes to our emotional needs, so you have shown both great sensitivity and great courage to arrive at this place.

I urge you to continue to be kind to yourself in this process by being patient and curious, and be ready and willing to forgive yourself for any missteps or struggles that you may encounter. Self-forgiveness is another challenging thing, especially for those of us who are prone to self-criticism, perfectionism, and feelings of shame. Chapter 13 delves more deeply into the topic of forgiveness, but I offer a short self-directed forgiveness practice here that you may want to keep handy as you proceed.

Prepare yourself for the possibility that you may, through your deep desire to relieve your stress, lift the veil of sadness, lighten the burden of anxiety, or relieve your heart of guilt and shame, occasionally move too quickly or take on too much. We all can get zealous and overconfident at times, especially when it comes to the possibility of feeling better, and so we may overstep our capacity in the moment to manage our most challenging emotions.

TIP

Instead of giving up if you feel an increase in your emotional pain beyond what you feel you can reasonably manage, I recommend that you first take a moment to forgive yourself for being human and for wanting so much to be free of suffering that you made a temporary wrong turn. You may have gotten stuck, touched a raw emotional nerve, or been fleetingly reminded of past failures or challenges. Consider taking a moment to offer yourself this wish before you continue and return to it if you need it later:

> *May I be patient and kind and forgiving of my urgent intention for relief of my pain. May I forgive myself in advance for any hurt that I may unconsciously cause myself in this process, and allow myself to proceed slowly and patiently.*

With all this in mind, I invite you to roll up your emotional sleeves, reconnect to your warm intention to treat yourself with compassion, and get to the task at hand: finding tools for working with your difficult emotions.

Mindfulness Tools for Meeting Emotions

In Chapter 4, I share the practice of mindfulness after introducing you to it as one of the three components of self-compassion in Chapter 1. You have probably discovered that the capacity to bring yourself to the present moment, to let go of judgment and simply become aware of what is arising, is a powerful practice all by itself. Mindfulness allows us to resist and overcome our instinctual reactivity and tendency to allow our amazing human minds to wander off into the past, into the future, and into fantasy, fear, and frustration. A simple practice of steadying your attention by resting in awareness of the process of breathing can create a kind of solid base of operations for anything you may endeavor to do.

Yesterday my wife asked me to make a home improvement on the outside of our house. In order to do this, I needed to set up a ladder to reach the project in question. The first thing I needed to do was to place the ladder on solid footing.

Not being a fan of teetering precariously in high places, I spent more than a little time finding just the right orientation for the four legs of the ladder to build a solid foundation that would support me. This is one function of mindfulness: to set a solid foundation of awareness upon which everything, including self-compassion practice, can rest. As I'm sure you have gathered about this practice of self-compassion, there are more than a few opportunities to face emotional challenges, and having a firm base is a great place to prepare for and respond to these challenges when they arise.

Name it and you can tame it

Under normal circumstances, we are not prone to pausing long enough to name an emotion when we feel it. You may be out for a leisurely walk with your dog (as I am on occasion, with our two corgis), and an unexpected thunderstorm with torrential rain may appear and drench you both. When this happens, you wouldn't typically say, "Oh! Rainstorm!" as if you or the dog needed to know the name of what's happening. You would just do what needs to be done in the moment to weather it, escape it, or dance in it, whatever is your preference.

The same is true of emotions. Most often, at least when you are experiencing them alone, you don't stop and say, "I'm angry." Instead, you may just let that anger propel you into a pattern of thinking, behaving, and experiencing further emotions (like outrage, indignation, or resentment).

But what if you *did* pause long enough to notice exactly what it is you are feeling and name it for yourself? Would it be helpful in some way? As it turns out, neuroscientists have wondered about this and conducted experiments to see exactly what happens in your brain when you name the emotion you are experiencing. In 2007 David Creswell discovered a significant effect of labeling difficult emotions in the activity of the amygdala. The *amygdala* is a brain structure that can be considered the primary source of our "fight or flight" reactions. It alerts us to danger when we encounter it. Creswell found that the amygdala becomes less active when we label emotions, thereby being less likely to trigger the full cascade of sympathetic arousal that I discuss in Chapter 4. Furthermore, he found that this labeling seemed to also support the brain's capacity to regulate and manage these emotions when they arise.

A simple way of encapsulating these findings and this approach is "Name it and you can tame it." Like most clichés, this one has a basis in truth but also has science backing it up to boot. When one can notice the presence of an emotion (and these emotions can be sneaky sometimes), we can pause and gently say to ourselves, "This is frustration" or "Anxiety is arising." Remember that saying "I am frustrated" and "I am anxious" are unfortunate ways that our language fuses us with our feelings and complicates matters (see Chapter 4), implying that you and your emotions are the same, which you are not.

The result of labeling emotions when they arise is that you begin to create a little space around them so that you can see that you and your emotions are separate and that what is actually happening is that this particular emotion is visiting you in this moment. This gives you a tremendous advantage in working with the emotion because you can see the space between you and the feeling, and in this space is where you can alter your relationship to the feeling. As the psychiatrist and Holocaust survivor Viktor Frankl once said, "Between stimulus and response there is a space. In that space is our power to choose our response. In our response lies our growth and our freedom."

Feel it and you can heal it

One of the reasons that we don't typically name our emotions when they arrive at our doorstep is that they very quickly trigger a lot of thinking and a variety of bodily sensations that capture our attention instead. When someone cuts you off in traffic, you may be vaguely aware that you are angry and perhaps feeling frightened, but mostly you are focused on thinking about how insensitive or careless the other driver was and how you could have been killed. You feel your own body's reaction to the adrenaline dump you just experienced, with your heart pounding and feeling shaky. Emotions tend to have both physical and mental components like this, and they often dominate your awareness in these moments.

Sometimes in self-compassion courses when someone says they felt anxious, I ask what can be a crucial question: "How did you *know* that you were anxious?" The answer to that question often starts with a thought, like "I was afraid that I might have to testify in the trial" or "I knew I didn't want to go there." But if I gently persist with someone who offers up a thought and ask, "So that was a thought; were you aware of anything in your body at the time?" people usually can identify a sensation like a rapid heartbeat, flushing, or tension in the neck. Sometimes they are still feeling these sensations long after the thoughts came and went.

If we are trying to sort out and contend with a challenging emotion after identifying and naming it, we then have two choices of targets to work with in order to potentially transform that feeling: thoughts and bodily sensations. You have your choice, but you may have already discovered that the thing about your thoughts is that they are slippery, shifty, clever characters that move and transform and are hard to pin down. When you say to yourself, "You shouldn't worry about this," your devious mind will issue up an argument like "Why shouldn't I worry about this?" and when you formulate a response, it will shift again to "Well, but if this happens, then *that* will happen. Then I have to worry about *that* instead." You will never prevail in this conversation with yourself because your mind always knows what you are about to say and is ready with a response that trumps it.

Thankfully, your body moves much, much slower and therefore is an easier target to focus and direct your attention toward. When you can locate and anchor your emotions in your body, and then hold them in mindful awareness, quite often the difficult emotion begins to change on its own by virtue of the attention. In some ways, locating the sensation is a kind of proxy or stand-in for the emotion itself, so that you can practice your self-compassion on it, so to speak. When you can settle your attention on a specific location in the body that calls for your attention, you can rest just a bit and begin to bring some warmth to the body that can, over time, become the warmth that you may offer your whole self.

REMEMBER

It is important to note that people vary quite a bit in their ability to actually tune in and detect bodily sensations, especially when they are experiencing strong emotions or when they have had previous issues (like trauma or illness) involving their physical body. If you are someone who has difficulty with this (regardless of the reason), my recommendation is to explore it gently but be willing to let go of it if it becomes a struggle. (Remember, "If it's a struggle, it's not self-compassion.")

There is some benefit to being able to be informed by your body's sensations, and you can cultivate the capacity over time if you like, but you do not need to put extra pressure on yourself to feel something just now when you don't. (Practicing the Compassionate Body Scan from Chapter 4 can, over time, help you to attend more fully to the sensations of your body.)

Self-compassion tools for strong emotions

There is an old saying that "the Gulf Stream can flow through a straw provided the straw is aligned to the Gulf Stream, and not at cross purposes with it." In the Five Stages for Encountering Emotions that I review in the previous chapter, you may notice a progressive lessening of resistance to the emotions over time. This is a gradual, stepwise process of realizing that when we resist the reality of emotions, we are at cross purposes with them, and that it may be possible to come into harmony with them instead. This is not a process of denial or stuffing down emotions, but it isn't plunging headlong into them either. Instead, you discover how to let them flow through you when they come, so they don't blow you over with their intensity.

REMEMBER

Difficult emotions become more transitory (meaning they flow through you more easily as they come and go) when you can adopt a loving, accepting relationship (over time) with them.

Once we have built the solid platform of mindfulness, through naming emotions and locating them in the body, we have the sense of safety and courage within ourselves to warm up our awareness and tap into our tenderness toward ourselves simply for feeling these feelings. When we can do this, we are able to give ourselves what we need in these moments because we are not running away from, avoiding, or trying to control what is arising within us.

Just as you have many options for how you can treat a good friend compassionately when they are having a hard time, you have a variety of options at your disposal for ways to treat yourself. If your friend has just scored poorly on an entrance exam to medical school or law school, you might offer them a warm embrace or a hot cup of tea (physical compassion) or comfort them with encouraging words and validate the pain of disappointment they are feeling (emotional compassion), or simply validate their pain and help them see it in the larger context of common humanity (mental compassion). These are not hard and fast, discrete categories, but you can see that your options are varied, and this applies to meeting your own difficult emotions as well. Thus, when you are asking yourself "What do I need?" you have a whole menu of possibilities to offer yourself when you are struggling.

Physical self-compassion can be referred to as softening. When we notice a painfully tense neck in a stressful situation, we have the possibility of meeting that pain with compassion by releasing it and letting go of the tension. This might take the form of a warm comforting heating pad or the gentle touch of a self-massage (or inviting someone else to massage it). As I discuss earlier in regard to mindfulness where we "feel it to heal it," this very literal softening (or even just softening around the edges) of a place in the body where the emotion manifests can soften our relationship to the emotion itself in a very direct way.

The most obvious manifestation of *yin* self-compassion is in the emotional self-compassion of soothing ourselves when we suffer. Again, because these types of compassion are not discrete, soothing can come not only in the form of a gentle caress of our hand on a painful or tense part of the body, but it can also come as some comforting words of compassion for ourselves, like "I'm so sorry you feel this way," or "I'm here for you to support you." Why wouldn't you meet yourself with the same tenderness and warmth that you offer a loved one?

REMEMBER

From a mental perspective, simply allowing the discomfort to arise and making metaphorical space for it to come and go can be a powerful practice. Too often when difficulty arises as an unexpected visitor to our doorstep, we mentally contract and have the urge to grab it by the scruff of the neck and promptly escort it out to the metaphorical trash can. Instead, if we can create a little space around it and let go of needing to get rid of it, we see it in a different light. In this moment we are not surrendering anything; rather, we are giving up the need for anything to be any different in this particular moment. Allowing is not a defeat, but it is a transformation from being one (or both) of the battling chess pieces (mentioned in the previous chapter) into being the board itself.

Putting it all into practice: Soften, Soothe, and Allow

PLAY

Softening . . . soothing . . . allowing. Physical . . . emotional . . . mental. This is a remarkable array of resources already at your disposal to begin to work with your challenging emotions in more fruitful, harmonious, and compassionate ways. The following exercise, adapted from the Mindful Self-Compassion program, brings together your mindfulness tools of naming and locating emotions, alongside your self-compassion tools of softening, soothing, and allowing. It is presented as a sequence, but you can approach it all as an experiment and an adventure (like everything else in this book) and see what happens with each element. You can find out what works for you and what doesn't, and see what it is like to slowly begin to be with (or even dance) with your emotions in a new way. Be patient, go slow, and most of all, be kind . . . to yourself.

A note about this practice: I am presenting this practice like a formal meditation with a structure and sequence in order to help you become familiar with it, but it is also intended to be an informal practice, meaning that over time you can deploy it in a moment of difficulty. In this sense, it is what I would call a "pocket practice" because you can keep it in your metaphorical back pocket to bring out at a moment's notice. There may be times when you want to return to these pages and step through the whole practice, but you may also find that, on the fly, you can pause and simply say "soften-soothe-allow" or even just "soothe" with the warm touch of your hand to your heart or some other place on your body. This is where you can customize the practice to suit your needs so that you can access it when you really need it, which is what self-compassion is really all about. It all depends upon what you need in a moment of difficulty.

One more thing: As I introduce you to this practice, I ask you to call to mind a problem or situation that generates some difficult emotion so that you can practice these skills. Please honor where you happen to be at this moment as to whether the timing is right. If you do choose to proceed, start slow, and pick a situation and level of intensity that is right for you, knowing that this is just to familiarize you with the practice and get a felt sense of it. Most importantly, the intention here is *not* for you to continue to practice by calling to mind difficult situations to bring up suffering to work with. Life does a really great job of serving up these opportunities on its own, and the intention is for you to have this practice in your back pocket for when these inevitable moments of difficulty arise.

Take some time now to find a comfortable position for your body. It is extremely important that you create an inner and outer environment of ease and comfort when you are practicing with difficult emotions. (This is an act of self-compassion in itself.) As you settle in, you might offer yourself some soothing or supportive touch simply to remind you of your own presence and that you, like anyone else, are worthy of kindness, patience, and respect.

Choosing a situation to work with

Allow yourself to recall a *mildly to moderately difficult situation* that you may be going through right now — a work challenge, stress in a relationship, or maybe a health issue you are facing. Take some time to reflect on the problem, being sure to choose a situation that generates at least some stress in your body when you think of it but doesn't overwhelm you. For the purposes of exploring this *yin*-based practice for the first time, it is probably best not to choose a situation that makes you feel angry or one where you feel a need to stand up for yourself or protect yourself.

Sink into the problem in your mind's eye, getting a clear sense of who is involved, what's been said (or unsaid), what happened, or what *might* happen. Give yourself plenty of time to relive and register the experience in your mind.

Naming the emotions

As you explore this situation in your mind's eye, see if you can notice what emotions come with this reliving of the experience. Take your time and let the emotions come to you, rather than searching them out if they are not immediately apparent. Are you noticing worry, confusion, sadness, grief, fear, longing, despair? Perhaps something else?

If you aren't quite clear which emotion or emotions you are feeling, that's fine for now; simply experiencing it is enough. And if there are many emotions arising as you recall the situation, see if you can name the most prominent or strongest emotion associated with the situation and work with that for the balance of the practice.

Take the time now to repeat the name of the emotion to yourself, but be sure to use a tender, understanding voice, as if you were validating it for a friend who was feeling it. Something like "Oh, that's disappointment," or "You're feeling grief right now." Let yourself hear yourself speaking the name of the emotion and notice how it feels to do this. Take your time. There's no rush.

Finding emotion in the body

When you are ready, expand awareness to your whole body just as it is in this moment. After a bit of time has passed, you may refresh the image and felt sense of the difficult situation in your mind, and slowly scan your body for where you may feel the emotion most readily. You can mentally scan your body from head to toe, pausing anywhere you encounter any tension or discomfort, feeling whatever is there to be felt, and nothing more. Again, there is no hurry. Take your time and explore your whole body.

If you can, choose a single location in your body now where the feeling expresses itself most strongly, whether it is a familiar or surprising place in your body. Maybe you notice some unusual muscle tension, some heat, or an ache in the stomach or in your heart.

When you identify a location, see if you can warmly and kindly incline your attention toward that particular part of the body. See if you can experience the sensation directly, as if from the inside, rather than *thinking about* the sensation. If this is too much right now, you can certainly ease up and notice a general sense of unease or discomfort, whatever seems right to you in this moment.

Softening, soothing, and allowing

As you have a mental and physical awareness of the particular location in your body where the emotion seems to be manifesting, begin to *soften* into it. Let the muscles soften and relax, as if you were easing them into warm water. Softening . . . softening . . . softening. Remember that you are not trying to change the feeling at all, but just holding it in a tender way. If softening is difficult, you may want to try softening a little bit around the edges at first.

Take your time, know that you cannot rush this process; instead, let it happen through your own kindness. If at any point you feel it would support you or comfort you, you can open your eyes if they are closed or even let go of the practice for now and feel your breath or the soles of your feet. This is a gentle introduction to a practice that may take some time to fully resonate for you.

If you feel ready to move on, now turn your attention to *soothing* yourself just because of this challenging situation. You may want to place a hand over the part of the body that feels uncomfortable right now and simply feel the warmth and gentle touch of your own hand. If this is an image that works for you, you can imagine warmth and kindness (*your own* warmth and kindness) flowing through your hand and into this one particular area that needs some tenderness right now. Sometimes thinking of your body as if it were that of a beloved child or another being you care about can help you find the right tone. Soothing . . . soothing . . . soothing.

You may try soothing yourself with some comforting or reassuring words that you need to hear right now. What do you need to hear that would soothe you in this moment? What would you say to soothe and reassure a dear friend who was struggling in the same way? Perhaps something like "I really care about you and I'm so sorry you feel this right now," or "I know it's hard, but you've got this. I'm here for you." Maybe you can offer yourself a similar message, something like "May I be kind to myself in this difficult moment."

Give yourself all the time you need to feel your own tender kindness and soothing. There is no need to rush or move on if this practice is landing for you and helping you to soften your heart and soothe yourself in the midst of difficulty. But whenever you would like to continue to explore your many options, move on to *allowing* the pain or struggle to simply be here, because it is. Make some room for it and release any need for it to go away. Allowing . . . allowing . . . allowing.

What would it be like to let go of needing anything . . . to be any different . . . in this moment? Allow yourself to be just as you are just now, just like this, if only for this one moment in time. Allowing . . .

Softening . . . soothing . . . allowing. Softening . . . soothing . . . allowing. Take all the time you need, without rushing or feeling pressure of any kind, to simply explore and try out these approaches on your own. Softening, soothing, allowing. The feeling may shift or change location, or it may stay where it is; either is okay, and you can simply stay with it regardless. Softening, soothing, allowing.

When you feel ready to release the practice, simply widen your attention to your whole body in this moment. Allow yourself to feel whatever you feel and to be exactly as you are just now. Take this precious time to dwell in the presence of your own good company for a time.

Give yourself plenty of time to settle, reflect, make notes, and savor or register the experience of this practice. There is no need to rush into labeling, describing, or putting words to any of the experience. That will happen in good time. Just let the practice continue to work in you over time.

TIP

Inquiring: What did you notice about working with your emotion in this way?

When you are ready to explore your experience, it may be helpful to consider each of the components and what you observed.

Were you able to find a name or label for the most difficult emotion? How was that?

What was it like to explore your body to identify a physical sensation associated with the emotion? Were you able to locate someplace where you felt it in your body? If you weren't able to locate it, how did you respond? (Sometimes, with certain emotions, our body in essence "numbs out" in response to that emotion. If that was the case for you, just know that this is a sign that you have touched a sensitive area and can continue to work with it patiently and kindly over time. As always, go slow and be patient, and perhaps you can work with the overall sense of uneasiness that may arise in those moments instead.)

Did you have any sense of anything changing when you *softened* into that location? How about when you *soothed* yourself for simply having the feeling? Was *allowing* something that you found supportive or helpful in some way?

TIP

While not being too quick to dismiss any of the elements of this Soften, Soothe, and Allow practice, take the time to experiment with it and customize it to suit you. If you found some elements more helpful than others, you may explore those further or focus on some more than others. You can also feel free to alter the order of soften, soothe, and allow to suit your own needs.

Shame: The Most Challenging Emotion of All

Of all the emotions that humans experience, perhaps the most painful, insidious, and life-limiting is the emotion of shame. As I explore in Chapter 5, although the experience of shame can be quite lonely and isolating, the reality of shame is held by our common humanity. This is just one of the paradoxes of this complicated experience that is worth unraveling here so that you can find a way to work with shame like all the other emotions you face as a human being with feelings.

I briefly define shame in Chapter 5, but it's worth returning to that definition, which is "a complex combination of emotions, physiological responses, and imagery associated with the real or imagined rupture of relational ties" (from the article "Shame: Countertransference identifications in individual psychotherapy" by William K. Hahn). That's a lot of fancy terminology to describe something that has no actual words to it. Shame is not a verbal experience so much as a visceral and emotional one, and so the focus in this chapter is as much on the experience of shame as on the definition of it. I provide some concepts that may incline you to look more kindly on this tricky emotional roller coaster.

Imagine for a moment that you are an insecure teenage boy (is there any other kind?) and you've barely made it on to your high school basketball team, all gangly, pimply, 6 feet of you (yes, I'm referring to myself here). You finally get into a game and find yourself at midcourt in the midst of a scuffle for the ball and, miraculously, you come up with it. With a rush of excitement, you twirl around and make a beeline for the basket. The cheers of the crowd are like a wall of indistinguishable sound urging you on, your tunnel vision narrowing so the only thing you see clearly is that hoop with the bright white net beneath. You begin your semi-graceful ascent as you launch a layup that gently swishes through . . . the net of the opposite team's basket.

Imagine the feeling of this embarrassing public blunder, feeling as if your internal organs are dissolving like a sandcastle in the tide, the intense flush as your face feels on fire, and the frantic wish that you could just disappear. Got it? Now *that* is the feeling of shame (with a little guilt and humiliation thrown in for good measure). In that one awful moment, you are acutely aware of believing you see yourself through the eyes of the whole world: as an imposter, a hopelessly inept athlete, a ridiculously stupid person, deeply unworthy of love or appreciation. There is no lonelier experience than believing that your deep dark doubts about yourself have now been exposed to the world for all to see.

This is the painful essence of shame, and as I note in Chapter 5, it is rooted in the deepest, darkest fears that humans can have: that we may be unlovable (often framed as a belief that we are, indeed, unlovable), and therefore our lifeline (like that of the spacewalking astronauts) has been cut and we will be left adrift to perish. This is how it feels to have shame. Your experiences of shame may be much deeper and more painful, but the essence is all in this simple story. In a moment of shame, you feel the painful trifecta of guilt, blame, and isolation. What could be worse than that? Not much, really.

Give yourself a little time to reflect on your own experience of shame. I don't mean to imply that my experience on the basketball court is identical to yours, and (as they say in car commercials) your "mileage" may vary.

TIP

How do *you* know when you are feeling shame? You may know it by a physical reaction such as hanging your head, fidgeting, faking a smile, getting angry, mumbling, talking too much or going silent, or even spacing out. How does shame make you feel in those moments? Foolish, silly, inept, clumsy, vulnerable, embarrassed, or even unworthy or unlovable? All of this, taken as a shame package, a shame sandwich if you will (where even the bread tastes bad), boils down to the same core set of feelings: guilt, blame, and isolation.

But what if you took a closer look at those feelings to test them out. Are they really what they tell you they are? Upon closer inspection of them, if you are willing to bravely explore these excruciating feelings, like so many other things that you have already explored in this process, you will find something very different within them.

Note: While I have already credited the Mindful Self-Compassion program and my dear friends and colleagues Dr. Kristin Neff and Dr. Christopher Germer for much of what I know and share in this book, I must give extra recognition to Chris for his pioneering and insightful work on shame and self-compassion in particular. He has been an inspiration and a mentor for me in many ways, but especially in learning about this important topic.

The three paradoxes of shame

As you previously discovered about shame, it arises from a very simple but profound wish that every human carries with them as their means of survival: the wish to be loved. When we are loved, all things flow from that — from our infancy through to our death, every one of us goes through life just wanting to be loved, whether we recognize it or not. This love is not just a romantic ideal (and you can easily use the words "appreciated" or "to belong" instead of "love"). It actually represents the lifeline that brings us what we need in life, from food, clothing, and shelter to the support and protection of being in community and a part of the human tribe. When we see that the love of our fellow humans is what we need to survive, we can see that potentially losing that bond has very high stakes.

Shame and love are two sides of the same survival coin, and if you can remind yourself of this reality, you can begin to open the door to exploring and managing shame. Shame is that fear (often held more like a rigid belief) that there is something fundamentally wrong with us that makes us unlovable. In other words, we believe that we are too flawed to be loved by others, and hence, vulnerable to being rejected, ostracized, or banished from the community. If we go through life believing this and trying desperately to hide that shameful thing that we don't want anyone to know, every failure, misstep, or error can feel like the one thing that will expose our emotional house of cards, and all will be revealed when it collapses and we are seen for who we "really" are. In my painful basketball analogy, I was afraid of being seen as inept, clumsy, or stupid. You can substitute your own shame-based fears here.

The isolation one feels in a moment of shame is easy to imagine when shame is framed as the universal wish to be loved. In that moment of embarrassment for me, I felt uniquely flawed and irretrievably inept, which led to feeling incredibly alone and isolated from anyone in that gymnasium (with all eyes upon me, which actually compounded the feeling). The paradoxical thing about feeling isolated in moments of shame is that, in actuality, *every single human being on the planet* feels shame sometimes because we all share that wish to be loved and connected.

In fact, while the story I told myself on the court that day in that terrible moment was that people were looking at me in disgust and anger and betrayal, in fact, I suspect that nearly every one of them was imagining how terrible it must have been to be me in that moment. Everyone there could relate to my pain through their own experience of shame, and ironically, when I felt most alone, everyone in the room was sharing the common experience of shame. This awareness of the common humanity of shame begins to help us turn the tide on the feeling as it exposes the fallacy of our core beliefs about ourselves as being uniquely bad, stupid, or unworthy.

The final paradox of shame is that, as we are experiencing it, it feels entirely permanent and fixed, like the final straw that will finally break the camel's back of our illusion of belonging. I imagine if someone had asked me after that fateful basketball game if I would go on to write a book in which I would honestly recount this horrendous experience, I would have just laughed . . . or cried. But in truth, shame is a burden carried only by a part of ourselves (that part that fears we will be found to be unworthy) and only for a limited period of time until it fades. Shame, like every other emotion that arises, persists and falls away as an ephemeral phenomenon that is simply a part of the impermanence of life itself.

SHAME IS NOT THE ENEMY

Over the years I have had the wonderful opportunity to learn from and befriend a number of colleagues from Asian countries such as Korea, Japan, Vietnam, China, and Singapore. One of the more interesting conversations I have had with these beloved and wise friends is on the topic of shame (I guess this means I'm kind of a self-compassion nerd if this is the topic of my favorite conversations!). Anyway, these colleagues point out that shame actually holds a valued place in many Asian cultures, and they point out that shame itself is not the enemy.

Specifically, if you look at shame as being a kind of reflection of the fear of being disconnected from others, then in a society that values and celebrates connection, shame is the force that draws people together. When you walk on the streets of Tokyo as I once did, you see the drivers obeying the traffic lights, the pedestrians following the signs and lights, and no litter anywhere. These are all signs of the positive power of shame to encourage conformity, not standing out from the herd, and being respectful of every other human. People do not want to feel shame because of how painful it is, and so they follow the rules and conform to society's expectations in large part.

So shame can be an adaptive emotion or a pro-social emotion in many situations, which is all the more reason not to treat it as something to be eliminated or eradicated as part of our new self-compassion practice. We are just bringing a warm and kind awareness to the arising of shame and finding ways of relating to it that do not limit us or cause us unnecessary suffering.

Interestingly, the three paradoxes correspond quite nicely with the three components of self-compassion when you begin to see self-compassion as a powerful antidote for shame. The antidote for feeling blameworthy is self-kindness, the antidote for the sense of isolation is common humanity, and the antidote to seeing an experience as fixed and permanent is mindfulness. Pretty cool that it lines up that way, isn't it? You can see how this works in the following informal practice called the Self-Compassion Break for Shame.

What underlies the phenomenon of shame?

As I believe I have made quite clear, none of us is to blame for having shame, and we have clearly inherited this tendency toward wishing to be loved. For this reason, the British psychologist and founder of Compassion-Focused Therapy, Paul Gilbert, says "shame is not our fault, but it is our responsibility." In other words, we come by it honestly, but that doesn't mean we can't acknowledge and work with it in productive ways that reduce our troubles and struggles and give us more ease and peace. In order to work with shame, it is helpful to recognize what maintains and drives our shame so that we can begin to address those forces in a meaningful way.

Shame is likely to emerge whenever you face difficult circumstances, such as losing your health, wealth, relationships, or meaningful work, or when you suffer bias or discrimination based upon your identity (for example, race, gender, sexual orientation, ability, or socioeconomic status). In those moments of distress, we are prone to asking, "Why me?" and the feelings that come up are likely to trigger a downward spiraling chain reaction.

The downward spiral to core beliefs

We say or think "I feel bad," which leads to "I don't like this feeling," which triggers "I don't want this feeling," leading to the thought "I shouldn't have this feeling," dropping down to "Something's wrong with me to have this feeling," and finally landing at "I'm bad." Sometimes this can be a short and wild ride from "I feel bad" to "I *am* bad." With shame, all roads lead to those core beliefs that we are somehow unworthy or fatally flawed and thus unloved or unlovable. Often referred to as negative core beliefs, they echo in the backs of our minds for years and years as doubts about ourselves that suddenly feel completely solid and true in our most vulnerable moments.

The negative core beliefs that people hold are actually not that numerous (usually numbering around 10 to 15 total) and include thoughts like "I'm defective," "I'm unlovable," "I'm helpless," I'm a fraud," "I'm stupid," or "I'm a loser."

Chris Germer points out that even if we hold one of these core beliefs, we are not alone, because we share it with about half a billion other humans on the planet! What would you consider your top one or two core beliefs that come up for you in challenging circumstances? Sometimes determining this takes some patience and reflection.

If you can identify a negative core belief, see if you can resist the temptation to outright dispute that belief. Like trying to direct compassion to any other thoughts (as I note earlier), trying to challenge a negative core belief that has been with you a very long time (perhaps since childhood) and trying to change or eliminate it is a tricky business. It is actually transformative enough to simply be able to name it and validate it in some way. You can even simply say something kind to yourself like "You feel like you're unworthy of love. That must be *so* hard!"

Shame is like mold: It thrives in darkness

The reason that simply acknowledging negative core beliefs is powerful is that shame does best when it is unexamined. It works its devious plan to undermine and shortchange you by working undetected in your psyche, so anytime you shine light on what it is up to, it loses its grip on you (remember Toto pulling back the curtain in *The Wizard of Oz?*)

Silence and darkness support shame in persisting, and self-compassion shines the light of mindfulness and the warmth of compassion on it to begin to shift that relationship. Because we fear that our core beliefs will be exposed and we will be rejected if that happens, the challenge is to first admit that we have these beliefs and then bring compassion to ourselves for suffering all these years with these limiting, painful stories. At some point in our process, if we feel safe and brave enough, we can even share our self-doubts with others to further the process of shining light on shame.

One way of working with shame and reshaping your relationship with it is to see that not only is it a universal human experience, but it only applies to just one part of who you are. Remember that I am not suggesting that you eliminate shame, but only that you understand and align yourself with it so that it does not cause you so much suffering. After all, you still just wish to be loved.

Richard Schwartz, the developer of Internal Family Systems theory, has described our psyche as being made of many parts. We have lovable parts and unlovable parts, wounded parts and compassionate parts, critical parts and trickster parts, and so on. When we are engulfed in shame, we are so absorbed in the one part that is hurting that we believe that we are globally flawed and unlovable. Self-compassion embraces *all the parts* of yourself in one fell swoop. The old saying goes "I'm not perfect, but some parts of me are excellent." See if you can remember that the next time you feel shame.

Practice: Self-Compassion Break for Shame

It is entirely possible to use shame in the Soften, Soothe, and Allow practice that I introduce earlier, and the Mindful Self-Compassion program has a modified version of that practice specific to shame. The approach is the same, but given the complexity of the emotion of shame, my advice is to go slowly and patiently and decide what is right for you.

The informal practice that follows (also drawn from the Mindful Self-Compassion program) is a bit briefer and a nice doorway into working with shame in a less ambitious way at first. It will look and feel familiar to you because it is a modification of the standard Self-Compassion Break, so you may find it easier to start with this and then move on Soften, Soothe, and Allow as you feel some willingness to move forward.

As with other practices, I ask you to call to mind a situation where you felt embarrassment or a little bit of shame, but my intention is not for you to continue to practice by calling these things to mind. It is intended as a "pocket practice" that you can utilize when these moments happen spontaneously in your life. Believe me, life will serve them up on a regular basis, so there will be no shortage of opportunities for practice!

Embarrassment and shame reside on the same continuum, with shame usually being more intense and painful. But embarrassment is a good place to start, although you may notice that something that initially seems embarrassing may slip into something more like shame as you look closely. Be patient and go slow with this practice.

When you are ready, call to mind an event in your life, clearly in the past, when you felt embarrassed or mildly ashamed. For example:

>> At a work meeting it was pointed out by a supervisor that your performance was not as strong as that of a colleague.

>> You complained about someone in an email but accidentally sent it to that person.

>> You lost your temper in a stressful moment and said something you regretted later.

Mindfulness

Allow yourself to fully drop into the situation and to remember how you felt at the time. Take plenty of time to return to the experience as it unfolded. Notice how embarrassment or shame feels in your body.

See if you can name the experience for yourself in a kind and gentle way: "Shame . . . ahhhh, this is how shame feels."

See if you can explore your body and discover where you feel this shame the most.

Allow yourself to experience whatever comes up, perhaps just creating a little extra space within you to hold this experience.

Common humanity

Know that what you are experiencing now is part of the human experience. Everyone feels shame, and anyone would probably feel as you did in the same situation.

You may also be feeling isolated and alone at this moment, which is the nature of shame. But shame is a universal emotion, and *everyone* feels it sometimes.

See if you can pause and acknowledge that you feel like this because you, like everyone else on the planet, *just want to be loved.* Or to be *appreciated,* to *belong* — whatever word fits for you. Shame happens because we want so much to be loved and appreciated by others.

See if you can connect with that wish *beneath* the experience of shame. Can you give yourself *permission* to do so?

Self-Kindness

See if you can respond to shame in a new way. Can you give yourself some kindness simply *because* you're having a moment of shame?

If it feels right to you, please go ahead and place a hand on the part of your body that feels shame the most. Maybe send kindness through your fingers into that part of your body that is holding shame for you, or gently rub that part of your body.

You may imagine a dear friend who found themselves in the same embarrassing situation as you. What would you say to comfort or support your friend? Can you say the same words to yourself? Can you whisper the same words into your own ear?

When you're ready, let go of this particular practice and allow it all to settle just a bit. Take your time to pause, take notes, and honor however you feel in this moment.

Inquiring: How was it to work with shame in this way?

Consider the following questions:

>> What did you notice as you did this Self-Compassion Break for Shame?

>> Could you notice shame manifesting in your body?

>> Were you able to create a little space around the shame?

>> How was it to remember that you are not alone while feeling shame?

>> Did you have any sense of feeling the wish to be loved?

>> How did it feel to offer yourself kindness (in any form) in this practice?

I invite you to consider trying this practice a few times in various situations, keeping in mind that it is built around the same three components of self-compassion: mindfulness of what is here; acknowledging the common humanity of the moment; and bringing kindness to ourselves for the pain we are feeling. This can make it easier to remember the steps in a moment of suffering when you may not have a copy of this book nearby!

4
Turning Challenge into Opportunity

Explore the challenging path of finding and practicing forgiveness.

Find out how to locate and appreciate your deep sense of belonging, wherever you go.

Discover the fullness of what can be possible when you connect with savoring, gratitude, and self-appreciation.

Chapter **12**

Transforming Challenging Relationships

It may seem paradoxical to say this after spending so much time and energy exploring our common humanity, but in many ways we are still all so different from each other that it may seem like a miracle that we get along at all! Looking at our many differences — genes, culture, age, sex, gender, family background, spirituality, dreams, and aspirations — we can begin to see why so much of our stress and suffering arises from relationships. The French philosopher Jean-Paul Sartre famously said, "Hell is other people," and you probably have had more than a few moments when you would have raised a beer (or fine French Bordeaux) to old Jean-Paul to heartily concur.

There are many classic bar scenes in movies, but my favorite comes from *The Muppet Movie*. Kermit the Frog is sitting at a piano bar drowning his sorrows over his latest tiff with Miss Piggy, and Rowlf the Dog is behind the piano tending to Kermit. Once Rowlf realizes that Kermit's concerns are about his relationship, he draws him into a song that I think highlights the paradox of relationships in general: We experience some pain in being connected to others, and we feel the pain of potentially losing those same relationships. As the Muppets point out, "You can't live with 'em, you can't live without 'em. There's something irresistible-ish about 'em. We grin and bear it cause the nights are long, and we hope that something better comes along."

"Something better" than other people is unlikely to come along (although pets are a close second!), so our task becomes how to navigate the tricky but incredibly fulfilling territory of interpersonal relationships. As Kermit says in the song, "There is no solution, it's part of evolution." So, to again quote Paul Gilbert on our evolutionary inheritance, "It's not our fault, but it *is* our responsibility."

The self-compassionate approach, not surprisingly, is to follow the pain of relationships, and in this case that pain comes in two opposite kinds of pain: the pain that we feel when we are rejected by others or feel separate or alone (often in the form of anger), and the *empathic distress* that arises when we experience the difficulties of others with whom we are connected. The pain of disconnection (anger) and the pain of connection (empathic distress) are each a part of being in this interconnection with others, and both can benefit from the kind attention of self-compassion.

REMEMBER

The purpose of this chapter is actually *not to repair challenging relationships* but instead to determine how to meet and understand the pain (and occasional anger) that we all feel in those relations in order to respond in a healthier way. It entails further building the resource of self-compassion so that it is available in your relationships rather than healing old wounds.

Connection as the Foundation for Human Life

Humans are social beings, and it isn't as superficial as the fact that we just have fun hanging out with each other. We actually need each other to survive and to thrive. From the moment of conception to the day of our death, we rely on our connections to other people, whether they are obvious or not, and whether we acknowledge them or not. In a very obvious way, newborn humans are completely vulnerable and reliant on someone caring for them to survive. As we grow older, we rely on each other in slightly more subtle but very real ways, whether it is to learn from each other, to encourage and support each other, or to provide the things each of us needs for survival.

We may live alone, but unless we live in a cave and forage for food, someone built the structure we live in, grew the food we eat (or the seeds we plant), assembled the clothing we wear, and compensated us in some way so that we could get what we need in life. There is no denying our deep bond to each other, even if that bond is also a source of pain from time to time.

In *collectivist cultures* (which is what most east Asian cultures tend to be), there is a greater awareness of this interconnection among us, and this web of humanity is honored and supported. However, most of us in the West are far more aware of the *rugged individualism* of our culture and how the emphasis is much more on self-reliance and independence than in other cultures. This is not to suggest that one is better than the other, but the differences are striking and noteworthy. (Interestingly, my experience shows that there is just as much interest in self-compassion, and a lack thereof, in Eastern cultures as there is in Western cultures, so simply embracing a collective culture does not ensure that you will be kind to yourself.)

All of this leads to the importance of cementing in our awareness the very fact of our human existence: that we are deeply and profoundly connected to each other in meaningful ways. This connection affords you the inner safety and courage to act boldly and stand up for change, as well as supports you when you struggle and fail and fall short.

As you begin to feel a part of a vast web of interconnection with all other humans, you can begin to cultivate a more compassionate stance toward yourself when your bonds with others lead to pain, struggle, and stress. This is because you realize that pain in relationships is a natural consequence of the importance *of* those relationships. We feel pain when we are rejected simply because we value *being* connected, just as we feel the pain of grief because of our love for the one we lost. We feel the pain of others because we are uniquely wired to be able to resonate and respond to the emotions of others so that we are more closely attuned and able to help each other. Our connections are valuable, and like anything we value, it hurts to lose them.

I am willing to admit that at first glance, there may be what I call the "woowoo factor" or what my wife calls "hooey" when you read about us all being interconnected. But if you are having that sort of reaction, see if you can let your initial cynical impression subside and consider the primary sources of joy and suffering in your life. What is it *about* those things that brings you those feelings of joy and suffering, and how many of them have to do with other people in some form or another?

I am writing this book in the middle of the COVID-19 pandemic, and the fact that I cannot gather in close proximity with my loved ones and friends just reminds me how much I value and treasure their presence in my life. I also know that when my wife returns home from an outing with our dogs, my heart fills with joy and a smile overtakes my face because of the reconnection. There is nothing magic or woowoo about this. We are deeply coupled to our human family, and the bond goes both ways, as they are connected to us as well.

Practice: Giving and receiving compassion

As with many of the practices in this book, this meditation is drawn directly from the Mindful Self-Compassion program, with minor modifications to make it more accessible in the form of this book. It is a core meditation in that program and brings together a focus upon the breath and the integration of lovingkindness and compassion into a powerful meditation that will help you to stay in connection with others while still practicing compassion for yourself. Some have nicknamed this practice "loving others without losing yourself."

This gentle linking of breath and compassion may be new territory for you, but see if you can be patient and curious about how it unfolds. If you are one of those skeptics I just mentioned, see if you can meet the arising of your own skepticism with some kindness and tolerance, much the way you met your inner critic in Chapter 9. Acknowledge that the inner skeptic is a close friend of your inner critic and is looking after you in its own way so that you don't get hurt or betrayed. Trust that you are in good hands here, with me as your guide, and this can be an experiment in your own mind. Nobody will know you are doing this meditation, and if it doesn't resonate, you can let it go.

Take some time to find a comfortable place to sit for a period of time and allow your eyes to close if you are willing. You may offer yourself some soothing or supportive touch just to reconnect with your warmhearted intention to meet yourself with kindness and compassion.

Savoring your breathing

Slowly allow your attention to turn to your breathing (if it hasn't already) and simply allow yourself to be a watcher of the process of breathing for awhile. You may begin to notice how your breath nourishes your body as you inhale and how it soothes and cleanses your body on the exhale. Inspiration . . . and expiration.

Letting go of needing to control or direct your breathing in any way, simply allow your breath to find its own natural rhythm. Notice how it feels inside your body to be breathing in and breathing out. You may even allow yourself to be very gently rocked and caressed by the cadence of your breathing.

Warming up your awareness

Gently allow your attention to rest more squarely on just the in-breath for a time, savoring and appreciating the sensation of breathing in, one breath after another. You may even have a sense that each in-breath energizes your body in some way.

If you like, as you continue to breathe in, see if you can breathe in *kindness and compassion* for yourself. Feel whatever you feel as you do this, but it may be a quality of kindness and compassion, a sense of warmth or ease, or maybe a word or an image flowing in on your breathing.

After a time, shift your focus to your out-breath, feeling your body breathing out and the ease of exhalation. Ahhhhhhhhh . . .

When you feel ready, call to mind someone you love or someone who is dear to you who is struggling and needs compassion just now. Visualize this person clearly in your mind and begin directing your out-breath toward this person. Simply offer this fellow human being the ease of breathing out.

If you like, send kindness and compassion to this person with each out-breath, one breath after another. (If you find it a bit easier at first, you can direct the breath out to others in general rather than choosing a particular person at this point.)

Exploring self and another together

Widen out your focus again to the full sensation of breathing both in and out, savoring the sensation of the full cycle of breath.

As you become settled in this wider view, begin to explore breathing in for yourself and out for the other person (or persons): "In for me, and out for you," or "One for me, and one for you." As you breathe, draw kindness and compassion in for yourself and send something good out to another.

You are free (and encouraged) to adjust the balance between breathing in and out to whatever feels just right to you. For example, it may be "five for me and one for you" or "one for me and two for you," or it can simply be an even flow, whatever feels right.

Not getting too tangled in the details but letting go of unnecessary effort, allow the meditation to be as easy and uncomplicated as breathing itself.

Allow your breath to flow in and out the way the ocean flows in and out. A limitless, boundless flow of compassion. Let yourself be a part of this limitless, boundless flow in an ocean of compassion.

Give yourself all the time you like to savor and practice, to breathe and be, and when you are ready, release the practice and rest quietly in your own body and notice what is there and how this practice was for you. You may want to make a few notes for yourself or simply reflect. Take your time and see what unfolds.

Inquiring: What was it like to share your compassion?

When you are ready, take some time to consider what you observed in this practice. As I note earlier, this practice brings together a lot of what you have learned so far, and I can tell you that my own experience of this practice the first time I did it was a bit disconcerting. It was a lot to keep track of, and I kept finding myself holding my breath or trying to control or direct my breath. It took awhile for me to let go and let the breath do what it did, while I simply allowed the compassion to flow in and out.

REMEMBER

This practice forms a nice foundation for becoming more aware and appreciative of our connections to others. It can be fruitful to return to when we are feeling isolated, alone, or disconnected in some way — not to change how we feel, but to meet ourselves in the midst of our feelings and remind us of our deep connections.

Anger: The Pain of Feeling or Fearing Disconnection

"I really hate the layout of your office."

These were the first words out of my brand-new client's mouth when she sat down. Stella was her name, and she was clearly unhappy and angry. She had been referred by a colleague who said she had some "anger issues" that he thought I could help her with. I was new to private practice and happy to have a referral. But not quite so happy upon meeting Stella.

To my credit, I buckled in for the wild ride that was my session with Stella, where she went on to angrily berate the parking lot at my office, my fees, and then, as we moved into the intake therapy session proper, virtually everyone in her family and around her in her life. I was barely able to get a word in as she continued to express her angry venom at virtually everything.

Finally, with only a few minutes left in the session, as I was reeling from Stella's onslaught and a bit confused as to how to intervene, she paused to catch her breath. I still didn't know what to say, and I'm embarrassed to admit the first words I did utter, but here they are: "You seem angry."

Well, that prompted a pretty snide and angry and sarcastic response as well, but I was able to get her to pause a moment and I said (as if I had much more clinical experience than I did): "It's been my experience that anger is almost always a reaction to feeling vulnerable or afraid. I wonder if that resonates for you at all."

A long pause ensued (by far the longest period of silence in the session), and then she looked me in the eyes with the first bit of tenderness I had witnessed and began to silently cry. It went on for a few minutes and I simply let her cry, offering tissues but mostly being present to her suffering, with warmth. That moment is seared into my memory, and I can recall all the details now as I write these words.

Stella ultimately wrapped up the session with a bit more anger, and sadly never returned. I often wonder about her, and I hope she found another compassionate ear who could help her hold her pain.

REMEMBER

But the lesson for me has been profound. Anger is always sending a message and, in a weird way, it's not what it's about. What I mean by that is that anger is more like what you might call a "secondary emotion" and not a "primary" one. Anger is a *reaction* to something deeper that you feel and mainly serves the purpose of protecting us by redirecting attention away from the deeper pain of disconnection.

When you feel disconnected (rejected, betrayed, lost, or alone) all kinds of emotions can arise in response to those feelings, and anger and panic are among the most common ones. If you return to the metaphor of our human connections being like the space-walking astronaut's lifeline, then imagine how you would react if you feared that you *were* that astronaut and your connection to the "mother ship" was threatened. With your very existence hinging on the uninterrupted flow through that lifeline, your reaction would probably be swift, decisive, and intense. Anger is one option; panic, outrage, indignation, resentment, and annoyance are other "hard" feelings that could arise in those moments.

But allow me to unpack those moments of disconnection just a bit. If you accept that our connections are deeply important to us as humans, then it follows that we all want to protect and nurture those connections like precious jewels. We lock these jewels away in the safety of our hearts so nobody can steal them, but now and then we feel an intrusion or a threat to the security of our connections. You get passed over for a promotion, your partner breaks up with you, or you find that a trusted friend has betrayed your confidence. These are all legitimate reasons to get angry (legitimacy isn't the point here), but what is helpful to appreciate is that the anger serves an initial purpose in these moments. The anger protects us from a transgressor, someone who has threatened the integrity of our connections to others or to them.

When anger serves us

It is extremely helpful to acknowledge that anger itself is not the problem, in the same way you have learned that resistance, backdraft, and difficult emotions are not the problem. In fact, it's worth exploring how anger serves and protects us in various ways. You can think of anger as a burglar alarm for your heart, doing what it can to alert you of intrusions into your safe and brave inner space so that you can respond accordingly. Anger can arise in the service of yang self-compassion and serve some positive functions.

For instance, anger is helpful in situations like:

» If your partner releases your child from a timeout that you had imposed, your partner has overstepped their boundaries and violated yours in the process, undermining your authority. The anger that arises in you at that moment is a sign that something is wrong and needs to be addressed.

» If you are a victim of domestic abuse and you have finally had enough of your partner's abusive behavior, anger can energize you to protect yourself, stand up for your rights, and perhaps escape the situation. This is a form of fierce self-compassion as the anger helps you reduce harm to yourself and others.

» When you witness injustice in any form, your righteous anger and indignation can support you in taking action on behalf of those who have been mistreated or harmed.

When anger harms us

The "problem" with anger is not its mere existence, but more a function of the relationship we have with it (where have you heard this before?) and to what degree it then lingers and poisons other aspects of your life and erodes your sense of safety internally and in the world. Anger can become corrosive, disruptive, and problematic in some ways, like these:

» When people are chronically or repeatedly angry, it has significant negative health effects on blood pressure, risk of heart attacks and strokes, and stress-related digestive issues.

» Anger can be a powerful poison in relationships and get in the way of us being able to form new relationships. Who wants to date an angry person who snaps at everything and gets into fights?

>> After having established the power and potential of mindfulness and being in the present moment earlier in this book, you can easily see how anger takes one out of the present moment pretty easily and out of one's own experience. We become so focused on the offender and what they did (in the past) that it is difficult to remain grounded in the present moment.

REMEMBER

The long-term effects of anger are that, in your earnest endeavor to protect yourself from disconnection, your protective feelings of anger harden and petrify into chronic bitterness, pessimism, and resentment.

These "hard feelings" are very resistant to change. Because they are so entrenched in our hearts and our psyche, we haul them around long after we no longer need them to deal with specific situations. The old sayings are that "anger corrodes the vessel that contains it" and "anger is the poison we drink to kill the other person."

Meeting anger with self-compassion

A powerful way of sorting out whether the anger you are experiencing is helping you or perhaps is no longer serving you (in other words, has hardened into bitterness or resentment, or is impeding your ability to move forward in relationships and in life) is to begin to explore it mindfully and self-compassionately. Rather than *reacting* to anger, mindfulness allows us to *respond* instead, and purposefully and patiently responding to anger begins to reveal the underlying message of anger related to the fear of disconnection.

Beginning with validation

Anger is a tricky emotion because it signals so much more, and it is also so physiologically activating (and uncomfortable) that we often slide right past the emotion itself to focus on the target of our wrath instead. This is further complicated by the very real possibility that we may feel some guilt or shame over even feeling anger to begin with. Women in particular are often socialized to believe that they are not entitled to anger or that anger isn't an "appropriate" emotion for women to even feel, much less express. And, like members of other groups that have experienced a great deal of discrimination, anger can come at a very high price, including further disconnection or rejection by others.

There is a yang-like quality to validating your anger because you are standing up for the truth of your anger, the logic of becoming angry in the first place because you've been injured, and your own self-worth as a human being. While this is logical, it is not always easy, but it serves to ground you in the reality of the situation fully and give you a virtual platform from which to explore the feeling more deeply.

For many, just the process of validating one's own anger is a huge accomplishment for the time being, and in the exercise ahead, if this is true for you, know that you can take credit for doing a difficult thing in the service of ultimately being able to work with anger more effectively. As always, be patient, go slow, and remember that if it's a struggle, it's not self-compassion.

Finding the soft feelings behind hard feelings

The challenge, if you are willing to proceed from validating your anger, is to stay present "in the fire" long enough to see what is underneath. We tend to direct our anger outward toward the object of the injury or threat to protect what has been wounded inside of us in that moment. So, our hard feelings are protecting softer, more tender feelings of fear, loneliness, loss, or vulnerability underneath.

Remember how Stella responded to my suggestion that *her* anger was covering up a feeling of vulnerability? In retrospect, that may have been just a bit too much for her to digest in that moment, explaining why she did not return, but the revelation did seem to touch a raw nerve for her. But Stella's lesson may be a guide for you, in that you don't need to rip off the covering shield of anger to expose what is underneath. Self-compassion is not so much about *mining*, but more like *melting* instead.

The challenge then becomes how you may begin to gently explore a potentially tender part of yourself, the way you would tend to a beloved child who was injured on the soccer field or your treasured pet with a thorn in its paw. It is important to know that validation of your hard feelings (like anger) and tending kindly to the injured part of you can actually co-exist. By validating the anger, you are saying that you are fully justified to have felt the anger. That justification puts aside rightness and wrongness so you can tend to the result of that injury instead.

You do not have to forgive the person who hurt you or even fully appreciate the initial injury that triggered your anger in order to simply tend to what needs attention inside you. The circumstances don't matter when you are feeling wounded, vulnerable, or afraid; only the quality of your attention toward yourself matters in those moments.

Uncovering what underlies your soft feelings

"Why would I want to uncover these really tender and vulnerable feelings under the self-protective hard ones?" you ask. Good question. The answer lies in your willingness to continue to approach this practice with some sense of adventure, curiosity, and patience, because when you are willing to see the lost, scared, vulnerable part of yourself, you begin to discover what you really *need*. In much the same way as you discover your core values in Chapter 8, you can often find underneath the painful feelings an indication of what is most important to you.

Take the example of finding out that your girlfriend has invited someone to your birthday party that you really do not like or respect, and you feel you have been pretty clear in your views on this person, even though you know that *she* happens to like this person. This is the straw that breaks the camel's back for you, in that you have seen a pattern of her not listening to or honoring your views or opinions, and you react angrily. The two of you end up in a big fight.

By validating the anger and finding the soft feelings underneath the hard feeling of anger, you may help to slowly melt the anger and see that underneath it is a feeling of being disrespected or even disregarded. But underneath *those soft feelings* is the simple need to be heard and respected. As a person, you really need to feel heard, seen, and respected by the people around you. Nothing unreasonable about that, is there?

Responding compassionately to ourselves

As I discuss in regard to shame in Chapter 11, at our very foundation we all just want to be loved, and this is perhaps the most universal need of all. It is easy to see how that need to be loved underlies the need to be heard, seen, and respected, and applies to the need to be validated, connected, or known as well.

In the kinds of situations that I have described in this section that trigger anger in one way or another, if you look closely enough, you see the simple desire to be loved. Most often in these situations, we are seeking this love from the other person (which is reasonable), but when we do, we overlook the possibility that we could also provide this love *for ourselves* in a way that is not contingent on getting what we seek from the other person.

Perhaps in the immediate aftermath of an incident where you have felt as though your connection was endangered or ruptured by another person, it is wise to let that anger signal the injury, empower you to respond appropriately to protect yourself, or stand up to prevent further harm from taking place. But when that anger lingers on unresolved and you carry it with you long after the incident has passed, you may be able to see how self-compassion can play a role in dissolving or melting the anger. At that point the anger is no longer serving its purpose (and may in fact be poisoning your life in other ways).

TIP

When you can see the soft feelings that were triggered by the situation and the need underneath, you can explore how it may be possible for you to meet those needs yourself. Perhaps that other person is or was not capable of meeting that need for whatever reason, but the best news about self-compassion is that it is unconditional. This means that regardless of whether the people around you can meet some of your needs, your compassion is always available to you.

Practice: Meeting Unmet Needs

In the following exercise, entitled Meeting Unmet Needs, again drawn from the Mindful Self-Compassion program, I walk you through these steps in a formal exercise. In the course itself we move through this process pretty quickly, but since you are encountering it in book form, I encourage you to give yourself plenty of time and space to walk through it step by step, and perhaps return to it over and over to allow the slow and steady melting to take place.

As always, be patient and willing to be a steady but slow learner, remembering the exhortation to "walk slowly, go farther." And please keep in mind that the purpose of this exercise is not to try to fix old relationships, but instead to find out how to respond to them in a new, more self-compassionate way.

Begin by taking a few slow, deep, mindful breaths and allow your body and mind to settle. When you are ready, call to mind a *past* relationship that you still feel angry or bitter about. Let this be a relationship that was mildly to moderately disturbing and not one that was traumatic or abusive (for now). It is important that, for this exercise, you choose a relationship that resulted in anger over how you were treated *that no longer serves a purpose* and that you are ready to let go of.

TIP

It can often be very helpful to focus in on a single specific event in that relationship that still troubles you and may be representative of the larger issues in that relationship. This will allow you to stay focused and follow the exercise, as long as it is not too easy or too tough when you call it to mind. Take the time here to call this situation to mind, imagining it as vividly as you can and getting in touch with the anger and feeling it in your body.

Validating the anger

Understanding that it was completely natural for you to have felt anger in this situation, you may say something to yourself to remind you. You could say, "It's okay to feel angry! You were hurt! This is a natural human response," or something like "You're not alone. Lots of people have felt just the same way in a situation like that."

Really take the time to *fully validate* your experience of feeling the anger itself, without getting too caught up in the details of who said what or who did what to whom. Let those details slide into the background while you validate your feelings unconditionally.

Simply getting to a place of being able to validate your anger is a huge accomplishment in itself, and the self-compassionate thing to do at this point is to pause here for now and let that validation sink in. You may have even suppressed this anger in the past. Right now the best thing you can do is to feel it fully.

You may want to support and encourage yourself by giving yourself a strong yang-like supportive gesture such as a fist over the heart to signify your strength and resolve. Or you may feel that drawing on yin self-compassion by soothing yourself with an open palm on the heart or gently stroking your body in some other location is what you need. You decide what you need just now.

Finding softer feelings

Consider for a moment whether you are willing to move forward and are certain that the anger you feel is no longer protecting you in the way that it once did. If you'd like to release it, then you can begin to explore what may be underneath.

Take some time to see if you may discover some soft feelings (like hurt, fear, loneliness, sadness, or shame) behind the hard feelings of anger.

If you identify a soft feeling coming up for you, try to name it in a warm, understanding tone of voice, the way you might do so for a dear friend — something like "Oh, that's fear" or "You're feeling sad right now." Let yourself have plenty of time to simply feel the feeling that is visiting in this moment because it is here, releasing the need to make it go away or to change in any way. At first, you may simply want to pause at this particular stage and take the time to get to know this soft feeling that has been hiding behind the hard one.

Finding unmet needs

If you are inclined to move on after giving some time and space to the softer feelings, you are invited to begin to release the specific storyline of this particular hurt. Even though you are likely to have very specific and strong thoughts of right and wrong, guilt and blame, see if you can let those thoughts float into the background as you ask yourself the following question:

What basic human need to I have, or did I have at the time, that was not met?

Allow the question to linger in your awareness and see what possibilities may arise when you give them space. Some possibilities may include the following:

>> To be seen

>> To be heard

>> To feel safe

>> To be loved

>> To belong

>> To be accorded dignity

>> To have justice or fairness

>> To feel special or validated

>> To be free

Again, using a warm and understanding tone, try naming the unmet need in a gentle and understanding voice. Just as in previous steps, you may choose to pause here to attend to the unmet needs if you like. Doing so is a radical act of self-compassion too. There's no need to rush on to the next step.

Responding with compassion

If you are inclined to continue, you may consider reconnecting with your intention to be kind and patient and compassionate with yourself by placing a hand on your body somewhere that is supportive and encouraging, or giving yourself a few words of kind encouragement (for example, "You've got this, my friend."). You are acknowledging here that even though you wished to receive kindness or love from another person, that person was unable to do so for a variety of reasons outside of your control.

Thankfully, you have the unconditional and ever-present resource of your own compassion as well. As a result, you can begin to meet your needs more directly, avoiding the middleman (or middlewoman), if you want to think of it that way. What is it that you longed to hear from the other person? Can you begin to say it to yourself?

If you needed to be seen, your compassionate voice could speak to the wounded part of you: "I see you."

If you deeply needed to be respected, you can say, "May I know my own value."

If you needed to feel connected, your compassionate part could say, "I'm here for you" or "You belong."

Or if you simply needed to feel loved, see what it would be like to say, "I love you" or "You matter to me."

This is an opportunity to say to yourself, or just one aspect of yourself, right now, what you may have been longing to hear from someone else, perhaps for a very long time.

Words are one thing, but action is something else. How did you want to be treated by this other person? Might it be possible to commit to taking at least one small step in the direction of caring for yourself as you always wanted to be treated by others?

Even if you find yourself struggling to give yourself compassion for your unmet needs just now — maybe you feel confused or are having difficulty finding an unmet need — you can give yourself compassion for that struggle as well.

Take your time, letting this process again be a melting and not a mining exercise. Linger with each step to let the practice do its work and hold yourself tenderly in it all. You have reached the end of this particular exercise, and you can allow yourself to be just as you are, knowing you can return to this process again as needed. Hold it all lightly and patiently.

Inquiring: What did you discover?

Obviously, this is an exercise with a lot of steps, and as a result, leaves you with a lot of different things to contemplate, consider, and observe. You don't have to rush to make sense of it all, but it may be helpful for you to have the structure of the exercise laid out in a series of reflective questions to consider. There are no wrong answers here, but only unlimited opportunities to understand, appreciate, and make room for self-compassion in meeting anger.

>> How did it feel to validate your anger?

>> Were you able to find any soft feelings behind the anger? If so, which ones?

>> Did you discover a deeper, unmet need?

>> What was it like to begin to meet that unmet need with self-compassion?

>> Where are you now? What do you need?

TIP

The next section moves on to the other pain we experience in relationships, the one of connection, but I strongly suggest that you pause here, put down the book, and give yourself something good (we call this behavioral self-compassion) like a cup of tea, a good rousing jog around the neighborhood, or an episode or two of your latest binge-watch. You deserve to reward yourself for doing this deep, powerful, and sometimes draining work.

There is no gold medal for practicing self-compassion, so you won't win an award for going through this book faster than anyone else. Let yourself be the tortoise rather than the hare . . . a self-compassionate tortoise doesn't always win the race, but it finds joy in the journey, nonetheless. (If you're wondering if a tortoise can have common humanity or not, you're overthinking this whole metaphor. Take a break and ease up, my friend!)

When Being Connected to Others Hurts

"I feel your pain."

This overused cliché is often used ironically to signal someone who is only pretending to know what another is feeling, but it is a cliché (like most) that actually has its roots in common experience. Emotional experiences of other people can actually be quite contagious, and you can probably think of several situations in which you have been around people experiencing strong emotions (both pleasant and unpleasant) and have had some experience of actually feeling what they are feeling. This is much more than simply *understanding* what they are feeling. It's not a cognitive experience so much as an emotional and visceral one. If you have ever held someone who has just suffered a terrible loss like the death of a loved one, you obviously *understand* the logic of *why* they are feeling this profound and intense grief, but you likely also feel the gut-level pain of loss in the pit of your stomach or the helplessness of despair in your heart. We are touched emotionally by the experiences of the people around us, and there is good reason for this, as we explore later in the chapter in the section "How and why connection can hurt."

Being connected to other people has both its joys and its sorrows for sure, but all in all, we are better off being connected and attuned to others than we would be with the opposite. If you find yourself wishing you weren't connected to others because of the potential that you will feel the pain of another's suffering, think about whether you would like to throw away your mobile phone just because sometimes people call you with bad news. Or perhaps you would prefer not to have nerve endings at the tips of your fingers because it hurts when you burn them on a hot frying pan. These difficult experiences are protective and informative experiences as well, if we can see them this way, and the same can be true of our ability to register the struggles of the people around us.

So I invite you now to explore the "you can't live with 'em" part of Kermit and Rowlf's dilemma described earlier, to see how you may bring self-compassion to bear on managing this intimate association that you have with others, particularly when they struggle and suffer and you feel their emotional pain.

How and why connection can hurt

The fact that humans can feel the emotions of another person is undeniable, but the explanation for how that happens — and even more interestingly, *why* it happens — is important to understand. Then you can begin to find a new way of relating to these feelings, allowing you to navigate this web of interconnection with a greater degree of ease. This also helps you to be better able to maintain your own well-being while simultaneously being a better and more compassionate partner, parent, boss, or friend.

Significant evidence suggests that humans are neurologically wired to be able to sense the emotions of other people (to be empathic), although neuroscientists disagree on exactly what that mechanism is and how it works. For our purposes here, we don't need to grasp the subtle anatomical issues at play. We can use the concept of *mirror neurons* as a relatively simple way of understanding what happens, even if we don't exactly know the "how" of the process.

In the early 1990s, a team of neuroscientists in Italy made a fascinating discovery while studying the brains of macaque monkeys. These scientists found that certain groups of neurons in the brains of the monkeys fired not only when they performed an action (like grabbing an item) but also when the monkey watched someone *else* perform the same action and even when the monkey only *heard* the action being performed. This has led to a whole field of study built around these mirror neurons that appear to be the conduit between ourselves and others. Scientists disagree about the exact functions, mechanisms, and purpose of these mirror neurons, but the connection itself is undeniable.

For the purposes of exploring our connections with other people, mirror neurons can explain the pain of connection quite well. If you are attuned to another person, say your partner for example, and your partner comes into the kitchen as you are preparing dinner, you may be able to feel their emotional state of anger. Of course, there are many cues that you may garner from them to sense their emotional state, such as their facial expression, body posture, or saying "I'm very angry with you right now," but many times we sense their anger without any of these not-so-subtle cues. And you may have had this experience even with people you don't know at all but simply encounter on the bus, at the DMV, or at the next table in a restaurant.

You know from your own experience how emotions can be contagious as well. If you are a parent, you may have noticed how your kids can often take on your mood and, conversely, you may have noticed how you can "catch" their mood. Any parent who has ever made the long drive home with a sweaty athlete who ended up on the losing end of a sports contest knows this feeling (however much you may have tried to "look on the bright side" and introduce ice cream into the equation to perk up said athlete).

In intimate relationships it is even easier to pick up on this emotional resonance. Imagine the scenario where you are in a bad mood and you try to hide it from your partner. Your partner comes in none the wiser after a relatively good day and immediately senses something is wrong, feeling wary and perhaps a bit grumpy as a result. "What's the matter?" they say in an edgy voice. "Me? What's the matter with you?" you reply. And so it goes, into a downward spiral that isn't pretty and probably all too familiar.

This interconnection is clear when you consider that, given this state of affairs, others are partly responsible for our state of mind, but equally true is the fact that we are also responsible for theirs as well. Mirror neurons are two-way streets.

SELF-COMPASSION BREAKS IN RELATIONSHIPS

Once you begin to recognize the potential for a downward spiral in your relationship (and really, who hasn't had that experience of an all-too-familiar troublesome interaction with our loved ones?), you have the opportunity to break the pattern or "go off script." As I have quoted Paul Gilbert before, "It's not your fault, but it is your responsibility."

Rather than getting entangled in the downward spiral, one way to tap into self-compassion in that moment is to call to mind the Self-Compassion Break from Chapter 1. If, in a moment of difficulty, you can have the presence of mind to pause and mentally step away from the conflict for even a brief moment, you have done the most difficult part of cultivating a more self-compassionate stance in the relationship.

From that perspective of having paused, you can simply put your hand on your heart or some other soothing place (if that is not provocative to your partner) and acknowledge that "This is a moment of suffering . . . suffering is a part of any relationship . . . may I be kind to myself in this moment . . . may I give myself the compassion that I need." It can be that quick if need be, or you can take more time if it is available.

As an additional resource, you might also consider the "in for me and out for you" breathing practice that I introduce as part of the Giving and Receiving Compassion practice earlier in this chapter. This practice can be particularly supportive *while* you are interacting with the other person because it helps you maintain your emotional balance while in contact with them, helping you keep a compassionate frame of mind.

If you have an opportunity to try this in a moment of relationship challenge, observe carefully how your shift in mood, temperament, and attitude may have an impact on the other person. If this is not your go-to strategy in such moments, it may confuse the other person at first, but try to persist and see what unfolds between you. When you "break script," the other person almost always follows suit because otherwise, it gets awkward when they are reactive and you are compassionate.

With the reality of this "sixth sense" established (although some are more sensitive to it than others), the question becomes, "Why do we have this capability?" By this point in this book, you probably aren't surprised to hear that experts believe we humans have the capacity to feel the emotional experience of others because we are wired to be connected and we need each other to survive. Thus, the mother of a newborn is better able to successfully care for her baby if she can sense the baby's needs and emotional state. As we grow older, we need to understand and cooperate with each other in order to survive and to thrive. In fact, while most people associate Darwin with the idea of "survival of the fittest," he actually more highly valued *cooperation* over competition as a key factor that helps a species survive.

Because we are wired together to empathically resonate with others, not only is it evolutionarily adaptive to sense, understand, and cooperate with others, but it also means that we can have a role in reversing the aforementioned downward spiral and turn it into an upward spiral. We actually have the possibility to catch ourselves in a familiar downward spiral, cultivate compassion (for ourselves and for the other person), and engender feelings of kindness and concern that lead to a shift in our own attitude that can lead to a similar mood adjustment in others.

REMEMBER

In the end, the two-way street of mirror neurons points you to the inevitable conclusion that the best way to have good, harmonious, and productive relationships with other people is to cultivate compassion in the face of suffering — both your own and that of others. Positive emotions flow from goodwill, and all of this leads to positive interactions with the people around you.

Burnout and the myth of "compassion fatigue"

Perhaps one of the most challenging aspects of this phenomenon of empathic attunement is when we empathically resonate with people who are suffering. When you are in a role of providing care to others (whether professionally or just personally), you are likely to make contact with people who are struggling, afraid, dependent, needy at times, helpless at times, and generally distressed. Of course, people in the helping professions (like physicians, psychotherapists, nurses, and coaches) are most often in these kinds of relationships, but all of us have some caregiving role (as parents, children of elderly parents, friends, spouses, or in community service). The fact that we empathically resonate with others is often what draws us to these roles in the first place. But if we are not able to manage it effectively, it can lead us down a road to caregiver fatigue or burnout.

Caregiving fatigue as a sign of being human

Too often, we are intimately familiar with caregiver fatigue because we have experienced it firsthand or have seen it in our friends or colleagues. Characterized by frustration, irritability, absentmindedness, avoidance, loneliness, worry, disrupted sleep, and even resentment, caregiving fatigue is all too common among those who care for people who need help and support.

It's easy to fall into the trap of believing that caregiving fatigue is actually a weakness or a unique failing on your part, but it's actually a sign of being human. What I mean by this is that, as humans, each of us can hold only so much empathic distress. Think of it like a goodwill bucket that you carry, which is slowly filled by the suffering you encounter. If you don't do something to periodically empty your goodwill bucket, it eventually becomes too heavy to carry and you drop it. With emotions, when the weight of distress becomes too great, you begin to resist it, which leads to more fatigue, and ultimately you simply shut down.

This is why I recommend opening and closing (as discussed in Chapter 3) as a self-compassionate means of balancing your capacity to manage pain. The very sad outcome of this resistance and shutdown when we are caring for other people is that you can begin to resent the very people for whom you are caring. Imagine how it might feel, especially if you consider yourself a particularly compassionate person, if you found yourself having resentful thoughts toward your aging mother or your deeply depressed client.

Learning to breathe underwater

If you have ever suffered from caregiver fatigue, you have probably been the recipient of some very well-meaning and heartfelt advice. "Get some exercise," some people say, or "Set better boundaries with your clients," they advise. "You really need to take a vacation; it will help you get your head on straight again," say friends. "You are in need of some serious self-care, my friend. How about booking a spa day soon?" There is absolutely nothing wrong with any of this advice, but it does pose a very real and practical problem. Imagine you're a therapist in a psychotherapy session and someone is pouring out their heart to you and it's really getting tough to hold it all. You can't very well just say, "Sorry to interrupt, but your story is really freaking me out and I need to step out for a few minutes to get a back rub from my colleague."

Self-care off the job is one thing (and certainly important), but how do you meet yourself and the distress you feel when you are immersed in the care of other people? As some have described it, you have to learn "how to breathe underwater."

Especially if you are in a caregiving situation where opportunities for respite and time away are limited to nonexistent (like a sole caregiver for an aging demented parent, for example), you have to find a way to sustain and nourish yourself *while* providing care and comfort to another person who may very well be demanding a great deal of your energy and compassion. As flight attendants advise in their safety briefings, you must put the oxygen mask on yourself first, so that you can then help a child with theirs.

Boundary-making

If caring for someone else is taking a toll on you (or you are subject to this experience of caregiver fatigue at times), you may actually have thought that perhaps you are *too* compassionate. If this idea occurs to you, the natural response is to throttle back on your output of compassion to compensate. However, this simply feels like you are being cruel in withholding the natural love and care that you want to provide. You face a real dilemma in these moments.

Another approach is to have better boundaries, which in many cases feels like constructing an impenetrable wall between you and the other person (especially in professional caregiving situations where you may have many people needing your attention). Mindfulness teacher Saki Santorelli writes in his book, *Heal Thy Self* (Harmony), of boundaries as traditionally defined as a dividing line or separation between two things. However, when we are deeply connected to another person, especially one who is suffering, it is basically impossible (and impossibly harsh) to break that connection. Nonetheless, it *is* possible to allow the boundary to be a place where you and the other person meet, a kind of flexible membrane where each can feel the presence of the other, but there is no blending of the two. This allows us to love another without losing ourselves in the process.

Just ahead I introduce you to a practice that begins to foster finding this balance between ourselves and the other person using self-compassion as the harmonizing factor that supports this balance.

Before you get to the specific practice I am recommending, it is important to dispel the myth of the term "compassion fatigue." This is a commonly used term that is actually a misnomer. When we are feeling depleted and overwhelmed as a result of our connection to another person or other people, ironically enough, it is because we need *more* compassion rather than less.

I explore the difference between empathy and compassion in Chapter 7, and it's worth reiterating here. Empathy is our human capacity to sense the emotions of another person, but compassion is so much more: It holds the suffering in the larger space of awareness and warmth coupled with the desire to relieve that suffering. Empathy is a one-way street (inward), and compassion is a two-way superhighway where we are in touch with the pain and warmly directing kindness back at the same time. This is why some may refer to caregiver fatigue as empathy fatigue, because when you cannot connect to the compassionate part of yourself that feels the pain and wants to relieve it, empathy becomes a tremendous burden that continues to fill your goodwill bucket to overflowing.

Practice: Compassion with Equanimity

PLAY

Don't let the fancy term "equanimity" fool you into thinking this practice drawn from Mindful Self-Compassion is esoteric or intellectual. The definition of *equanimity* is "mental calmness, composure and evenness of temper, especially in a difficult situation." When it comes to maintaining a warm and loving connection with someone who is suffering and may be draining and overwhelming you,

I imagine you would be happy to be a little more equanimous. I share the following poem I once wrote when I realized that the word "equanimous" was the only one I could think of that rhymed with hippopotamus. I had always seen hippos as quite mindful and equanimous, although apparently the equanimity is a myth.

The Hippo
The hippo floats in swamp serene,
some emerged, but most unseen.
Seeing all and only blinking,
Who knows what this beast is thinking.

Gliding, and of judgment clear,
Letting go and being here.
Seeing all, both guilt and glory,
Only noting. But that's MY story.

I sit here hippo-like and breathe,
While inside I storm and seethe.
Would that I were half equanimous
As that placid hippopotamus.

But I digress. This practice combines some guiding phrases with the Giving and Receiving meditation that I introduce at the beginning of this chapter. While I am introducing it here as a formal meditation, you can also do it as an informal practice in moments of difficulty, on the fly, to help tend to yourself when you're feeling symptoms of caregiver fatigue or burnout. I ask you to call someone to mind for the purposes of this first introduction of the practice, but the intention is that you won't have to try hard to call someone to mind later. Instead, when the occasion arises, you will have the practice in your "back pocket" to offer in a time when you are struggling.

When you are ready, take some time to make your body comfortable and at ease, taking a few conscious breaths to settle your mind and body and to find your way back into the present moment. You may even like to place your hands on your heart or in some other soothing and supportive place on your body that helps remind you of your intention to be kind and patient with yourself in this practice.

After taking the time to settle and fully arrive, call to mind someone you are caring for who is exhausting or frustrating you — someone you care about who is suffering right now. (For this first time through this practice, I recommend *choosing someone other than your own child*, as this is quite a bit more complicated and best saved for a time when you feel comfortable with the practice.)

Take some time to really visualize this person and the particular caregiving situation you find yourself in with them. Let the whole experience come alive in your mind and perhaps feel the struggle manifest in your body as well. Allow the struggle to be present for a time so that it really registers, and let go of particular thoughts about it for now. You can always ground your attention in your breath or the soles of your feet if this gets too intense, but remember you are only making room for an emotion that is already here anyway.

Now take the time to repeat the following phrases to yourself, letting them roll through your mind and land in your heart. Take your time and feel the importance and wisdom of these words.

> Everyone is on their own life journey.
>
> I am not the cause of this person's suffering, nor is it entirely within my power to make it go away, even though I wish I could.
>
> Moments like these can be difficult to bear, yet I may still try to help if I can.

You may want to offer these three "Equanimity Phrases" to yourself a few times to allow them to fully register.

Be aware of the stress you may be carrying in your body just now. Inhale fully and deeply, drawing compassion inside your body. Imagine filling every cell of your body with this loving compassion. Allow yourself to be soothed by inhaling deeply and giving yourself all the compassion you may need in this moment.

As you exhale, send out compassion and kindness to the other person who is coupled with your discomfort.

Begin to breathe compassion in and out, at your own rate and rhythm, simply allowing your body to breathe itself. No effort is required. Perhaps settle into supporting the breath with the words "One for me and one for you" or "In for me and out for you." There's nothing else to do but to breathe compassion in and compassion out.

Any time you may notice some holding or tension in your body, you may try inhaling some compassion for yourself and directing it to that area while continuing to breathe compassion out for the other person.

If you have the sense that you need to adjust the balance between yourself and the other person, feel free to do so, directing your breath a little more in one direction or the other. It might be "ten for me and one for you" or "one for me and two for you" or letting it be an even, steady flow of compassion.

You may notice how your body is being caressed from the inside as you breathe. Allow yourself the image of floating on an ocean of compassion — a limitless, boundless ocean that can hold all suffering.

And at a time of your choosing, return to the phrases once again:

> Everyone is on their own life journey.
>
> I am not the cause of this person's suffering, nor is it entirely within my power to make it go away, even though I wish I could.
>
> Moments like these can be difficult to bear, yet I may still try to help if I can.

Whenever you are ready, you can release the specifics of the practice and take some time to simply rest in your own experience of this moment, allowing yourself to be exactly as you are (however that is) just now.

Inquiring: What stood out for you?

Finding a kind of flow and balance between caring for yourself and another person is a labor of love that may take some time to bring about ease in these situations. I encourage you, as always, to be patient with yourself and to be curious about your experience. Consider these questions.

>> What did you notice as you called the person to mind who exhausts and frustrates you? What thoughts, what sensations in your body, and what emotions were present?

>> How was it to offer yourself the Equanimity Phrases?

>> Were you able to breathe compassion in and out, for you and the other person? Did you experiment with adjusting the balance?

I have met many people who have taken those Equanimity Phrases and posted them someplace where they can see them on a regular basis. People who work in healthcare or mental health in particular often find that just reminding themselves that "everyone is on their own life journey" can be a kind of "mini-reset" of their roles and expectations for their work. Take the time to customize this practice so that you can make it easily accessible when you need a course correction or an attitude adjustment.

Finally, always remember that caregiver fatigue is not a problem, but rather a sign that you are human and that you are worthy of your own compassion to help you be compassionate to others. The cliché is "you need to be compassionate toward yourself if you are going to be compassionate to others," but this is actually not true (as you may have noticed way back when we explored how you would treat a friend in Chapter 1). However, compassion for others is definitely *not sustainable* unless you include yourself in the circle of compassion. Put that oxygen mask on yourself so you have it on when you are caring for others, and you can paddle together on that ocean of compassion.

IN THIS CHAPTER

» Exploring the basic principles of forgiveness

» Uncovering some surprising features of forgiveness

» Practicing five steps on the path of forgiveness

Chapter **13**

Forgiving Without Forgetting

Wikipedia defines forgiveness as "the intentional and voluntary process by which one who may initially feel 'victimized' undergoes a change in feelings and attitude regarding a given offense, and overcomes negative emotions such as resentment and vengeance." Sounds simple enough; why don't you just do that and let me know how it goes?

This is very succinctly and directly stated and captures the essence of what forgiveness involves. One could say forgiveness is giving up all hope of a different past. But all of this clarity actually obscures the hard reality that forgiveness is a remarkably complex and thorny emotional challenge that confounds the best of us.

I can say here and now that I will not solve it in this chapter either, but I hope to be able to shed some light on how self-compassion can support anyone in the *process* of forgiveness. It's important to begin by seeing that forgiveness is indeed a process and not a fixed place or destination. Again, as I have pointed out in several chapters thus far, self-compassion is a gradual process of *melting* over *mining*, which is why self-compassion can be helpful.

Whole books are written on the topic of forgiveness, so we just scratch the surface here. But if you would like to move at least a little bit in the direction of forgiveness, these pages can provide you some guidance.

Twelve Principles of Forgiveness

Buddhist teacher and psychologist Jack Kornfield has written and spoken extensively on the topic of forgiveness, and he often speaks in terms of 12 foundational principles of forgiveness. These principles, or steps in the process, can provide you some signposts on the road of forgiveness. Each represents a process in itself to explore and consider.

1. **Begin by knowing what forgiveness is and what it is not.**

   This is the education stage of forgiveness where we recognize the reality that it does indeed mean "giving up all hope of a different past" and that it does *not* include having to forget the offense (more on this later).

2. **Take the time to sense the suffering that lack of forgiveness is unleashing on you.**

   Feeling the weight of holding back on forgiveness allows you to see that it is not in your own best interests and is not compassionate to yourself.

3. **Reflect on the benefits of being able to uncover your loving heart.**

   Once you recognize the burden of holding back on forgiving, you can help yourself remember what it is like to have a loving heart unburdened.

4. **Consider letting go of your loyalty to your suffering.**

   You may be clinging to your wish that circumstance had been different or the offense had not been made, and you may feel a sense of loyalty to the wound you experienced. (Think of the character Gollum in *Lord of the Rings* who evolves into a monster as he protects and treasures his "precious" ring.)

5. **Pause to appreciate that forgiveness is a process.**

   As noted earlier, we are melting and not mining. Forgiveness has various layers to be gently peeled back over time.

6. **Set the compass of your heart and psyche *toward* forgiveness.**

   Much as you identify your core values as a means of reducing struggle and finding ease, setting a steady course in the general direction of forgiveness lets you "move at the speed of trust," as motivational speaker Stephen Covey says.

7. **Remember that forgiveness has inner and outer forms.**

   I focus on the inner journey of meeting the pain underneath forgiveness with self-compassion, but often some form of overt action may also be called for. This may include prayer, ritual, making amends, or any one of a number of outer actions.

8. **Start with what's easy for you.**

   Just as you did in the Lovingkindness for a Loved One practice in Chapter 6, where you began with directing lovingkindness toward a beloved being, you can "warm up" by forgiving people who are easier to forgive and work your way up to the more challenging.

9. **Be willing to grieve and let go in the process.**

   More than just a process, forgiveness is a process of renewal and rebirth in a way. The butterfly ultimately needs to shed the cocoon, and you will need to let go of the past to some degree in order to be free of its burden. This is not easy, by the way (that's why it's way down here at Step 9!).

10. **Recognize that forgiveness is a whole-person process.**

    If you've ever heard someone say, "I forgive you" and known that they were not sincere, it is probably because they hadn't fully forgiven yet. You can feel it in your body when you are holding back on forgiveness, and you can also feel it when you let go. The trauma that is often underlying the need for forgiveness often resides in the body, and making room for this possibility allows for deeper healing.

11. **Shift your identity to forgive.**

    As you begin to tap into your sense of common humanity and feel less alone and isolated through self-compassion practice, you begin to see that there are large parts of who you are that are not touched by what has happened to you. As you realize this, you realize that you do not have to be defined by your experiences unless you choose to be.

12. **Put forgiveness in perspective.**

    Even though our personal "drama" may be incredibly painful and profound, we realize over time that life is so much bigger than our "little stories." It is not just "your hurt" but the hurt of humanity. Everyone who loves is hurt in some way. If you experience loss, it is not just your pain that you feel; it is the pain of being alive. In this you begin to feel your innate connection to everyone.

The Self-Compassionate Path of Forgiveness

The 12 principles of forgiveness are certainly logical and clear, but you may find yourself wondering how to accomplish such a monumental task when you consider any hurt or wound that you may be considering forgiving. Before embarking on a particular self-compassion practice meant to support you in the process of forgiveness, it would be helpful to get clear on a few things.

REMEMBER

The central tipping point (and the reason it is often so hard for most of us to start down the road of forgiveness) is that we cannot forgive others or ourselves unless we first open up to the hurt that we experienced or may have caused.

You have heard a message like this again and again in this book: You have to feel it to heal it. And frankly, you may be getting a bit tired of that message, but it really is underlying all the work you are doing here. To forgive others we have to face the fact that we were hurt, and to forgive ourselves we must be open to the guilt or shame that we may feel for having hurt others or betrayed ourselves in some way.

One way of tipping that balance toward setting a course for forgiveness is to completely let go of the falsehood that by forgiving you must accept bad behavior, or that you must at least forget the harm that was originally inflicted. "Forgive and forget" is the old saying that has set up countless people over many years to further resist forgiveness and shout "I will *never* forget!"

Forgetting is not required, or even expected. The wound or the pain of the transgression was real and deserves to be honored, but that does not mean you have to give it the power to define or limit you. This is all about perspective, as Jack Kornfield noted in Principle Number 12.

Quite often, the harm that we experience from other people feels uniquely personal and intentional but is usually the end result of a whole complex series of causes and conditions that converged in an unfortunate situation that led to you being harmed. This does not excuse the person who caused that harm, but it does hold them in a certain context that helps you see more clearly all the various contributing conditions that led to their bad behavior.

The developer of Non-Violent Communication, Marshall Rosenberg, famously said ". . . expression of anger is the tragic expression of an unmet need." The poet Miller Williams wrote in his poem "Compassion," "What seems conceit, bad manners, or cynicism is always a sign of things no ears have heard, no eyes have seen. You do not know what wars are going on down there where the spirit meets the bone."

Practice: Five Steps to Forgiveness

Chris Germer has distilled this process down to a manageable reflective process that you can try to begin to ease in the direction of forgiveness. As always, there is no benefit in rushing this process or pushing through it to the end. Let it be a process of unfolding, a melting rather than a mining, and be curious and attentive to your needs as you go along.

When you are ready, take some time to close your eyes and call to mind a person who has caused you pain in the past and you *may* (emphasis on "may") be ready to begin to forgive.

As you have the person in mind, it may be helpful to choose a specific event in that relationship that was mildly or moderately disturbing for you. You can always return to more difficult incidents, but keeping with Jack Kornfield's advice, start with something a bit easier first.

Step one: Opening to pain

As you call to mind the person and the situation, see if you can remember it as vividly as possible, allowing yourself to revisit the pain that this person caused you. You may feel this pain in your body somewhere, and if you do, see if you can observe it as it is without shying away or distracting from it.

Step two: Self-compassion

As you hold the pain you are experiencing in awareness, see if you can validate the pain the way you would for a dear friend who was struggling with the same feeling. You might say to yourself, "Of course you feel this way right now. You were hurt! This is painful!"

Let the words, and more importantly the love beneath the words, sink in. Continue giving yourself compassion in whatever form you like. You may place your hand on your body someplace empowering or soothing, and imagine kindness streaming through your hand and into your body. If words are what you need in this moment, perhaps offer yourself lovingkindness phrases like "May I be safe," or "May I know ease," or "May I be kind to myself just now." Take all the time you need. The pain has been with you for a very long time, so you don't need to rush the healing process.

As you are ready and holding yourself tenderly in this difficult moment, ask yourself, "Am I ready to forgive this person?" Take some time to let the answer arise. If your answer is no, then you can simply continue to give yourself compassion for your struggle and your pain. This is enough for now.

Step three: Tapping into wisdom

If you *truly believe* that you are ready to forgive this person, see if you can see the person's actions in the larger context. Perhaps you can understand some of the forces that made this person act badly, like the fact that they too are an imperfect human being and subject to making mistakes sometimes.

Or perhaps there were environmental factors that influenced what happened. These could be things that were beyond both of you or perhaps beyond your collective understanding at the time. Maybe the other person was under a lot of stress at the time, or maybe their life journey included financial stress, a difficult or abusive childhood, low self-esteem, or cultural factors. Again, none of these circumstances excuse the bad behavior itself, but they allow you to see the situation from the larger perspective. Perhaps this person was trying to live their best life, with authenticity and integrity, but the two of you simply ended up at cross purposes.

REMEMBER

Regardless of the particular factors that contributed to the pain in this situation, the pain itself is still quite real.

Step four: Forming an intention to forgive

If you feel ready, begin to offer forgiveness to the other person, perhaps saying the phrase: "May I begin to forgive you for what you have done, wittingly or unwittingly, to have caused me pain." Perhaps offer this phrase of forgiveness a few times to try it on for size and see how it lands for you at this time. You can always return to this another time if you discover that you are not quite as ready as you thought you might be. Or just continue to offer the forgiveness.

Step five: Protecting yourself

Allow yourself to learn in this process of forgiveness, if it feels right, resolving to never be hurt in this way again. You can make a contract with yourself to never be hurt like this again, by this or any other person, at least to the best of your ability. This is the strength and resilience in forgiveness.

Inquiring: How was it to begin to forgive?

This forgiveness practice is rarely easy and is best viewed as a single step in the direction of forgiveness. In an incredibly touching poem called "Prayer Before the Prayer," authors Desmond Tutu and his daughter Mpho Tutu write of the tentative and tender nature of this process, "I am at the prayer before the prayer of forgiveness."

Consider the following questions:

» What did it feel like to re-contact the pain that you experienced? Were you able to contact it and stay with it?

» Were you able to offer yourself compassion in the midst of this pain?

>> Were you able to achieve any degree of perspective over the circumstances or historical factors that led to this person's hurtful behavior? If you were, did that shift anything for you?

>> Did you find the forgiveness phrase, especially "wittingly or unwittingly," ease your process in any way?

As with everything else in self-compassion practice, I hope you took your time, were patient and kind with yourself in this process, and are willing to revisit this practice as part of your process of forgiveness.

Chapter **14**

Cultivating a Sense of Belonging

Think about how you describe yourself to others for a moment. What are the various labels and descriptors you may use to give people a sense of who you are? You might describe yourself as a plumber, an Asian-American, a Democrat, 42 years old, Presbyterian, and so on. You may also have other descriptive labels for yourself that you only share in certain, more intimate situations, such as your sexual identity, your health status, or your life history (like trauma, oppression, or discrimination). I call all of these your identities, and they are important to acknowledge because they make up your sense of who you are.

As a multi-faceted human being (which we all are), you hold a variety of identities that contribute to describing you. You are comprised of the sum of your parts, both those you inherited and those that come from your experience on this earth. One way that these identities help to make you feel unique is the way in which these various identities intersect. In other words, you might identify as a Latinx queer Catholic, or a woman with chronic pain and a history of childhood abuse.

REMEMBER

The various identities you hold intersect to create a quite unique sense of who you are as a whole person.

Each identity that you hold can be incredibly influential and important to you and may have afforded you opportunities as well as burdened or limited you in some important ways. Most of these identities likely have this double-edged sword quality. For example, your race may be quite precious to you because of the history of generations of those who share that identity, but it may also have led to you being oppressed or discriminated against. This can be true of many identities — even some like a history of trauma or chronic health issues — but the silver lining in those identities may be harder to identify or appreciate at first.

It is well beyond the scope of this book to delve into the specific thorny issues of these various identities and how to come to terms with them. They often touch on deeply emotional and closely held aspects of yourself that deserve careful attention that I can't provide here. However, my purpose in bringing them up is to explore how self-compassion can support you in a way that reaches *beyond* these aspects of your identity to looking at the whole package of who you are. Don't get me wrong: I am not suggesting that you overlook or minimize or deny the various identities that you hold; instead, I am advocating for cultivating a place in your heart and in your practice that allows all of these identities *to belong*, and for you, as the holder of these identities, to feel as if *you* belong too.

Putting Your "Whole Self In"

Allowing all of yourself to truly deserve and receive your own compassion is kind of like the "Hokey Pokey" if you think about it. Do you remember this song from your childhood? I remember standing in a circle as a 10-year-old and the teacher playing a scratchy record on a bulky phonograph (a clue to my age!) where we were instructed to "Put your left arm in, put your left arm out, put your left arm in, and you shake it all about. Do the hokey pokey and you turn yourself around. That's what it's all about!"

This raucous activity progresses through all your various parts (with much giggling and silliness) and culminates with "Put your *whole self* in." What I'm suggesting is that self-compassion can help us to include our whole selves within the circle of our own compassion and can protect us against becoming overly preoccupied and limited by certain aspects of our identity that may very well describe us partially but need not define us at the same time.

Let me share a noteworthy example of how these identities can limit you if you become too focused upon them and lose sight of the larger picture. I was once teaching a Mindfulness-Based Stress Reduction course to a group of about 25 people. The group seemed to be coming together nicely, and there was quite a mix of ages, ethnicities, and life experience in the room. I was feeling good about how the course was going.

At the end of the second session, Carole, an older woman with anxiety who tended to sit near the door for each session as a way of contending with her anxiety, approached me with her course materials clutched in her arms in front of her. She asked to speak privately with me, and when we were alone, she tried to hand me her materials and said, "I love this course and I'm getting so much out of it, but I really think I don't belong here." I asked her why she would say that, and she replied, "Well, like I said, I'm getting a lot out of it, but I look across the room at Isaac and I think 'he deals with chronic back pain every day of his life' and I can't imagine what that would be like. All I have is anxiety. His situation is so much worse than mine that I just don't feel like I deserve to take up space in this class when there are people who are much worse off." I reassured her that she was certainly worthy of her own kind attention and eventually convinced her to stay.

But what was striking was what happened at the end of the third session, when Isaac took me aside as everyone was filing out of the room. He looked conflicted, and I had noticed he was much quieter in class this week than he had been in previous weeks and spent part of the class reclining on the floor to relieve a bit of his pain. He said, "You know, Doc, this mindfulness stuff is really good stuff. I've been listening and reading and meditating and it seems to be helpful, but I can't help feeling that I really don't belong here in this class. I've had this pain for years, and I've come to just deal with it like an annoying monster that lives in my body. But then I see Carole and hear what she goes through with all that anxiety and I think, 'How does she do it? I'd be a hot mess if I had that kind of feeling all the time.' I've only got some chronic pain, and here she's got this terrible anxiety. I don't really feel like I deserve this class when there are people like her wanting to be in here."

I *so* wanted to put the two of them together in a room and share what they had shared with me, but confidentiality would not allow that. Yet this very clearly demonstrated to me how two people who suffered with very different, but equally worthy, challenges were actually excluding themselves from a profound opportunity to get some much-needed relief based upon the value they placed on one aspect of their identity. Both Isaac and Carole were discounting themselves and were focusing solely upon evaluating their pain and their anxiety (respectively) to determine their relative worth and worthiness.

REMEMBER

Quite often those who hold identities that are under-represented in certain settings have been conditioned by experience to be particularly aware of how they are different from others rather than their common humanity. If you have felt excluded or minimized because of an identity you hold (such as being a person of color or being gay, in the dominant culture), you've had a lifetime of encountering environments that are structured for the comfort and inclusion of the dominant identity (white or heterosexual, in this example) and not for you. You would naturally then be more inclined to focus on how you differ from others than on how you might be the same. This is a huge inclination to overcome, but self-compassion can provide the means.

Your identities describe you but need not define you

In the end, beyond the various identities that intersect to shape your overall identity, you are still a member of the human race and therefore worthy of kindness, compassion, and love, just like every other human being. What I am suggesting is that these identities do *describe* you but do not have to *define* you.

Too often you may have trouble looking beyond some of these identities (especially the ones that loom large in your awareness because they have led to pain or hurt) to the larger appreciation of your common humanity. Held within the context of your shared human experience, you can see these identities as simply a part of that experience and equally worthy of being included, tended to, and appreciated.

Can you take a radical stand by being willing to embrace these identities? Self-compassion can help you do that by giving you the inner safety and brave space to hold whatever you feel or experience as a human being. As I have established earlier, we humans are over 99.9 percent the same from a genetic perspective, but oh how we like to cling to that 0.1 percent that we perceive makes us separate and different! Even if you look beyond genetics to life experience, religious preference, and other identities, these elements are obvious ways in which we are different but totally overlook the ways in which we are substantially the same.

This is not to say that you shouldn't want to delve deeply and cling tightly to a certain deep connection to, for example, your family heritage or others who share your gender-expansive identity. This actually can foster your sense of belonging and give you a sense of acceptance and pride that can ultimately support you in embracing the entirety of who you are.

TIP

The trick here is to acknowledge your intersecting identities, without becoming preoccupied with any of them. The question becomes whether you can honor these identities by saying "this, too, is true of me" and maintain your awareness of the larger context of your whole self as well. "I am Latin, too." "I am also a Muslim" or "Among my experiences was being the victim of a violent crime." When you broaden your perspective on yourself and your identities, you allow yourself to own them without *becoming* them.

FOR THE TRAUMA SURVIVOR

Psychologist David Treleaven is the author of the highly informative book *Trauma-Sensitive Mindfulness* (W. W. Norton & Company). He offers a few tips for those whose identities include the experience of trauma. If you're someone with a trauma history (which is the case for many of us), it's useful to learn how to focus on good parts of your history — not just what was hard and overwhelming. This isn't in the service of skipping over your trauma, but rather is intended to open up space for you to continually heal and integrate it. Here are a few ways you can practice self-compassion with awareness of trauma:

- **Widen the aperture:** If you're turning and facing your history, see if you can widen your focus. Here you're making room for what's been hard and also what's been joyful, life-affirming, and resilient. You may even include times that have been neutral. The more you can widen your focus as a trauma survivor, the less likely you are to over-focus on traumatic events — something that can limit your capacity for self-compassion.

- **Acknowledge, but don't necessarily engage:** If you encounter traumatic memories or sensations at any point in your practice, you don't always need to engage with them. Parts of you can be highly identified with being a "trauma survivor," and sometimes it's most useful not to fully engage and get caught in the weeds. Sometimes you may simply bow to the memories and narratives you encounter inside (as you will in the practice later in this session) and then carry on, acknowledging their presence with self-compassion.

- **Connect with others:** Trauma can make you feel separate, isolated, and alone. One thing that can be helpful with trauma and self-compassion is to remember that many other people have experienced similar pain in their lives. This is not to discount your trauma, but to connect with a bigger field of awareness. You are actually part of a huge collection of human beings who have had traumatic experiences and claim this particular identity.

Humans are relentless evaluators

Couple this propensity to get hung up on your differences with another interesting human tendency — the human drive to compare ourselves to others and then to evaluate ourselves relative to other people as well — and you start to discover the downside of becoming preoccupied with your identities as defining characteristics, just as Carole and Isaac did.

The tendency to compare ourselves to others is just the way we are wired as human beings. Some believe that this is the last vestige of our need to find our place in the "pecking order" of our herd or tribe, which again ties us to our evolutionary roots around trying to remain safe and secure within our human family. In other words, this is still about our innate human wish to be loved, and therefore protected and connected.

Carole and Isaac each felt quite isolated in their particular brand of suffering, such that they overlooked the obvious fact that they are also humans like everyone else, and equally worthy of love and affection. In fact, even focusing on the identities of Isaac having chronic pain and Carole suffering from anxiety, we can see that each shared these identities with literally tens of millions of other humans who claim the same identity. The one thing that they most identified with and led them to feel isolated from others actually bound them to millions of others!

The Power of Belonging

Kenji had grown up in a really tough family setting. His parents were first-generation immigrants, and they were both forced by necessity to take jobs well below their training and education levels in order to support themselves and their growing family. This situation was a constant strain upon the family and especially frustrating for Kenji's father. Kenji's temperament, even as a small child, was sensitive. He was prone to expressing emotion and was also quite creative and drawn to aesthetic pursuits. His father was literally the opposite of this in many ways and had become a hard, judgmental man who valued hard work, logic, and stoicism. Needless to say, Kenji felt a lot of disapproval, and his father was quick to judge him and frequently made angry, devaluating comments to Kenji, telling him he was lazy, worthless, and weak.

I met Kenji in a workshop on self-compassion for men, and he introduced himself by describing this childhood experience as the source of his own self-loathing and lack of self-compassion. The way he spoke of this identity of having had a harsh, judgmental childhood felt like a big, heavy bag that he had been lugging around for most of his life. He expressed this with a lot of shame and spoke hesitantly as he shared it, as if others might also devalue him for saying it aloud. It was not unlike the way I've heard others describe a past traumatic event in their life, and indeed, this was traumatic to Kenji. The group just listened warmly and attentively as many heads nodded (even if Kenji didn't see this because he spoke with his head down). The safe space had been created in the room, and Kenji was brave enough to trust it.

A few minutes later, my colleague led the group in a short self-compassion meditation that invited people to engage in a Self-Compassion Break and to call to mind a recent difficult situation, to acknowledge common humanity, and to place their hand on their heart (or elsewhere on their body) in a supportive touch. When we inquired into the experience afterwards, Kenji raised his hand, saying that he had had a difficult time with the practice. He said, "I was following along and could feel my internal struggle, but when you asked us to put our hands on our hearts and to give ourselves some kindness or affection, I simply couldn't do it. I just didn't feel worthy of my own love and affection in the situation I recalled, and I literally couldn't place my hands on myself that way."

He started to move past that very poignant statement to say what happened next, but my colleague Daniel perceptively paused him for a moment. Daniel said, "Wait. Just a second, Kenji. Could we go back just a bit? Do you think that right now, in this moment, you could offer yourself your own kindness and compassion? Could you even just say 'I'm worthy of my own love and affection'?"

Kenji looked doubtful but determined. He dropped his eyes and slowly opened his mouth to speak. "I am worth. . ."; he couldn't finish. He took a deep breath, paused, and tried again, without success. The anticipation in the room was growing and we could all feel it, and perhaps all the focus on him was making Kenji feel even more isolated and different from everyone.

The silence went on a bit longer, and then, in a moment I will never forget, one of the men across the circle spoke up. "Kenji, you're worthy of *my* love and affection." Then another man cleared his throat and said, "Kenji, you're worthy of *my* love and affection." Slowly, one by one, every man in the room acknowledged Kenji and repeated this expression of love and belonging. Every man in the room had heard Kenji's story, and yet none of them had experienced exactly what Kenji had experienced in his life. But all felt connected and had no doubt that Kenji belonged in that circle with them.

The other members of the group helped Kenji to honor his life experience (in inviting him to tell his story) and encouraged him not to cling to his feeling of thinking he was fundamentally unworthy, undeserving, separate, or beyond salvation. By reminding him of his common humanity through their expressions of solidarity and support, they made it possible for him to include himself in the circle of his own compassion. Nothing was denied, overlooked, or dismissed about Kenji's identity, but instead the group said "This, too, is true of you," and embraced him, nonetheless.

You may not have a circle of people around you to provide this safe and brave space as these men did for Kenji, but you do have a growing practice of self-compassion that is available to you.

How you resemble an iceberg

You've probably heard the famous quote by John Donne that states, "No man is an island of itself; every man is a piece of the continent, a part of the main." This is another way of pointing to our common humanity. It's a good reminder as you consider seeing yourself as part of a larger whole, even if you hold certain individual identities or experiences. But while you are not an island, you *could* consider yourself an iceberg instead.

What I mean by this is not that you actually *are* an iceberg, of course, but that you (like all humans) *resemble* an iceberg in an interesting way that is worth exploring as part of being willing to acknowledge your intersecting identities without being defined by them.

If you begin to look at your various intersecting identities such as race, ethnicity, gender, body type, and so on, you can also notice that some are more likely to be visible and easily known to other people, while many more identities are not at all visible or easily recognized by others (for example, sexual orientation, life history, illness, socioeconomic status, political affiliation, gender identity, and so forth). Certainly, reflecting on these visible and hidden identities can be fruitful when you are gathering with other "icebergs" (also known as people). They can help you to be sensitive to the needs of other people who may hold wounds or insecurities or long histories of oppression around some of these hidden identities that you might unintentionally insult or violate in some way. For example, you might inadvertently refer to a hurtful stereotype about a certain religious group or tell an inappropriate joke that reflects poorly on a certain gender identity or nationality. So, having this sort of self-awareness of your own "iceberg essence" is useful in social situations.

But if you take the time to reflect on the iceberg of your own identity and look a bit closer, perhaps even taking an inventory of your various identities (something few of us really do in any systematic way), it may be a way of simply acknowledging that each of these is true of you, but also that none of these defines who you are by itself. Once you can begin to simply acknowledge and embrace or befriend these identities, you make room for them to belong in your life and for you to put your whole self into the circle of your own compassion. (Admittedly, this is not always easy, but it can be done in the same way you did this with difficult emotions with the Five Stages of Encountering Emotions in Chapter 10.)

Next, I guide you through a reflection on the iceberg of your identities, and then we slowly begin to embrace that iceberg (an odd metaphor, but you know what I mean) with a self-compassion practice of making room for our identities called the This, Too Meditation.

Reflection: Naming your identity iceberg

Note: This is a modification of an exercise that is done in a variety of settings to sensitize people to their various identities (visible and invisible) and is also an optional part of the Mindful Self-Compassion program. The original source is unknown.

Take a moment to think about the shape of an iceberg, which typically consists of a point at the top and a large percentage of the irregular shape below, with a water-line about one-third of the way down from the top, as shown in Figure 14-1.

When you are ready, pause and take some time to reflect on some of your identities that spring to mind. Write them in the appropriate place inside the iceberg based upon whether they are visible or largely invisible. You can start with some of the identities I mention earlier, but you can think beyond these examples too. For instance, you might list "Sensitive" or "Widow" or "Intuitive" if these are labels that apply in your case. Take your time with this and consider yourself from all different perspectives.

Once you feel that the iceberg is complete, take some time to look at it in its entirety and read through the various identities you have listed.

When you are ready, move through each identity and take some to reflect on whether that identity has afforded you any benefits in your life (like opportunities, privileges, or protection) and if it has, place a "B" next to that particular identity.

Once you have gone through all the identities, move back through the list and consider whether any of the identities has limited you in any way, perhaps due to bias, prejudice, or discrimination. Place an "L" next to any identity that you feel has limited you in some way.

It is entirely possible that several of the identities will have both a "B" and an "L" next to them. It's worth reflecting on these in particular as you go through this process.

You might take a moment just to honor this collection of intersecting identities that you hold. Feel the "fullness" that you may experience from having put onto paper a number of identities that you may have carried all your life and never specifically identified or acknowledged.

You can also take a moment to fully appreciate the benefits that have accrued to you over a lifetime because of some of these identities.

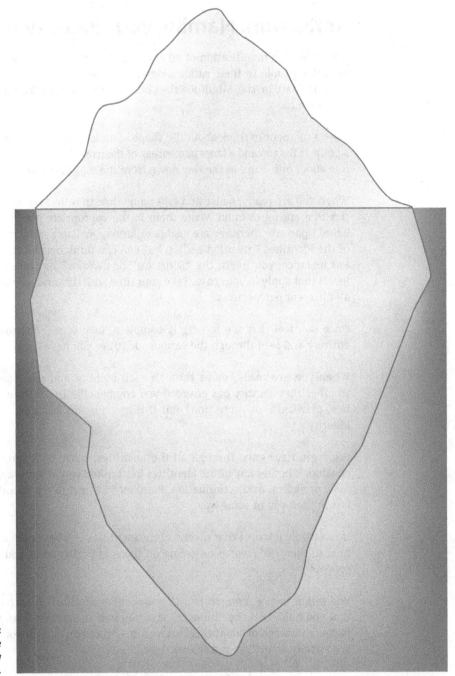

FIGURE 14-1:
Most of the
iceberg is below
the water line.

It is also worthwhile to pause and honor the burden and pain of the limitations you have experienced as a result of certain of these identities. This doesn't excuse anyone or anything and does not assign blame, but simply acknowledges how hard it has been to hold these identities and perhaps the long legacy (in some cases stretching back long before you were born) of pain, oppression, or discrimination that is the heritage of certain identities.

Consider the weight of certain identities, and how some have lifted that weight repeatedly and developed strength, courage, and resilience as a result of facing this oppression and adversity. Have you, in some way, developed some resilience or fortitude or wisdom as a result of this experience? Take the time to make room for this as well.

Give yourself plenty of time to reflect and hold all that may have been stirred up by this iceberg exercise. Perhaps you would want to take a break before moving on to the practice below, or you may be ready to bring self-compassion into the process. What do you need in this moment? Either is okay.

Practice: This, Too Meditation

When you are ready, take some time to make yourself physically comfortable, or at least as comfortable as you can be. Perhaps allow your eyes to close, at least at first (before reading the rest of the meditation) to settle your mind and body and to tune in to your body as it breathes.

Take some time to comfort and soothe and encourage yourself with some kind, supportive touch. Perhaps place one or both hands over your heart or some other place on your body that feels supportive and encouraging and reminds you of the intention to meet yourself kindly and warmly in this practice.

A journey in your mind

When you are ready, take a little mental journey through a beautiful environment of your choosing. Just sense yourself easing into a mountain meadow, or a sunny, sandy beach or a safe and comforting indoor space that is familiar, supportive, and safe for you. Take some time to simply meander mindfully through this space, appreciating the beauty and ease of a space that you have created for yourself.

As you move through this imagined space, encounter, one by one, the various identities that you identified in the Iceberg Exercise, like old friends with whom you have recently become reacquainted. You might form a mental image of a person (or yourself) who represents that identity for you, or maybe a word denotes that identity, or perhaps some other symbol, for you, symbolizes that identity. You may prefer to simply say the name of the identity to yourself (silently or out loud) to acknowledge it.

Greeting each identity gently

See if you can pause and warmly greet each identity, perhaps bowing or offering a smile of acknowledgement or even welcome if that feels right. As you come into contact with this identity, perhaps name it in a gentle, understanding voice and follow that with "This, too, is true of me." Or simply "This, too." So, this might sound like "I am Latinx. This, too, is true." Or "History of abuse. This, too." Return your hand to your body in some form of supportive touch, if that feels right.

Take your time to allow this encounter to unfold in its own time. When the time is right, return to your gentle journey, always supported by your breath and your intention to be kind to yourself as you encounter the next identity in similar fashion.

Continue wandering and encountering and supporting yourself while acknowledging the truth of each of these identities. Take your time, pause when it feels right, and resume when you are ready. At any time, you can step out of this process and pause or leave the practice, or at least move to the closing elements of the meditation. Let your own heart be your guide as to what is right for you in this moment.

Opening up and closing the practice

When you feel ready to begin to conclude the practice, allow yourself to leave your imagined space and return to an awareness of your own self, your whole self, sitting here in this moment. Perhaps gently sweep your attention across your body, taking note of whatever sensation you may be experiencing just now and giving yourself whatever you may need. It may be further soothing or supportive touch, perhaps breathing in compassion for yourself, or saying a few words of encouragement like "This was hard, but you've got this." Remind yourself that these identities that you greeted *describe* you but do not *define* you. Maybe say, "These, too, are true. But I am more than these things," if that supports you and helps you see yourself in the larger context.

Allow yourself to be exactly as you are in this moment and to feel exactly as you feel. Be patient and kind with yourself, your *whole* self.

TIP

You might like to pause and reflect, take some notes, or do something to care for yourself like having a cup of tea, taking a little walk, or petting your dog or cat. These things can help you feel the fullness of your being and the ways in which you look after yourself when you need it.

Inquiring: How was it to greet your identities?

This experience of identifying and acknowledging our various identities can be quite challenging for some, eye-opening for others, and downright pleasant for still others. As they say in the car commercials, "Your mileage may vary." Whatever the experience, take some time to consider what you found out. What did you discover? What surprised you?

Was there anything that you found you could let go of as a result of this reflection and practice? For example, perhaps you found that you had always thought of yourself as a "chronic pain patient" but discovered that there was more ease in thinking of yourself as simply a "person who experiences pain." Often when we see that things that have become part of our identity are simply experiences we have had (albeit sometimes very difficult and painful experiences), we are able to shift our relationship with them, perhaps to set them down and stop carrying them as burdens (or at least lighten the load a little bit), and instead simply acknowledge that "This, too, was true of me."

I once had a woman in one of my courses who came in with quite a pronouncement one week. The group had been tending to what they take in (in a physical but also a metaphorical sense) on a regular basis and simply noticing this.

Kathleen came in and announced, "Everybody knows that I'm The Diet Coke Lady. My friends, my co-workers, everyone knows that I've always got a Diet Coke nearby, and I probably drink five or six of them in a day. I have been The Diet Coke Lady for probably 15 years.

"This week I started to pay close attention to what I'm taking in, and each time I ate or drank anything, I really tried to pay close attention to how it tasted, how it felt in my mouth, how it felt inside my body, the whole thing. I did this with my Diet Coke as well. And you know what? I discovered *I don't actually like Diet Coke!*" The group laughed (and so did I) because in that moment we all appreciated the power of a simple label to overcome the actual reality. By seeing the truth of her situation (her dislike of Diet Coke), her identity shifted to one of being "someone who used to think of myself as The Diet Coke Lady." This did not deny the reality of her past experience, but it allowed her to honor and hold it in a certain way that did not burden or define her in the same way.

When it comes to the experiences you have had, or the preferences you have espoused or the habits you have formed, you are free to form your own definitions of yourself that honor them without letting them limit you. A dear friend told me a story recently about being in the hospital and sharing a room with a man he didn't know. My friend overheard a nurse asking his roommate a series of standard intake questions. She asked the man, "Are you a smoker?" and he replied, "No." She seemed surprised for some reason, but then asked a follow-up question: "Have you ever smoked?" and he replied, "Yes." "When did you quit smoking?" she inquired. "Yesterday," he replied.

Just imagine how that might feel in that moment if you were that man. What he reported to the nurse was absolutely true and he was refusing to be burdened by the label of "smoker" that had been true of him for many years but may very well have made it even harder for him to maintain his abstinence. He could have said, "I am someone who was a smoker," which is a self-compassionate way of accurately describing himself without defining himself and opening up the possibility of continuing in life as a nonsmoker (or former smoker).

REMEMBER

It isn't always true that simply noticing an identity will change it or even dissolve it, but there is some benefit in looking a bit closer and not letting it define you, even if it might describe you. This is an incredibly powerful act of self-compassion in and of itself.

Chapter **15**

Overcoming Our Ancient Brains: Opening to the Good

If you pause and reflect on your process thus far in this book, whether you went systematically chapter by chapter, or bounced around and skipped a few things, there has been a decided emphasis on pain, struggle, and distress. Frankly, some form of pain, suffering, and distress is probably what drew you to this book in the first place, as it is a very strong motivator. So it's natural that this is where I focus your attention. We sometimes joke that the Mindful Self-Compassion program should have more accurately been named the "Opening to Pain and Suffering Program," but we were pretty sure that that would be a bonehead marketing move that would have scared most people away!

But when you step back a bit and look at your experience of life, you realize two things about pain and suffering. The first is that, while it certainly tends to take up a lot of your attention, there is a lot more to your life than this. You have joys as well as sorrows, you have pleasure in addition to pain, and you have ease as well as dis-ease. The things that get you up in the morning and going about your business are the things that bring you joy. It could be the cat who entwines herself around your ankles as you prepare her food bowl, the partner whose smile fills you with warmth, or the sunlight through the trees on your evening stroll. These are the treasures of each life and truly our reason for living, even if much of our energy may be taken up with addressing the things that get in the way of these joys of life.

The second thing you may realize about your attention to your pain and suffering is that you are paying attention to them because deep down, you desire something else. In other words, it is actually your deep commitment to finding joy, to being happy and free from suffering, that causes you to be so energized by your struggles and obstacles and problems. One could say that each of us suffers because we are committed to joy.

When you go to the doctor with a pain in your back, you are going there because you value being pain-free. When you go to your therapist with depression, you want to be happy. If you are outraged at injustice, discrimination, or marginalization, it is because you deeply value a just, fair, and equitable society. It is these core values (covered in Chapter 8) that alert you when they are not being followed or fulfilled.

I take some time with you now to more pointedly bring these things to the forefront of your awareness again so that you more clearly remember why you embarked on this journey to begin with.

Making Room for Joy

As you look more closely, you discover that underneath the tendency to focus upon the problems or challenges in your life is an even deeper and more profound commitment and desire for happiness, joy, and fulfillment. These parts of your life not only energize and sustain you every day, but they also support you in this training process for self-compassion. Think about it: When the going has gotten tough along the way (and admit it, it has sometimes), a desire for something else has kept you putting one foot in front of the other. When people climb Mt. Everest, there are certainly always challenges, pitfalls, and tragedies that may happen, but it is the periodic glimpses of the top (or the imagined triumphant moment of arriving there) that keeps them going.

Ask yourself: What has sustained and energized me so far in this process? Was it a vision of yourself successfully and confidently making a big presentation at work? Was it the loving gaze of a partner, parent, or child with whom you want to connect more deeply and meaningfully? Perhaps it was the felt sense of inner strength and resilience that can lead you to triumph over rigid old patterns of self-loathing and criticism. Give yourself some time to see what gets *you* out of bed in the morning, and what gets *you* to pick up this book and explore a few more pages and practices. Having a clear sense of purpose and vision for what you want to manifest in your life then begins to make room for it in your psyche.

If you haven't quite connected yet with the thing that sparks joy in you, it's worth taking a bit more time before moving forward. Sometimes people embark upon this journey of self-compassion largely driven by their struggles and pain and then generate a certain amount of forward momentum or feeling of commitment to the process and forget the deeper reasons for *why* they are even doing this. Whatever it is that may give you joy may feel as if it has gone dormant inside of you, but trust me, it's in there. James Baraz is a meditation teacher who has written a number of very good books (and offers an online course) on "awakening joy," and thankfully, most of his methods are actually quite simple but powerful means of accessing this joy within you.

The poet Mark Nepo says, "We waste so much energy trying to cover up who we are when beneath every attitude is the want to be loved, and beneath every anger is a wound to be healed and beneath every sadness is the fear that there will not be enough time." Much of what you have done over the past several chapters of this book has been to gently and slowly melt these layers and uncover who you really are, with courage and curiosity, and to embrace that deep desire to be loved. Nepo goes on to say, "Our challenge each day is not to get dressed to face the world but to unglove ourselves so that the doorknob feels cold and the car handle feels wet and the kiss goodbye feels like the lips of another being, soft and unrepeatable." What better reason to get up in the morning than "the lips of another being, soft and unrepeatable"? Your reason may not be lips, but it may be equally powerful and inspiring to you.

TIP

Take some time to "unglove" yourself and see what you encounter that moves and inspires you. This is another process of melting over mining, and you can take your time. When you identify something that sparks joy, you may even consider "What is under *that?*"

For example, maybe cooking your favorite foods (in my case it's Indian food) brings you joy. What is it *about* cooking those foods that gives it such meaning? Maybe it is the virtual symphony that you conduct to bring together disparate ingredients into a coherent and tasty whole. Maybe it is the feeling of caring for the people you are feeding. Or perhaps it is feeling appreciated by those same people — a feeling of belonging and worthiness. Let yourself explore these things that spark joy, so they are front and center in your mind and heart.

The Teflon Versus Velcro Conundrum: Accurately Appraising Experience

As I establish in Chapter 4, the mind loves to wander. It is one of the first things that new meditators discover about their minds and is often the most challenging part of beginning a practice of mindfulness and self-compassion. Your mind may have wandered just since starting this paragraph, for all I know, and I wouldn't blame you for it. This is just what minds do.

But what I didn't explore previously is exactly *why* the mind wanders, and the answer to that question actually addresses why sometimes it is so hard to identify our great pleasures and sources of joy in our lives. Once you understand the nature of the mind and why it does what it does, you can begin to unlock the potential for making changes and shifts in your way of viewing the world to make room for the positive, the joyful, and the fulfilling things in your life.

Have you ever noticed the kinds of things that tend to capture your attention in a day? You may focus in on one experience, like getting an employment review from your boss. She sits down and says some very official-sounding things and then pulls out a long form with numerous checkboxes and columns and rating schemes. Together you make your way through the various domains of responsibility in your job, and she ticks off one line at a time: "Excellent at teamwork, excellent at communication, strong at follow-through, needs work on organization, excellent at problem-solving, strong on leadership." A pretty solid evaluation, all in all, but what will you remember and ruminate on the rest of your day? Probably that "needs work on organization," right? This is the way human minds work.

You see, our minds are not trouble *makers*; they are trouble *finders*. Evolutionarily, our brain has had to be occupied in the primary and ultimate task of keeping us safe and alive. For centuries and generations, Job One of a human was to simply survive, and in order to do that, one had to be on constant alert for threats and problems. The more lackadaisical and happy-go-lucky of our ancestors were the ones who fell off cliffs, ate the poison mushrooms, and were consumed by predators while marveling at a magnificent view. The Nervous Nellies, on the other hand, were always on alert and more often avoided catastrophes of various sorts because they were constantly on the lookout for dangers. Thus, we are the descendants of the Nervous Nellies, and as a result we have inherited their nervous, scanning, observant brains.

As I note in Chapter 4, when the mind is wandering, there is a specific set of structures in the brain that "wire together" to urge the mind to wander, and together they are called the *default mode network* (DMN). This DMN is, as its name implies, our default mental stance when we go about our daily routine. Basically, this DMN is constantly looking around us (and within us) for threats, danger, and problems in order to anticipate, solve, and avoid any harm that may come to us. It is our neurological line of defense against the world. The DMN is looking for dangers and not daisies, problems and not poppies.

Scientists refer to this as the *negative attention bias,* and every human comes by this bias honestly. When you are presented with a set of data, like your work evaluation, your mind will naturally look for the problems and not the successes. It's a natural and understandable expression of your negative attention bias, but that doesn't mean that you are doomed to this bias forever.

Rick Hanson, a neuropsychologist, author, and Buddhist teacher, says, "Our brains are Velcro for negative experiences and Teflon for positive ones." One particularly challenging aspect of this tendency of our brains is that when we tap into anger or fear (which is what happens when we detect a threat or a problem), it automatically narrows our perceptual field (we get tunnel vision) so we can address the problem. Everything else (the positive) gets crowded out. Thankfully, if you make room for positive emotions like love and joy, you actually broaden your awareness to free you up to see new opportunities and creative solutions. Helen Keller once wrote, "When one door of happiness closes, another opens, but often we look so long at the closed door that we do not see the one that has been opened for us."

The purpose of this chapter is to help you overcome this negative attention bias and to purposefully shift attention to positive experiences, not to cancel out or avoid or dismiss the unpleasant and painful ones, but to purposefully create a more equitable and accurate awareness of the two sides of experience by making room for the positive.

Cultivating Happiness by Embracing Your Life

Our brains have well-worn pathways leading us to problems, threats, and pessimism, but neuroscientists are clear that we can lay down new pathways of joy and satisfaction if we are patient and persistent in forming these new habits. Not that long ago, we were told that our brains were relatively fixed and unchangeable, but the wonders of modern technology have allowed us to look more deeply at the brain and observe it in real time, such that we can see that the things we do in our daily activities have an impact on the brain.

Studies show how long-time meditators actually are able to preserve cortical thickness in their brains relative to non-meditators. In a classic study of London cabbies (well before the onset of Google and GPS), researchers found that those drivers who had spent years learning the complex map of London streets actually had a *hippocampus* (the structure in the brain devoted to spatial intelligence) that was significantly larger than that of regular citizens. Other studies have also shown that regular meditation practice can impact the relative contribution of areas of the brain devoted to positive and negative emotional states, such that the meditator has easier access to the positive ones. (These same studies note improved immune functioning as well.)

So this evidence suggests that, just like our muscles, we can impact the functioning of our brain through intentional activity. It doesn't happen overnight (there is no pill you can take to change your brain in this way), but with systematic "brain training" you can get out of those well-worn grooves of the negative attention bias and forge new pathways that make room for the positive, the fulfilling, and the joyful.

Specifically, there are three kinds of positive experiences that one can cultivate with intention, and I introduce you to all three in the following sections, along with specific practices designed to cultivate these experiences. These experiences or practices are savoring, gratitude, and self-appreciation.

Savor the flavor . . . of life

Going back to the analogy of our brains being Teflon for positive experiences, perhaps we could extend it to say that we can intentionally peel off that coating to our brains and let things stick a bit longer and make an impression. When it comes to cookware, this is a dishwashing nightmare, but when it comes to your brain, we can call it savoring — allowing the pleasant experiences that arise to actually remain with us and stick to our awareness in a way. It's probably best to leave this analogy behind at this point, but I think you see what I'm driving at. With intention, we can actually use our mindfulness to become aware of pleasant things when we happen upon them, pause, and let them make an impression on us and register in the brain as just what they are: pleasant experiences.

I happen to live on a beautiful stretch of the Oregon coast, and we have an amazing view to the west over an iconic bridge to the Pacific Ocean beyond. The sunset views are amazing, but there have been moments when my wife will exclaim, "Check this sunset out!" If I'm preoccupied with something else, I might politely look up, see the view, and smile appreciatively before moving on to whatever seemed so important at the time. That is decidedly *not* savoring, but it's often what we do when we encounter things that are pleasant, beautiful, inviting, or pleasurable in some way. Savoring would be me actually stopping, turning to face the sunset, and allowing it to simply land in my consciousness and make an impression on me.

Think of the difference between passing someone in a subway tunnel and meeting someone for the first time on a Match.com date. The former is gone in an instant, but the latter is likely to make an impression because you are simply opening up to them and taking them in (while surreptitiously checking to see that their clothes are clean or listening for references to living in their parents' basement, perhaps. After all, this could be your soulmate!).

Research suggests that simply savoring our positive experiences increases happiness and satisfaction, and even savoring positive memories increases activity in brain areas associated with positive emotions and resilience. And the really good news is that you don't have to go looking for these positive experiences, because they are happening to you all the time if you open up to them. Right now, I am sitting at my computer, but I just took a sip of cool ice water that was delightful in my mouth and going down my throat. The fir tree outside my window is swaying gently in the breeze in a rhythmic way, and I can see a photo of my son and I smiling into the camera in bright red sweaters from a few Christmases ago.

You don't have to look for transcendent, euphoric experiences but simply lower the bar for what you find to be pleasant and enjoyable. The poet Mark Nepo says, "The key to knowing joy is to be easily pleased." Can you let yourself be "easily pleased"?

TIP

A wonderful opportunity to practice savoring is with food and eating. Perhaps resolve to eat your very next meal or snack mindfully and with the intention to savor the aspects of it that are enjoyable, tasty, or pleasant. Let all your senses get involved and notice the sights, sounds, smells, tastes, textures, and so on that come into your awareness. When something piques your interest or sparks a little bit of joy, pause and let it land. Allow the experience to register.

Practice: Something to savor

The following is another practice drawn from the Mindful Self-Compassion program. In that program it is referred to as a Sense and Savor Walk, but the good news about this particular version is that you can do it anywhere, and you don't even have to walk if you don't want to. However, if you have access to a pleasant, relatively peaceful, natural setting like a garden, backyard, or park, it can be especially enjoyable. And if you don't have this available to you just now, you can simply let your mind wander (as you know it does!) around the space you are in in a similar fashion.

The invitation here is to allow yourself and your imagination some time and space to wander. Imagine that you and your attention are like a honeybee or a butterfly in a beautiful garden, simply flitting or buzzing from thing to thing that captures your attention. Take your time and when something captures your fancy, pause and simply take it in. Be sure to engage all your senses if you can and let the thing make an impression in your mind.

Stay with each experience as long as you like, lingering longer than you usually would to truly savor and appreciate the experience. When it feels right, disengage and flit on to something else that captures your heart. Let this be a light and easy practice that is not about *trying* to enjoy yourself but about letting pleasure come to you.

Recognize the pleasant thing when it comes into your field of awareness, allow yourself to be drawn into it, savor it for as long as you like, and then let it go as you move on. Like a bee that fills up with nectar and returns to the hive to deposit it before going for more, you can pause when you feel full, let yourself feel the fullness, and then move on to the next thing.

Take all the time you can and let it be a luxurious experience like soaking in a warm bath after a long day.

Inquiring: What was it like to savor?

Without having to analyze your experience of the Something to Savor practice, what comes into awareness when you reflect on it? What did you notice? What did you discover?

Did you face any challenges in this practice? Were you able to notice the habits of the mind, perhaps pulling you away to other experiences, other times, problems, or worries you may have? Remember, you are just now beginning the process of retraining your brain to open up to the positive and the pleasant, and you have had a lifetime of practice looking for problems and threats. See if you can be patient with yourself. Know that as you continue to purposefully practice in this way, you can build new neural pathways that align you with the good, the pleasurable, and the joyous.

Gratitude and well-being

Gratitude is like savoring on steroids (well, without all the nasty side effects). What I mean by this statement is that the foundation or first step of accessing feelings of gratitude is to actually notice the positive things in your life. Just as compassion cannot arise without mindfulness (actually being aware that suffering is present), gratitude cannot arise unless you are mindful of the gifts and treasures that you have received.

A CHOCOLATE MEDITATION

Who can resist a headline like that?

As you have no doubt discovered by now, the practice of self-compassion is so much more than a "feel-good" practice and involves a fair amount of courage and willingness to embrace all the facets of life: the painful and the pleasurable, the dark and the light, the bitter and the sweet. In the end, self-compassion is really about embracing all of your life and meeting yourself kindly and firmly in the midst of it all. Even this chapter on opening to the good is really about including the good alongside the rest and appreciating the whole package that is you.

Finding the balance between the two sides of the coin of life is not always easy, and this is a brief, fun meditation that you can do to get a felt sense of what doing this can be like. You need to have a piece (or a few pieces) of bittersweet chocolate for this practice. No need to feel guilty about going to the store to purchase chocolate; just tell yourself (and the checkout clerk) that this is important homework.

When you are ready, pause for a moment and consider that our perceptual system thrives on contrasts. In order to know dark, we have to know light (even when it comes to chocolate!); to know good, we must also know bad. As Chris Germer has said, "We know the toe is soft because the rock is hard." Therefore, our lives as humans are always bittersweet, just like this particular dark chocolate.

Break the chocolate into three pieces and place the first piece in your mouth. First, focus your attention on the bitterness, perhaps noticing where bitterness arises in the mouth and on the tongue. Take your time and eventually swallow the chocolate.

With the second piece, let your attention rest on the sweetness this time. Notice whatever unique qualities arise around sweetness and see if you can fully savor it. Again, take your time and swallow when you are ready.

Finally, with the third piece, see if you can embrace both aspects, the bitter and the sweet, in your awareness. Feel the tender flowing dance between these two different qualities, just like the ebb and flow of bitter and sweet in your daily life. See if you can find an appreciation for the interplay of these two tastes and how together they are much more complex and fuller than they are separately.

This is the essence of our human experience, and making room for the fullness of experience is the ultimate goal of self-compassion practice in many ways.

When you notice the pleasant things in your life and let them register with you as you savor them, you are likely to further appreciate the causes and conditions and people that led to that moment and your opportunity to experience it. As you begin to appreciate this interconnection between your pleasant moment as it is and a whole series of events and conditions that went into it, a natural sense of gratitude for all of it arises.

For example, perhaps you find yourself savoring a remarkably warm, savory, and buttery croissant with your coffee this morning. (Mmmmm, I'm getting hungry just thinking about it and wishing I had one! But I digress.) As you notice the flakiness of each morsel and appreciate the taste exploding on your tongue and the feeling of satisfaction as you swallow, you may slowly begin to broaden your attention. You may become aware of the person who brought you the croissant, the person who lovingly prepared it, the person who milked the cows to make the butter, the cows themselves, the sunshine and water that fed the wheat and nurtured the cows, and on and on. This is more than just an intellectual exercise; it's a heartfelt appreciation for the interconnection between all things and how nothing arrives without a whole confluence of factors arising.

There is growing evidence that the systematic practice of gratitude (usually in the form of keeping a daily gratitude journal in which you note ten things you are grateful for each day) can have a significant effect on well-being. Research suggests that a regular practice of gratitude reduces stress and depression, increases optimism and overall well-being, and leads to healthier lifestyle choices and behaviors (such as healthy eating, improved sleep, and enhanced physical health).

REMEMBER

It's important to notice that one thing that differentiates gratitude from savoring is the interpersonal aspect of it. It may seem quite solitary to reflect on things you are grateful for, but by doing so you are dispelling the illusion that we are separate from others and therefore isolated. So practicing gratitude actually enhances your sense of common humanity and connection with others, which really makes it a *relational practice* in the end.

Practice: Gratitude for little things

This simple practice gives you an opportunity for further pausing and reflecting on the pleasant and positive experiences. It also serves to formally begin practicing gratitude as a precursor to making it a part of your routine as you create these new neural pathways for taking in the good.

Take out a piece of paper (sometimes "going old school" and actually writing these things down with a pencil on paper helps you cement them in your mind) and pause to reflect. Taking your time, write down ten small and seemingly insignificant things that you are grateful for. Think of things that you often overlook but actually make you feel grateful when you think of them. Think small and remember Mark Nepo's words, "The key to knowing joy is to be easily pleased."

You might think of wheels on suitcases (as I have often done), the smell of hot popcorn, a familiar jazz riff, or your dog's wagging tail when you come home — whatever springs to mind. You may even call the thing to mind, savor its impact on you, and then write it down.

Once you have ten things on your list (it shouldn't take long), take a little time to go back and wander through your list.

Inquiring: How did it feel to practice gratitude?

What did you notice as a result of doing this simple gratitude practice? Perhaps you noticed feeling a bit happier, more relaxed, or at ease as a result of reminding yourself of your many blessings and the things that led to you experiencing them. Maybe for this moment you were able to resist the negative attention bias for a time and see things more clearly.

Note that sometimes you may feel a bit worse after this practice if you judge yourself for not being happier or feeling more grateful than you are. This is not unusual, but rather something to tend to. See if you can use different language than simply, "I am not grateful enough" or other judgmental phrases. Consider saying to yourself, "I have not been as grateful for things as I could have." Phrased this way, you are simply saying how it has been for you and leaving yourself free to change that pattern over time, whereas a blanket statement about how you are (for example, "not happy enough") dooms you to repeating that pattern.

TIP

This gratitude exercise is essentially the procedure for keeping a gratitude journal. If you make a commitment to keeping a small journal, perhaps beside your bed or someplace where you will make it a part of your routine, you simply take the time each day to record the things that you are most grateful for. Nothing more. The science is clear that you will likely derive a benefit in terms of better mood and well-being as a result of doing so. Many couples also find that keeping a joint gratitude journal that they complete together each day is a beautiful bonding experience that helps make it a more social and connecting experience.

Who have you missed? Appreciating our own selves

It is entirely likely that, as you assembled your gratitude list in the preceding section, there was one thing missing: your own good personal qualities. As is the case with compassion, most people forget to include themselves in the circle of gratitude or appreciation and tend to focus outside of themselves or on others. You can be grateful for so many things in your life, and yet your tendency may be to overlook our own good qualities. Your tendency may very well be to criticize yourself instead and focus on where you feel you are inadequate or in need of improvement and simply take your good qualities for granted. The end result of this tendency is that you end up with a skewed view of who you are. It's like the false humility when we wear a new piece of clothing and someone compliments us on it and we respond, "Oh, this old thing? It's nothing. I just had it lying around."

How many of these positive qualities do you find yourself struggling to acknowledge? Do you have difficulty receiving compliments when people offer them to you? Many people find that, consistent with the negative attention bias discussed earlier, compliments seem to bounce right off while the slightest negative feedback becomes our preferred topic of rumination for quite some time. It feels downright uncomfortable for many of us to even think about what's good about ourselves.

You may wonder why it's so hard to accept compliments, and the answer is probably familiar to you. Usually, we don't want to alienate our friends by appearing to brag about our good qualities, or we've been taught that if we somehow raise up these qualities, we are then subject to being knocked off a pedestal. Many of us heard this morsel of wisdom from our parents when we crowed about something we felt we did well: "Don't get too big for your britches, young man!"

You may think that this is a cultural issue and that certain cultures celebrate self-appreciation better than others, but this appears not to be the case. In fact, I have been quite amused when I have asked various groups all over the world about why it's so hard for us to appreciate our own good qualities, and they often respond the same way. They say something like, "You don't understand. You see in *our* culture, we have this thing that we call _____ and it means that you should not try to stand out or hold yourself above other people because you will suffer as a result."

The amusing thing is that everyone thinks that their culture is uniquely different in this way, but they all describe essentially the same principle. It is referred to as the "Tall Poppy Syndrome" in some countries, wherein you don't want to be the tall poppy in the field because that is the one that gets cut off! And in this analogy, you can hear the evolutionary roots of the phenomenon. If you are a member of a herd that gains its safety from togetherness, the last thing you want to be is the one that stands out from the herd or the tribe, because that means you are vulnerable to predators. We just can't seem to shake our evolutionary roots, can we?

REMEMBER

When you are aware of your common humanity, however, you realize that everyone has strengths and good qualities, and it facilitates each person in being able to appreciate them. When you acknowledge this truth, then you realize that it does not mean that you are superior to others or the only person who has this trait, just that this, too, is true of you.

Furthermore, we come by these strengths and qualities, to some significant degree, because of multiple factors outside of ourselves, including other people who may have taught, nurtured, mentored, or inspired us. By recognizing the contributions of others when we appreciate our good qualities, we are actually honoring those people and their gifts as well, and honoring our interconnection with them too.

Self-appreciation is certainly not selfish at all; it actually provides the emotional resiliency and self-confidence that we need to engage with and support other people in a sustainable and meaningful way.

When you can appreciate your own good qualities, you are better able to support others in doing the same. As a parent, supervisor, mentor, or friend, your capacity to appreciate your own strengths is a powerful embodiment of self-compassion that is felt by those who look to you for inspiration and guidance.

Practice: Appreciating your good qualities

Once again, this is an exploratory practice that is drawn from the Mindful Self-Compassion program, intended to begin to foster awareness of, and appreciation for, your own good qualities. This can be a novel sort of reflection for some people and can even activate some painful emotions. As always, please give yourself what you need at any point (after all, that's what self-compassion is all about!) and be patient and kind with yourself.

Take some time to put aside distractions, find a comfortable position for your body, and allow your eyes to close or your gaze to soften so that your attention is directed inward. Perhaps notice your breath moving in and out and allow yourself to ride on the flow of breathing. You may even place your hand on your heart or some other supportive or soothing place on your body to remind you of your intention to be kind, patient, and curious.

When you are ready, see if you can call to mind three or four things that you appreciate about yourself. At first, the things that come to mind may be more superficial in nature, but be patient and willing to probe a bit deeper to see what you really, deep down, like about yourself. Keep in mind that this is a private exercise, and you won't have to share any of what you come up with, so you can be truly honest with yourself.

At first, tuning in to what we really like about ourselves can feel awkward or even a little bit uncomfortable. If this is the case for you, then remember to go slowly, be patient, and respond to any discomfort with whatever you may need in that moment. Simply give yourself the time and space to feel whatever you're feeling and to be exactly as you are.

Keep in mind that when you acknowledge these good qualities, you are not saying that you *always* show these qualities or that you are any better than anyone else. You are simply noting that this, too, is true.

Take your time, but when you have accumulated a few things, see if you can choose to focus in on just one of them that resonates for you just now.

As you hold this quality in awareness, see if there are any people associated with this good quality for you. Perhaps friends, parents, teachers, even famous speakers or authors may come to mind — people who were a positive influence in your life in some way. You may even visualize each of these positive influences in your mind's eye and send *them* some warmth and appreciation as well.

Our encounters with influential people in our life are not always pleasant or easy at the time, but they can make us better and stronger people as a result. Sometimes we grow and develop out of hardship that another person put us through. If there was someone like this in your life who ultimately made you a better person (whether it was their intention or not), can you acknowledge this as well?

By honoring ourselves for these qualities and acknowledging those who influenced us, we are also paying tribute to them.

Give yourself time to savor this opportunity to simply feel good about certain aspects of yourself. Let the experience fully register and sink in. Take all the time you need to let self-appreciation take root in your heart.

Inquiring: What was it like to appreciate your own good qualities?

As you reflect on this experience, consider that this may be a new practice for you, and whatever you discover is worth exploring patiently and kindly. As I note earlier, we get a lot of conditioning to ignore or overlook our positive features and talents, so it takes some time to develop some ease and willingness to shift these patterns.

What came up for you as you beheld these positive qualities?

Was there anything noteworthy about including those who may have contributed to your having these qualities? Did this make the practice easier or harder to do?

Which exercise was easier for you: gratitude or self-appreciation? Why do you think that was?

Do you feel an inclination to return to this (or any of the practices in this chapter) over time? Remember, you have had a lifetime of experience to develop your negative attention bias, and that means it will take some patience, persistence, and time to develop new habits of mind and heart.

5

The Part of Tens

Find ways to continue to explore and study self-compassion.

Explore ways to support yourself in the continued practice of self-compassion, even when it gets hard.

Discover ways that self-compassion can positively impact your relationships and deepen your connections.

Pick up some small, quick, and easy self-compassion practices that can make a big difference.

IN THIS CHAPTER

» Exploring the Center for Mindful
  Self-Compassion

» Discovering books and other
  resources for learning more

» Linking to websites, blogs, and apps
  to support your practice

Chapter **16**

Ten Paths for Further Practice and Study

t seems that perhaps you are on to something here with self-compassion practice, right? Maybe a few light bulbs went on during the course of reading this book and trying out the practices, or maybe it was more like a floodlight. Whatever the case, you are keen to go further with exploring how you can become more self-compassionate, or you simply want to sustain the practice over time. Take some time to browse through this chapter to see what catches your eye, as there is a little something for everyone here.

The Center for Mindful Self-Compassion

The Center for Mindful Self-Compassion (CMSC) exists with the sole purpose of being the "global leader in self-compassion training" and is the home of the Mindful Self-Compassion program. The website (centerformsc.org) is a virtual treasure trove of information, resources, and materials to support you in your practice and exploration of self-compassion. You can find recorded meditations, listings of self-compassion-related books, and teachers of the MSC program around the globe; take Live Online MSC courses; and discover other special programs constantly being offered by the center and its teachers.

As the executive director, I am admittedly biased, but CMSC is really the world-wide hub for all things self-compassion related. Take some time to explore it and discover its riches, perhaps subscribing to the CMSC newsletter or even looking into how to become a teacher of MSC as well.

But most of all, I highly recommend that you consider continuing your journey of self-compassion by taking the eight-week Mindful Self-Compassion course (online or in-person) or seeking out a five-day MSC Intensive course if that suits you better. These can all be found on the CMSC website.

Three Core Books on Self-Compassion

CMSC has an extensive listing of interesting books published about self-compassion at centerformsc.org/cmsc-library/. But I would highlight three as key to getting a firm appreciation for the practice and the MSC program:

>> *The Mindful Path to Self-Compassion: Freeing Yourself from Destructive Thoughts and Emotions* by Christopher Germer (The Guilford Press) offers a clinical psychologist's perspective on self-compassion as a means of contending with the challenges people face in life. Drawing on Chris's decades of experience as a therapist and a meditator, this book is an eye-opening read because it explores the paradox that you have discovered here: We all want to avoid pain, but letting it in and responding compassionately to ourselves for experiencing it is an essential step on a path to healing.

>> *Self-Compassion: The Proven Power of Being Kind to Yourself* (William Morrow Paperbacks) is an extremely accessible and inspiringly candid account of Kristin Neff's journey to becoming the global authority on self-compassion. Drawing on her personal experience, Kristin really shines light on how one can meet self-criticism and offset its negative effects through moving toward self-compassion and away from the limited usefulness of a focus on self-esteem. The book includes exercises and action plans for putting self-compassion into action.

>> *The Mindful Self-Compassion Workbook* by Kristin Neff and Christopher Germer (The Guilford Press) is a rich companion book to the MSC course itself, but is designed to be used as a self-paced learning and practice guide. The book is more closely aligned with the specific organization of the MSC course and provides many opportunities for journaling, practicing, and exploring various aspects of self-compassion practice in a very practical and easy-to-follow form.

Self-Compassion-Based Retreats

A recent study suggested that most people would rather get an electric shock than be alone with their own thoughts, so the idea of joining a residential silent meditation retreat may sound like a nightmare to some. However, it may sound like a dream to others. The reality is that, like mindfulness and self-compassion practice itself, it has aspects of the whole range of the enjoyment spectrum. But in the end, having uninterrupted time to cultivate a warmer, more supportive, and kinder relationship with yourself can be a tremendously revitalizing and healing experience. Like all things in this book, I recommend that you go slow and be patient with yourself in choosing a retreat, but don't let all that silence scare you!

You can often find daylong or weekend retreats as a nice introduction to retreat practice. Most meditation retreats combine sitting and walking practice with talks by the teachers and sometimes other activities like gentle yoga, usually in a remote setting with healthy food and spartan living quarters. Five- and seven-day retreats are quite common as well and are often quite affordable, many being offered on a dana (donation) basis. Simple internet searches can find retreats near you that are primarily mindfulness and self-compassion-based. Look for a focus on mindfulness and compassion meditation and those that incorporate large periods of silence and contemplation. CMSC has a page devoted to retreats offered by MSC teachers around the globe and is a good starting point: centerformsc.org/course/category/silent-retreats-offered-by-msc-teachers/.

Community of Practice

Thus far you may have found this journey of self-compassion to be a rather lonely one as you made your way through this book. As I note elsewhere, it can sometimes be hard to get a strong sense of common humanity if you are feeling isolated or separate from others (physically or emotionally). Humans are social beings, and we thrive in community with others where we can feel understood, accepted, embraced, and supported. Even in the somewhat solitary practice of meditation, it helps to commit to participate in some sort of ongoing practice group or experience.

You might reach out to MSC teachers in your area (search the directory on the CMSC website) or other meditation teachers or centers to see if they host ongoing meditation or study groups. CMSC also hosts ongoing free online drop-in groups called the Circles of Practice for those newer to the practice of self-compassion as well as others for "graduates" of the MSC course. These sessions are led by highly experienced MSC teachers and are simply a virtual space for people to gather and practice together with a brief opportunity for people to discuss, ask questions, and connect. For more information, check out `centerformsc.org/msc-circle-of-practice/`.

Websites, Audio, Apps, and Other Technology

The online practice groups just mentioned are one way of making use of technology to support your ongoing practice. We are all so enmeshed with our technology today — with smartphones, smart watches, constant Wi-Fi access and all the rest — that it's worth noticing your relationship with it, in the same way I suggest you look at your relationship with yourself, your emotions, your thoughts, and your sensations. Rather than fully resisting technology (remember, what you resist, persists!), I encourage you to explore how technology can support you in your practice.

At a very basic level, searching out websites and blogs devoted to mindfulness, compassion, and self-compassion can be quite fruitful and lead you to all sorts of tips, tricks, insights, and ideas to keep you motivated and informed.

One way to help provide some structure and focus to your ongoing practice is to listen to guided meditations. You can certainly listen to the guided audio practices included with this book, but there are also numerous such meditations in other locations online. Again, CMSC hosts a page on the SoundCloud site that not only houses meditations by MSC co-founders Chris Germer and Kristin Neff, but also many Certified MSC teachers' meditations, including those in quite a number of different languages. See the site at `soundcloud.com/centerformsc`.

Smartphone and smart-watch apps are proliferating rapidly, and a comprehensive review of them is well beyond the scope of this book. Some of these apps (Insight Timer and The Mindfulness App are the most popular) provide links to literally thousands of meditations, but also tap into common humanity by letting you know how many people are meditating along with you at any given time and where they are in the world. Other apps, like Headspace, Calm, and MindFi, are a bit more ambitious and attempt to harness the technology to give you a more structured and sequential experience to meditation training. While their focus (at the time of this writing) is more on mindfulness, this provides a solid foundation and support for your self-compassion practice.

CDP: Deepening Your Practice Beyond MSC

If you are a lifelong learner of self-compassion and have had the opportunity to take the Mindful Self-Compassion course, you may want to delve into the Community for Deepening Practice, which is a program designed to be a "deeper dive" into the MSC program to explore, elaborate, and enhance what has been learned in the course. In the CDP you join a cohort of no more than 19 other participants who meet weekly in large- and small-group configurations over the course of eight months. The CDP is led by skilled and Certified MSC teachers and includes a rich online environment for ongoing support, encouragement, and dialogue. This is a unique opportunity to drop a bit deeper into the lifelong practice of self-compassion. Find it at www.befriend-yourself.com/.

Fierce Self-Compassion

One of the challenges to finding out about self-compassion is that many people (as you may well know from your own experience) have certain misconceptions and misunderstandings about what it actually is. Furthermore, many people see it as primarily a soft, nurturing, soothing practice, when in fact, it has a quite strong, vibrant, and empowering side as well. I refer to this as the yang side of self-compassion in this book, and Kristin Neff's book entitled *Fierce Self-Compassion* (Harper Wave) is a compelling exploration of this more active side of the practice. It compels you to act courageously to protect yourself from harm, say no to others so you can meet your own needs, and motivate necessary change in yourself and in the larger society. This book brings a fresh perspective, especially for women, and explores ways to reclaim your power and embrace fierceness as a part of your true nature.

Self-Compassion for Kids and Teens

Okay, this one isn't for you, unless perhaps you are a teenager. But if you aren't one, you *were* one, and you know it's damn hard to be one. Perhaps you've even found yourself wishing you had learned to be mindful and self-compassionate early in life, especially as an angst-ridden, conflicted, sensitive pre-adult. My dear friends and colleagues Karen Bluth and Lorraine Hobbs have developed a remarkable teen version of MSC called Making Friends With Yourself that speaks to teens in developmentally appropriate language and incorporates practices that actually resonate with them. If you have a teen, know one, or know someone who does, I highly recommend this program to plant the seeds of self-compassion at a crucial age. Check it out at centerformsc.org/msc-teens-adults/.

Dr. Bluth has also written two helpful books aimed at teens: *The Self-Compassionate Teen: Mindfulness and Compassion Skills to Conquer Your Critical Inner Voice* and *The Self-Compassion Workbook for Teens: Mindfulness and Compassion Skills to Overcome Self-Criticism and Embrace Who You Are.* Both books, published by Instant Help, aim to support teens and their parents in their navigation through this challenging time of life.

For younger kids and their parents, Certified MSC Teacher and child therapist Eileen Beltzner has written a playful and engaging book to explore mindfulness and self-compassion together. *How to Tame the Tumbles: The Mindful Self-Compassionate Way* (from Mosaic Press) charts the bumpy emotional journey of Esmeralda Anastasia Pookapoo and how she develops the ability to regulate and manage her feelings with her friend Pookie the dog. In a warm and engaging way, this book for kids can even help adults appreciate their own emotional "tumbles."

Self-Compassionate Parenting

How many times have you heard the old adage that parenting is the hardest job on the planet? I can attest to that from my own experience, and we get very little but on-the-job training to even *be* a parent. Certified MSC teacher and clinical psychologist Susan Pollak has a remarkable book called *Self-Compassion for Parents: Nurture Your Child by Caring For Yourself* (The Guilford Press) that helps you explore the at first counterintuitive idea that treating yourself with kindness can actually translate into what you offer your children. Susan has included short, accessible meditations and other practices to support you in being your best self, for your own well-being and for your child.

The Best Self-Compassion Resource Ever

You. That's right, you. So often we have conditioned ourselves to look outside ourselves for the answers, the solutions, the education, or the guidance from others. All of this is indeed available to you if you are resourceful, curious, and persistent, but one of the great things about self-compassion is that it shows you how to become self-reliant when it comes to emotional needs and challenges, in much the same way that you have probably learned to be self-reliant as an adult in the world to meet your needs for the basics. When you are hungry, you know how and where to get food. When you are in need of a place to live or clothing to wear, you know that you need money, and you know how to acquire it so that you have these things.

Self-compassion teaches you to ask yourself, "What do I need?" Little by little, you learn how to answer that question and provide what you need for yourself. Maybe what you need is a compassionate kick in the pants to get up and take action. Self-compassion helps you do that. Maybe what's called for is a warm caress and gentle words simply validating your pain. Self-compassion helps you do that. Your task is simply to remember to actually ask yourself the question. It's not as easy to remember as you may think, but when you ask, you can usually find the answer within.

The next time you find yourself seeking, striving, or reaching for something in a moment of difficulty, see if you can remember to give yourself a moment to answer the question: "What do I need?"

You'll be glad you did.

Chapter **17**

Ten Tips for Keeping Up Your Practice of Self-Compassion

Like most new routines, self-compassion is relatively easy to start, but the real test is whether you are able to sustain it to help slowly bring about new ways of behaving and responding to your challenges. You have had a lifetime to develop the tendency to be self-critical, prone to shame, and perfectionistic, so nobody expects you to change overnight, with one Self-Compassion Break, or even after going through an entire book like this one. It takes time, practice, patience, warmth, and persistence. You've got those, because you're here at the end of the book wondering how in the world you will ever keep this up and make needed change.

Before I offer some suggestions, please take a moment to recognize what's going on here. I'm willing to bet that before you picked up this book you were curious, perhaps willing to explore this practice with some skepticism, and not entirely convinced that self-compassion was for you. But now, here you are, a few hundred pages later, wondering with just a hint of anxiety in your heart if you might be able to continue this practice in some way because something struck you, shifted in you, or moved you in some way.

I have some ideas and suggestions for how you can keep it up, but just pause for a moment to appreciate whatever it was that struck you that has you contemplating your next move. Take a moment to reflect on your process in going through this book and recall the moments that really stand out for you. What were the experiences, the insights, the words, or the actions that set of a spark of awareness, a hint of relief, or a glimpse of light at the end of this particular tunnel? Take some time to savor that moment (or moments) and consider the essence of it. Whatever it was that happened, whatever light bulb blinked on or load was lifted, let that be your guide. That, whatever *that* actually is, is the thing that will be like a guiding light and a beacon for your continued journey. You can always come back to that moment of shift or engagement, to remind you of the power of this practice.

Note: For this and subsequent chapters, I reached out to my self-compassion teacher colleagues for ideas, tips, tricks, and hints. I am forever grateful to all my community of colleagues at the Center for Mindful Self-Compassion who have taught me so much, and I note the specific individuals who provided the inspiration where possible.

You Don't Have to Do Them All

While I presented quite a collection of different exercises, meditations, and other reflections in this book, you should feel free to pick and choose like you would at a delicious buffet. Take it all in, give them all a reasonable try, but then decide what works for you. My colleague Clark Freshman likened this to a breakfast buffet when he was a kid. He said he'd look at all the delightful offerings, from delectable fruit to fresh waffles, but then he'd invariably pile his plate with bacon. You have full permission to have all the "bacon" in this practice you want (Mmmmm, bacon. But I digress.) If you found the Soften, Soothe, Allow practice to really support you, by all means, soften, soothe and allow away! (And truth be told, if you find that "soothe" is your form of Clark's bacon, go for it!)

Another beloved colleague, Oori Silberstein, says it's like inviting a friend over when a cousin gives you a whole box full of sweaters they no longer want. You have a sweater-trying party and you decide which ones don't fit, which ones are too itchy, and so on. You may find only one that feels "just right." Consider your party a success and go with it. Sweaters, bacon, self-compassion: Whatever works for you is okay.

Furry Friends Are the Best

The powerful thing about self-compassion (over self-esteem) is that it is entirely unconditional. You offer yourself compassion regardless of the circumstances, without an agenda of changing anything, and you accept yourself just as you are in each moment. For humans, this is not an easy thing, no matter how romantic and lofty it may sound. But many of us have tremendous role models in unconditional love around us. In fact, I have one curled up at my feet right now.

Our furry pet friends are often in our lives precisely because they always love and accept us as we are. Charles Yu said, "If I could be half the person my dog is, I'd be twice the human I am." Our pets can be our teachers of unconditional love, and we can aspire to their level of achievement in that regard. Laila Narsi says "snuggling up with a furry friend, looking into their eyes and receiving unconditional love, realizing that the friend's eyes are a reflection of my own self-compassion" is a powerful lesson in how we can all be with ourselves.

TIP

If you have a pet, take the time to be with them and notice how you feel when you are in tune with being accepted, appreciated, and not judged in any way. This can create a kind of benchmark by which you can measure your own efforts at being self-compassionate — not as a goal to strive for, but a deeper appreciation of what it feels like to feel accepted.

The Self-Compassion Workout Approach

I often think of the practice of self-compassion as just that, practice, like what you would do physically to get in shape or prepare for an athletic competition. If you haven't exercised your compassion for awhile, it may be a little flimsy or flabby or weak, but if you begin to, as David Fredrickson says, "use light weights and easy reps," you can begin to reverse the trend and strengthen the love muscle, so to speak. You are motivated enough to take action to make a change. I know this about you because you went to the trouble of purchasing this book and have read large parts of it, so you are willing to make a commitment to change.

But that may also mean that you are a person who boldly acts to get things done, so you may be a bit on the ambitious side. You may be the person who strides into the gym in your shiny new spandex workout outfit and grasps the biggest weight on the rack because someone cute might be watching, even if you had a bit of trouble pulling the glass door of the gym open a few minutes earlier. Step away from the heaviest weight unless you are an incredible hulk and go for the practice that you can get behind, or even adjust the intensity of one of the bigger practices to a level where it stretches you but doesn't overwhelm you. Ambition can be positive, but it can also set you up to struggle or feel overwhelmed. Remember the circles around the sweet spot of tolerance from Chapter 3, and make sure that you're just outside the circle of safety and into the circle of challenge.

Cultivate a Base of Kindness

Admit it; you've wondered now and then if all there is to self-compassion practice is meeting suffering, stress, pain, and difficult emotions. There's that negative attention bias I explore in Chapter 15 again, and it's a pretty sneaky tendency that keeps popping up just when you think you've overcome it. But the good news about self-compassion is that one of its components is self-kindness. Simply being kind to yourself actually builds your capacity to access that kindness when you *really* need it: in times when you are struggling. It's like weaving a parachute. If you are planning on jumping out of an airplane with a parachute but need to make your own chute, then you'd best start weaving it well in advance and not upon takeoff, right? You are better off weaving your parachute morning, noon, and night, day after day if you want it to be functional when you take the leap. It's the same with lovingkindness, and there are lots of ways to practice that.

TIP

My clever friend Julie Potiker advised me to "put a sticker on your bathroom mirror (like a smiley face) and greet yourself with a warm "I love you, doll face!" every day. I told her that "doll face" didn't work for me, but I'd be willing to try "big guy." Laila Narsi suggested pausing now and then to place your hand on your heart and say, "May I accept myself as I am," or simply leave a few love notes to yourself around the house. Or consider doing what Sondra Gudmundson suggests: "At the end of the day, as you retire to sleep, feeling the warm touch of your hand on your body, say 'Goodnight tender heart. I see you. I feel your presence through each beat. I'm here for you, and I wish you a good night's sleep.'" Cultivating this inclination of the heart toward kindness makes it more available to you in those tougher moments.

It's Better Together

Just like venturing into any new territory, it's advisable to have a traveling companion. In this case it can be helpful to have a "self-compassion buddy" with whom you can commiserate and celebrate, as well as someone from whom you can gain a little motivation — someone who isn't quite as sneaky as your inner critic or inner trickster. A self-compassion buddy won't undermine your motivation by saying just the right thing to take you off the hook when you really think you should be practicing. Your buddy doesn't judge you, but they do want the best for you, so they tell it like it is. They remind you that they care about you and don't want you to suffer, and *that's* why they're texting you on a Saturday afternoon to ask if you've meditated today.

You don't have to adopt your self-compassion buddy or invite them to family reunions. Maybe you just have an agreement to send a daily quick WhatsApp message or text to each other as a simple reminder that they are in your thoughts. Perhaps you meet now and then for coffee to be with each other and to truly *feel felt*, as psychiatrist Daniel Siegel says.

REMEMBER

We need frequent reminders of our common humanity, and simple points of contact like this are enough to snap us out of the trance of isolation and back into the human race.

Everybody Must Get Stones

Quite often when you have a moment of difficulty or you find yourself spiraling into reactivity, more than anything else you need to find a way to first ground yourself. This is one of the many benefits of mindfulness practice because it takes us out of the past and future and directly into the present moment. You can do this through focusing on your breath or even outside of yourself on nature or the view out your window. In the Mindful Self-Compassion course, we actually give each participant a small, polished stone that we call the "Here and Now Stone" to be the external focus of attention in a challenging moment. We encourage people to keep the stone on hand, perhaps in a pocket or some accessible place, and to pull it out and pore attention into the texture, the shape, the color, and the weight of it.

This is not a distraction away from the moment but a deep dive into it instead. You are allowing yourself to be absorbed in what is immediately in front of you rather than letting your mind spin out into all sorts of imagined future scenarios or troubling experiences of the past. See if you can find a simple object like a "Here and Now Stone" to keep with you and help you ground your attention.

Practice Behavioral Self-Compassion

Long before you ever knew what self-compassion was, you actually already knew how to practice it to some degree. Think about how you tend to take care of yourself, comfort yourself, or soothe yourself when you are having a tough day or are facing a particularly difficult challenge. Maybe you make yourself a cup of tea, take a short walk, or pet your dog (my corgis get the benefit of my difficult moments on a regular basis). These are what Chris Germer and Kristin Neff call *behavioral self-compassion* because they are the actions you take to give yourself what you need in a moment.

If you do it intentionally (with the intention to respond to what you need because you are struggling), then it is behavioral self-compassion, and therefore, a worthwhile practice. The key is to do it with awareness and actually, intentionally savor the experience as you do it. So if binge-watching a new TV show or having a bowl of Ben & Jerry's Cherry Garcia ice cream is your "thing" in a moment and you do it mindfully, then you're good to go. If, instead, you find yourself doing these things ten episodes in or halfway to the bottom of the quart, not so much. See if you can pause and ask yourself the magic question of self-compassion: What do I need? And then respond to it with the things that are already tools in your self-compassion toolbox, perhaps from long before you knew you had one. And be sure to savor the experience.

Cultivate Gratitude in Connection

In Chapter 15, I raise the concept of the negative attention bias and how we are much more prone to looking for problems or difficulties than we are toward making room for the positive and the joyful in our life. One aspect of self-compassion is to maintain a balanced perspective of ourselves so that whatever perceived flaws or challenges we have, they don't swell up to fill the whole of our awareness. This is not about being in denial of real problems to be solved or weaknesses to be overcome, but rather to see that in addition to these issues, there are other things in our lives and ourselves that are worthy of appreciation and savoring.

Taking the time to feel gratitude for things in our life (as I note in Chapter 15) has been shown to be quite powerful for people's mood, quality of life, and even their physical health. You can "multiply" the effect to some degree by not only taking time to consider what you are grateful for, but also sharing that gratitude with others. Find a "gratitude buddy" with whom you can exchange a daily gratitude email or text message and then share three things you are grateful for each day. These are things in your life and not necessarily about the other person. Just sharing your joy and appreciation not only restores your balanced view of your life and yourself (mindfulness), but it reminds you of your connections to others (common humanity), and in a way is a thoughtful gift to yourself each day (self-kindness). All the factors of self-compassion rolled up in a nice neat daily package!

Be Willing to Start Again . . . and Again

The good news about self-compassion practice is that even when you stop doing it regularly, and then you realize that you haven't been doing it — bingo — you can resume! And not only that, but if you find yourself beating yourself up for not practicing self-compassion (really the height of irony if you think about it), you can give yourself compassion for that hardship as well! You really can't lose with self-compassion practice, and there is no point where, even if you haven't used it, you actually lose it. It's always there.

In fact, what would it be like to let go of thinking of self-compassion as a task that needs to be done (like washing the dishes) or a long-term commitment (like joining a gym or getting married)? What if, instead, you simply committed to do your best at being kind to yourself whenever you notice that you are not? Sometimes the whole idea of incorporating a new habit or routine in your life can just feel like too big of a burden all at once. And another nice feature of self-compassion practice is, as my colleague Chris Germer says, "Once you start, self-compassion actually enhances rather than undermines motivation."

You may start practicing because what I have written here makes sense or what you have discovered from the research motivates you, or because a friend or therapist recommended it to you, but the only thing that will sustain your practice is feeling the effects of having actually *done* it. A therapist friend has a sign in her office that sums this up: "People change, not when they see the light but when they feel the heat." You will be able to make the change not when you see that it's good for you, but when you feel the warmth of your own tender beating heart.

If It's a Struggle, It's Not Self-Compassion

I say this all the time in my Mindful Self-Compassion courses, and it is remarkably hard to remember when you are one who is inclined to "try hard" when you take on a new thing. When you find yourself "trying" to practice self-compassion or straining to meet yourself with kindness, you may want to remind yourself that the very act of forcing something is counter to your intention. As I noted early on, if it's a struggle, it's not self-compassion. See if instead you can make your practice as pleasant as possible. If you are a parent and your child has ever had a temper tantrum (and whose hasn't!), think about how you met it. You met it with tenderness and kindness and as much patience as you could muster, because you knew that berating or criticizing or shouting at your child was only going to achieve the opposite of your intention. This is true in really difficult, challenging moments of intense painful emotion, but the principle still applies in less intense moments.

TIP

Develop the practice of checking in with yourself from time to time, perhaps using the tone of voice and choice of words you would use with a friend whom you are concerned about. For example, if I sense my adult son is having a hard day, I might say, "Hey big guy! How's it going?" in a light but caring tone. Maybe it's more like "How's your heart today, sweetheart?" or "Is there anything you need, my friend?" Find a way to let the practice be light and easy, as much as possible, like a cool breeze on a hot day. It's not the solution to all your problems, but it's a little tender kindness when you need it most. You don't have an agenda for change or an attempt to distract; you're simply offering a kind gesture because the moment is hard.

Chapter **18**

Ten Ways Self-Compassion Can Improve Your Relationships

n Chapter 12, you focus your attention on how to transform challenging relationships (and really, aren't *all* relationships challenging, when you think about it?). One thing that often comes up for people as they are learning self-compassion and considering how it works in relationships is really how complex our relationships can be. It's hard enough coming to terms with yourself and all the tricks and shenanigans that your mind and heart play as you go about your daily life. And then the whole thing gets exponentially more challenging when you begin to engage with another human being, who also has to contend with their own inner circus of emotions, thoughts, and sensations.

Really, practicing mindfulness and self-compassion while engaged with another person is like ninja training: a whole other level and seemingly almost unfathomable if you think about it too much. Do yourself a favor and let go of trying to sort it out with your intellect and logic, because the issues are much better addressed through simply embodying self-compassion, being kind and patient with yourself (and the other person), and feeling your way into each relationship. What does this look like? Well, here are a few ideas for how you can bring self-compassion into your connections with others.

My dear friend and favorite MSC co-teacher Michelle Becker is the founder of the Compassion for Couples program (wisecompassion.com/compassion-for-couples) and has an insightful and fascinating podcast called Well-Connected Relationships (wisecompassion.com/join). She and I talked about ways of integrating self-compassion into relationships, and some of what she suggested is in the following points.

Finding Out What *They* Need

As you well know by now, the quintessential question of self-compassion that you should always ask yourself in a moment of difficulty (or really, anytime) is: What do I need? As you may also know, that answer varies from time to time, based on the situation. Well, if you are going to direct compassion to your partner, spouse, or friend, it may help to know what *they* need. Specifically, even the basic things that we prefer in order to soothe, strengthen, comfort, or console ourselves vary from person to person. Assuming you want to be as supportive and compassionate as you possibly can for the important people in your life, it may be a worthwhile investment of time and warmth to ask them what comforts and soothes them. What are the words or phrases or tone that they need to hear in order to calm their nervous system or empower them to take care of themselves or make change?

Some of us are "touchy" people (in a good way), and a sweet warm hug really hits the spot. For others, words really matter, and we need to hear things that are actually spoken out loud so that they make an impact. For example, someone who feels the power of words and finds them motivating and reassuring may not realize that your warm gaze was an expression of support, or they may not notice the thing that you did for them that you felt was an act of compassion. And of course, for others, the preferred modality is taking observable action.

TIP

Gary Chapman's book *The 5 Love Languages* (Northfield Publishing) does a beautiful job of helping couples identify how to express themselves so that they are heard by their partners. This is in the same vein. Take the time to check in with your partner and explore together how you each prefer to receive compassion from the other.

Adopting a Shared Road Map

In Chapter 8, I discuss discovering your core values and how self-compassion can facilitate this process such that you can reduce the suffering and struggle in your life and achieve greater satisfaction. Uncovering your "inner compass" by exploring what is deeply meaningful to you can really be a powerful reset and get you on the path to greater internal harmony and purpose. When you are in a relationship, it becomes important to assure that you and your partner have some sense of each other's core values and are not at cross purposes wherever possible.

This is not to say that your map of core values needs to perfectly overlay that of your partner. In fact, that sounds rather boring in a way; instead, each partner needs to have a deep appreciation of the other's "life road map" so that you can support each other in moving in valued directions. I have a colleague who is a therapist and MSC teacher, and also an amazing quilter whose basement is jam-packed with fabrics, quilting paraphernalia, and machines. Her husband is a physician who owns his own airplane and loves tinkering with it and taking it places. They have been happily married for 40+ years. Her values focus on creativity, artistic expression, and helping people. His values focus on travel, mechanical processes, and helping people. Thus, they have shared values and divergent values. The key here is to take joy in each partner's values and their accomplishments even if you don't share those particular values. This is how it works with this couple.

Taking some time to reflect on your respective core values and then sharing them in a heartfelt way can foster compassion and self-compassion in the relationship. You might consider the ten dimensions of life around which our lives as humans typically revolve, take some time to explore what you value in each domain, and then share your work with your partner. These dimensions are as follows: work/career, family of origin, intimate relationships, citizenship, health, social connections, personal development, spirituality, leisure time, and parenting.

First ask yourself, "What's most important to me about this dimension?" Then ask yourself, "Is there anything deeper underneath that?" Repeat that reflection until you feel you've reached "bedrock" and write down what you came up. Make your way through all the dimensions and then compare notes with your partner.

What do you notice about similarities and differences? Perhaps ask each other what you can do to support your partner in their core values? Does this reflection uncover areas of conflict for the two of you that you can explore now to prevent future pain? What is surprising to you about your partner's values? This simple shared exercise can go a long way toward deepening your relationship and finding harmonious ways of being compassionate to each other.

Reversing the Downward Spiral

You know the drill: You come home in a foul mood after a difficult day at work and your partner senses that you're out of sorts. He says, "What's wrong with you?" out of genuine concern. You are predisposed to react badly because of your day and say "Me? What's wrong with me? What's wrong with *you*?" And then you're off and running into a downward spiral of reactivity and recrimination. The fact that we have the means of sensing each other's emotional states (remember mirror neurons from Chapter 8?) just adds to the complexity of these interactions, and we can literally feel each other spiraling down in these moments.

The good news is, of course, the same reality as the bad news: Your mirror neurons are two-way streets. We can feel the pain of our partner, and they can feel our pain. Which of course means that you both have the capacity to feel each other's goodwill and compassion if you can manage to deploy it in these moments. "Self-compassion *now!!*" you may shout, but unless you have a genie in a bottle with a spare wish or two, this rarely works particularly well.

However, practicing a Self-Compassion Break may very well do the trick in this moment. When you find yourself in a heated discussion, you can simply excuse yourself from the situation, offer yourself some soothing or supportive touch, and remind yourself that "This is a moment of suffering . . . Suffering is a part of any relationship . . . May I be kind to myself and give myself the compassion that I need." Whether or not your partner knows about the Self-Compassion Break, once both partners feel their sympathetic nervous systems deactivating and no longer feel threatened (in whatever way), then the conversation can continue.

REMEMBER

The way that you disengage from a heated moment to practice self-compassion is important to consider. It can be perceived as "checking out" in a passive-aggressive way if you don't clearly let your partner know that you simply need a minute to pause and reflect. Perhaps you could simply say: "I need to pause for a moment," or "Can I just take a moment to myself to collect my thoughts?" Also, the very act of checking out of a difficult downward spiral is an act of self-compassion in itself, so don't discount the value of simply doing that even if a self-compassion break does not automatically follow in every situation.

You can also practice the Self-Compassion Break together if you are both familiar with it and inclined to do so. This can be a beautiful harmonious dissolution of tension and hard feelings if done with care and patience.

Giving and Receiving Compassion to and from Your Partner

Relationships are like cars or bridges: In order for them to function well, they need continuous care, careful attention, and periodic maintenance. Perhaps not the most romantic analogy, but there is a modicum of truth in this. Naturally, the usual flow of close relationships involves an ongoing exchange of warmth, kindness, and compassion, as this is the lifeblood of strong, healthy relationships. But you can also be more purposeful in cultivating and nurturing the bonds you have between you by finding ways to practice mindfulness and self-compassion, both together and apart.

Going back to the practice of Giving and Receiving Compassion in Chapter 12, you may find that when you have the inclination, simply calling your partner to mind and practicing "one for me and one for you" or adjusting the balance to accommodate whoever seems to need it the most right now is also possible. Simply breathing "in for me and out for you" tends to strengthen the sense of connection to the other person and allows us to love the other without losing ourselves, which is a delicate balance to maintain in most relationships. Take the time to deliberately cultivate compassion for your partner, drawing from the "ocean of compassion" that is available to all of us, and practice offering a little for them and a little for you. Perhaps it is a bit like bathing in the ocean of compassion together. Whatever image suits you is fine. The key is that you share the experience, even if you are the only one formally doing it.

Savoring Each Other

Before you let your imagination run wild with this particular title (although my imagination leads me to some rather delightful possibilities for connection if you want to indulge your own), I'm suggesting that you endeavor to overcome your negative attention bias together by practicing the "Something to Savor" practice from Chapter 15. Engaging together in a pleasurable activity like wandering in nature, flitting from thing to thing like a distractible butterfly or adventurous toddler, can really be a way of resetting your nervous system after a difficult situation. It can simply cultivate a baseline of calm and opening to the good that you can often lose track of in your busy daily lives.

Enter into the walk without expectations or thoughts of achieving anything and see if you can simply engage in the practice with an open mind and heart. Let go of doing it for a purpose, other than its own sake, and see what happens. Perhaps there will be moments when you find yourselves savoring the same bright flower and other times when you wonder what in the world your partner found attractive about a rotting log or why they wanted to taste a blade of grass. Let go of being concerned about each other's motives and simply experience the fullness of savoring. And if you happen to find yourself savoring each other (in whatever form), then go with it! Who am I to judge?

Maintaining Your Relationship to the One in the Mirror

This is just a reminder that self-compassion is essentially a practice of tending to perhaps your most intimate relationship: the one with yourself. For some reason, we seem to get so easily lost in the fray when we are engaged with other people, and you can easily overlook yourself when you are focused upon improving or repairing your relationship with another. Remember that the greatest gift you can give the people around you is to also love and make room for yourself so that you can tend to many of your needs with your own kindness.

When you are in a relationship, especially when your partner is suffering in some way, you can tend to overlook your own needs and even to assume too much responsibility for the other person's well-being at the same time. Going back to the Compassion with Equanimity practice from Chapter 12, you can remind yourself of those equanimity phrases to find just the right balance between yourself and the other person, forgive yourself for wanting to do more than you can, and comfort yourself for how hard it can be to be in a relationship sometimes. Remember the phrases: "Everyone is on their own life journey. I am not the cause of this person's suffering, nor is it entirely within my powers to make it go away, even though I wish I could. Moments like these can be difficult to bear, yet I may still try to help if I can."

By remembering that we are each on our own life journey, you can begin to sort out the areas where you can make a difference and the areas where you have no control. Wisdom is what allows you to differentiate those two areas, and the continued practice of self-compassion contributes to that wisdom. Be wise, be kind, and be clear on what is your life's journey and what is someone else's. This practice, in addition to helping you meet your own struggles with kindness, also empowers the other person to locate their own source of inner strength and resilience by giving them the opportunity to find it on their own.

REMEMBER

Just as in parenting, we all have to learn to step back and let our loved ones learn, always standing by to support and cheer them on, but letting them find their own way. This is the foundation of healthy mutual relationships, where both partners are empowered to be fully themselves.

Making Room for Humor and Joy

We often get the advice, "You need to work on your relationship," which sometimes has the tone of "You need to scrape barnacles off the boat twice a year." Who wants to "do work" on their relationship like it's a pesky mold problem in your basement? On the other hand, most people don't object to tending to the garden or playing ball with a child, even though these are both "work" that lead to good outcomes. So could you make the effort you put into your relationship a bit lighter and effort*less* instead?

My colleague Emma Willoughby provides a delightful example of making room for lightness in the midst of a difficult situation. She says, "Me and my dear heart do the 'big feelings dance' in tricky relationship times. It's basically doing a Self-Compassion Break combined with ridiculous dancing. When big feelings arise, stop, notice, and whoever notices first starts the dancing and the other has to join in. Dance it out and connect up and giggle again!"

REMEMBER

Obviously, every relationship is different and can tolerate different forms of humor, so it's best to sort these things out in advance. Silliness, distraction, and sarcasm are very different ways of accessing humor, but which one is right for you needs to be sorted out with your partner. The risk, of course, is that your humor may be perceived by your partner as dismissive, hurtful, or demeaning if you haven't found just the right way to express it.

I once had a dear friend with whom I had talked about the value of letting go in moments when we are clinging to something difficult. I used the simple hand gesture of holding my fist out, palm up, and slowly releasing the fist in a gesture of release. It conveyed the point, but at a later date when she was getting really worked up about something we were discussing, I chose to share that gesture with her as a moment of levity. She reacted with an entirely more pointed hand gesture that I won't describe here, but suffice to say that I may have made a poor choice in that moment to suggest letting go. The good news is that we both burst out laughing right afterwards!

Being Better Together but Good Apart Too

The best relationships are the ones where people thrive as individuals, each in their own way, and together there is a certain amount of awesomeness that happens as well. In fact, the success of most relationships is a curious interplay between independence and interdependence, such that when you are following your core values and pursuing your dreams as individuals you are actually able to contribute more to the relationship because you are feeling nourished and focused and fulfilled. At the same time, when your relationship feels as if it is "firing on all cylinders," it provides a solid platform and even a launching pad to pursue what matters most to you.

REMEMBER

Making your relationship strong involves making sure that you are acting self-compassionately and finding time and space away from your partner to make your own way in the world. At the same time, when your partner seeks to do the same, your opportunity is to recognize that this is an act of self-compassion on their part and to cultivate what the Buddhists call *mudita* or "sympathetic joy." This is essentially taking joy in *their* joy, delighting in *their* delight, and lovingly encouraging *their* blossoming because their joy is intertwined with yours.

This might look like encouraging your partner to take that pottery class, knowing that this is something she longs to do as a creative outlet, even though your particular interest is more in online gaming. When she is in class you feel happy for her even if you notice a nagging feeling of painful separation or perhaps some lingering threads from old wounds of having been excluded or overlooked. You can meet these with some kindness, maybe saying, "Ooh, this kinda stings a little bit. It's hard, but it's okay. My love is getting to do what *she* loves, and that makes me happy too." And that evening while you are online slaying dragons or piloting a fighter jet while your partner is watching TV, your enjoyment is enhanced because you know she is wishing you well and giving you space, and you feel a little less guilt for taking time away from her.

Finding Shared Lovingkindness Phrases

In Chapter 7 you have the opportunity to carefully reflect on the things you most need to hear, because as a human being, you really need to be reminded of these things. It can be a slow, luxurious process of asking yourself what you need, what you *truly need*, and what you need to hear, trying phrases on for fit and making adjustments. I have always appreciated Chris Germer's suggestion that when you hear these phrases, your immediate response is a heartfelt "Oh thank you. Thank you!"

Because you and your partner presumably wish the relationship well, you may consider collaborating on that reflection to see if you can come up with a set of shared lovingkindness phrases (perhaps in addition to any individual phrases you may develop) that you can share with each other. Simply being able to look someone in the eye and say, "May we be happy" is very powerful and connecting. With a little creativity and attention, you can really customize a set of phrases that suits the unique nature of your relationship.

REMEMBER

These are inclinations of the heart and not destinations, so "May we have three children, two girls and a boy" may be a bit too specific. Something like "May we know the joy of parenting" can align you with a deep shared intention without pinning it to a particular outcome. Other possibilities might be "May we find delight in our friendship" or "May we grow deeper in our faith together." Identify your own shared phrases and find opportunities to speak them or share them in other ways. You may want to send a quick text message to your partner when you think of it or put a sticky note on your refrigerator with your shared phrases on it. Let yourself marinate in the lovingkindness wishes for your bond with your partner.

Deepening Through Training in Self-Compassion

I have already extolled the virtues of the Mindful Self-Compassion course at numerous points throughout this book, and I have seen several couples go through the program together and be thrilled with the experience. In fact, I know several couples who not only took the course together but went on to go through MSC Teacher Training and now teach the course together.

TIP

Beyond the standard MSC course though, I highly recommend considering the Compassion for Couples program (https://wisecompassion.com/compassion-for-couples/) offered by Michelle Becker, which I reference at the beginning of this chapter. I have had the pleasure of teaching this course with Michelle and have been honored and touched to witness what happens for couples as they explore how to bring compassion into their relationship to not only heal wounds but also to go from good to great through tapping into their natural compassionate inclination. Often people need the structure of a formal course, combined with a certain sense of common humanity about the challenges they face. Having a group to support and encourage you (and remind you that all relationships have challenges and difficulties sometimes) really makes a difference. Compassion for Couples is a remarkable course designed by an extraordinary teacher.

Chapter **19**

Ten Pocket Self-Compassion Practices for Busy People

B usyness is an epidemic raging through our society, masquerading as an unavoidable feature of modern life. We wear the label of busy as a kind of badge of honor and justification for all manner of behavior, as well as an excuse for those things that we have not done or cannot accomplish. Busyness undermines our deeper values and erodes the quality of our life, and yet we can't shake it, and we (ironically) often try harder and work more to try to be less busy. The roots of busyness are deep and strong, maintained by processes as old as our evolutionary origins, as indelible as our childhood experiences, and as palpable as the simple need to be loved by others.

When it comes to self-compassion, this relentless condition of crazy busyness threatens to erode the best of intentions to create a more compassionate relationship with yourself. The good news about self-compassion (how many times have I written *that* phrase in this book!) is that being busy and being self-compassionate are not either/or propositions. You can be busy *and* practice self-compassion, and doing both makes you no busier than you were already. And lo and behold, it may actually result in you choosing to find ways to be less crazy-busy and bring more ease, peace, and patience into your life. Slow down for a moment and consider the following simple "pocket practices" to sprinkle seeds of self-compassion in your overgrown garden and see what sprouts for you.

Use the Smallest Unit of Self-Compassion

My friend Marissa Knox reminded me of a beautiful quote from Amy Burtaine: "The smallest unit of self-care is a single breath." Being able to see that even the simple act of taking a mindful breath is a tiny but radical act of self-kindness is an amazing reminder that self-compassion is simply a practice and not a destination or an obligation. Start small and grow from there.

Other simple reminders to practice a moment of kindness can include timers or notifications on your smartphone or a soothing and nourishing image as a background on your computer. The important thing here is that you do not discount the importance of these tiny moments. Chris Germer has said, "A moment of self-compassion can change your entire day. A string of such moments can change the course of your life."

Find Your Feet

So many of us are always on the run from here to there, when sometimes what we could really use is a moment of mindfulness, an opportunity to ground ourselves in the moment and feel the solid ground of the present moment so that we can actually notice what is arising and what is needed. So the next time you find yourself on the run and feeling a bit distressed (worried about the future, sad about the past, or preoccupied with a problem or challenge), see if you can remember to ask yourself a very silly question: "Where are my feet?" This is a powerful (and charmingly fun) way to invite yourself into the present moment, mainly because your feet are always *here*, wherever that happens to be.

Further opportunities are to see each footstep you take as a moment of awareness and mindfulness, even as you rush from place to place. I used to have a path that I walked at work that took me across a street that had a very marked crest in the middle, and each time I passed that crest, I used it like a mindfulness bell to remind me to drop into my body and my breath.

TIP

When you do have a bit more time and can walk in nature, seeing each footstep as a tiny expression of compassion for the earth and nature can be a deliberate way to cultivate some warmth and kindness while moving from place to place.

Listen to Self-Compassion

As we go about our busy days, many of us have found ways of keeping up and keeping entertained by listening to audiobooks, playlists, and podcasts. If certain songs bring you joy, inspire you to take action, or soothe you when you are struggling, consider putting together a playlist that is as close as your smartphone to address what you may need in a moment. There are many options for assembling these playlists, and if you create a few (for example, for times when you need some calm, times when you need a little motivation, or times when you just need some mindful distraction), you can simply tap-tap-tap your way into a self-compassion practice that is portable, super accessible, and just what you need.

TIP

The Center for Mindful Self-Compassion created this all-purpose self-compassion playlist on Spotify: `open.spotify.com/playlist/7AlezZhRrwJiWuWXnDHyl6?si=f3BDHkSHQCSNMAOYrkn4Xw&nd=1`. Or if that's too much to type, simply search for "Center for Mindful Self-Compassion" on Spotify.

Find Self-Compassion in a SNAP

Julie Potiker, a friend and colleague and author of *Life Falls Apart, But You Don't Have To* (Mindful Methods for Life Press), offers a simple acronym of SNAP for a brief practice when time is of the essence. Here are the four steps to remember in a challenging moment:

» **Soothing touch:** Finding that you are struggling, place your hand lovingly somewhere on your body that feels supportive and soothing.

» **Name the emotion:** Take a moment to identify what emotion or emotions are present and name them gently to yourself: "Oh, anger is here," or "I'm noticing embarrassment arising." (Note how you are not fusing yourself with the feeling through your language. In other words, you don't say "I'm angry" or "I'm embarrassed.")

» **Apply a practice:** Addressing the question of "What do I need?" you can respond mindfully by giving yourself a Self-Compassion Break, just a mindful breath, the Soften, Soothe, Allow Practice or something else that is called for.

>> **Proceed with self-compassion:** Feeling the impact of having acknowledged and responded to your difficulty, you have done a kind of mini-reset of your nervous system and can go forward a little less reactive and more grounded and kind.

Facing a challenging situation on the go can become easier in a SNAP.

Catch the Fleeting Moments and Transitions

Even busy people can overcome the negative attention bias that I discuss in Chapter 15. This one is just as simple as it sounds: Find the tiny moments to savor so that they actually make an impression on you. Each time you notice that someone is smiling, or someone lets you into traffic, or your Starbucks latte is perfect, pause just long enough to let it register. Feel what it feels like when things go well, which we don't often do. I saw a tweet lately that said, "My favorite childhood memory is when my back didn't hurt." Who has memories of things going as expected? See if you can make some positive impressions on yourself that you may even remember later!

TIP

Along with this, you can pay it forward by purposefully providing these opportunities for others. As my colleague Michael Murphy has said, "When I see a smiling person, I just assume it's meant for me because, well, why not? And I smile back at them. In traffic I find it helpful to leave a space in front so if someone needs it, they can slip in there. I might even get a friendly wave from them and arrive just a little bit happier at my destination."

Pinpoint the Unmet Need

Perhaps the most challenging experiences that we face as busy humans come when we encounter other people who are angry, resistant, or aggressive. These emotions are challenging even when we're sitting on a cushion, feeling fully resourced and as equanimous as can be. But when you encounter an angry colleague in the hall at work while you are rushing to an important meeting that started five minutes ago and your cup of tea is scalding in your hand, handling these experiences is nearly impossible.

In a situation like this, it's all you can do to simply remain composed. But if you can take a single self-compassionate and grounding breath, you may find a tiny opening between you and that person to ask yourself, "Where is this person's pain?" This is not easy — in fact, it is an advanced practice — but quite often one can identify the soft feelings underneath the bluster and the fury (as we do with the Meeting Unmet Needs exercise in Chapter 12 where we look at anger). If, even for a moment, you can connect to that person's feeling of hurt, fear, vulnerability, or pain, you will have fundamentally shifted the dynamic in a heartbeat.

As I note in Chapter 12, Marshall Rosenberg has said, "Every criticism, judgment, diagnosis, and expression of anger is the tragic expression of an unmet need." In the aforementioned situation, the person may be saying, "I can't believe you didn't stand up for me in that meeting with the boss. I thought I could trust you, but it turns out you're just a selfish jerk!" That's a statement that's bound to sting, but if you can feel the hurt arise, perhaps as a sensation in the body or the flush of anger, and you can give yourself the gift of even a single breath, you may have the time to see the unmet need in the other person. Perhaps they are feeling betrayed, vulnerable, or victimized in some way. Rightly or wrongly, it doesn't matter, because their emotion is real. Having an idea of their unmet need will open the door to a meaningful discussion because they will feel heard and they can hear you.

Maintain Connection Despite Busyness

There is something about being incredibly busy that leads to a certain feeling of loneliness. In fact, I have seen many people try to differentiate themselves from others based on their level of busyness. This usually sounds something like, "You think *you're* busy. I've taken one kid to soccer, the other kid to ballet, gotten my oil changed, made dinner for my family, and scrubbed three toilets today." It's like the "Busy Olympics," and everyone is vying for a gold medal to show how their busy is on a whole other level.

That silly competition aside, we can be busy and still remain connected to other busy people, and technology can actually help with this to some degree. Our busyness ebbs and flows, right? Sometimes we have frenzied moments, and then there are (however brief) periods of downtime or pauses between things. This may be during your commute, your walk across campus, or while you wait in the doctor's office. Those brief windows are great opportunities to pause and practice, and one practice can be a connection practice where you text a friend who is also trying to be more self-compassionate and mindful and struggles as much as you do. Your message might arrive in a stressful moment and provide just the relief and release they need, and you will feel better having connected in a small way.

TIP

A simple message like "Hey! Where are your feet?" or a simple smiling emoji can be a great gift of presence and kindness in the midst of a busy day. Build up a small network of folks who appreciate the value of being present and kind to yourself and drop an email, text message, WhatsApp, or even a sticky note (if you're old school) now and then. To feel connected to others when you are racing around like your hair is on fire can be a tremendously grounding and supportive experience. You crank out emails and chat messages all the time for other reasons; how about a little "Common Humanity Message" now and then?

Really Connect with the People You Meet

Following on from the previous suggestion, you may notice how connected you feel with the people you interact with directly. Whether in person or online, do those other people "feel felt" as Daniel Siegel says? Have you ever met someone who was physically in front of you but not there in terms of their attention or awareness? Have you ever *been* that person? I have, and I'm not proud of it. Afterwards I feel a certain amount of shame or embarrassment for having been preoccupied and not having given that person the full focus of my attention. This is especially upsetting to me because I know how it feels to be the person not attended to.

What if you formulate an intention to really connect with people you meet with, or to specifically aim to make eye contact with each person in the room at a meeting? See if you can stay with them long enough to really feel their presence and for them to feel your kind attention. This is a form of savoring practice that allows you to be fully present with people in a meaningful way. It also leads to more productive meetings, more loyal employees, and more confident and mature children. There is no downside to this practice of savoring people and holding them in awareness with kindness for both parties.

Remember What's Going on Here, with Me

I once saw a comedian riffing on the idea that men often are the ones who end up controlling the TV remote control and drive their partners crazy with their constant channel-changing even when shows are on. The comedian (a man) said, "You don't understand. It's not about *what's on* for us, it's about what *else* is on." This is the legacy of having an incredible human brain — we can be stuck in traffic and thinking about making love to our partner, or we can be at the beach thinking about our big work project coming up, or we can be eating our chicken and wishing we'd ordered the fish. Sometimes the capacity to take ourselves elsewhere can be super valuable, and sometimes it completely undermines our capacity to be fully present and therefore self-compassionate.

The next time you find yourself in a meeting and thinking about a *different* meeting, see if you can invite yourself back into this one and be just a little bit curious about what led you off. If you were annoyed with something someone said, can you pause long enough to just acknowledge that what they said hurt and give that hurt a little space? Alternatively, if the *other thing* you are preoccupied with is upsetting or stressful to you, can you pause long enough to drop your attention into your body in *this* moment long enough to soothe, comfort, or strengthen yourself just because it's hard?

REMEMBER

Being fully in the present whenever possible is obviously quite helpful, whether in a meeting or on the freeway, but more importantly, it facilitates you being more self-compassionate because you can track your own inner process more clearly and respond to moments of difficulty with an openness and willingness that just isn't available when you are distracted. Give yourself the gift of at least a modicum of your own attention whenever you can. You do deserve it, you know.

Exercise the "Beautiful No"

My dear friend, colleague, and inspirational guide Amy Saltzman has an amazing gift for sharing mindfulness, especially with kids and teens, and we have collaborated joyfully on many projects over the years. She knows well that I have what I call a "pathological inability to say no" to things. This inability, which has gotten me into some real pickles but has also opened up some tremendous opportunities (which is why I continue to say yes instead), has been a challenge for me because of how incredibly busy it makes me. We co-chaired a big mindfulness conference a few years in a row, and the first year at the end of a very successful event I was going on about what we should do next year and she put a hand on my arm and said, "Maybe you could just proceed by finishing the outbreath first." Point well taken.

Wise Amy introduced me to the parallel concept to "finishing the outbreath" of things, which is to learn to exercise the "beautiful no." She points out that saying no to some things allows us to say yes to other things, and also makes sure that the things we *do* commit to are done well and with our full attention. Do you find yourself, like me, a victim of FOMO? This is the Fear of Missing Out on things, and these days it's rampant. Why do we obsessively check Facebook, Twitter, Instagram, and so on? Because we don't want to *miss anything* or we want to know *what else is on* as I note earlier.

If you are like me, you get excited about things and are afraid that this particular opportunity will never come along again, so you literally feel compelled to say yes in order to make sure you don't miss anything. I have begun to learn (after working *way* too hard at times) that saying no to some things can actually be a beautiful thing that brings about its own sense of relief, ease, and happiness. Saying no can be a radical act of self-compassion because you respect yourself enough to treat yourself as a precious, limited commodity. Which you undoubtedly are, because we all are.

REMEMBER

When you exercise the beautiful no, you also get the opportunity to experience a different phenomenon: JOMO, or Joy of Missing Out. What openings might be created for joy when you say no? How might you be able to do what you do with more care, commitment, and passion because you aren't pulled to do something else as well?

TIP

And if "no" all by itself is just a bridge too far for you, maybe you can start with "not right now" and see how that works out. Baby steps. It's worth giving it a try.

Index

S

About the Author

Dr. Steven Hickman has been a practitioner and teacher of mindfulness and self-compassion for over 20 years. As a licensed clinical psychologist and associate clinical professor in the UC San Diego School of Medicine, Steven first began practicing mindfulness as part of his training to become a Mindfulness-Based Stress Reduction (MBSR) program teacher. He taught that program for 15 years, during which time he established the UC San Diego Center for Mindfulness and its Mindfulness-Based Professional Training Institute. That center (and Dr. Hickman) has become a world leader in the field of teachers of mindfulness- and compassion-based programs.

In 2012, Steve first learned of the Mindful Self-Compassion (MSC) program developed by Dr. Christopher Germer and Dr. Kristin Neff, and immediately gravitated to that program and their work. He found that MSC had a remarkably transformative effect on people and committed to supporting and growing that work through teaching MSC. With his expertise as a trainer of teachers of mindfulness, he was invited by Drs. Germer and Neff to join them and colleague Michelle Becker to co-develop a teacher training program in MSC.

His involvement with MSC grew over the years, and in 2018 he became the executive director of the nonprofit Center for Mindful Self-Compassion, dedicated to creating a more compassionate world through the dissemination of self-compassion practice worldwide in many forms. He has traveled extensively around the world teaching MSC and training teachers of that program, as well as speaking and training on related topics. He is a widely sought-after speaker and presenter in the field, and he writes routinely for a number of publications, including *Mindful* magazine. Steve is now retired from UC San Diego but still serves as the founding director of the Center for Mindfulness there as it continues to grow and thrive as a world leader in the field.

He lives with his wife Shelley and two corgis (Murphy and Rocket) in beautiful Newport, Oregon. He has three young adult children, affording him ample opportunities to practice what he teaches.

Dedication

So many people could be the focus of this particular spotlight of dedication, but as I write this, my beloved mother Fran Coverdell is on a gentle but clear decline into the end of her life and will likely not be with us when this book is published. She taught me by example to be curious, to believe in myself, and to always find a way to smile and laugh no matter what. Her love, her intelligence, and her creative spirit will live in me and through me for all the days of my life.

Author's Acknowledgments

It's hard to know where to start in thanking the people who made it possible for me to write this book, but I really feel I have to start with my dear friends and colleagues Chris Germer and Kristin Neff. They went from names on the covers of amazing books to revered colleagues to trusted and treasured friends over the years. I will be forever grateful that they invited me into this journey with them and have shown their trust in me by inviting me to lead the organization they created, to speak on their behalf at times, and to periodically nudge me into the spotlight alongside them. Kristin teaches me every day how to have a "soft front and a strong back." Chris is one of a small circle of men I consider my "brothers from another mother" who is quick to acknowledge what I do well and there to listen to me when things are tough. I love you guys and will always be grateful for your teaching, which is to say, how you are as human beings and professionals.

It took me awhile to find her, but my beloved wife and soul mate (see page 149 of *Eat, Pray, Love*) Shelley Wistar is my inspiration, my sounding board, and my companion in life's adventures. She is endlessly patient with me and my musings, doesn't let me indulge in silly self-deprecation, and believes in me even when I'm having my doubts. With a heart as big as the world, the enviable capacity to strike up a conversation with anyone, and eyes that sparkle and shine with laughter and mischief, Shelley shares her strength, her love, and her brain with me daily.

My first "brother from another mother" and the Other Guy, Allan Goldstein, holds a unique place in my heart and in this book that only he could hold. A true friend who is faithful, patient, kind, and willing to call me out when I need it, Allan has been a treasure, a teacher, and a drinking buddy for all of the contemplative portion of my life. We got into a lot of mischief and tomfoolery over the years, and together we created an amazing center at UCSD, but mostly we had fun and kept each other honest and true to our practice. I love you, man.

Jon Kabat-Zinn has been a powerful force in my practice and my life, and his tremendous generosity, humility, and wisdom have guided me every step of the way in this work. Jon has the rare ability to lead from beside us all and inspire us to do our best work as teachers and as humans. Amy Saltzman has been a trusted advisor and dear friend who reminds me regularly to exercise the "beautiful no" (except when it came to the offer to write this book!). Susan Woods challenges me to be my best and reflect long and hard on who and what I am, while simultaneously sharing a certain brand of humor that keeps us both sane.

Michelle Becker is the ultimate connector and facilitator of good things. She has made opportunities happen for me in many ways, including first introducing me to MSC and Chris and Kristin. By far my favorite co-teaching companion and fellow traveler (literally), Michelle's wisdom, grace, and inspiration have shaped me into who I am today and how I express myself on these pages. And the twinkle in Michelle's eye is a thing to behold, and to instill just the slightest nervous twitch, because it's going to make me laugh, make me think, and probably get me into more mischief. Just the way I like it.

My CMSC colleagues are part of my extended family, and I am grateful for the contributions of several close colleagues who have supported and led me in various ways to grow this amazing organization. Aimee Eckhardt for her wise vision and warm heart; Natalie Bell for her powerful presence and clear vision; Gail Stein for her no-nonsense ability to get stuff done and her willingness to indulge my crazy impulses; and a whole worldwide community of amazing teachers, trainers, and MSC graduates who make it all worthwhile. May you all keep up the good work and share it widely.

I also want to thank my son Ben Hickman for being the fine young man he is becoming and for being my mindfulness teacher for all his life. I smile every time I think of him, and he inspires me to always be my best and do good work. Thank you to my beloved siblings Melissa Carey and Chris Hickman, with whom I have grown closer in recent years. I appreciate both more and more each day as we reacquaint ourselves with each other. And the late addition to our family, my half-brother Tom Powell. What a gift to get an "auxiliary sibling" so late in life!

The very last thank you is to LouAnne Foley, my high school English teacher, whose good humor and teaching magic inspired me to write *and* be funny. I will be forever grateful for that gift. All in all, I am a lucky man who has had a tremendous opportunity to share this work through this book.

Publisher's Acknowledgments

Acquisitions Editor: Tracy Boggier
Project Editor: Tim Gallan
Copy Editor: Christine Pingleton
Proofreader: Debbye Butler

Production Editor: Tamilmani Varadharaj
Cover Image: © Liliboas/Getty Images

Leverage the power

Dummies is the global leader in the reference category and one of the most trusted and highly regarded brands in the world. No longer just focused on books, customers now have access to the dummies content they need in the format they want. Together we'll craft a solution that engages your customers, stands out from the competition, and helps you meet your goals.

Advertising & Sponsorships

Connect with an engaged audience on a powerful multimedia site, and position your message alongside expert how-to content. Dummies.com is a one-stop shop for free, online information and know-how curated by a team of experts.

- Targeted ads
- Video
- Email Marketing
- Microsites
- Sweepstakes sponsorship

20 MILLION PAGE VIEWS EVERY SINGLE MONTH

15 MILLION UNIQUE VISITORS PER MONTH

43% OF ALL VISITORS ACCESS THE SITE VIA THEIR MOBILE DEVICES

700,000 NEWSLETTER SUBSCRIPTIONS TO THE INBOXES OF *300,000* UNIQUE INDIVIDUALS EVERY WEEK

# of dummies

Custom Publishing

Reach a global audience in any language by creating a solution that will differentiate you from competitors, amplify your message, and encourage customers to make a buying decision.

- Apps
- Books
- eBooks
- Video
- Audio
- Webinars

Brand Licensing & Content

Leverage the strength of the world's most popular reference brand to reach new audiences and channels of distribution.

For more information, visit dummies.com/biz

PERSONAL ENRICHMENT

9781119187790	9781119179030	9781119293354	9781119293347	9781119310068	9781119235606
USA $26.00	USA $21.99	USA $24.99	USA $22.99	USA $22.99	USA $24.99
CAN $31.99	CAN $25.99	CAN $29.99	CAN $27.99	CAN $27.99	CAN $29.99
UK £19.99	UK £16.99	UK £17.99	UK £16.99	UK £16.99	UK £17.99

9781119251163	9781119235491	9781119279952	9781119283133	9781119287117	9781119130246
USA $24.99	USA $26.99	USA $24.99	USA $24.99	USA $24.99	USA $22.99
CAN $29.99	CAN $31.99	CAN $29.99	CAN $29.99	CAN $29.99	CAN $27.99
UK £17.99	UK £19.99	UK £17.99	UK £17.99	UK £16.99	UK £16.99

PROFESSIONAL DEVELOPMENT

9781119311041	9781119255796	9781119293439	9781119281467	9781119280651	9781119251132	9781119310563
USA $24.99	USA $39.99	USA $26.99	USA $26.99	USA $29.99	USA $24.99	USA $34.00
CAN $29.99	CAN $47.99	CAN $31.99	CAN $31.99	CAN $35.99	CAN $29.99	CAN $41.99
UK £17.99	UK £27.99	UK £19.99	UK £19.99	UK £21.99	UK £17.99	UK £24.99

9781119181705	9781119263593	9781119257769	9781119293477	9781119265313	9781119239314	9781119293323
USA $29.99	USA $26.99	USA $29.99	USA $26.99	USA $24.99	USA $29.99	USA $29.99
CAN $35.99	CAN $31.99	CAN $35.99	CAN $31.99	CAN $29.99	CAN $35.99	CAN $35.99
UK £21.99	UK £19.99	UK £21.99	UK £19.99	UK £17.99	UK £21.99	UK £21.99

dummies.com

dummies®
A Wiley Brand

Learning Made Easy

ACADEMIC

9781119293576
USA $19.99
CAN $23.99
UK £15.99

9781119293637
USA $19.99
CAN $23.99
UK £15.99

9781119293491
USA $19.99
CAN $23.99
UK £15.99

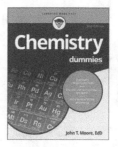

9781119293460
USA $19.99
CAN $23.99
UK £15.99

9781119293590
USA $19.99
CAN $23.99
UK £15.99

9781119215844
USA $26.99
CAN $31.99
UK £19.99

9781119293378
USA $22.99
CAN $27.99
UK £16.99

9781119293521
USA $19.99
CAN $23.99
UK £15.99

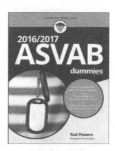

9781119239178
USA $18.99
CAN $22.99
UK £14.99

9781119263883
USA $26.99
CAN $31.99
UK £19.99

Available Everywhere Books Are Sold

dummies.com

dummies®
A Wiley Brand

Small books for big imaginations

9781119177173
USA $9.99
CAN $9.99
UK £8.99

9781119177272
USA $9.99
CAN $9.99
UK £8.99

9781119177241
USA $9.99
CAN $9.99
UK £8.99

9781119177210
USA $9.99
CAN $9.99
UK £8.99

9781119262657
USA $9.99
CAN $9.99
UK £6.99

9781119291336
USA $9.99
CAN $9.99
UK £6.99

9781119233527
USA $9.99
CAN $9.99
UK £6.99

9781119291220
USA $9.99
CAN $9.99
UK £6.99

9781119177302
USA $9.99
CAN $9.99
UK £8.99

Unleash Their Creativity

dummies.com

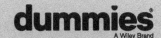